A.H. FOX

THE FINEST GUN IN THE WORLD

A.H. FOX

THE FINEST GUN IN THE WORLD

MICHAEL McINTOSH

THE DERRYDALE PRESS
Essex, Connecticut

THE DERRYDALE PRESS

Published by The Derrydale Press
An imprint of The Globe Pequot Publishing Group, Inc.
64 South Main Street
Essex, CT 06426
www.globepequot.com

First edition copyright © 1992 by Michael McIntosh
Revised edition copyright © 1994 by Michael McIntosh
First Derrydale Printing 2016

All rights reserved. No part of this book may be reproduced in any form or by any electronic or mechanical means, including information storage and retrieval systems, without written permission from the publisher, except by a reviewer who may quote passages in a review.

British Library Cataloguing in Publication Information Available

Library of Congress Catalog Card Number: 92-74033

ISBN: 978-1-58667-138-9 (pbk.)
ISBN: 978-0-92435-724-4 (cloth)
ISBN: 978-1-58667-139-6 (e-book)

*Temples are to be dedicated to the gods,
and books to good men.*
Aristides

This one is to the four Headricks:
Bill and Donna
Bill and Ethel

And to Susan, as always

	Introduction	ix
	Acknowledgements	xiii
	Prologue	xvii
1	On the Cusp	21
2	Fox Gun Company, Baltimore	25
3	Matters of the Heart: Fentress	39
4	Pigeons in the Park	41
5	Philadelphia Arms	61
6	A Difficult Birth	77
7	A Gun for Teddy, Guns for the Grand	97
8	New Guns, New Men	109
9	Matters of the Heart: Ellen	131
10	"The Most Perfectly Proportioned Small-Gauge Gun"	135
11	Over Here, Over There	149
12	Triggers, Accolades & Flare Guns	165
13	Singular Guns	181

14	"The Finest Car in the World"	191
15	Super-Fox	211
16	El Dorado & the Grail	237
17	Pleasure Palace, House of Cards	243
18	Quiet Days in Pleasantville	263
19	Savage Years	277
20	Specials & Oddments	307
21	Matters of the Heart: Velma	327
22	Sunset and Evening Bell	329

Appendix I: The Paper Trail	335
Appendix II: Chronology	365
Appendix III: Grades & Models by Year	375
Appendix IV: Sources	379
Appendix V: The Fox Gun Reborn	380

Index 395

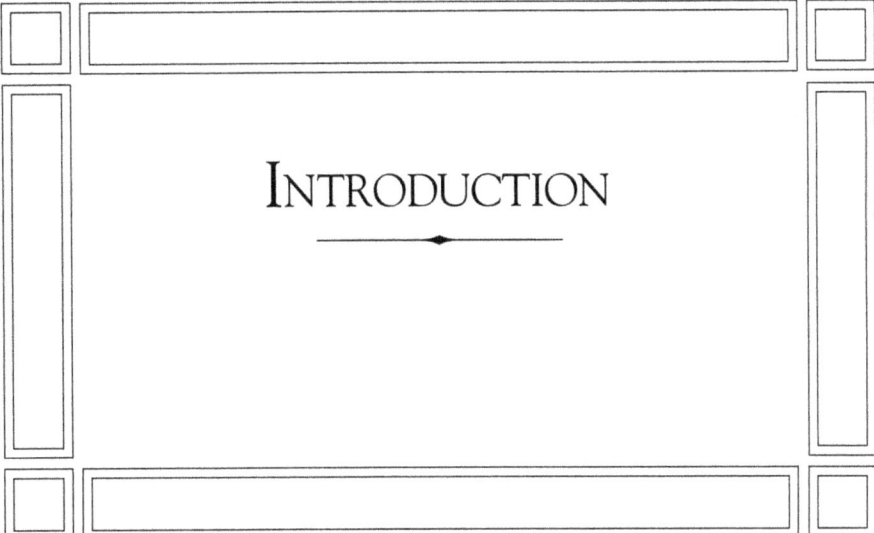

INTRODUCTION

It's funny, sometimes, how these things begin. In the late 1970s, I wrote a slim little book on American shotguns, in one chapter of which I had this to say about Ansley Fox: "Ansley H. Fox is in many ways the Invisible Man of American gunmaking. We know very little about his professional career, even less about the man himself." I didn't know it at the time, but those two sentences were the beginning of this book.

In the winter of 1984, about a year after I became shotgun columnist at *Sporting Classics*, then-managing editor Joanna Craig asked if I had any interest in writing a feature story on Fox guns. Those two sentences were the first thing that came to mind, apparently, because I remember answering without a moment's prior thought that I'd like to combine a discussion of the guns with a biography of Ansley Fox—or at least attempt to give the invisible man whatever substance I could find. By the time the story appeared in print, in the September/October issue of 1985, I was thoroughly fascinated with Ansley Fox, and this book was inevitable.

I won't bore you with the details of how the picture of the man gradually began to resolve out of the flotsam and minutiae of history, except to say that I have been continually astonished at how many details of a life can survive in one sort of record or another and how one thing can lead to another. I was extremely fortunate—purely by accident or instinct, more often than not—because for a long time, everything I touched seemed to lead in just the right direction. The blind alleys were mercifully few and mercifully minor.

The sense of discovery was tremendously exciting. As if out of nothing, a human being emerged, a man whose follies and failures loomed as large as his virtues and successes. In the process, I learned first-hand the obsessive passion that drives biographers, and there were times when sheer fascination with the man threatened to subsume the other themes upon which this book is built. Here was a man born more than a hundred years ago, a man who died when I was three, and he was virtually coming alive before my eyes and in my mind. I cannot begin to describe the feeling.

Naturally enough, the trail took some odd and ironic twists. You'd think that learning a man's full name would be one of the easier tasks a biographer should face. Perhaps it is, but it wasn't so for Ansley Fox. Even when the *Sporting Classics* story went to print, I still didn't know his middle name. Everywhere, it seemed, he was Ansley H. Fox or simply A.H. Fox; even his death certificate bears the initial and not the name. Finally, combing through the archives at the court house in Philadelphia, I made a discovery: You can die in New Jersey without a middle name, but you need one to get a divorce in Pennsylvania. The trouble is, though, it doesn't have to be spelled correctly, so I spent a couple of years believing I was dealing with the life and times of one Ansley Hermon Fox—because that's how the clerk who typed the papers decreeing the divorce of Ansley and Fentress Fox put it down. And I didn't know it was wrong until I got a look at what must be one of only a very few instances when Ansley Fox signed his full name in his own hand. Sometimes, all you can do is shake your head in utter bemusement.

Ultimately, the project took on a third dimension that expanded it to almost unmanageable proportions. I have come to believe that guns are as much artifacts of their historical context as they are artifacts of human hands and spirit. We can appreciate them for intrinsic merit, which is the *what* of their existence, but we can never fully appreciate the *why* unless we have some understanding of the world in which they were created. This becomes even more important in dealing with the history of a manufacturing firm, because its activity and even its very existence is directly shaped by the social and economic environment of its time.

And what a time it was. The span of Ansley Fox's life, 1875 to 1948, represents the most influential seventy-odd years in the history of the United States and indeed, the history of the world. In those years, our country went through change of a scope difficult even to imagine. Ansley Fox's life began four years before Edison invented the incandescent lamp and ended six years after the first nuclear reactor was built. When he was born, the automobile did not exist, and when he died, Volkswagen Beetles had already been imported to America. In 1875, no man had ever flown in a machine heavier than air; by 1948, a man had flown a jet aircraft faster than the speed of sound.

In those years, the world went through two wars of unheard-of proportion, the greatest empire of modern time went from full flower to virtual collapse, the United States' role in the world community changed forever, and economic depressions bedeviled Europe and America. Those also were the years that spanned the American Industrial Revolution, and Ansley Fox was in the thick of it. In some ways, his life was a testament to Calvin Coolidge's slogan: "He who builds a factory builds a temple."

In many ways, Ansley Fox was a synecdoche of America—restless, full of confidence, always willing to push the envelope to new limits. He helped shape the times, and the times shaped him.

So, I have built this book on three themes. It is a history of the Fox gun and a biography of Ansley Fox, both woven into the context of American history and such world events as affected the United States in important ways. Such an enormous amount of material naturally has posed some difficult problems in choosing how to organize it. I decided early on that a strictly chronological approach would be cumbersome and ultimately confusing where the guns are concerned, but by the same token, a piecemeal approach of focusing too narrowly on each model and grade would destroy the coherence of the historical dimension.

In the end, I chose to attempt chronology in a modified form, to allow history and biography to unfold period by period and yet to carry certain subjects, such as the Super-Fox and the single trap guns, to their conclusions virtually all of a piece. The story therefore moves ahead of itself at times and then returns to the central structure. As a quick reference to salient facts, I've made up a chronology, which is Appendix II, and a chart showing the period when each grade and model of gun was listed in company literature; this appears in Appendix III.

It's been a long time a-borning, this book. Seven years is a substantial chunk of any working life, and they've brought some changes. I started this project on an electric typewriter and finished it on a word-processor. When I started it, writing was a part-time job; now it's a full-time career. In these years, I've been divorced and remarried and known the feelings that come when parents die, shared pain and happiness with the people I love. Some time back I reached the point of ambivalence toward my work with Ansley Fox and his guns, anxious on the one hand to bring it to a close but at the same time of half a mind to just go on tinkering with it forever. Some of my colleagues and friends think I've done that already. But just as everything begins somewhere, so there must be endings, too.

All along, I have sought to create something of broader scope than simply a litany of how long Sterlingworth barrels were or when the K Grade single trap was discontinued, although that information and much more like it forms a vital part of this book. The fact is, though, there's more to it than barrel lengths and chokes and checkering patterns. All that is part of a larger story, one that touches upon our own heritage, upon our own identity as shooters and hunters and collectors and even as Americans. That's the story I have attempted to tell.

Copper Creek Farm, Camdenton, Missouri
April 1992

A Note on the Second Edition

Nineteen ninety-three proved to be a momentous year both for the Fox gun and for this book. Bookwise, the first printing of the trade edition sold out in mid-December. To say that I'm pleased by the reception it's had is to understate the case—just as it is to say that I'm grateful for all the kind words and support.

At about the same time the last copies went out the door at Countrysport, the first of the new Fox guns came to life in Connecticut, marking the first time in more than a generation that a high-quality double gun has been manufactured in the United States. An astonishing event.

The combination of a sold-out book and the gun's rebirth presented an opportunity to bring Fox history fully up to date—as well as to repair the typos and bobbles that managed to elude everyone's eyes the first time around. Thus the new Fox guns are now noted in the appendices, particularly in the all-new Appendix V, which tells their story as it has unfolded up to now.

I hadn't anticipated a revised edition quite so soon, but as Ansley Fox discovered long ago, history moves at its own pace—and it's our job to keep up as best we can.

Copper Creek Farm, Camdenton, Missouri
February 1994

ACKNOWLEDGEMENTS

No book of this size and scope could be written without assistance from others—in this case, many others. The following people and organizations rendered invaluable help, providing advice, information, encouragement—and in some cases, all three.

John Allen, Game Fair Ltd., Nashville, Tennessee; Dr. William Andrews; *The Atlantic City Press*, Atlantic City, New Jersey; Roger Batey; Fran Batson, National Archives, Philadelphia Branch; Ed Beaulieu; Bob Beaulieu; Mitzie Bielin; Bryan Bilinski; Ray Borges, The William F. Harrah Automobile Foundation, Reno, Nevada; Brad Bowling, Krause Publications, Iola, Wisconsin; Braxton Bragg; James J. Bray; Maxine Brennan and Antoinette Adam, The Historical Society of Pennsylvania, Philadelphia, Pennsylvania; Gurney Brown; Dr. Paul G. Brown; David Brydon; The Circuit Court for Baltimore City, Baltimore, Maryland; Tracy P. Clark; Debbie Colaniro, The Antique Automobile Club of America, Hershey, Pennsylvania; Frank Conley; Daniel and Joanna Cote, *The Double Gun Journal*; James Curry; Col. Blair J. Davis; Van T. Davis; Lon W. Deckard; A.W. Dippold; Dr. Henry Domke; William Donne; Tony Galazan; Dick Graves; Jim Gereno; Herman Gilbreth; Day Goldy; Jess Guy; Bill Habein; Amelia Haile, The Baltimore County Historical Society, Baltimore, Maryland; Dyrk Halstead; Hal

Hamilton; Don Hardin; R.W. Harris; Jack Haugh; Peyton Hawes-Dunn; Thomas N. Hopper; James Hornor; Herb Houze, The Buffalo Bill Museum; Paul Jackson; Marcus Jacobs; Hal Jaques; Andy Keedy; James Kelly; Catherine Kennedy, The Enoch Pratt Library, Baltimore, Maryland; Pat Kennedy; Adna Karns and Carol Klaus, *The Sporting Goods Dealer*; Michael Kobos; William A. Langelatti, Office of the Prothonotary, Philadelphia Court of Common Pleas; Millie Link, Amateur Trapshooting Association, Vandalia, Ohio; Tom Loughmiller; Ted Lundrigan; The Maryland Center for Health Statistics; Bernie Matthys, *The American Field*, Chicago, Illinois; Howard McBride; Daniel McCombs; M. McGovern, The Orphans Court, Philadelphia, Pennsylvania; Bill McPhail; Jerry Minton; Burton Moore; The New Jersey Department of Health, Bureau of Vital Statistics, Trenton, New Jersey; Francis O'Neill and Isabella W. Athey, The Maryland Historical Society, Baltimore, Maryland; Stephania E. Papi, Department of Health and Mental Hygene, Division of Vital Records, Baltimore, Maryland; Dan Papp; Bill Paquette; Windi Phillips, Sotheby's; Frank Pisciotta; Allen H. Pressley; Mike Prisco; Jack and John Puglisi, Puglisi's Gun Emporium, Duluth, Minnesota; Lou Razek, Highwood Bookshop, Suttons Bay, Michigan; Talley Riddell; Jim Rhoades; Donald Rooney, The Atlanta Historical Society, Atlanta, Georgia; Jack Rowe; Richard Ryherd; Lewis and Janet Schiller; Robert Schilling; Walter Schmidt II; Ned Schwing; The Secretary of State, Trenton, New Jersey; David Seymour, Harleigh Cemetery, Camden, New Jersey; Jim Sisson; Jim Smith; Steve Smith; James A. Stahl; James W. Stone; Richard B. Sydnor, Jr.; Dana Tauber; Jack Tramonte; David Trevallion; Robert Urich; The U.S. Patent and Trademark Office, Washington, D.C.; Terry D. Voss; Stan Watson; Steve West; Barrett J. Williams; Steve Wirth; Charles Wroten; and Vern Young.

Some chapters were previously published, in somewhat different form, in *Sporting Classics*, *The American Rifleman*, and *Shooting Sportsman* magazines. To the editors, my thanks.

David Noreen contributed time and energy far beyond the call of duty. Likewise, I owe truly special thanks to Roe S. Clark for his unstinting kindness and unflagging patience.

Without my dear friends William H. and Ethel Headrick, William W. and Donna Headrick, there would be no book at all—and, considering all that's happened over these seven years, probably no author as well. Take even a casual browse through these pages and you'll see why Bill Headrick is the finest gun photographer in the business. What's not so readily apparent—but which lies nearer to the heart of things—are all the years of good food and good talk and good whiskey, of ever-helpful critique, of support and solace and shelter from a world of storms. There is more to thank them for, and more thanks are due, than I have the words to say.

And so as well for Susan, who saw it through.

"The unequalled success of the A H Fox Gun is due to its unequalled quality"

Ansley H. Fox

Prologue

He was born on the cusp between two worlds, at a moment when history was about to pause, take stock of things, and change direction like a great, groaning shift of geologic plates. Behind lay the old feudal culture of the South, devastated by war and reforged by the clumsy hammer of Reconstruction into a caricature of its conqueror. The vast western lands were largely claimed but far from won. Less than a year before his birth, two mining engineers attached to an expeditionary cavalry troop under George Armstrong Custer found and reported gold in the Black Hills, holy ground of the Sioux nation.

In the Northeast, factories sprouted and grew like grimy moss. Elsewhere, life moved with the cycle of the seasons, its tempo set by the plowhorse.

In the year Ansley Fox was born, the Pullman parlor railway car was put into operation, and the *New York Daily Graphic* published the first newspaper cartoon strip. The first no-hit nine-inning baseball game was played, in Philadelphia, the first no-run nine-inning game in St. Louis, and in New Haven, Yale and Harvard played the first football game in which both teams wore uniforms. G.F. Green patented the electric dental drill.

That year saw the first running of the Kentucky Derby and the first book manuscript ever written on a typewriter, a novel titled *The Adventures of Tom Sawyer*.

On Ansley Fox's first birthday, Custer and the Seventh Cavalry struggled briefly and to the death against legions of Sioux and Cheyenne on a dusty Montana hilltop near the Little Bighorn River.

Ahead lay the twentieth century, its seeds already rooted—the new America where technology would blossom, an America that would prosper and consume and grow restless. He would be restless along with it.

A.H. Fox Gun Company, CSE Grade   WILLIAM W. HEADRICK

1
ON THE CUSP

In 1872, Addison C. Fox lived in a rented room at Mrs. McKinley's in Atlanta. He was thirty-six, born at Leesburg, Virginia, and had come to Georgia with his brother Amos. Both worked at the firm of Redwine & Fox, wholesale and retail druggists, purveyors of paints, oils, and window glass. The Atlanta city directory describes Addison Fox as a pharmaceutist, Amos as a druggist.

At about that time, Addison Fox met and married Louisa Ansley of Augusta, Georgia. They moved to Decatur, a few miles east of Atlanta, and on Friday, June 25, 1875, Louisa bore a son whom they christened Ansley Herman.

Addison Fox was by then a practicing homeopathic physician. Amos apparently preferred a commercial, public life; he pursued various interests in oil for many years, became Postmaster of Atlanta in 1894, and in 1896 held a seat on the board of directors of the Confederate Veterans Home. Addison Fox, on the other hand, seems to have been content to concoct his medications and ply them in the private, often intimate world of physician and patient.

Insofar as a man's choice of career is a clue to his nature, Ansley Fox seems to have synthesized something of the contrasts between his father and uncle. Like Amos, he was a buyer and seller of things, a businessman with an eye always cocked for opportunity. But, perhaps more like his father, he also clearly possessed some powerful sense of quality, some seemingly inexhaustible appreciation for beauty and craftsmanship. There is little evidence that he ever was content to turn out products solely for the sake of profit. He was fond of describing the things he made as the finest of their kind. Whether they were is less important than the fact that Ansley Fox wanted them to be.

Addison Fox left Atlanta sometime between 1876 and the end of the decade, moving his family to Maryland, where a second son, Harry, was born in 1880. The 1892 Baltimore city directory shows Addison Fox, physician, living at 508 West Fayette Street, keeping office hours from eight until ten o'clock each morning, from three to four in the afternoon, and again from five until seven in the evening. His consulting rooms no doubt were in the family home.

The 1880s were not without misfortune for the Fox family. According to census records, Addison Fox had a new wife by 1900–Henrietta Polk, born in Virginia in 1864. It was a time when women often married young and just as often died young; Louisa Ansley Fox may well have been one of them. Census records show three more children born to Addison Fox–Beaulah in 1891, Sharon (a son) in 1896, and Raphael in 1897. Henrietta Fox unquestionably was the mother of Sharon and Raphael and possibly bore Beaulah as well

Ansley Fox seems to have owned an affinity for guns early on. According to a sketchy biography by M.H. Wright, published in the October 1908 issue of *Field & Stream*, his fondness for firearms was "passionate" and was fostered by an uncle who taught him to shoot a rifle at the age of ten. If the uncle was Amos, these would have been inconvenient lessons, for Amos Fox still lived in Atlanta. In any event, the passion for guns clearly was genuine. Lots of boys have it, and few ever lose it entirely. Indeed, guns and shooting would preoccupy Ansley Fox for at least half his lifetime.

Wright goes on the say that from an early age Ansley Fox's marksmanship "began to attract attention among his neighbors," which could mean anything from real skill to a penchant for shooting lightning rods from rooftops or plugging neighborhood cats. Perhaps it was both, for there is ample evidence that he became a brilliant shot.

Again according to Wright, Ansley Fox's proficiency with a gun prompted him to earn a living as a market hunter for three years following the end of his public-school education. If this is true – which I doubt– he likely was moved more by the seemingly endless supply of game around Chesapeake Bay than by any pressing need for a livelihood. Market hunting was seasonal and at best offered scarcely more than a subsistence. But the romance of it might have been wonderfully appealing to the adolescent son of a comfortably well-off and probably somewhat indulgent family.

All in all, Ansley Fox's market hunting, if indeed he did any, probably was more a lark than a living. What is most important – and most certain – about these years in the last decade of the century is that Ansley Fox became an inventor and, for the first time, truly stood in the public eye.

Baltimore Arms, Trap Grade — WILLIAM W. HEADRICK

2

Fox Gun Company
Baltimore

During the latter half of the nineteenth century, the armsmaking world turned itself inside-out. In a wave of creative energy that swept through Europe and England like an electric current, the muzzle-loading gun gave way to the breechloader, the hammer gun to the hammerless action, black powder to nitro. The first ripples started in France, and in England grew into a groundswell that reached America while Ansley Fox was still a schoolboy.

Until the mid-1880s, the hammer-gun reigned almost unchallenged in the American gun trade. Dan Lefever was the first important American maker to take the hammerless action seriously, although his 1878 hammerless breechloader was not the first such gun built in this country; that distinction probably belongs to Charles Edward Sneider of Pratt Street, Baltimore, who was building hammerless doubles at least two years before Lefever's appeared. But Sneider and his guns made little impact on the market and even less on history, and when Lefever's masterpiece, the Automatic Hammerless, appeared in 1885, it was the only high-quality, American-built hammerless gun available. The first L.C. Smith hammerless went into production a year later, followed in turn by similar designs from Parker in 1889, Baker in 1890, and Remington in 1894.

And eighteen-year-old Ansley Fox had some ideas of his own. On May 2, 1893, he applied for patent protection on a break-action gun in which hammers concealed inside the frame were cocked by leverage from the barrels. The patent, No. 522,464, was issued July 3, 1894.

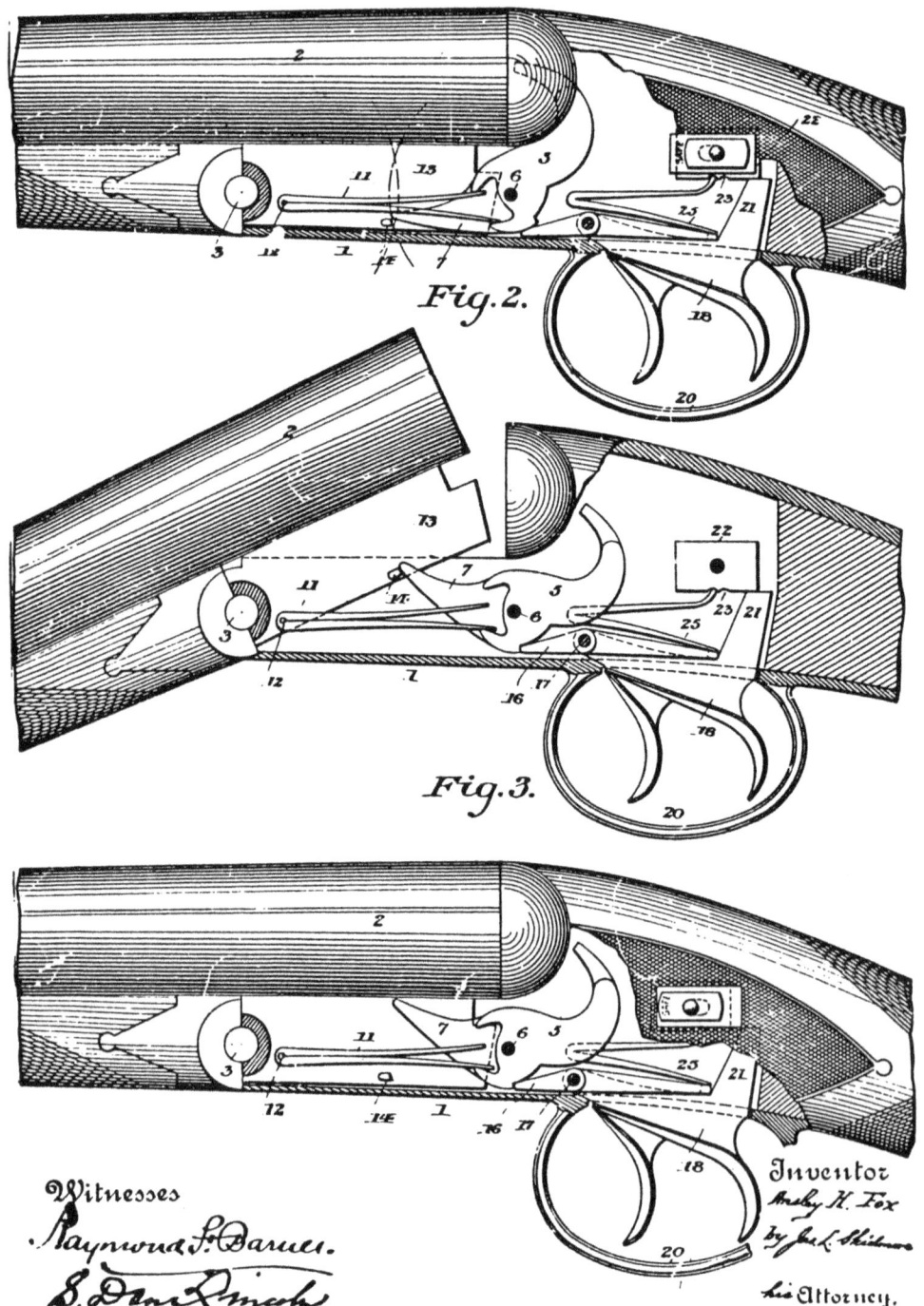

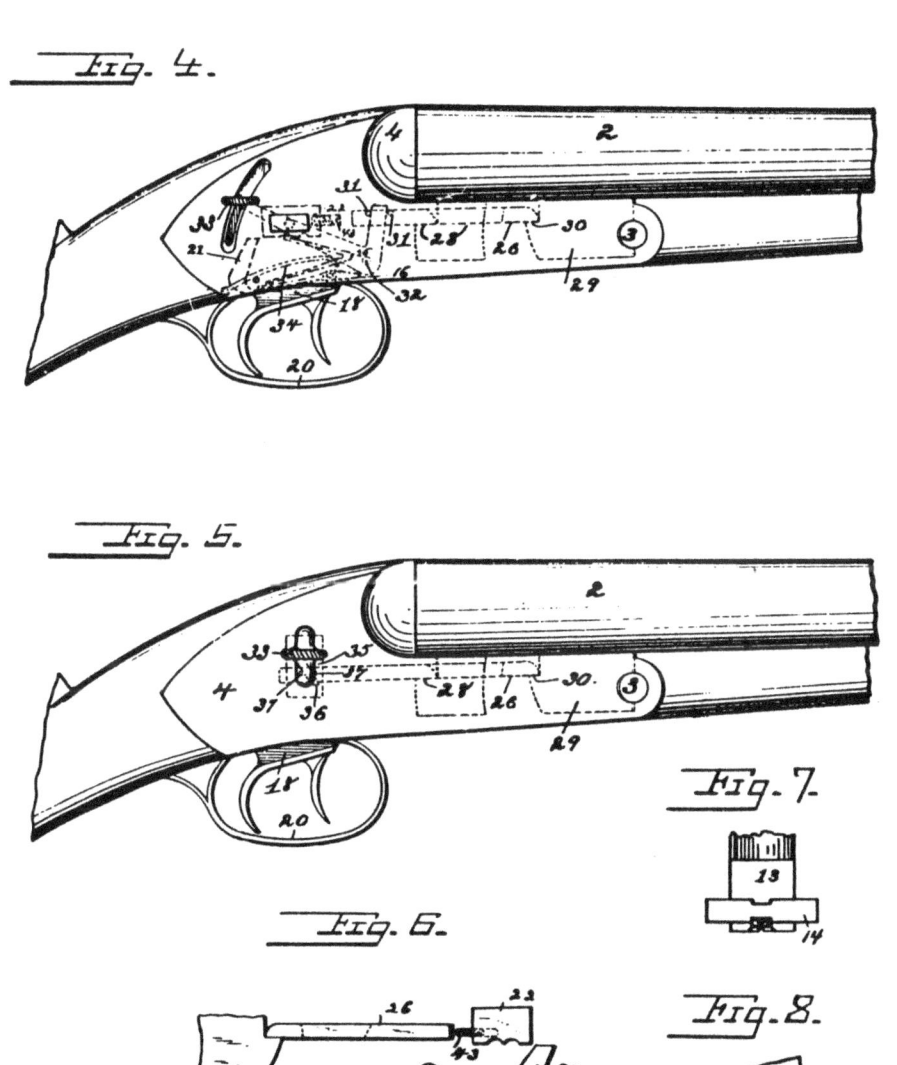

(No Model.)
A. H. FOX.
BREECH LOADING BREAKDOWN GUN.
No. 522,464.   Patented July 3, 1894.

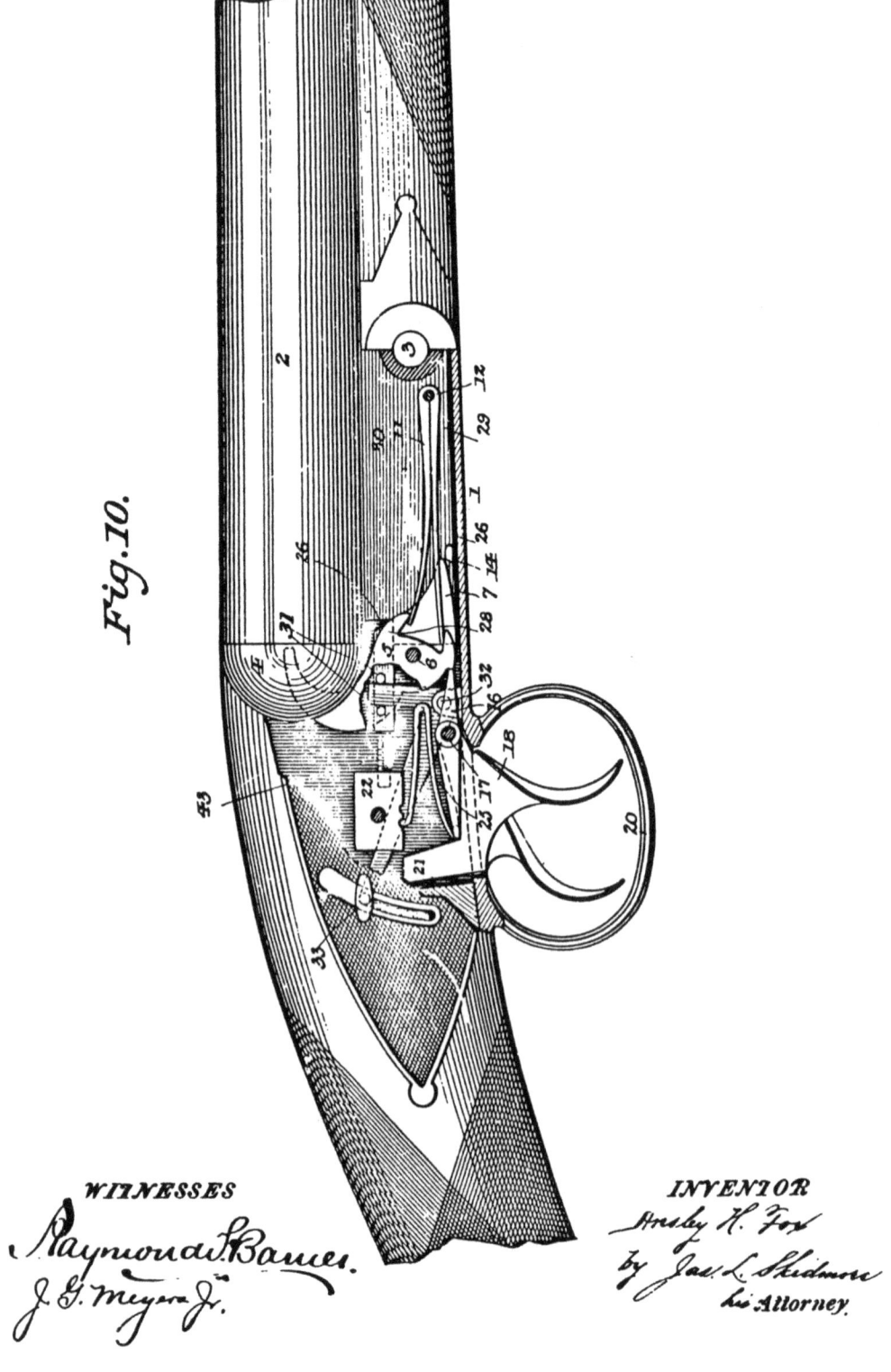

Fig. 10.

WITNESSES
INVENTOR
Ansley H. Fox
by Jas. L. Skidmore
his Attorney

Actually, the patent covers a number of features, most of them decidedly odd even in an age of odd guns. The action is remarkably simple—hammers with integral strikers, and sear linkages connected directly with the triggers, all powered by two leaf-springs. The safety is an intercepting block mounted in the left side of the frame, much on the order of W.W. Greener's arrangement. The bolting system is presented in two variations. One is a thumb-lever on the right side of the frame, linked by toggles to a sliding underbolt; the other is more straightforward mechanically but even stranger in execution—a Purdey-type double underlug retracted by a thumb-wheel on the right side of the frame. Weird it is, but it also was innovative enough that the U.S. Patent Office accepted a total of nineteen features as patentable.

There is no evidence that the original design ever was put into production, but Fox wasn't finished with it. Over the next year, he refined his thinking and on July 16, 1895, filed application for a patent on an improved version. His intention, according to the patent papers, was to

> ...simplify and improve the cocking mechanism, provide improved means of holding the sears in engagement with the hammers, and to improve the safety devices for holding the triggers in safe position when desired. A further object of my invention is to provide the barrels with an improved form of rear extension adapted to register with a counterpart recess in the breech-block, in order to secure greater strength where needed, said extension being provided with a dovetail recess, to which is adapted a dovetailed extension on the forward end of the snap lever.

All told, he requested patent protection for twelve specific points of the design, and this was granted as Patent No. 563,193, issued June 30, 1896.

Overall, the idea is similar to Anson and Deeley's now-classic 1875 hammerless action and also to Greener's Facile Princeps action, invented shortly after the Anson and Deeley. In all three, the hammers are cocked by leverage coming directly from the barrel lump, rather than by intermediary levers or hooks. Perhaps the prophetic aspects of Fox's gun, and its earlier version, are the simplicity and the emphasis upon strength.

Ansley Fox had by that time taken up trapshooting, and a great many of his ideas about what a shotgun ought to be probably were shaped by that experience. Target-shooting is a brutal proving-ground for guns, and Fox no doubt saw first-hand what gunmakers of the future would face. He probably saw guns literally fall apart under the constant pounding. The new nitro powders were both more efficient and more powerful than black, and they bashed black-powder guns unmercifully. Frames cracked; fastening bolts and hinge pins wore quickly; unshielded firing pins allowed gases to flow back through the actions and wreak havoc upon buttstocks. Critical sear notches soon wore to the point that locks became dangerously unpredictable or wouldn't work at all. Springs broke by the dozen. The new ammunition clearly demanded new ways of thinking about how to design and build a shotgun.

Ansley Fox took his revised drawings to Joseph A. Geiji, a Baltimore gunsmith, who set to work on a prototype. The gun earned some notice even before the U.S. Patent Office approved the application.

In its issue of December 12, 1895, *Shooting and Fishing* published a description of the design, probably written by Ansley Fox himself. Dr. Samuel Fort described the new action in the March 7, 1896, issue of *The American Field*, calling Fox a "boy inventor" of nineteen—even though he was nearly twenty-one by then and stood almost six feet tall. The gun, Fort says, "bids fair to be a great success." The prototype "will be placed in active service, and experiments made to develop any weakness the action may have." Fort doesn't mention what the experiments were to be, but the gun clearly was meant to be used at the traps.

"There seems to be a growing tendency toward a return to the hammer gun," Fort goes on, "especially among the pigeon shooting fraternity, owing, it is said, to the inability of the average hammerless mechanism to remain adjusted, especially in point of trigger-pull; but this mechanism of Mr. Fox's would seem to obviate such vices, and the fraternity will watch with interest the planned trial of the action and the results of wear and tear."

Apparently, no one reported the results of the trial, whatever it was, but the gun must have shown to good advantage. Fort's article notes, "Industrialists have been interested in the action and a stock company will probably be formed here [in Baltimore] to push its manufacture. Failing this, it is the intention of the inventor to go West, probably to Chicago, and there to develop not only this, but several other equally notable inventions of which he is the author."

Those other inventions aren't specified—and apparently weren't patented—but as it turned out, Ansley Fox didn't have to strike out for the Wild West, not even as far as Chicago. In October 1896, Thomas Castle bought one-sixteenth interest in the Fox patent for the sum of $150, which Ansley Fox used to buy shares in National Arms Company, incorporated December 9, 1897. The 1898 city directory shows National Arms located at 5 West German Street and Ansley H.

(No Model.)

A. H. FOX.
BREECH LOADING BREAKDOWN GUN.

No. 563,153. Patented June 30, 1896.

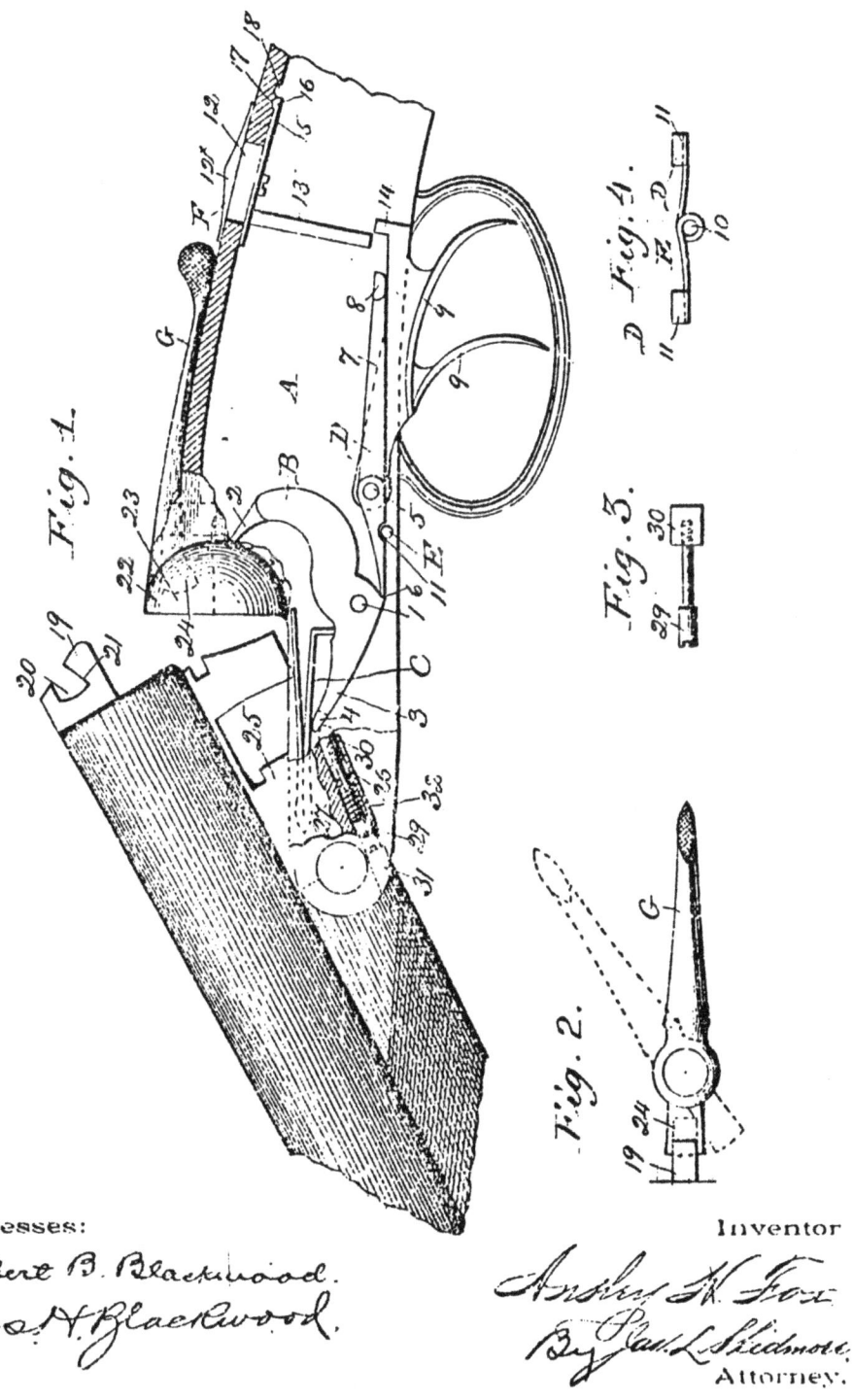

Witnesses:
Albert B. Blackwood.
Jos. H. Blackwood.

Inventor
Andrew H. Fox
By Paul L. Sidmore
Attorney.

Fox as president. Ansley Fox, Addison Fox, Chapin A. Ferguson, John Prosser Tabb, and Ernest E. Hummer all served as directors.

Exactly what they directed isn't clear, for there is little evidence that National Arms ever built any guns. (This National Arms Company is not to be confused with a Brooklyn, New York, firm of same name, which manufactured Moore's-patent revolvers from 1864 until it was bought out by Colt in 1869.) The one thing National Arms is known for certain to have done is change its name to National Gun Company in 1898 and presently cease to exist altogether.

Presumably, Ansley Fox needed more capital than National Arms possessed and had struck a deal with Burr Howard Richards and his son Burr Howard, Jr. In the transfer of assets from National Arms to National Gun Company, Fox obtained a majority of stock, which put him in a position to sell the patents to Burr Richards for $49,950 in stock and $50 cash. Thus, on July 25, 1898, Fox, the two Richardses, Joseph Burton Pleasants, and John Prosser Tabb signed papers incorporating the Fox Gun Company of Baltimore City, capital stock valued at $15,000. The papers were filed at two o'clock the following afternoon, making the incorporation official.

Both the 1899 and 1900 Baltimore directories show the Fox Gun Company on Stockholm Street at the corner of Leadenhall. Burr Howard Richards is listed as president, Ansley Fox as secretary, and Burr Howard Richards, Jr., treasurer.

The company did well at first, at least in attracting favorable attention. An article from a Baltimore correspondent in the premiere issue of *The Sporting Goods Dealer*, October 1899, says: "The Fox shot gun, invented and patented by Ansley Fox, one of the most promising young trap shots of this state, is being manufactured here now, but the trouble is that he can not manufacture the guns fast enough to supply the demand."

A handful of these guns still exist—twist-barreled 12-gauges marked *Fox Gun Co. Balto. Md. U.S.A.* on the left side of the frame. Most, but not all, are stamped with the 1896 patent date. No record remains of how many were built; the highest serial number I know is 875, an A Grade of which only the frame remains. Curiously, No. 866 also exists as a frame only.

Whatever his actual role in the Fox Gun Company, Ansley Fox spent much of his time shooting pigeons at trap tournaments around the East, no doubt demonstrating the Fox gun. Then came the first in what would be an almost life-long series of disappearing acts.

A journal report dated August 9, 1900, says that Ansley Fox had "become a professional. He has been engaged by the Winchester Repeating Arms Co. of New Haven, to represent its shotgun and ammunition." There is good evidence

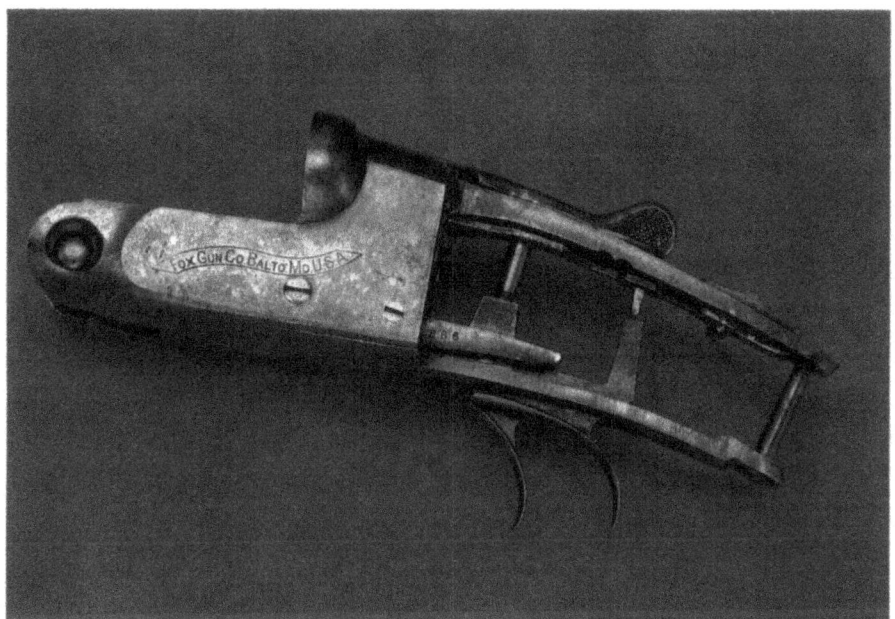

Gun frame, Fox Gun Company, Baltimore   WILLIAM W. HEADRICK

that he similarly represented DuPont powders and ammunition during the next year or so.

There was a restlessness in Ansley Fox. What prompted him to abandon the Fox Gun Company of Baltimore is as elusive as what moved him from one business to another through most of his life. The common assumption has been that he simply was an inept businessman. That view stems from typically fatuous comments by E.C. Crossman in a February 1920 article in *The Sporting Goods Dealer*, and it's been fostered by nearly everyone who has since written about Ansley Fox.

But it doesn't fit the facts. That Fox was able again and again to secure heavy investments in his ventures is hardly a sign of ineptitude.

So what moved Ansley Fox? A powerful will, for one thing, probably supported by a healthy ego. It seems clear that Ansley Fox answered only to himself. He wanted to make high-quality items that bore his name, and nothing less would do. Sometimes, not even that would do, it seems, for he set out to dominate every market he entered, no matter what the product. He was a man frequently out of sync with his time, sometimes ahead, sometimes behind. His markets often either were not ready for Ansley Fox or had already left him for something else.

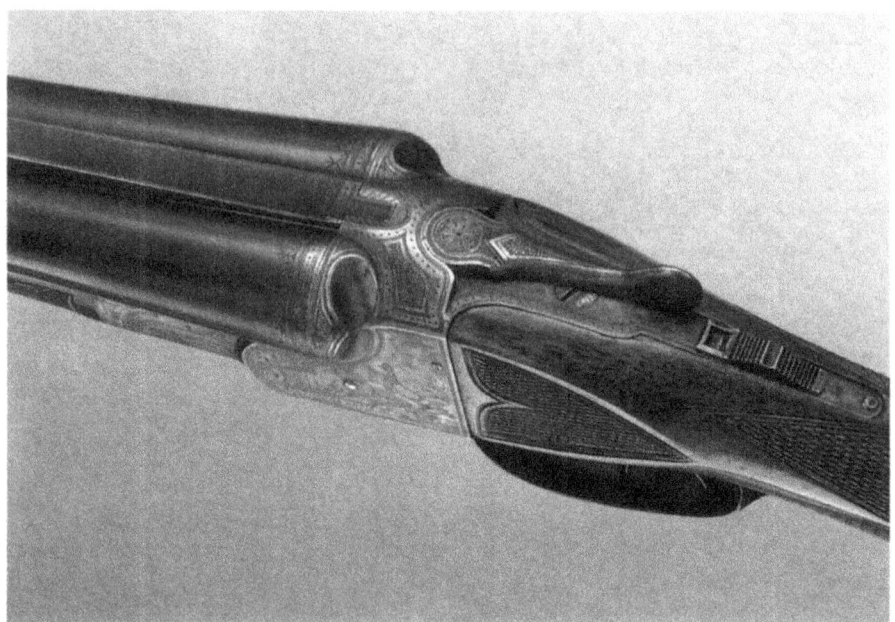

Baltimore Arms, Trap Grade, designed by Frank Hollenbeck — WILLIAM W. HEADRICK

The answer may be simpler yet. Ansley Fox may well have been one of those gifted people who can throw off brilliant ideas like sparks from a grinding wheel but who quickly grow bored with the day-to-day business of nurturing the results. Had anyone bothered to ask Ansley Fox what was his favorite venture, the answer might have been the same as Picasso's when asked which was his favorite painting: The next one. It also seems possible that the Fox Gun Company simply failed to dent the shotgun market deeply enough. At the turn of the century, as now, "news" articles in the trade journals often were written by the manufacturers themselves, and the reports of Fox Gun Company's early success may have been largely wishful thinking.

Certainly, competition was fierce in the firearms industry. Parker was riding high, dominating the market, its factory reportedly working double shifts. A great many of the best professional trapshooters—such luminaries as James A.R. Elliott, Rolla Heikes, and Fred Gilbert—used Parker guns, and Parker made the most of that in its advertising. Ironically, even Ansley Fox would shoot a Parker in at least one major tournament.

L.C. Smith guns were popular, too, with Hunter Arms reportedly working around the clock to meet the demand. Lefever Arms and Syracuse Arms claimed a fair share of sales as well. Dan Lefever was heavily advertising his new boxlock gun. All in all, it was a tough world for a newcomer with yet another double gun to sell, and perhaps Fox and his partners discovered that they really could manufacture them fast enough, after all.

The split with the Richardses may have been at least partly personal as well, or maybe it was entirely personal. Guns subsequently produced by the Richardses under the Baltimore Arms stamp owe something to Fox's design, but they owe even more to the work of Frank Hollenbeck, an excellent designer who had left Syracuse Arms and who in only a few years would start his own gun company in Wheeling, West Virginia. The Baltimore Arms rib extension and cross-bolt fastener are entirely Hollenbeck's, covered by a patent issued to him February 13, 1900.

So perhaps the Richardses wanted an updated gun; they certainly were in a position to insist on it if they chose. Ansley Fox may have refused to revise his design, prompting the Richardses to bring in Hollenbeck. That much is speculation. What is certain is that Ansley Fox was gone by the middle of 1900.

The Richardses regrouped, and the company became Baltimore Arms. The city directories of 1901 and 1902 list the address as Sharp Street at the corner of Stockholm. Burr Howard Richards, Jr., now served as president, Bedford Glascock (spelled *Glasscock* in some sources) as secretary-treasurer, and E.M. Crenshaw as vice-president and assistant secretary. If you were new-fangled enough to have a telephone, you could reach the company offices by asking Central for Henrietta 235.

A 1900 Baltimore Arms catalogue shows guns available in three grades: A, fitted with twist barrels, at $35; B, with "three-blade Damascus" barrels, at $45: and C, with a choice of twist or fluid steel barrels, at $80. They came in 12-gauge only, both barrels bored full choke "for close, hard shooting." Other borings were available on request.

The Sporting Goods Dealer of September 1901 tells of Mr. B.H. Richards, Jr., making the rounds with a $150-grade Baltimore Hammerless gun. The company, the story says, had been "a trifle backward in getting the new guns out," was having trouble meeting demand. That may be true, but "being unable even to show samples for a time" might also describe a little firm hanging on by its fingernails.

Baltimore Arms advertising appears in the January, September, and October 1902 issues of *The Sporting Goods Dealer*, showing two gravure cuts, two different grades of gun, all with Damascus barrels and engraved frames. They essentially are Parkerlike in the contours but also somewhat Foxlike in profile. According to a July 1903 *Sporting Goods Dealer* article, production had doubled each year. By then, there were five grades—A, B, C, Trap, and D—ranging in price from $33 for an A Grade to $175 for a D Grade.

The end came swiftly. In November 1904, trade-journal reports indicate that Burr Howard Richards had been appointed receiver for Baltimore Arms on petition of creditors. The principal creditor was Bedford Glascock, erstwhile officer of the firm, who claimed that payment had been refused on $25,700 in notes. Total indebtedness was estimated at $80,000, assets "much less."

Baltimore Arms appears in the 1905 city directory, but it's a moot point, because there is no evidence that the company actually operated after 1904. At least part of the remaining inventory ended up in New York City, at the Charles J. Godfrey Company, 4 Warren Street. In October 1904, Godfrey advertised a number of Baltimore Arms 12-gauge guns with Best English Stub Twist barrels at a discount price of $22. Apparently, they sold less than briskly; another Godfrey ad from November 1905 offers 12- and 16-gauge, steel-barreled Baltimore Arms guns, accompanied by heavy canvas cases and wooden cleaning rods, for $19.50 apiece.

(Later still, toward the end of 1908 and in January 1909, Godfrey placed ads in *National Sportsman* announcing "a limited number of Fox double barrel shotguns of $50 grade with Krupp steel barrels," a sole-leather case, three-piece cleaning rod, and a hundred black-powder cartridges—all for $35. We'll never know exactly what the guns were, possibly leftovers from Philadelphia Arms, but the illustrations show Baltimore Arms guns.)

The fate of Baltimore Arms was not unlike that of many another small company at the turn of the century, amounting to little more than a footnote in history. In the Fox story, it represents both a beginning and a portent of things to come.

BE Grade 20-gauge, 1917 WILLIAM W. HEADRICK

3
Matters of the Heart: Fentress

She was sixteen when they married. Ansley Fox was twenty-three.

Fentress DeVere Keleher was born in North Carolina in 1882. How and when she met Ansley Fox has long since faded into the shadows of history, but meet they did, and the Reverend Mr. J.C. Hummer married them in Baltimore on June 29, 1898.

Ansley Fox moved out of his father's house at 313 North Carey Street and installed his bride in a home of their own a block north. Along with Fentress, he acquired her mother, Virginia Edwards, and her seventeen-year-old brother, Manley Edwards.

In December 1899, Fentress bore a son, christened James Addison Fox. The 1900 census, which misspells Ansley Fox's name as *Ansel*, shows them all living together, happily or otherwise, at 421 North Carey Street. Now, that whole block has been replaced by the freeway section of U.S. Highway 40.

And there were dark days. Infants are delicate creatures in a hostile world, and as infants often did, James Fox died before 1900 came to an end. No doubt the family grieved deeply. Fentress, for whatever comfort it may have been, became one of a vast sisterhood. A few years later, living in Philadelphia, she found kindred hearts among her closest neighbors. Julia Mooney, who lived next door, had borne six children and buried four of them. Clara Gamble and Eliza Brown, across the street, had, like Fentress, mourned their only children.

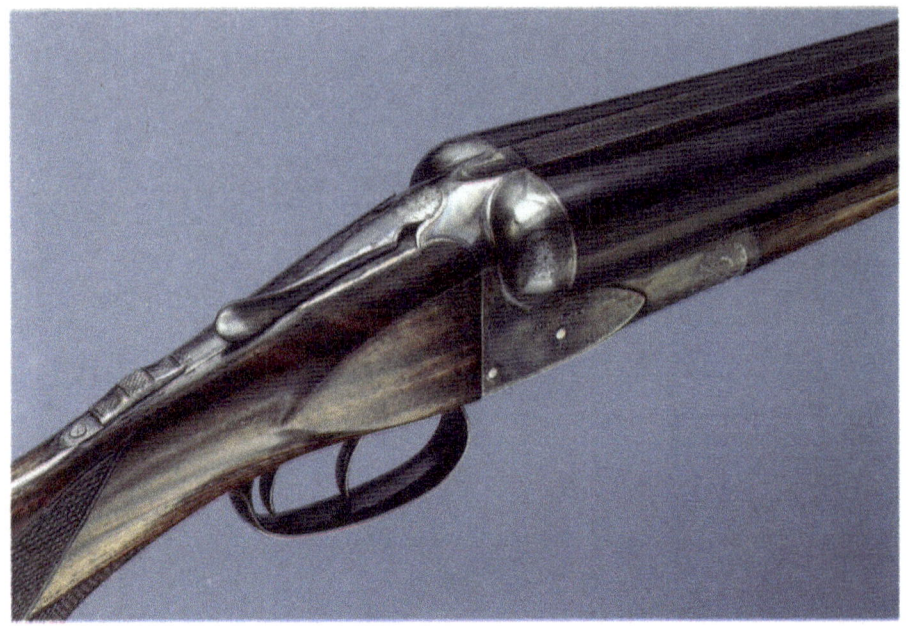

AE Grade 12-gauge, 1910 WILLIAM W. HEADRICK

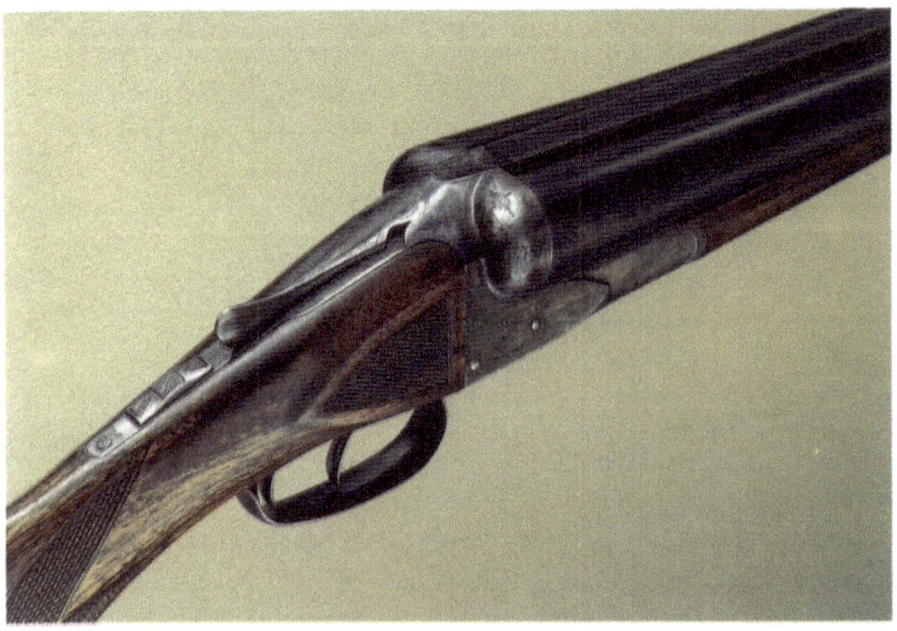

BE Grade 12-gauge, 1910 WILLIAM W. HEADRICK

4

Pigeons in the Park

According to a brief piece in *The Sportsmen's Review* of June 9, 1900, Ansley Fox took up trapshooting in 1897. Actually, he was a trapshooter well before that, and a member of the Baltimore Shooting Association at least as early as 1896. But exactly when Ansley Fox discovered an abiding fondness for formal shooting is less important than what he did with it, because he became for a brief while one of the finest pigeon shots in America.

As with so many things of Ansley Fox's time, the turn of the twentieth century found the sport of trapshooting in transition, and he would find himself, as usual, astride the border between two worlds.

The original trapshooting target was a wild bird—wood pigeons and Lincolnshire blue rocks in England, where the sport began, and the passenger pigeon in America, where trapshooting was introduced about 1830. Fifty years later, the passenger pigeon was so bedeviled by habitat destruction and by year-round harvest for the wild game markets that obtaining enough birds to supply even a modest tournament was nearly impossible.

The game no doubt contributed to the pigeon's eventual extinction, but it never was a primary cause. Like the buffalo, the passenger pigeon simply was too plentiful to survive the American penchant for overuse.

Trapshooters tried any number of substitutes, live and inanimate—from blackbirds, purple martins, starlings, sparrows, and even bats, to discs and balls of glass, paper, pitch, resin, and clay.

For some time, glass balls were the principal alternative to live birds, and they were the targets of choice in some of the most famous exhibitions of marathon shooting ever known in America. But glass balls offered little by way of a genuine challenge to wingshooting skill, and for that, clay targets soon came to the forefront.

They weren't much different from the targets we know today, but what finally made them better than anything else at simulating the flight of a live bird was the increasingly sophisticated mechanism of the trap. Between 1880—when George Ligowsky of Cincinnati secured patents for the now-familiar domed clay disc and a machine to throw it—and the turn of the twentieth century, patents were issued for more than forty different clay-target traps.

The first nationally advertised tournament using clay targets was held in Chicago in May 1884, sponsored by the Ligowsky Clay Pigeon Company. So few shooters showed up that it scarcely was a contest at all. A more successful—and certainly more auspicious—affair came in February 1885 at New Orleans. Attendance once again was less than overwhelming, but the great names were there—Adam Bogardus, Dr. F.W. Carver, James A.R. Elliott, Frank Parmelee, Harvey McMurchy, and others, many of them not only splendid shots but also representatives of the arms, ammunition, and target-equipment industry. Within two years, targets were an established sport in their own right.

Along with it eventually came governing bodies to establish rules and lend some consistency to the game. The most important of them were closely tied with the arms industry. The American Shooting Association, founded February 11, 1889, was the first to exert any real influence over the sport. By 1892, the Interstate Manufacturers & Dealers Association had replaced the ASA, and in 1895, the name was changed to the Interstate Association. For many years it was the principal force in defining the game.

Meanwhile, the diehard live-bird shooters finally settled for domestic pigeons, larger and a bit slower than their wild cousins but worthy targets nonetheless. Clay targets eventually won out almost entirely, but trapshooting at live birds continued past the turn of the century—and indeed, it still survives as the premier form of organized shooting. Spend an afternoon in a pigeon ring, and you'll never again be wholly satisfied with target games.

In the Grand American Handicap tournament, the two forms briefly overlapped. The first Grand American at targets was shot in 1900, and the last Grand using live pigeons was held in Kansas City in 1903.

Those shooters who were veterans at the turn of the century—men like James Elliott, Rolla Heikes, William R. Crosby, Fred Gilbert, Charles Budd, John Fanning, and others—naturally were live-bird shooters. The first great target shots were yet to appear. Only a handful of the older men ever were able to shoot equally well at both.

By the mid-1890s, Ansley Fox had built some reputation around Baltimore as a pigeon shot. Samuel Fort had wrapped up his 1896 *American Field* article by observing that young Fox was "something of a shot, but, having devoted more of his time to developing his mechanical ideas than to shooting, does not rank as an expert. No doubt in time this will be rectified."

The time came in the fall of 1898. On October 6, Ansley Fox delivered a middling performance in the Maryland and District of Columbia Live Bird Championship, the first live-bird tournament at Monumental Shooting Park in Baltimore. It was a fifteen-bird event, and Ansley Fox killed eleven from a handicap distance of twenty-eight yards.

Five days later, he entered the sixth annual tournament of the Baltimore Shooting Association. It was a four-day affair, two days at targets and two at live birds. Ansley Fox shot poorly on Tuesday and Wednesday, at one point breaking only five in a fifteen-target event. But on Thursday afternoon, he killed all seven pigeons in the Baltimore Introductory, sharing top money with four other shooters. Later in the day, he killed ten straight at thirty yards rise in the Suburban Sweepstakes, finishing in a three-way tie for first place.

The main event came the following day, Friday, October 14. Shooting at a handicap rise of twenty-nine yards, Ansley Fox killed twenty-four of twenty-five pigeons and won the Maryland Handicap. It turned his $25 entry fee into $150 in prize money and his local reputation into a brief moment of national fame.

As the century came to an end, it was clear to all but the most obtuse that major tournaments in the none-too-distant future would be clay-target affairs. Ansley Fox presumably shot quite a few clays over the coming months. He was a member of the Baltimore Shooting Association, successor to the old Baltimore Gun Club. At that time, the club grounds comprised several acres of leased land in Pimlico, a northwestern suburb about half an hour by trolly from the center of Baltimore. In addition to its live-bird traps, the club also owned three target traps, and there Ansley Fox learned the game of the future.

The knack for shooting clay targets came, but it came slowly. At a two-day tournament in Portsmouth, Virginia, on September 6 and 7, 1899, he turned in mediocre scores. Each day comprised ten events with 150 targets all told. On the first, a sweltering Wednesday, Ansley Fox got off to a slow start, breaking six of ten targets in the first event and seven of fifteen in the second. He shot better after that but finished the day with only 108 broken targets and a seventy-two-percent average. H.C. Bridges, a North Carolina man who shot under the name "Tarheel," lost only nine targets and was high gun for the day.

Ansley Fox was more consistent the following day, but he also was consistently a few targets off the pace. Both his total score, 119, and his average, seventy-nine percent, were better but no match for the competition. Hood Waters, a veteran trapshooter who also lived in Baltimore, took high honors with 132 breaks and an eighty-eight-percent average.

It seems likely that Ansley Fox did most, if not all of his tournament shooting in the last two years of the century with a gun of his own design. It was common practice then, as later, for manufacturers to sponsor professional shooters who could demonstrate guns and ammunition in competition, and the companies squeezed every winning performance for as much advertising mileage as it would bear. A healthy portion of the reputation that Parker guns enjoy to this day was built by professional gunners and reported at every opportunity in the company's advertising.

By the spring of 1900, Ansley Fox had broken away from his partners in the Fox Gun Company of Baltimore, and the parting apparently was rancorous enough that he refused to shoot publicly with the guns they'd built. When he went to New York to shoot in the Grand American Handicap, Ansley Fox took along a 7 $1/2$-pound Parker 12-gauge and a few cases of Trap Brand shells loaded with 3 $1/2$ drams of E.C. powder and an ounce and a quarter of No. 7 $1/2$ shot.

The sky in New York was perfect that April week, marred only by a brief rain squall on Tuesday noon. New Interstate Park in Queens, which only a year before had been a truck garden, was still under construction, but it showed every promise of becoming the premier trapshooting arena of the East. There were four sets of traps, an elegant hotel and casino, boardwalks and promenades. The Grand was a social as well as a sporting event, and a correspondent to *The Sportsmen's Review* would later remark with pleasure on the number of ladies who came to watch the gunners work.

Mr. Howard D. Bates, who did his shooting in a black wool suit, vest, and bowler hat, would take the Grand American trophy home to St. Thomas, Ontario, after winning a shoot-off against James R. Malone of Baltimore.

For Ansley Fox, it was a rite of passage, the first test of his skill against the finest shots in North America. He was twenty-four, and no doubt he was as nervous as any young man with good sense ought to be.

The game was live pigeons, 14,000 of them shot by week's end. On Monday, it was eight birds at thirty yards rise in the Interstate Park Introductory. From a field of 100, Ansley Fox was one of twenty shooters who shared second place for missing a single bird. Twenty-four men split top money. Whatever he thought of his own ability—which probably was quite a lot—Fox must have known then that he was in the big-time game.

He shot better that afternoon, in the Borough of Queens Sweepstakes, killing all twelve of his birds at thirty yards rise. So did sixteen others, among them Rolla Heikes, one of only a few older professionals to shoot equally well at both live birds and clays. Later that summer, Heikes would win the first Grand American trophy for clay-target shooting.

In the Nitro Powder Handicap next day, Ansley Fox shot with a coolness beyond his years. He killed all sixteen birds in the event at a handicap rise of twenty-eight yards and shared high-gun money with fifteen others from a field of 163.

A north wind under a bright sun lashed the shooters on Wednesday, the first day of the Grand American Handicap. It was strong enough at times to sweep a dead bird over the boundary fences; at other times, it lay meekly, scarcely affecting the flight of the blue, black, and dun pigeons that had been hand-chosen for strength and speed. Mr. J.M. George, the first shooter of 211, fired the first shot at ten o'clock that morning. Fox finished the day in a twenty-three-way tie for first money, with sixteen birds straight.

Thursday's weather was no better. The event was twenty-five birds, handicap rise, for the Grand American trophy and all the marbles. Ansley Fox missed the eighteenth, a fast, right-quartering driver out of trap No. 2 in the second set. With it went any chance of winning the Grand. He finished straight in the sixteen-bird miss-and-out against twenty-five others who had tied at twenty-four birds dead and won $121.65 as tenth money. The wind finally died late in the afternoon.

Not many people came to watch Friday's shooting. At twenty-nine yards rise, Ansley Fox missed two of the fifteen birds in the Consolation Handicap, an event that probably had little consolation in it. But he killed twelve straight in the Auld Lang Syne Sweepstakes that afternoon, one of only five shooters in fifty to do so. Next morning, he packed his gun and his grips and caught the Baltimore train. He had fired at 104 pigeons in five days and had lost only four. He finished the week with a ninety-six-percent average—the highest of anyone who had completed every event—and took home nearly $400 in prize money. The experience was beyond price.

He chose not to enter the clay-target events in the Baltimore Shooting Association's annual spring tournament, held the week after the Grand American. By Thursday, April 12, when the live-pigeon events began, the fine spring weather that had blessed the Grand was only a memory. A chill north wind brought heavy rains interspersed with drizzling mist and brief flurries of snow. On that Thursday morning, the *Sportsmen's Review* writer said, rubber shoes were much in demand.

Ansley Fox killed thirty-two pigeons that day, the only shooter to turn in a perfect score in all three events. Not even James Elliott, arguably the finest pigeon shot in North America and the only one to hold all the important live-bird championships at the same time, did as well. Even so, Ansley Fox wasn't a clear winner; he shared top money with seven other shooters in the first event, with five others in the second, and with six in the third.

He didn't shoot as well in the Maryland Handicap next day, but no one else did, either. There were no perfect scores in the event, which called for twenty-five birds at handicap distance. Shooting from thirty yards rise, Ansley Fox lost the seventh and twenty-third birds out of bounds and missed the fifteenth altogether. Even so, he and two other men collected $21.65 apiece in sharing third money, winning more per man than the six who finished second. Four men shared first-place money at $40.60 each. At day's end, Ansley Fox once again owned the highest average of anyone, finishing at 94.7 percent.

Whatever his reasons for deciding not to shoot in the target events, it wasn't for lack of confidence. A month later, on Tuesday, May 15, he was shooting targets at Monumental Park in Baltimore, at a tournament sponsored by the Standard Gun Club. Someone observed that shooting doubles was the most difficult test of a gunner's skill and offered a bet that Ansley Fox couldn't break forty-three out of twenty-five pair.

No one had ever shot that well at double targets, and when Ansley Fox went out to settle his wager late that afternoon, the consensus was that he wouldn't, either. Odds in the side-betting instantly ran into double digits. What happened next made headline copy in newspapers and sporting journals over half the country. A Baltimore daily, reporting with the breathlessness of a dime novel, had this to say:

> *The first ten were ground up to powder without a miss, and, after a few minutes' rest, he started on the second string of ten. When this ten had been completed the score showed not a miss, and when, after the third ten had been shot and still not a miss, the shooters present began to realize that something out of the ordinary was going on. The fourth string of ten was shot, and when this string ended with the score still clean, excitement ran high. All eyes were now turned upon the young Baltimorean, who seemed to be the coolest man in the crowd. With unerring aim, and with quickness that was simply wonderful, the last ten were broken, and with it the world's record for double target shooting. After many congratulations, Mr. Fox's*

friends asked him to shoot at fifty more birds to see what he could run his already phenomenal score up to. He then broke forty-eight out of his next fifty doubles, which score beats the best record ever made by any other shooter. The grand total of 98 out of 100 birds, double style shooting, has never been equaled in Europe or America.

Ansley Fox was on a roll. The following week, on May 23, he broke 152 of 165 targets in an Interstate Association shoot at Richmond, Virginia, losing high-gun honors by a single clay. Early in June, at a tournament that was part of the Maryland Sportsmen's Show at Electric Park in Baltimore, he won the show championship, the Maryland state championship, and the high-average trophy, with ninety-six percent.

Sometime during that spring, Ansley Fox signed on with Winchester Repeating Arms as a professional shooter, joining the ranks of those who by virtue of exquisite skill were employed by gun and ammunition manufacturers simply to shoot matches and earn high averages in tournaments. In the shooting world, these men were the elite, the famous. Newspapers and trade journals chronicled their performances with great affection and detail, and their employers' products shared the lustre of their reputations.

Though it became Ansley Fox's job to promote Winchester products, he continued for a while to use a Parker gun. He did, though, accept consignments of Winchester cartridges loaded with E.C. powder and marketed under the "Leader" trade name.

Following a common practice of the time, he often shot under a nickname, and from the spring of 1900 until the end of 1902, many of the trapshooting scores reported under the names "Winchester" or "Leader" were those of Ansley Fox.

He was Leader at the first Grand American Handicap at targets, held June 11-15 at Interstate Park. He and four other Baltimore men—Hood Waters, J.R. Malone, H.E. Lupus, and E.H. Storr—shot as a squad, calling themselves the Oyster team.

Rolla Heikes, whom the other shooters called "Pop," did the best shooting the first day, breaking 174 of 175 targets in ten events. Ansley Fox broke 144 and finished well down in the standings.

He shot better the following morning but not much, breaking seventy-five of eighty-five targets in five events. In the Preliminary Handicap that afternoon, he was still off his game. Shooting from twenty yards, he broke seventy-eight of 100 and finished far out of the money.

Thursday was a close and sultry day, dampened occasionally with light rain and twice by downpours. The Grand American Handicap, 100 targets at handicap distance, got under way at two o'clock in the afternoon, with seventy-four shooters entered. Rolla Heikes won the trophy with a score of ninety-one. Ansley Fox, shooting from nineteen yards, broke eighty-six. Heavy rain ended the day before all the ties were broken; after the shoot-off next morning, Fox collected $32.55 as tenth money.

He once again shot poorly in the Consolation Handicap that afternoon, breaking only sixty-seven of eighty-five targets. He finished the tournament with an 84.2 percent average in all of the non-handicap events, only sixteenth-best and far off the pace set by old Pop Heikes' 95.6.

Ansley Fox clearly was off his game, clearly struggling. There are two likely explanations. The simplest is that he just needed a rest, needed a break from endless hours on the trains, from living in hotels, and from the exhausting concentration and physical stress of tournament shooting.

It's also possible that Ansley Fox was fighting to absorb the death of his son. No death certificate exists for James Fox, neither in Baltimore nor in Philadelphia. He was alive in mid-April 1900, when U.S. Census information was gathered, but apparently he died before the Foxes moved to Philadelphia in 1901. Because Ansley Fox's name appeared frequently in the sporting press in 1900 and 1901, we have a more detailed picture of his activities during those years than at any other time in his life. He disappears from view twice in 1900, first in midsummer, again in early winter, and both times for several weeks. It seems likely that during one or the other of those periods he was at home in Baltimore, giving Fentress what comfort he could and dealing with his own grief.

In any case, after the Grand American target tournament in June 1900, Ansley Fox isn't mentioned in the sporting press until *The Sportsmen's Review* reported on a tournament held at the Newport Gun Club, Newport, Vermont, on August 7 and 8. By then, he was a celebrity. The *Review* article says:

> *The assemblage of famous shots was a remarkable one for this vicinity, and one that will not be forgotten by the people who saw them. When such men as Fanning, Dickey, Hull, Leroy, Hallowell, Fox, and numerous experts of that class meet in a tournament, depend upon it there will be some good shooting going on.*

Whatever the expectations were, Ansley Fox didn't altogether meet them. Of 115 targets in seven events on August 7, he broke only ninety-eight, finishing fifth among forty-three shooters. Next day, he finished second in a program of six events, breaking ninety-one of 100.

It was a slow start perhaps, but the rest, if he took one, did Ansley Fox some good. Late in August, he set a new record for trapshooting in Carroll County, Maryland, breaking 109 of 110 targets in a tournament at the Westminster Gun Club. He ran sixty-nine straight, missed a target, and finished with another forty straight. At a Baltimore shoot the following week, he broke 146 of 150 on Monday and eighty-two of eighty-five the next day.

Shortly after, Ansley Fox headed out on a winter tour through the South. At a two-day tournament in Chattanooga in early September, he broke 182 of 200 targets for a three-way tie in first place. By that time, professional shooters were ineligible to share in purses or sweepstakes at tournaments sanctioned by the Interstate Association, so Ansley Fox was shooting only for the price of the targets, for the greater glory of Winchester Repeating Arms, and for his own love of the sport. Next day, he broke 172 of 200 to finish fifth.

The day after that, there were four events at live pigeons, and Ansley Fox shot in two of them. He killed all seven in the first event and nine of ten birds in the third. It must have seemed like coming home.

On September 19, he began two days' work in Pensacola, Florida, at the Dixie Gun Club Tournament. He won high overall average, breaking 120 of 140 targets in nine events. There were two live-bird events that afternoon. From twenty-eight yards rise, Ansley Fox scored eight of ten in the first, losing the third pigeon dead out of bounds and missing the fourth. In a miss-and-out shoot afterwards, he and a local man named Forbes traded kill for kill until Ansley Fox missed the eighteenth bird.

He and Forbes went at it again next day, first at targets, then at birds. Fox outshot him through the first eight of nine events and went into the last one with a four-target lead. Forbes was consistent; Ansley Fox was not. He lost seven of the last twenty-five targets and finished runner-up by two.

Ansley Fox shot in only one of the two live-bird events later that day. From twenty-eight yards, Fox, Forbes, and a Florida amateur named Bates all killed ten pigeons straight. That evening, Mr. T.E. Wells took Ansley Fox and three other visiting professionals aboard his launch for a tour of Pensacola Bay.

On October 13, he was in Altoona, Pennsylvania, for a live-bird handicap tournament at the Altoona Rod and Gun Club. He and another Baltimore man named Schultze were handicapped at thirty yards, the farthest of any among the twenty-eight shooters. It was a fifteen-bird event, and Ansley Fox killed twelve to finish in a six-way tie for third place. He joined in the target shooting afterwards, leading the entire field with seventy-four of eighty.

He was in Atlanta ten days later, for a three-day target and live-pigeon tournament sponsored by the Peters Cartridge Company. He shot brilliantly, finishing High Gun overall in two days of target shooting and a day in the pigeon ring. Of fifty pigeons, he lost only one, a bird that fell dead beyond the boundary fence. The shooting finished so near sundown that most of the men shot the last ten-bird race from their knees, the better to silhouette the birds against the sky. Ansley Fox and two others killed all ten.

Somewhere along the way, Ansley Fox acquired another nickname, this one "Hazel." What it meant is anyone's guess, but it clearly was an affectionate title, for Ansley Fox was popular among shooters. As a *Sportsmen's Review* writer notes in reporting the Peters Cartridge tournament: "Jolly, genial Fox ('Hazel') made friends with everybody, besides winning the first average."

After the Atlanta shoot, Ansley Fox apparently did little tournament work for the remainder of the year. This was the longest of his two absences from the sporting scene in 1900, and it, rather than his midsummer break, may have been prompted by his son's death.

When he came back, he came back with a flourish. On January 7, 1901, Ansley Fox killed a spectacular 129 of 130 birds in a live-pigeon shoot at Interstate Park in New York. He killed the first ninety-one straight. The ninety-second fell inside the ring, but it had enough strength left to flutter over the boundary fence when a dog was sent to retrieve it; under the standard rules of trapshooting, it was counted lost. Next day, after watching James Elliott win a two-man match against R.A. Welch for the DuPont live-bird trophy, Ansley Fox killed nineteen in a twenty-bird event.

He was still shooting from a handicap rise of thirty yards and still using Leader shells, but Winchester apparently had persuaded him to give up his Parker in favor of a Winchester Model 97. Presumably, he used a 97 for the remainder of his tenure as a Winchester representative, and if that were the case indeed, then Ansley Fox's trapshooting career reached a peak over the slender barrel and gawky profile of John Browning's best pump-action gun.

He had a bad day in Norfolk, Virginia, on January 24, killing only twelve of seventeen birds in three events, but over the following three months, Ansley Fox went on some binges of brilliant shooting. High highs and low lows were his trademark, it seems.

It began at the New York Sportsman's Show on March 2. The show was an annual, two-week affair held at Madison Square Garden, and at the turn of the century, it was the most important trade show of the American sporting-goods industry. All of the industry-sponsored trapsmen attended, and there was continual shooting on the Garden roof.

The shooting actually amounted to two extended exhibition contests, one the Sportsmen's Association Championship, the other a continuous match. The championship was shot at 100 targets per day with unlimited reentries allowed, so that any shooter making a bad start could drop out and start over, or he could shoot as many strings of 100 as he chose.

The continuous match essentially was an extended miss-and-out; the object simply was to make the longest run of consecutive hits. When a shooter missed, his score was tallied up to that point, and he started over. Medals were awarded in both events each day, and at the end of the show, the top four shooters in each were given prizes and trophies.

March 2 was a rainy Saturday, and shooting conditions at the Roof Garden were dismal. Rolla Heikes won the championship medal for the day with a score of ninety-four. Ansley Fox entered three times and finished fourth with his best score of eighty-nine. John Fanning won Monday's championship medal with a ninety-six, and Rolla Heikes' seventy-one was the high score in the continuous match. Ansley Fox shot two full rounds in the championship, eighty-four and seventy-four; the higher score was good for sixth place. His best run in the continuous match was only fifteen.

The rain stopped on Sunday, but the wind kept up, and by Tuesday afternoon, the weather turned cold as well. Rolla Heikes and Fred Gilbert tied for the championship medal at ninety-four, and Gilbert was high gun in the continuous match that day with a run of sixty-five. Ansley Fox shot 300 targets, improving his first-round seventy-six to an eighty-nine and a tie for third place, and improving that to a ninety and a tie for second. A long run of fifty-five won him second place in the continuous match.

Wednesday, too, was windy and cold. The continuous match was suspended for the day. Fred Gilbert shot a ninety-three to win the championship match. Ansley Fox once again shot 300 targets—two eighty-eights and a ninety— and tied in both third and fourth places.

By the following day, the wind had died, the weather was warm, and so were the tempers of the people who lived on Madison Avenue near the Garden. After four days of gunfire and stray shot sprinkling into the street below, the neighborhood complained so loudly that the shooting was called off at a quarter past eleven that morning and subsequently moved across the East River to Interstate Park for the duration of the Sportsmen's Show. No championship match was shot that day, but Ansley Fox won the continuous match with a string of forty-one.

On Friday, he won the championship match outright with a ninety-six on his second reentry. Gilbert took the continuous match with eighty-one.

Except for one score of ninety-five that earned a tie for fourth place, Saturday was a washout for Ansley Fox. On his first reentry in the championship, he missed an incredible seventy-four targets and turned in a score of twenty-six. He ran the first twenty-five targets straight in his third round, dropped to twenty-one and then to twenty and then withdrew from the day's match. His best run in the continuous match that day was twenty-nine, a far cry from Fred Gilbert's 139 straight.

The following week saw three new world records established. On Tuesday, John Fanning, Rolla Heikes, Fred Gilbert, William Crosby, and Frank Parmelee each ran twenty-five targets straight for a new record high score by a five-man squad. On Wednesday, Crosby broke 345 targets without a miss, far surpassing the previous record of 231, held by John Fanning. The same day, Parmelee and Gilbert each broke 100 straight, something that had never been done by two men shooting on the same squad.

Ansley Fox, too, had his moments, both good and bad. He broke no records, but he did win the continuous match on Thursday with a run of 125 straight. His other scores that week were largely undistinguished. Friday was the worst. He broke eighteen of his first twenty-five, withdrew and reentered, broke a nineteen and a twenty-three, withdrew and reentered a second time, turned in scores of twenty-four, twenty-two, and twenty-three and dropped out for the day.

In the final match on Saturday, March 16, Ansley Fox finished sixth with a score of ninety-one. Because he'd dropped out on Friday before completing a full 100-target round, the rules held him ineligible for the championship trophy. It wouldn't have made any difference if he'd stayed in. Fred Gilbert's superb shooting that week placed him well ahead of everyone else in the final standings. He, William Crosby, and John Fanning took the top three medals, respectively.

Two weeks later, Ansley Fox was back in New York, this time for the Grand American. By then, all the lavish accommodations at Interstate Park were complete—which was a good thing, because a week of villainous weather so bedeviled the Grand that shooters and spectators alike spent most of their time seeking shelter indoors. The writer who covered the affair for *The Sportsmen's Review* was as terse and grumpy as his counterpart the year before had been ebullient. "It is very greatly to be regretted," he wrote, "that the weather should have been so very inclement during this week of all the weeks in the year." Which is about as bitchy as you can be in the passive voice.

It started well enough. Ansley Fox killed ten birds straight in both the Park Introductory and the Borough of Queens Sweepstakes. But this was the Grand, and as usual, the heavy talent was in town—Fred Gilbert, Harold Money ("the shootin'est gentleman" of Nash Buckingham's stories), Rolla Heikes, James Elliott, William Crosby. Both Ansley Fox and Pop Heikes were handicapped at thirty yards, Elliott and Gilbert at thirty-two.

Monday was the only day that week with even a semblance of pleasant weather—a clear, bright sky and a gale-force wind out of the northwest that made sporty birds for shooters facing east. All of the shooting stations at Interstate Park faced east. Thirty-one of 136 shooters finished without a miss in the Introductory and only twenty of 182 in the Borough Sweeps.

Tuesday was goony-bird day, with heavy clouds and not a whiff of wind. The birds seemed to swim in the viscous atmosphere, lumbering up from the traps like barnyard chickens. The *Review* writer got almost testy about the number of perfect scores in the making. But he was able to report that the wind came back later in the day—out of the southwest this time—and brought all but thirty-one of 199 scores to ruin. That seemed to cheer him up.

By Tuesday evening, after two days' shooting, only three men in a field of 200 had not yet missed a bird: William Crosby, Howard D. Bates, and Ansley Fox.

Heavy rain driven by an east wind kept everyone indoors in Wednesday morning. Just after noon, tournament manager Elmer Shaner declared the opening of the Grand American Handicap postponed until the following day. The rain stopped half an hour later. To fill the afternoon, sixty-nine shooters got up a $5 miss-and-out, while six others shot two-man matches at the No. 2 set of traps. Ansley Fox and thirty-two others killed seven birds straight in the miss-and-out before sundown ended the sport.

The Grand began at nine o'clock on Thursday morning, April 5, in a sluicing rain. All told, 201 shooters started the event, which called for twenty birds that day, with the remaining five to be shot the following morning. Not even the strongest birds could fly well against the pouring, windless rain, and forty men, Ansley Fox among them, killed straight for the day. When the final, five-bird round was over on Friday morning, twenty-two straight scores remained. One of them belonged to Ansley Fox.

The miss-and-out shootoff for the trophy began at noon under clearing skies. In five days, Ansley Fox had fired at sixty-eight tournament pigeons and had killed every one. He was the only man to have come that far without a miss; Crosby had lost one bird and Bates two in the Handicap's first round.

His first bird was a fast driver, and Ansley Fox missed it twice. Eugene C. Griffith and J.L.D. Morrison shot their way through seventeen pigeons apiece until Griffith, an amateur who had shot fewer than 300 tournament pigeons before that week, won the Grand on the eighteenth bird.

It is the nature of shooting that the red gods seem to assign lost targets or apparently armor-plated birds to key moments in time—a fact that causes great gnashing of teeth among the young and a progressively fatalistic attitude among the veterans. In April 1901, Ansley Fox was about two months from his twenty-sixth birthday, young but with enough tournament mileage to know that he owed the gods at least one miss in a week's shooting. Still, like any of us, he must have wondered why it should have been *that* bird. He had never come so close to the Grand American trophy. He would never come so close again.

He entered the Baltimore Shooting Association's annual tournament on April 9. For the first two days, devoted to targets, strong crosswinds and unusually powerful traps kept everyone's performance below ninety percent. Fred Gilbert was high gun both days. Ansley Fox finished seventh the first day, sixth the next.

He didn't shoot in any of the three live-bird events on Thursday, and he might as well have passed up the Maryland Handicap on Friday. At a handicap rise of thirty-one yards, he missed the second, sixth, and seventh pigeons and withdrew. He shot in two miss-and-out events later in the afternoon, killing twelve straight in one and missing the first bird in the other.

Ansley Fox was a busy man for the next couple of months. On April 24 and 25, in a Peters Cartridge Company tournament at Binghamton, New York, he broke 331 of 350 targets to earn high-gun honors. On April 26, he shot in a 180-target tournament at Owego, New York, and was high gun once again with a stunning 176.

Ansley Fox shot both targets and live birds during the first two days of the New Jersey State Sportsman's Association tournament at Newark on May 7 and 8. From May 20 through 25, he shot in the Illinois State Sportsmen's Association tournament at Springfield. In a combination of live-bird and target events, his shooting was consistently good, at moments brilliant. He was in Circleville, Ohio, on June 4 for a three-day target tournament sponsored by the Ohio Trap Shooters' League, still shooting well but never quite well enough. A note in the *Sportsmen's Review* report observes that "Fox was a little out of form, as was also Ralph Trimble. The pace was pretty hot, though, maybe too hot." Maybe so. Ansley Fox broke a total 435 of 465 targets to finish sixth overall, only nine targets back from the winning score.

He found the competition considerably less intense in Warm Springs, Georgia, a couple of weeks later, at an annual affair sponsored by Mr. Charles L.

Davis. The first two days' shooting amounted to 175 targets each day, and Ansley Fox finished second overall on the first day, with 162. Next day, he shot into a three-way tie for fourth place with 155, only three targets behind the winner. In the next two days, shooting at thirty-two yards rise, he killed thirty-six pigeons in four events—straight scores in every one.

At the Grand American Target Handicap, held at Interstate Park in July, mosquitoes made almost as much news as shooters did. *The Sportsmen's Review* had this to say:

> *The Casino was also looking at its best, and a number of improvements were found to have been made, the chief one of which, however, was the placing of wire screens at all the doors and the doors and windows of the sleeping rooms. This was done merely as a precautionary measure, and not because it was thought they would be needed, for up to the week previous to the tournament no mosquitoes had made their appearance. But the extreme heat and mugginess of the weather brought them in innumerable numbers, not alone at the park, but in all parts of the city as well. Had due care been taken by those stopping at the Casino during the week, no one need have suffered, but by the careless leaving of the doors open and the displacement of the screens, the mosquitoes got into the building in such numbers that many who had been stopping there sought quarters elsewhere, but probably to fare no better.*

Unlike the mosquitoes, shooters arrived in quite numerable numbers—although attendance was healthy enough to account for 59,432 targets thrown between Tuesday morning and Friday afternoon.

The most formidable squad comprised industry professionals—Fred Gilbert, William Crosby, Rolla Heikes, John Fanning, and Ansley Fox, shooting as "Winchester." The Interstate Association had only recently adopted the now-familiar system of handicapping by distance, although it was short yardage compared with the current sixteen- to twenty-seven-yard standard. Some shooters stood as close as fourteen yards, and even the best professionals—Gilbert, Crosby, and Heikes—shot from only twenty-two yards. But given fast traps, hard targets, and relatively inefficient ammunition, it was enough; as the *Review* reporter notes, "It was an amateur tournament with the reversion of the old order of things—the experts being the contributors, instead of being the winners."

By the end of the week, none of the professionals won any of the major events. Eugene Griffith, who had won the Grand American at pigeons three months before, also won the Grand American target event. Ansley Fox, shooting from a twenty-one-yard handicap, turned in creditable but essentially lackluster performances.

No doubt he did a fair share of shooting over the next few months, but none of it was reported in the major journals. At some point during this period, Ansley Fox moved from Baltimore to Philadelphia, to 3534 Gratz, a quiet street that runs in fits and starts, a square or two at a time, north and south through the Germantown section of the city. His house still stands, a narrow, two-story row house with a bay window on the second floor and eaves trimmed in Victorian gingerbread woodwork. The 1902 Philadelphia city directory, the first in which Ansley Fox appears, lists his occupation as "salesman."

It's unlikely that we'll ever learn precisely why he chose to leave Baltimore at that particular time or why he chose Philadelphia as a destination. He clearly had no intention of spending a lifetime as a professional shooter and industry representative; if those years were meant to serve any larger purpose in Ansley Fox's life, it probably was to learn first-hand what the trapshooting world offered as a market for guns and how that market might be cultivated. Subsequent years would show that he took the lessons well to heart.

The decline of live-bird shooting was far advanced by 1902. A groundswell of anti-cruelty activism in the East had grown strong enough to disrupt the Grand American the year before and passionate enough that the New York state legislature passed a bill that banned pigeon shooting. Over the next few years, a number of other states followed suit. Ansley Fox no doubt felt a certain regret for the passing of a fine sport, but at the same time, he clearly recognized that target shooting would open an even greater range of opportunity for the arms industry. Pigeon shooting was expensive, and while its followers were many, their numbers were nothing like the legions that would embrace target shooting. More shooters meant more guns to be sold, and Ansley Fox intended to help fulfill the demand.

With Interstate Park no longer available for pigeon shooting, the Interstate Association looked west to Kansas City in 1902 for the tenth, and last, Grand American Handicap at live birds.

It was held at Elliott's Shooting Park, then situated in the Missouri River bottoms at the northeastern corner of Kansas City. Established in 1887 by James A.R. Elliott and his brothers, Bob and Dave, Elliott's would become the most famous and certainly the longest-lived trapshooting club in the Midwest. After several relocations to accommodate the sprawling growth of Kansas City, the park settled in Raytown, an eastern suburb, in 1934. It remained there, passing eventually out of Elliott family ownership, until bankruptcy claimed the grounds in 1983. The park closed down for good in 1985.

The 1902 Grand American was a mammoth affair by turn-of-the-century standards. Between the opening event on Monday, May 31 and the last shot on the following Saturday, 493 shooters tried their hands. Thirty-one of them killed twenty-five birds straight in the Grand; H.C. Hirschey of Minneapolis, who didn't miss a pigeon all week, won the shoot-off and the Grand American trophy. Ansley Fox, shooting a 7 $^3/_4$-pound Winchester gun at a thirty-one-yard handicap rise, lost one bird out of bounds, missed two others, and ended far out of the money—which amounted to $12,000 total purse.

He shot well in the other events. He was one of thirty-nine shooters to kill eight birds straight in the Missouri Sweepstakes, the last event of the week, but there was little glory at the Grand that year for Ansley Fox.

It was the same at the Grand American at targets in May, though a two-way tie for fifth place in the Grand was good for an additional yard of handicap distance, which put him at twenty-one yards for the last events. He fared no better in a Pennsylvania tournament the following week.

Early in September, Ansley Fox appeared at two more tournaments in Pennsylvania. He finished sixth in a three-day shoot at Erie City and third in another three-day affair at Du Bois. A month later, he took second place in two days of targets at the Baltimore Shooting Association tournament. On November 25, he finished fifth overall in a ten-event shoot at Rising Sun, Maryland.

Before the year was out, Ansley Fox's career as a professional shooter came to an end. For some months, he'd been at work gathering financial support for a gun factory, and as those plans came into place, he could ill afford the time spent on the railway cars and the firing line. In December 1902, he resigned his association with Winchester, presumably to devote full attention to the recently-founded Philadelphia Arms Company.

Still, professional or amateur, Ansley Fox loved to shoot. As a member of the Keystone Shooting League team, he entered the Pennsylvania State Tournament, held at the Florists' Gun Club grounds in Wissinoming, May 1903. He broke 278 of 300 targets in the open amateur events and finished eighth overall.

His shooting career served Ansley Fox extremely well. Over the next ten years, as his gunmaking career reached full flower, he would give the target-shooting world special attention as a market for Fox guns. And there, too, his approach would garnish tradition with innovation. At a big tournament these days, it sometimes is hard to find the shooting field among the rows of industry booths and tents and displays. That wasn't the case in Ansley Fox's day; gun- and ammunition-makers sent representatives but no formal displays of their wares. But in 1909, *The Sporting Goods Dealer* reported that the A.H. Fox Gun Company had set up a display tent at the Grand American Handicap tournament in Chicago. The reporter called it a novel way of promoting products.

All in all, Ansley Fox's tenure as a professional trapsman was brief and uneven. In a column of short comments published in August 1900, a *Sportsmen's Review* writer offered what probably was a more insightful view of Ansley Fox than anyone ever realized. "A.H. Fox," he said, "is real clever, and surprises the boys sometimes with his big scores. When at himself, Fox will give any of the crackerjacks a brush." And that, it seems, is how it was for Ansley Fox, not only at trapshooting but in business and at life itself—a losing struggle for consistency, marked with flashes of brilliance intense as lightning.

For whatever satisfaction trapshooting gave Ansley Fox, it also exacted a price. Like many another shooter of every era, the constant noise of gunfire made him nearly deaf. Perhaps, during reflective moments in later years, the hearing aid he wore reminded Ansley Fox of his shooting days and brought back faint echoes of the tension and exhilaration he once knew while shooting pigeons at the park.

In 1901, Ansley Fox moved to Philadelphia and lived for several years in this townhouse at 3534 Gratz, in the Germantown section of the city.

DAVID J. NOREEN

Philadelphia Arms Company C Grade WILLIAM W. HEADRICK

5

Philadelphia Arms

In the closing months of 1901, French artist Henri de Toulouse-Lautrec died from alcoholism, President William McKinley from an assassin's bullet. The new president, Theodore Roosevelt, hosted a black man, Booker T. Washington, in the White House, and thirty-four people died in New Orleans race riots as a result. George Eastman organized the Eastman Kodak Corporation, King Gillette marketed a hoe-shaped gadget called the safety razor, Walt Disney was born, and Ansley Fox designed a fastening system for a shotgun action.

He had two goals in mind. One was to create a mechanism that would lock the barrels firmly in place. The other was to improve the means by which the safety catch would engage each time the shooter opened the gun.

As the drawings show, he took a straightforward approach to accomplishing both. He was by then wholly convinced that a top hook and barrel extension offered a better, more durable fastener than a sliding underbolt. In this version, the hook is milled from a flat, thick semi-circle of steel and pivots on a vertical axis. A twelve-degree taper to the bearing surface compensates for wear.

At the turn of the century, the top-hook fastener was a well-seasoned concept. Westley Richards built the earliest version in 1862. In America, Dan Lefever had been using the vertical-axis hook since 1878, and both David Minier and Emile Flues would soon use it for the models of Ithaca guns that bear their names. Alexander Brown used the same principle in his 1883 design for the hammerless L.C. Smith, though his version rotates on a horizontal axis.

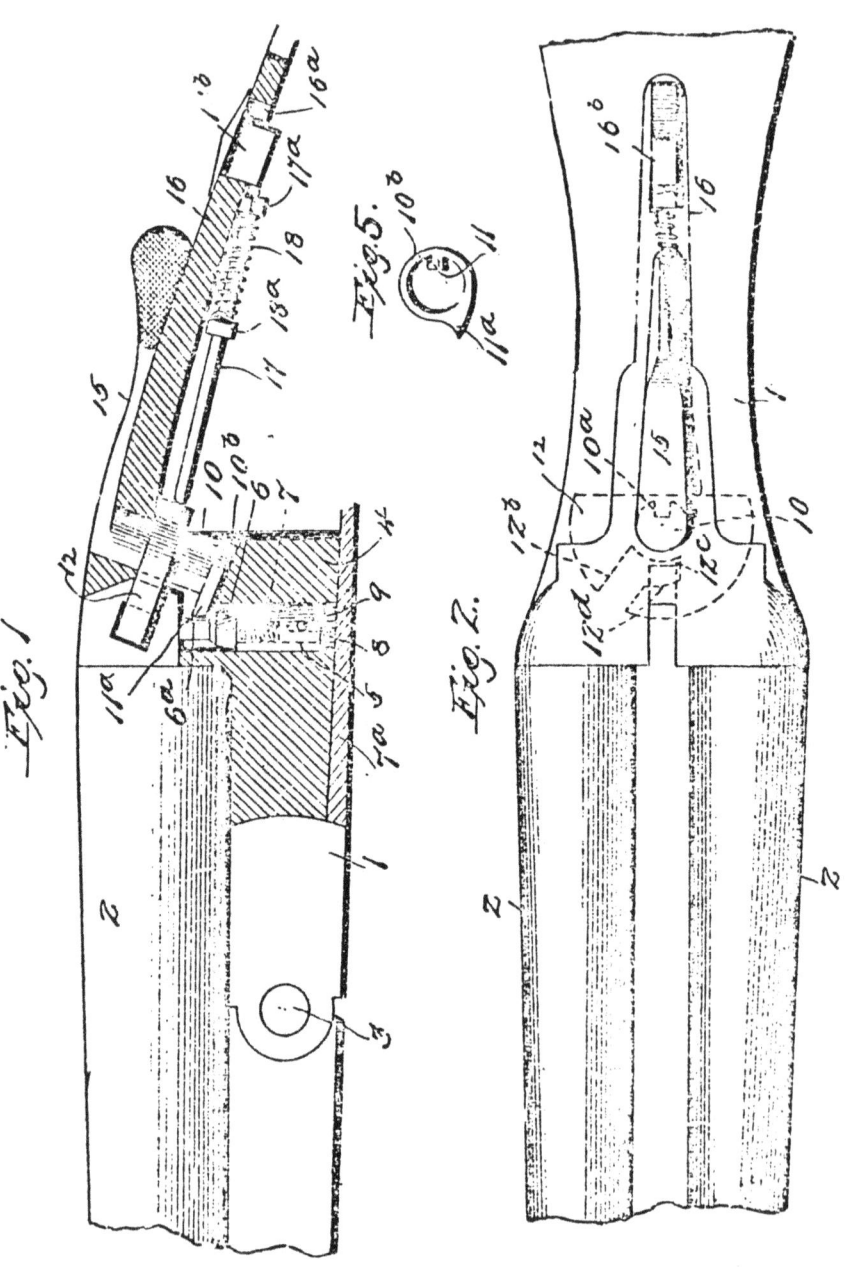

No. 714,688. Patented Dec. 2, 1902.
A. H. FOX.
BREECH LOADING FIREARM.
(Application filed Jan. 17, 1902.)

(No Model.) 2 Sheets—Sheet 2.

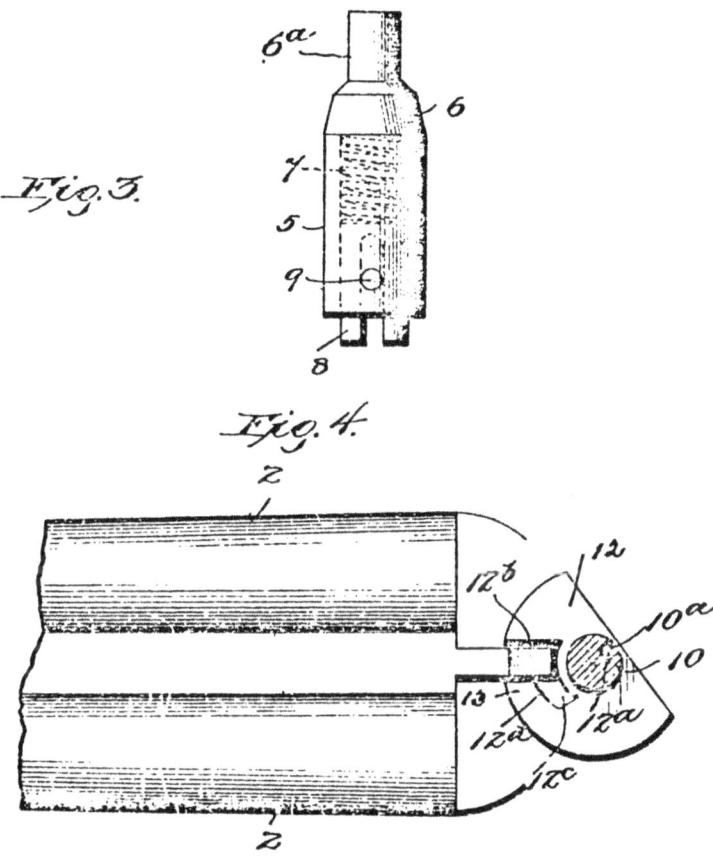

Witnesses

Inventor
Ansley H. Fox,
by Jas. L. Skidmore
his Attorney.

Unlike a sliding underbolt, which is simply cammed backwards as the gun is closed and then snaps forward by spring tension, a rotary top hook has to stay retracted as long as the gun is open. Otherwise, the rib extension cannot enter its slot in the standing breech. A top-hook system, therefore, has to include some means of holding the hook out of the way, but the catch must disengage instantly and automatically when the action is closed.

Ansley Fox solved that problem the same way most other double-gun designers have—with a spring-loaded stud inside the frame that pops up to act as a stop against the lower part of the top-latch spindle. The top portion protrudes into the rib-extension slot, and the extension itself disengages the stop by simply pushing it downward as the action is closed. In the 1901 design, the plunger assembly is more complex than it really needs to be, but it works, and Fox would use the same idea, somewhat simplified, in all of his later double guns.

The automatic-safety feature is a simple push-rod mounted between the top-latch spindle and the safety button. As the spindle turns, it cams the rod backwards and pushes the safety to the engaged position. A coil spring then pushes the rod forward, out of contact with the safety. Presumably, Fox added the spring as insurance against any chance of the rod binding the safety. Most American automatic safeties use push-rods, though few are spring-loaded, and Fox discarded the spring in later guns.

Ansley Fox submitted the drawings and written description of his gun to the U.S. Patent Office on January 17, 1902. When the patent, No. 714,688, was granted December 2, 1902, it protected five features of the bolting system, the spindle stop, and the automatic-safety linkage.

Having the patent in hand probably helped Ansley Fox convince investors that he could turn out an innovative, marketable product. He resigned from Winchester at that point and along with Alfred P. Shannon, C. William Haywood, Henry F. Kingsbury, and a man whose signature is illegible, incorporated Philadelphia Arms Company on November 5, 1902.

Although capital stock is quoted at 4000 shares with a total value of $200,000, the five men who signed the incorporation papers held only twenty shares among them, and the company's directors were not specified. The principal investor or investors clearly wanted to remain anonymous, and this no doubt is why Philadelphia Arms was incorporated in New Jersey, where state laws did not require extensive disclosures in setting up corporations. After New Jersey changed its laws some time later, a great many businessmen, Ansley Fox among them, found Delaware a similarly easy place to incorporate.

In any event, Philadelphia Arms incorporation papers list the New Jersey Trust Company, 417-419 Market Street, Camden, as the address and do not specify a place of business. The 1903 Philadelphia city directory lists no occupation for Ansley Fox, only his home address on Gratz Street. Presumably, he spent much of that year involved with the design and—after August, when the contract was signed—construction of a new factory building at North 18th Street and Courtland Street, near the railway just northeast of Wayne Junction Station. He also was engaged with the design for a new gun.

Although Fox assigned his 1902 patent to Philadelphia Arms, the guns themselves apparently were not built according to that design but rather on two patents issued August 16, 1904. The first of these, applied for on May 1, 1903, is No. 767,557, granted to Ansley Fox's brother Harry and assigned to Philadelphia Arms Company. It covers a cocking system comprising sliding, coil-spring-loaded rods and a roller-type cocking piece that rotates around the hinge-pin. (Most likely, Ansley Fox actually designed the system and for some now-obscure reason chose to have it patented in his brother's name. At the time, Harry Fox still lived at the Fox family home in Baltimore and was, according to the city directory, a student. Beginning in 1905, the directories show him as a physician, in practice with his father.)

The other patent, No. 767,621, was applied for on June 13, 1903, and was granted to Max Wirsing of Baltimore and also assigned to Philadelphia Arms. It covers an ejector system.

It's difficult to draw many conclusions on the evolution of Philadelphia Arms guns by looking at the guns themselves, simply because there aren't many floating around. None of the few I've seen are marked with any patent date other than August 16, 1904—and one, No. 1087, has no patent stamp at all. All I've seen incorporate the cocking system described in the Harry Fox patent, but the fastening system—a horizontally rotating top hook very similar to that of the L.C. Smith—is covered by a patent that never belonged to Philadelphia Arms Company at all. This is patent No. 796,119, applied for on December 29, 1904, issued August 1, 1905, to Ansley Fox and assigned to the A.H. Fox Gun Company.

But I'm getting ahead of the story. On October 27, 1903, Philadelphia Arms Company was incorporated in Pennsylvania. Directors and Subscribers to Shares are listed as follows: Ansley H. Fox, 201 shares; Philip F. DuPont, 100 shares; C. William Haywood, 99 shares; Douglas S. Daubt and Harry H. Fox, one share each. Capital stock is cited at $200,000. Ansley Fox is listed as president, DuPont vice-president and secretary, Haywood as treasurer.

Philip DuPont belonged to the chemical-manufacturing DuPont family, and he and Ansley Fox probably established an acquaintance during Fox's tenure as a professional shooter and industry representative. Given that and the decision

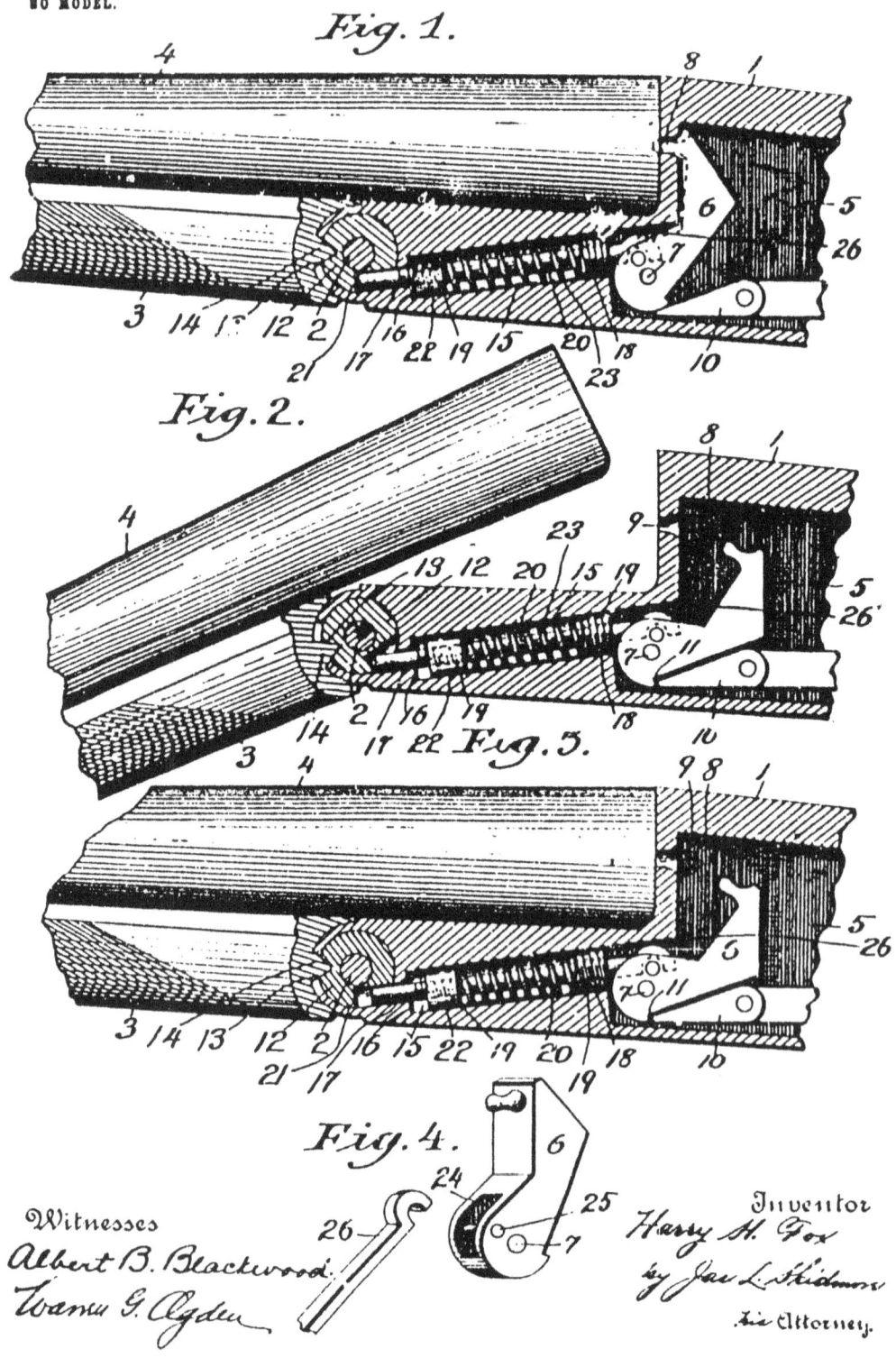

No. 767,621. PATENTED AUG. 16, 1904.
M. WIRSING.
EJECTOR MECHANISM FOR FIREARMS.
APPLICATION FILED JUNE 18, 1903.

NO MODEL.

Fig. 1.

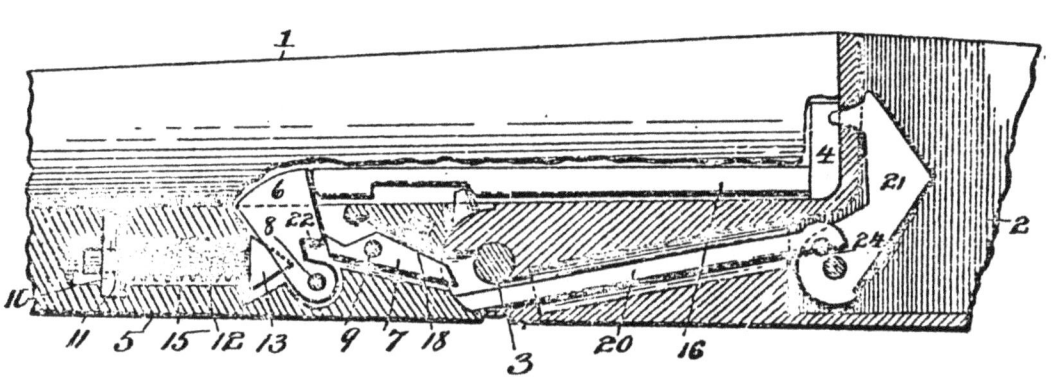

Fig. 2.

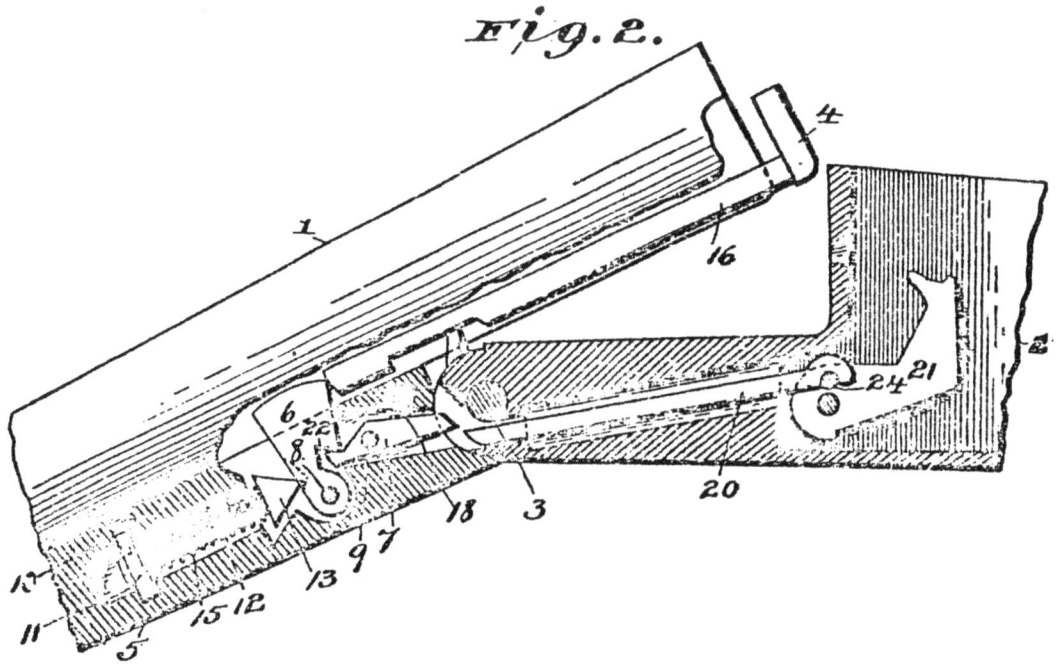

Witnesses
Jas. H. Blackwood
May M. Plyer

Inventor
Max Wirsing
By Jas. L. Skidmore
His Attorney

to incorporate in New Jersey, it's tempting to wonder if DuPont money wasn't involved in Philadelphia Arms from the beginning.

The earliest journal item on Philadelphia Arms that I've found appeared in the March 1904 issue of *The Sporting Goods Dealer*. "The Philadelphia Arms Co.," it begins, "has recently completed its new gun factory at Wayne Junction, Phila., and is now manufacturing the A.H. Fox hammerless gun... The factory is a two-story brick building 178 feet long by 60 feet wide and with the outer buildings and officers has about 15,000 feet of floor space... Deliveries will commence in July next at the rate of 15 guns a day." Prices, the story says, range from $50 to $500.

Ansley Fox knew full well what competition his new gun would face, and characteristically, he squared off to have a go at the alpha wolf. At first glance from any angle, you could easily mistake a Philadelphia Arms gun, with its rounded frame and dished sculpting around the hinge pin, for a Parker, and the similarities obviously were no accident.

Nonetheless, they're only skin-deep. The hammerless Parker of 1904 was a hellishly complicated piece. Fox's gun is considerably simpler mechanically, and of course, the fastening system is quite different from Parker's underbolt. Coil springs, moreover, are used throughout the Philadelphia Arms guns, as they are in all the later guns Fox designed.

Presumably, the company issued a catalogue in 1904, although I've never had the opportunity to see one. I do, however, have a copy of one dated 1905, titled "The A.H. Fox Hammerless Gun, Philadelphia Arms Co., Makers, Philadelphia, Pa., U.S.A." In layout and language, it's remarkably similar to the early A.H. Fox Gun Company catalogues, which comes as no surprise, and it offers the most detailed overview of the Philadelphia Arms guns we're ever likely to have.

List Price, $50.00

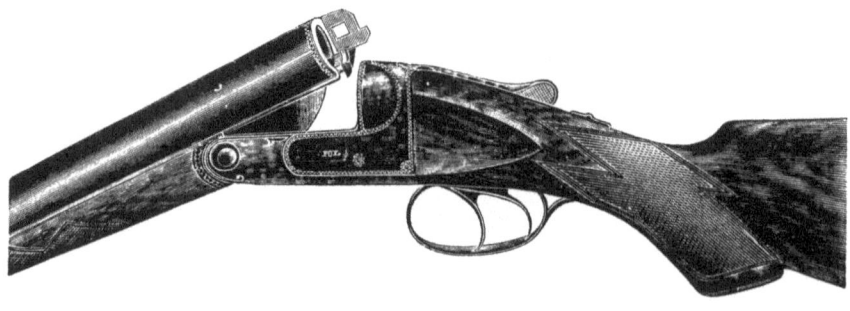

Grade A

The line comprised seven grades: A, B, C, D, E, F, and H. All were available with Krupp barrels, although Damascus barrels were optional in Grade C and above, and English-made Whitworth steel barrels were an additional option in Grade H. The only barrel lengths listed are twenty-eight, thirty, and thirty-two inches, and 12 the only gauge.

List Price, $75.00

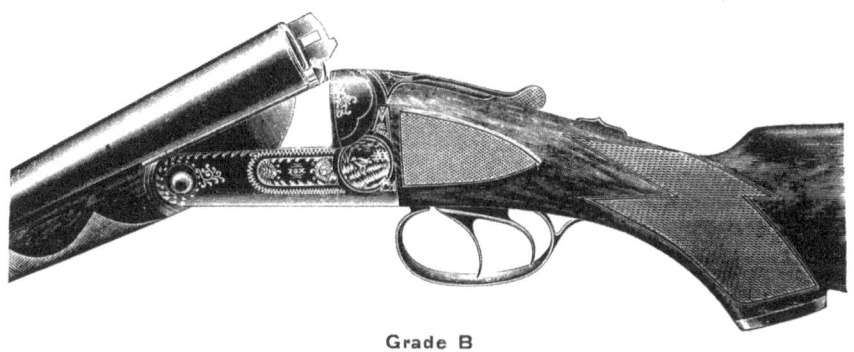

Grade B

Stocks are described as "English walnut" for all grades except H, which the catalogue says would be stocked with "the very finest Circassian." The A Grade came with pistol grip only, all the rest with a choice of pistol grip or straight hand. The F Grade stock is "inlaid with African buffalo horn and ivory tips," whatever that means. A hard-rubber buttplate is standard in all grades, but both grades F and H could be ordered with checkered butt and inletted buffalo-horn heel and toe plates. No beavertail fore-end is mentioned, only splinter-type with Deeley & Edge latch.

Similarly, there is no word of a single trigger. Ejectors are mentioned only on the order-blank page and nowhere else—not even in the list of replacement parts.

Only Grades A through E are illustrated, and as with the Fox Gun Company's GE Grade of later years, I have no indisputable evidence that Philadelphia Arms ever built an F or H Grade gun. In fact, I know of only two E Grades, one built for William Haywood and one for Philip DuPont.

(For all the similarities in appearance between Philadelphia Arms guns and Parkers—which today would land Ansley Fox in court so quickly that his underwear would have to catch the next taxi—it's worth mentioning that he did manage to scoop Parker by a good twenty years on one point, at least. The

A.H. FOX

Philadelphia Arms catalogue calls the Grade H "The Very Finest Example of the Gun Makers' Art." The 1926 Parker catalogue describes the Invincible "the finest example of the gun makers' art." Parker obviously took a lesson from Ansley Fox—though not one of punctuation.)

Exactly how successful Philadelphia Arms really was is difficult to judge. The guns were good enough, but economic conditions, which always profoundly affect sales of sporting and other leisure goods, were uneven. In the early years of the twentieth century, just as President Roosevelt and the Progressives were winding up for a round of trust-busting and regulating the business world, those who earned their wages from American industry found their purchasing power alternately stagnating and declining. Immigrants from eastern and southern Europe, arriving in ever-growing numbers each year, unwittingly served to keep wages low and to impede the unions' ability to organize.

List Price, $100.00

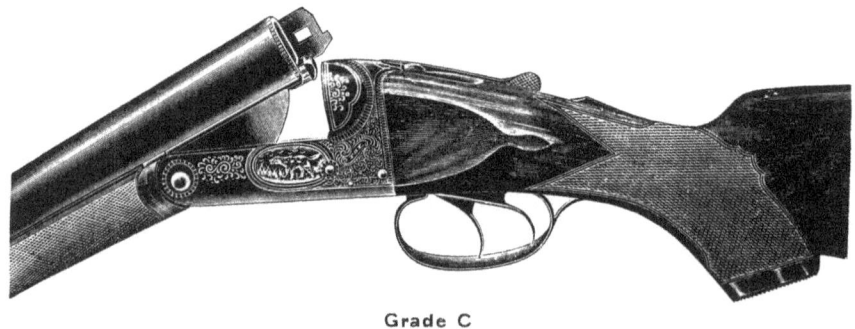

Grade C

As went the fortunes of the working class, so went the fortunes of the American gun trade. The best-heeled sportsmen in America obtained the majority of their guns from England and would continue to do so until at least the 1960s. This is why low- and medium-grade guns by every American maker vastly outnumber those of high grade.

Whatever the reasons, Philadelphia Arms was not destined for a long life.

In December 1904, Ansley Fox sent copies of the following letter to the trade journals and sporting magazines:

Philadelphia, Pa., Dec. 28, 1904

GENTLEMEN:—Please announce through your columns that I am no longer connected in any way with the Philadelphia Arms Company, of this city. I have resigned my position as president and general manager of that company, and have equipped a factory of my own, where I will manufacture a new double barrel, hammerless shot gun. This new gun embodies many valuable improvements and samples will be ready for the trade in January next.

Yours respectfully,
Ansley H. Fox

The official explanation for his seemingly sudden departure, published some time later, cites "business differences"—which of course is no explanation at all. Perhaps there were personality differences as well, or perhaps Ansley Fox realized that he had not yet come up with a product distinctive enough to create a market of its own. For all its intrinsic merit, attempting to sell a Parker lookalike against the real thing was perhaps a less-than-brilliant strategy, and considering that Philadelphia Arms carried an enormous burden of indebtedness, he may well have decided the only way to stay in the race was to change horses.

Moreover, Ansley Fox's declaration of being "no longer connected in any way" with Philadelphia Arms was somewhat disingenuous. He may have aban-

List Price, $150.00

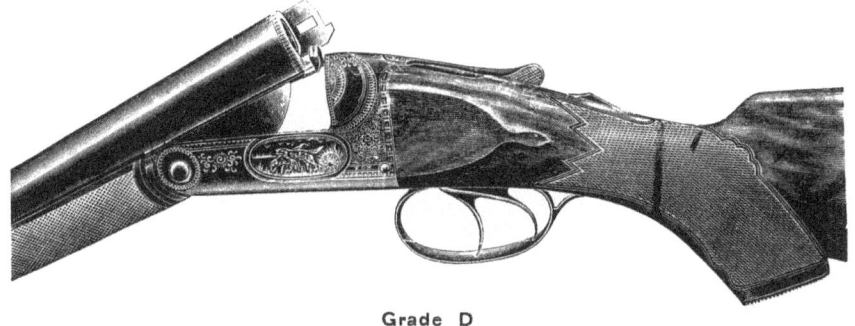

Grade D

doned any direct involvement in company affairs, but no evidence shows that he sold off his stock or severed any of his financial ties. In fact, subsequent events suggest that his real objective was to distance his name from Philadelphia Arms in the public mind.

Consider the facts. The earliest A.H. Fox Gun Company advertisement I've found appeared in *The American Field* of December 16, 1905, and no ad appeared in *The Sporting Goods Dealer*, which was the most important journal for the sporting-goods trade, until January 1906. According to all the ads, Fox Gun was located at Wayne and Bristol streets and was "Not connected with the Philadelphia Arms Company." Moreover, the "Notes" section of the December 16, 1905, *American Field* includes a little piece that begins: "Mr. Ansley H. Fox, president of the A.H. Fox Gun Company of Philadelphia, paid the American Field office a pleasant visit on Monday of this week. Mr. Fox reports that his company has just closed its first year of business with a highly satisfactory record and with still brighter prospects for the new year."

Now, on the other hand, the latest Philadelphia Arms advertising I can find appeared in June 1905, and this raises questions.

Ansley Fox's comments about a "highly satisfactory record" during Fox Gun Company's "first year of business" certainly are ambiguous, but he probably learned from his experience in Baltimore that to advertise a product without an inventory from which to fill orders was not a good idea, so it seems safe to assume that the new guns were being manufactured during 1905. There's no question they were manufactured during 1906. The question, for both years, is *where*?

And if Philadelphia Arms guns were being built after mid-1905, why were they not advertised?

Consider some more facts. A short piece published in *The Sportsmen's Review* of December 1, 1906, informs all interested parties that the A.H. Fox Gun Company "purchased the complete plant of the Philadelphia Arms Company... on the 25th of last month." The story, obviously a company press release, goes on to say "...we will now be able to manufacture the Ansley H. Fox gun in sufficient quantities to fill our orders promptly." Are we to infer from this that production was slow during 1906? If it was, why?

Ansley Fox's mention of "a factory of my own" in his December 1904 letter, strikes me as the final bit of disingenuousness. To put it another way, I don't believe it. If he had a new factory, what was the point of buying the Philadelphia Arms plant? Fox Gun could surely have obtained the Philadelphia Arms patents, and probably some or all of the machinery as well, without having to buy everything from the mailbox to the toilet paper.

List Price, $200.00

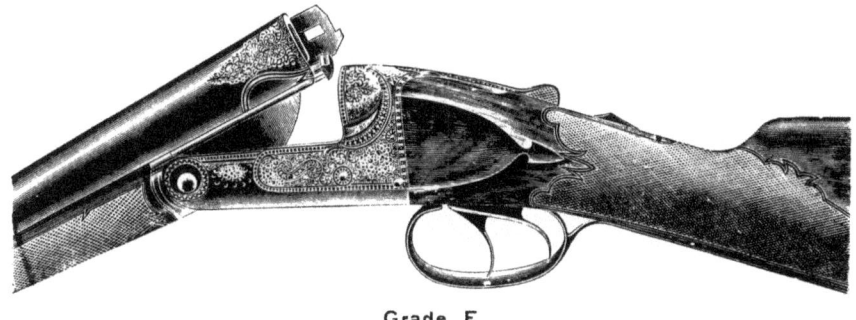

Grade E

It doesn't wash, from any angle. Under the boiler-plate and press-release gobbledygook, everything seems to point in the same direction: That the Wayne and Bristol address was nothing more than an office; that Ansley Fox retained his financial interest in Philadelphia Arms; and that the early A.H. Fox Company guns were manufactured in the Philadelphia Arms plant.

As a bit of hard evidence—not conclusive but certainly suggestive—I can tell you that the bird dog scenes on the trigger plates of William Haywood's Philadelphia Arms Grade E and A.H. Fox Company gun No. 35, which is stamped Grade "CS," are so nearly identical that they could only have come from the same engraver.

If I had to put it on a time-table, I'd say that Ansley Fox and his partners stopped manufacturing Philadelphia Arms guns at the end of 1904, spent the first six months of 1905 turning out as many A.H. Fox Company guns as possible while at the same time selling off as much of the Philadelphia Arms inventory as they could, and spent the rest of 1905 and part of 1906 completely retooling the factory to produce the new guns en masse.

Furthermore, I believe the Fox Gun Company advertisements disclaiming connection with Philadelphia Arms (which continued to appear in each issue of *The Sporting Goods Dealer* through March 1907) were mainly designed to distinguish the new gun from its Philadelphia Arms predecessor. (The Philadelphia Arms gun, remember, was officially called "The A.H. Fox Hammerless Gun," not the "Philadelphia Arms Gun.") It's the only explanation that fits all the facts.

Even though its continued existence was only a formality, Philadelphia Arms did not officially cease to exist until March 15, 1907—the same day that A.H. Fox Gun Company incorporated in New Jersey.

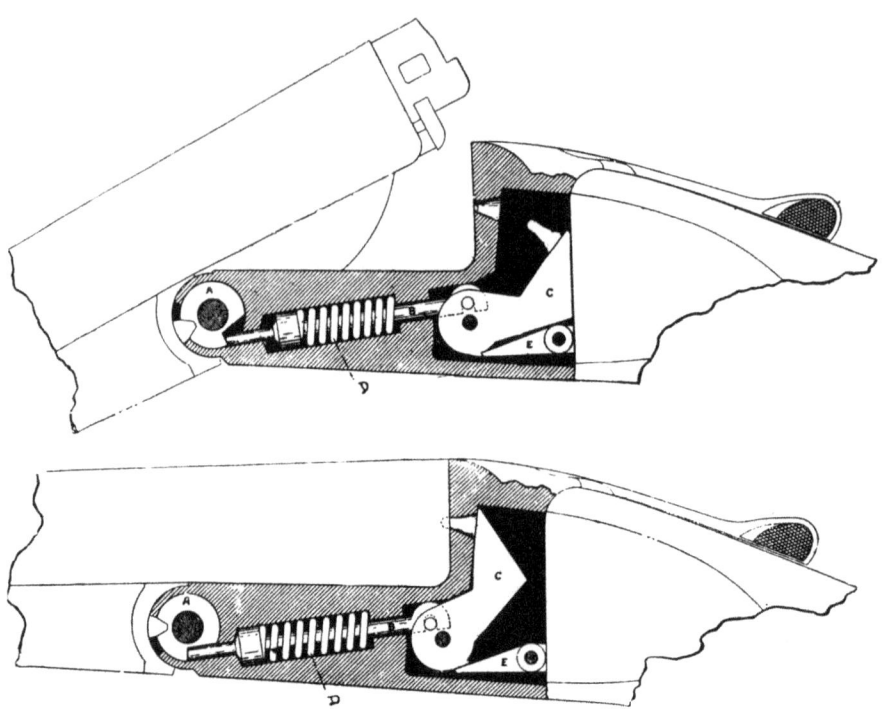

The first Fox cocking system, illustrated in the 1905 Philadelphia Arms catalogue.

It's a tangled web, this time of transition, and it isn't likely that all the strands ever can be sorted out. We probably never will know, for instance, exactly how many guns Philadelphia Arms actually turned out. The number may total 5000 or more, although the highest number I know for certain is No. 1845.

Any Philadelphia Arms piece is something of an artifact these days, not worthy of any great price unless of high grade, but certainly interesting. I know little about the two E Grades except that Haywood's gun has double triggers, extractors, and a straight-hand stock, but I do have notes on eleven others, all of which are 12-bores with Krupp barrels, double triggers, extractors, and splinter fore-ends. Otherwise, they are as follows:

    No. 203, A Grade, 30-inch barrels, pistol grip.
    No. 374, C Grade, 26-inch barrels (bobbed), straight hand.
    No. 454, C Grade, 32-inch barrels, straight hand.
    No. 802, A Grade, 28-inch barrels, pistol grip.
    No. 829, B Grade, 30-inch barrels, pistol grip.
    No. 1087, B Grade, 32-inch barrels, straight hand.

No. 1353, A Grade, 28-inch barrels, pistol grip.
No. 1505, A Grade, 30-inch barrels, pistol grip.
No. 1545, A Grade, 28-inch barrels, pistol grip.
No. 1676, A Grade, 30-inch barrels, pistol grip.
No. 1845, A Grade, 30-inch barrels, pistol grip.

Thirteen guns isn't much of a statistical sample, but it seems safe to conclude that Philadelphia Arms probably built no guns with single trigger or beavertail fore-end—which is no great surprise. Ejectors are more problematic; the company owned Max Wirsing's 1904 patent, but whether it actually built any ejector guns is doubtful—possible but doubtful. The absence of a half-hand stock does strike me as a bit odd, though, since the half-pistol grip is the standard for A.H. Fox Gun Company. But that, as they say, is another story.

A.H. Fox Gun Company CSE Grade, No. 35, and the 1905 Philadelphia Arms catalogue

WILLIAM W. HEADRICK

6

A Difficult Birth

The same tangle of events and murky interconnections that makes the Philadelphia Arms Company's final months a mare's nest of confusion also obscures the early days of its successor. According to M.H. Wright's "History of the A.H. Fox Gun Company," published in *Field & Stream* in October 1908 and reprinted two months later, slightly changed and without by-line, in *The Sporting Goods Dealer*, the Fox Gun Company had by 1905 "outgrown its quarters at Wayne and Bristol streets, as well as its capital; hence, in April of that year, a number of the wealthiest and best-known citizens of Philadelphia became interested in the business and the A.H. Fox Gun Company was incorporated with a capital of $100,000."

This sounds straightforward enough, but the facts aren't quite so clear-cut. Although the incorporation was bona fide (registered in New Jersey), the company did not quit the premises at Wayne and Bristol until early 1907, for that's the address given in the Philadelphia city directories during the first two years the A.H. Fox Gun Company is listed—1906 and 1907. As I discussed in the previous chapter, all the evidence suggests that Fox's disconnection from Philadelphia Arms was more apparent than real.

Whatever business maneuvering Ansley Fox performed between the end of 1904 and the first months of 1907, designs for the new gun were taking shape. On December 29, 1904, he filed application for patent protection on a fastening system, essentially the system used in Philadelphia Arms guns; this patent was granted August 1, 1905, as No. 796,119 and assigned to the A.H. Fox Gun

No. 796,119.
PATENTED AUG. 1, 1905.
A. H. FOX.
BARREL LOCKING DEVICE FOR BREAKDOWN GUNS.
APPLICATION FILED DEC. 29, 1904.

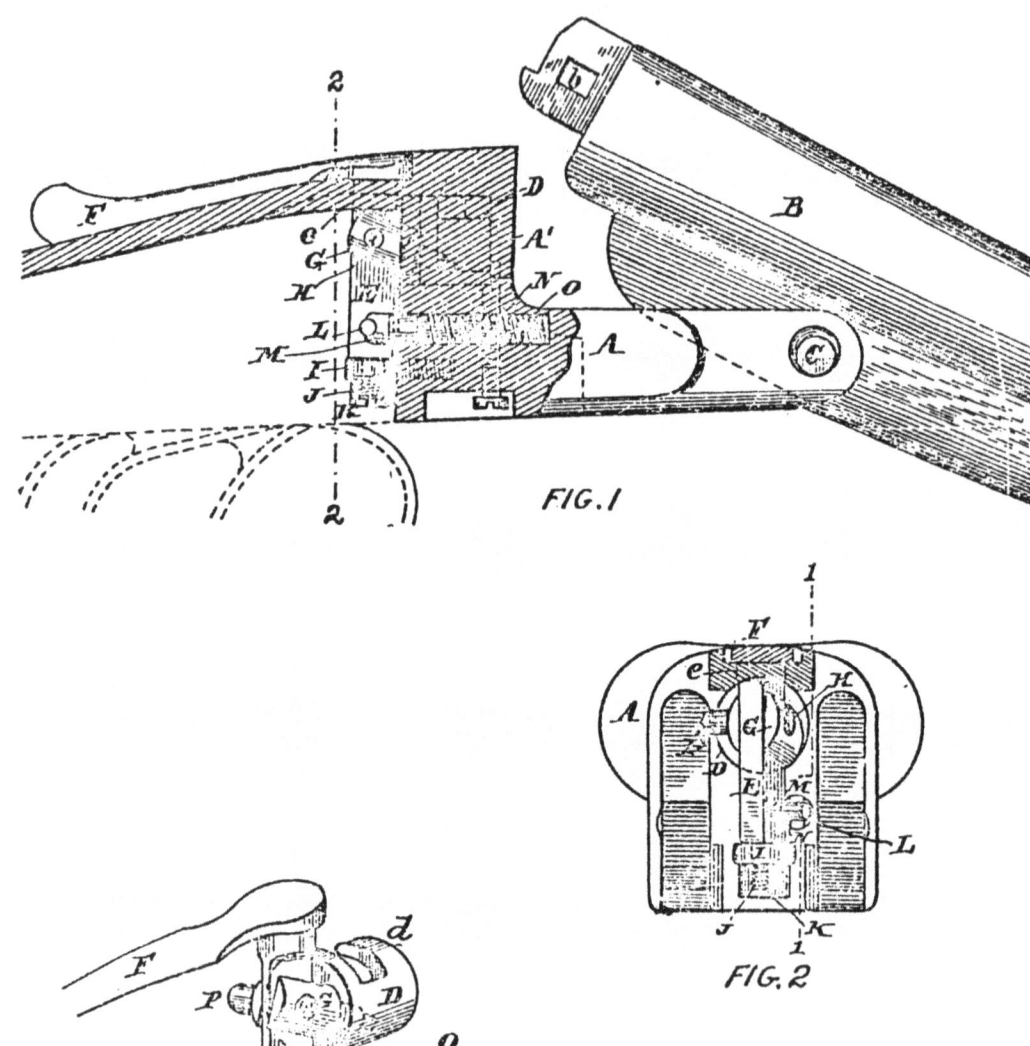

Attest
P. M. Kelly
M. J. Eyrl.

Inventor
Ansley H. Fox
By his atty

No. 810,046. PATENTED JAN. 16, 1906.
A. H. FOX.
BARREL LOCKING DEVICE FOR BREAKDOWN GUNS.
APPLICATION FILED AUG. 12, 1905.

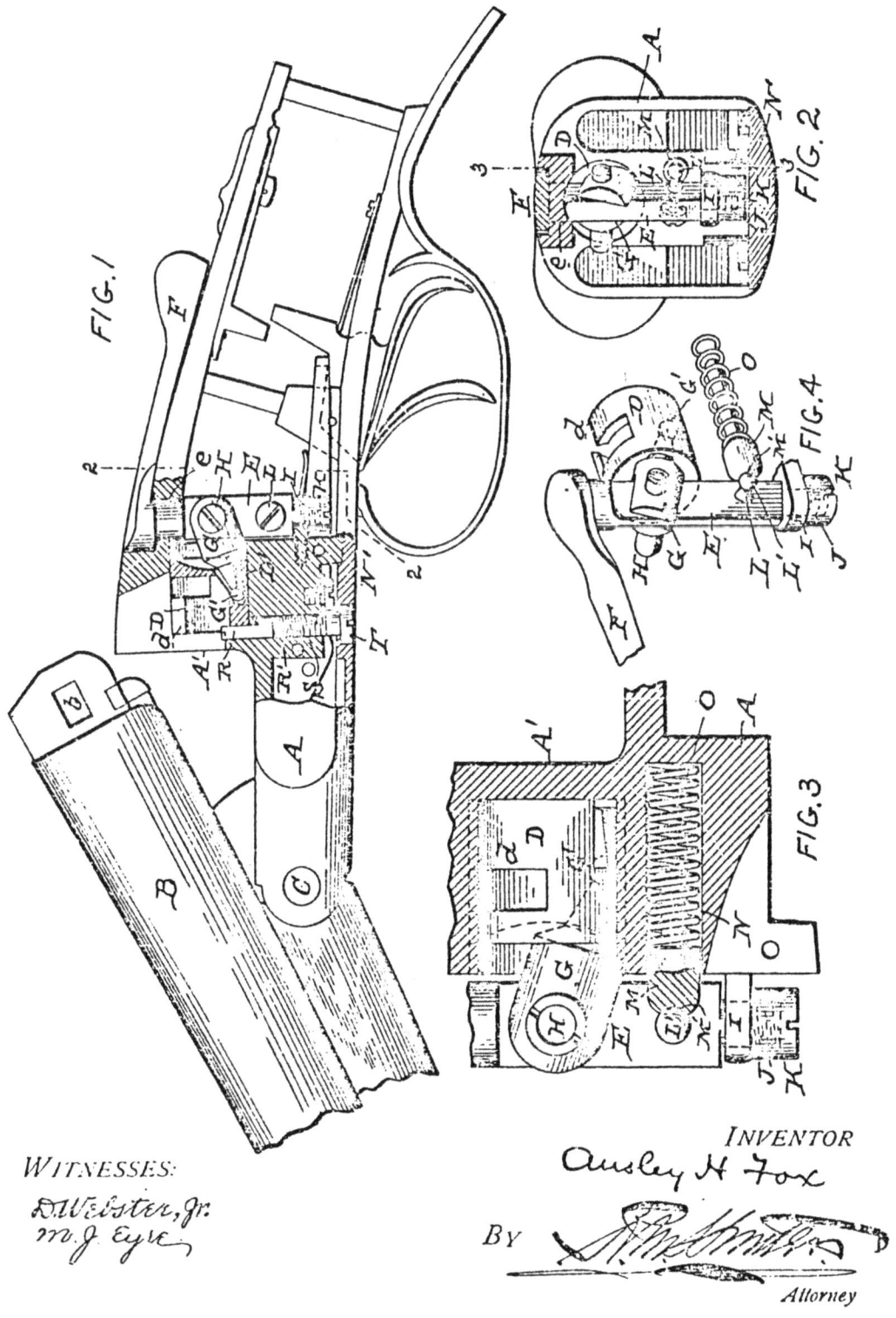

WITNESSES:
D. Webster, Jr.
M. J. Eyre

INVENTOR
Ansley H. Fox
BY
Attorney

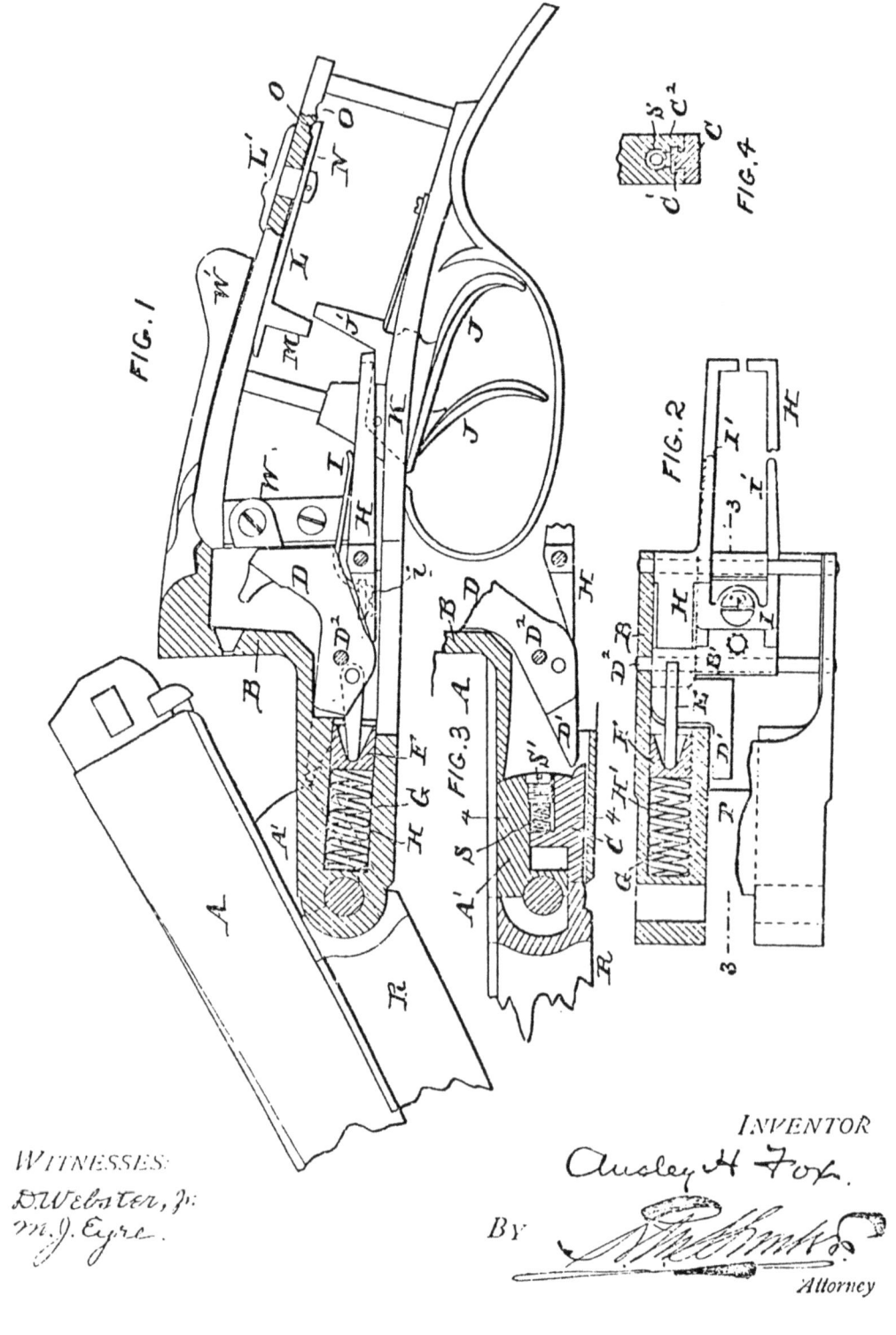

Company. Less than two weeks later, on August 12, he applied for a patent on improvements to the system. This one describes what was to become the classic Fox fastener with its rotary hook and single-bite barrel extension, and the patent, No. 810,046, was issued January 16, 1906.

The Fox gun's real heart is described in a patent application filed February 9, 1905, and granted October 17 of the same year. In the drawings and text of Patent No. 801,862, you can see the spring-loaded cocking slide fastened to the barrel lump and the three-part lockwork comprising only a sear, hammer, and coil mainspring.

Ansley Fox called it "The Finest Gun in the World," and in part at least, he was right. No Fox gun—indeed, no American gun—has ever approached the perfection of a London best nor the finest products of the various European trades, but by the same token, no boxlock action built anywhere exceeds the simplicity or reliability or sheer mechanical excellence of a Fox. No British or European boxlock is any better, and no American gun can even come close—not Parker nor Ithaca nor the Winchester 21 nor even Uncle Dan Lefever's great Automatic Hammerless.

This is not the time to catalogue all the Fox's virtues; I'll cover them all before this book is finished. For the moment, one little story should suffice.

If you're not already aware, it should come as no surprise that English gunmakers don't think much of American guns. The attitude stems in part from that wonderful British sense of nationalism (which a lot of people mistake for snobbishness, although it really isn't), but it also comes in part from the reality of things. Put two typical guns, one English and one American, side by side, and anyone who knows guns will have to admit that theirs are more highly refined than ours. That's just how it is.

Even so, quality tells. A few years back, I was standing in the tiny, unbelievably cluttered front shop at 79 Beak Street, London, talking with my friend John Wilkes, when I noticed a familiar shape among the guns standing in one of the wall racks. I asked John to see it, and he handed over a nice old XE Fox. Appropriate marks from the London Proof House showed that it had been living in England for some time. John said it was a customer's gun that had been in the shop for some minor repair. I asked him what he thought of it.

"Oh, quite good," he said. "The Fox and the Ithaca single trap are the only guns you chaps ever made that are as good as guns ought to be."

This is high praise from a man who, if you ask whether the price he's just quoted is in dollars or pounds, will likely say, "Pounds, of course; I don't trade in wog money."

A.H. FOX

I've asked any number of English gunmakers—those who actually do the hands-on work—what they think of American guns, usually for my own amusement and sometimes just to give them a chance to heap a bit of scorn on something besides each other, and almost to a man they've singled out the Fox as the only praiseworthy achievement of our gun trade.

Not that we should take their criticism too much to heart. After all, our guns always have been mass-produced for a more workaday market, and comparing any of them to a bespoken London best is largely an exercise in apples and oranges. The point is that not even the most chauvinistic gun man can deny the excellence of Ansley Fox's design.

In any event, the first of the new Fox guns were built during 1905—including a prototype 16-gauge, which is gun No. 17. Ansley Fox clearly was thinking of small-bores right from the start, although as we shall see, they didn't go into regular production until several years later.

The earliest advertising, which begins to appear late in 1905 and early 1906, shows 12-bore guns in grades A, B, and C. In the very earliest, D Grade is

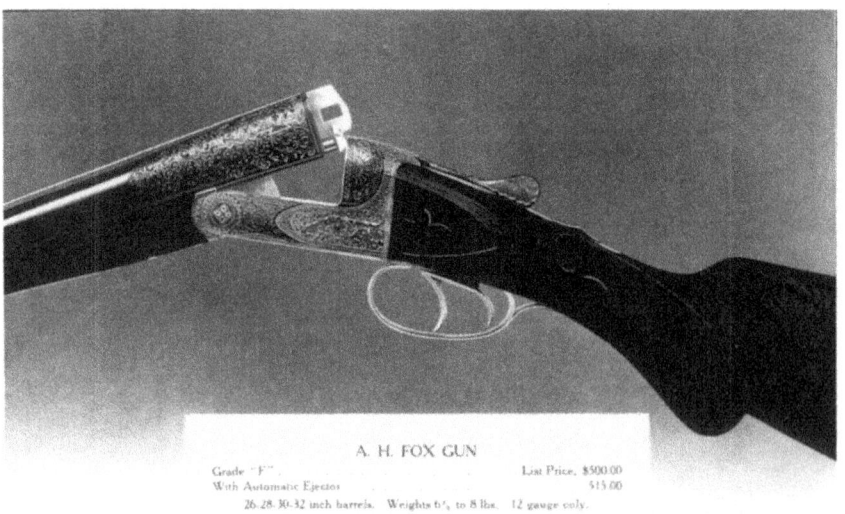

First illustration of the FE Grade, from the second Fox Gun Company catalogue issued in 1907.

mentioned but not illustrated. D Grade is illustrated in the first of two catalogues issued in 1907, and F Grade is first illustrated in the second.

Official announcement that inventory was available to the retail trade came in January 1906. A highly complimentary review in *The Sporting Goods Dealer*—clearly based on a company press release—praises the simple mechanics

A Difficult Birth

and compact frame, declaring, "In material, graceful lines and perfect finish the arm will compare favorably with the best of American or European make on the market." The piece also notes that both Krupp and Whitworth barrels were available. (Whitworth tubes are mentioned in both the 1906 and 1907 catalogues but not in 1908 or thereafter.) Fox guns, the story concludes, are manufactured in five grades at prices ranging from $50 to $500.

Besides manufacturing guns for the retail trade, the factory turned out a number of cutaways for salesmen's use. These were standard-production guns, numbered along with the rest, with windows cut into the frames so the salesmen could show the lockwork and other mechanisms. Exactly how many were built is unknown, and not all those that do show up in the records were noted by grade or shipping date. The majority almost certain were A Grades, although at least one was a B Grade. The lowest-numbered cutaway I know is No. 173, A Grade. Others are No. 432, A Grade, date unknown; No. 473, B Grade, date unknown; No. 7531, A Grade, date unknown; No. 7540, grade unknown, shipped June 25, 1907; No. 7552, grade unknown, shipped July 26, 1907; and No. 7628, grade unknown, shipped March 19, 1908. I haven't seen one, but I'm told that Fox later made some Sterlingworth cutaways, which is perfectly plausible, especially considering what the company hoped to accomplish with the Sterlingworth.

A Grade cut-away, No. 432. Salesmen used cut-away guns to show the lockwork and other internal mechanics.

CURTIS TATE

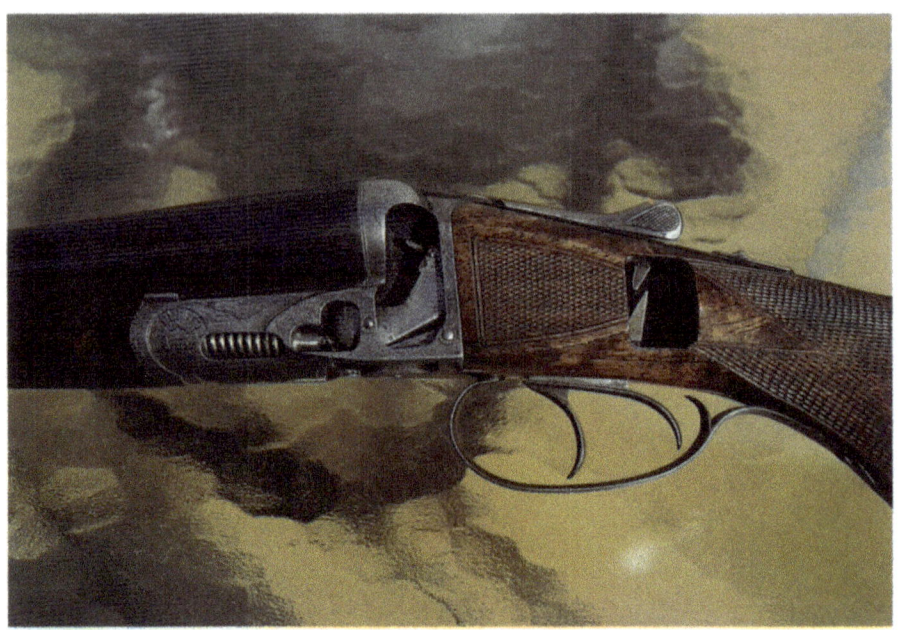

B Grade cut-away, No. 473. This is the only cut-away Fox known to exist in any grade higher than A.   CURTIS TATE

So far as I know, none of the factory cutaways had sections taken out of the barrels, which means they were fully functional guns, and indeed, many now show evidence of having been fired, some quite a lot. (At least one cutaway does have a slot cut in the barrels; this was done many years later, deliberately to render it incapable of firing.)

No. 7531 is possibly the strangest, because it's no longer a cutaway. All the openings in the frame have been filled in. Whoever did it clearly was a skillful metal-man—probably a factory employee who came across it in storage, or who decided to make himself a back-door gun.

The 1906 Philadelphia city directory lists Ansley Fox as president and general manager of the A.H. Fox Gun Company, William Lindig as vice-president and treasurer, and Frank J. Barthmaier as secretary. The 1907 entry is the same, except Ansley Fox appears only as president. By then, George A. Mosher was general manager, and sales manager as well. Mosher formerly had worked for both the Syracuse Arms Company and Lefever Arms.

At its December 6, 1906, meeting, the Interstate Association officially elected the A.H. Fox Gun Company to membership.

In early 1907, just as the Fox Gun Company announced a move into the factory formerly occupied by Philadelphia Arms, the gun made its first significant performances in competitive shooting. In a February 12 shoot held at the Point Breeze race track in Philadelphia, Mr. Fred Coleman turned in the only perfect twenty-five of the match, using an A Grade Fox. By May, Coleman had upgraded to a C Grade gun and used it to win a twenty-five-bird pigeon match held at Lebanon on the 24th. Shooting at thirty-two yards rise, he killed thirty-seven straight to take the match in a shoot-off. The news item, released by the Fox Company, reports, "Mr. Coleman has won every pigeon match he has shot with the A.H. Fox gun, one of his most recent victories being his defeat of the world-famous Captain J.L. Brewer, in which contest Mr. Coleman scored 94 to Brewer's 93 out of 100."

We'll never know exactly what business strategy Ansley Fox had in mind through all the jiggery-pokery he played with Philadelphia Arms, but the November 1906 "buy-out" wasn't the end of it. On March 15, 1907, the A.H. Fox gun Company was reincorporated in New Jersey and the Philadelphia Arms corporation was dissolved, its assets presumably taken over by Fox Gun. Six months later, on September 21, the company incorporated in Pennsylvania with a capital stock of $400,000. The Articles of Incorporation list the subscribers as Ansley Fox, 2734 shares: Frank J. Barthmaier, 133 shares; and James H. Eyster, also 133 shares. Directors, along with Fox, Barthmaier and Eyster, were Louis H. Eisenlohr, William H. Thomas, Harry L. Jenkins, Arthur Burton, William C.R. Reed, and Joseph W. Mills.

In return for all assets of the New Jersey corporation, Ansley Fox transferred 2600 of his shares in the Pennsylvania corporation, leaving him majority stockholder by one share.

The times were less than auspicious. On March 14, the day before the reincorporation in New Jersey, the stock market had suffered its worst crash since the Panic of 1901. Heaviest losers were the railroads—Union Pacific, Reading, and Great Northern—and the metals industry, notably American Smelting, National Lead, and Amalgamated Copper. The U.S. Treasury Department paid off $25 million in government bonds to help ease the blow, but no efforts were enough to stave off a second collapse on August 7, when stock prices once again sank to the levels they had reached in March.

Panic followed panic. In October, Charles Moore and Augustus Heringe attempted to corner United Copper and failed, sending Wall Street into a tizzy. Finally, on November 4, J. Pierpont Morgan invited the heads of all the major New York banks to a meeting in his library, locked the doors, and browbeat them into coughing up $25 million to shore up the stock market and the banking industry.

Morgan's move succeeded in returning some stability to the financial world, but the nation's economy was slow to recover. Inflation and unemployment both grew steadily, and as he had experienced in the early years of Philadelphia Arms, Ansley Fox once again saw the gun market dwindle. From 1907 to 1910, the Fox Company's production reportedly averaged only about 2000 guns annually.

Part of the problem lay with Ansley Fox's approach. In the January 1906 release to *The Sporting Goods Dealer*, the company is quoted as saying, "We have not taken cost or work into account in our efforts to make this gun superior to all others, but made the gun right first and figured the cost afterwards." It's a brave claim, certainly not unique. Every sort of business you can imagine has adopted a similar stance ever since commerce began, and usually it's been utter hogwash. In Ansley Fox's case, however, the events of an entire lifetime suggest he truly believed that quality is more important than manufacturing cost. The only hitch is the market. If you can sell your wares at a profit and in sufficient volume, then production costs aren't important; take away either factor, though, and you're sunk. Unfortunately, it's a hitch that tripped up Ansley Fox again and again. He seems to have truly believed that a high-quality item would sell regardless of how steep the price had to be, and when the market refused to cooperate, he found himself unable to lower the price without erasing his profit. One certainly cannot fault a commitment to quality, but in the face of reality, it was a blind spot that ultimately ended his career as a manufacturer.

Nevertheless, the Fox Company strove mightily to make The Finest Gun in the World finer still. Although Fox catalogues show ejectors as available options from the beginning, they aren't mentioned in any other company advertising until late 1907. The Fox ad in the October issue of *The Sporting Goods Dealer* reads in part, "Now Furnished with Automatic Ejector." The following month, the Fox offering is described as "an ejector with half the parts, twice the strength, all the certainly." Unfortunately, the ad copy is better than the product.

The first-generation Fox ejector system is described in a patent application filed July 24, 1907, by Ansley Fox and George A. Horne. Horne worked at Meriden Arms and, from 1888 until about 1904, at Syracuse Arms Company; he probably hired on at Philadelphia Arms about 1904. He worked for Fox Gun Company until about 1909, moved on to the New England Westinghouse plant at Meriden, Connecticut, and in 1917 became chief engineer and works manager at Hunter Arms.

Between 1896 and 1905, Horne earned six patents—three for ejectors, and one each for a "recoil-operated firearm," a "firearm safety device," and a

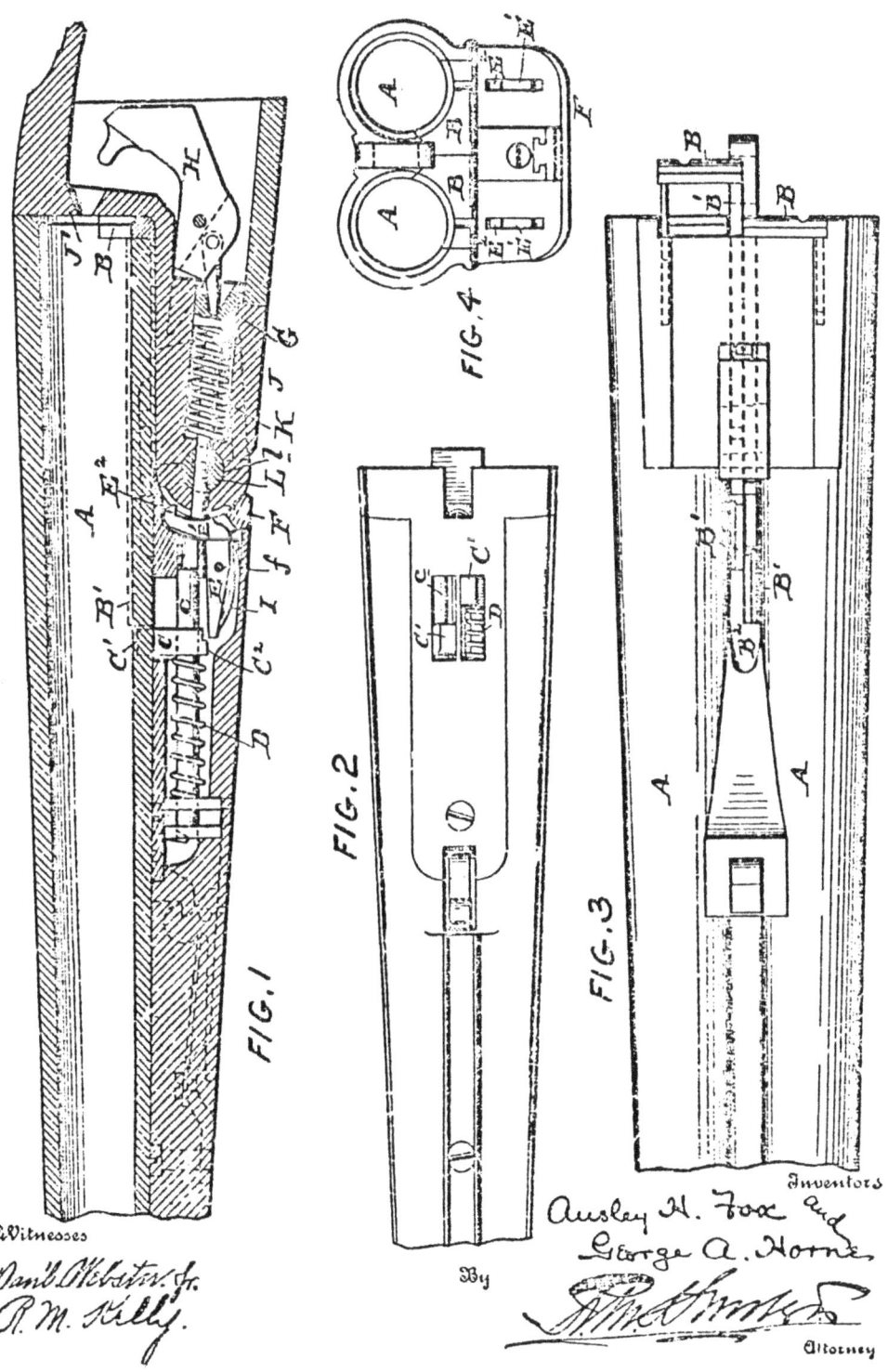

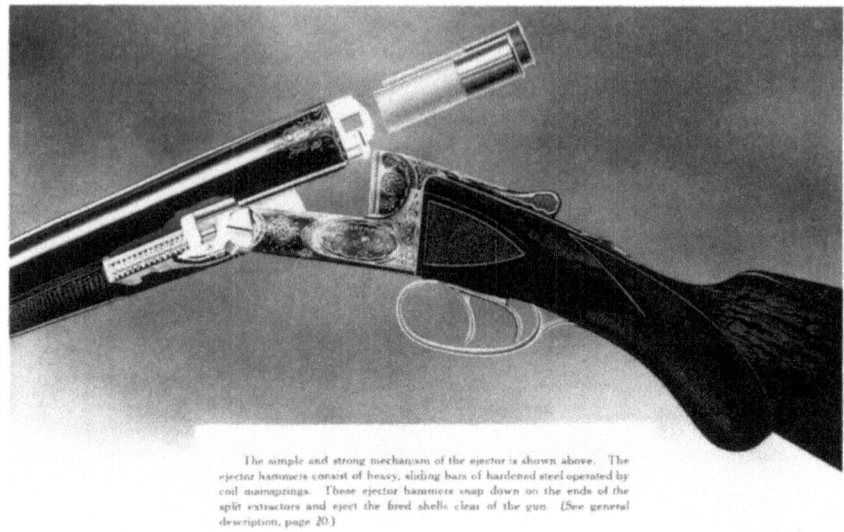

First-generation Fox ejector mechanism, from the 1907 catalogue

"breech-loading firearm." All of the ejector patents were assigned to Syracuse Arms, and the ejectors of most Syracuse Arms guns were made on Horne's patent of October 6, 1896.

The patent he and Ansley Fox filed jointly is for a "breech-loading gun," but the actual gun is the one described in Fox's patent of October 17, 1905, so the application really is for protection on the "ejecting devices." Presumably, these are primarily—perhaps entirely—Horne's design.

The system isn't entirely a bad one, but it had its flaws. The sears were a bit delicate, for one thing, and the company probably was forced to do quite a few repair jobs under the terms of its guarantee. The real shortcoming in Horne's design, which was very similar to the L.C. Smith ejectors of the day, is that the ejector springs are used to assist the extractors as well. If you open the gun without firing it, the extractors are mechanically cammed back for only about the first eighth-inch, and then the springs take over and push them to their full extent.

Spring-driven extractors may sound good in theory, but in practice they're a pain in the butt. Even though both Fox and Smith used coil springs, they weren't always strong enough to force a swelled cartridge out of a chamber, especially one with some grime and powder residue in it—and swelled cartridges were almighty common in those long-ago days of paper cases. The worst problem, though, is that the shooter has to compress the ejector springs every time he closes

A Grade 12-gauge, 1908 WILLIAM W. HEADRICK

Early BE Grade, first-generation engraving style WILLIAM W. HEADRICK

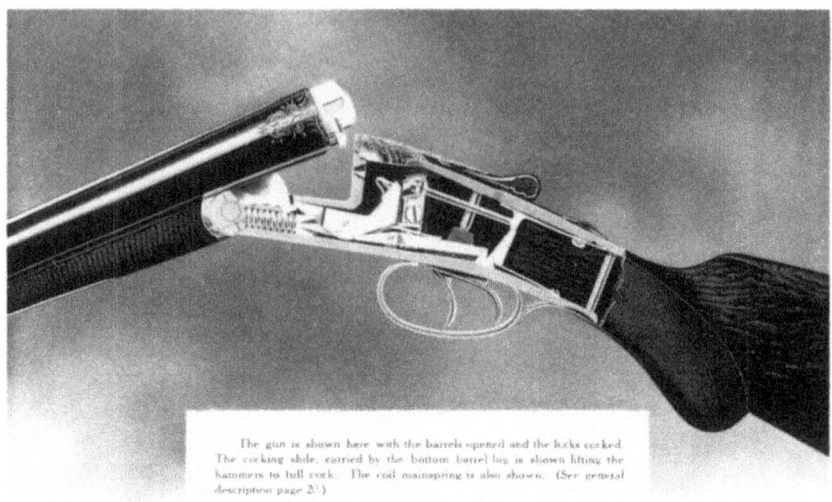

Fox Gun Company cocking system, from the 1907 catalogue

the gun, whether he's fired it or not. This puts unnecessary stress on the hinge and the fore-end, to say nothing of the shooter's forearms and wrists. Not good.

Even before the patent, No. 921,220, was finally issued on May 11, 1909, it was clear that the Fox gun needed a better system. Indeed, after December 1907, ejectors are not mentioned in any Fox advertising (except the catalogues) until a new design went into production in late 1910. More on that anon.

The financial upheavals of 1907 prompted Ansley Fox to brainstorm ways of riding out the hard times that appeared sure to come, including the possibility of moving the whole business out of Philadelphia. A one-sentence trade-journal item of February 1908 reports that "Mr. A.H. Fox... is endeavoring to secure a favorable site for his factory in Havre de Grace, Pa." Since there was no such town in Pennsylvania (and still isn't), the "Pa." obviously is a misprint for "Md." A similarly brief item published in August reads, "A report from Philadelphia states that the A.H. Fox Gun Company, of that city, may remove to Havre de Grace, Md."

I haven't a clue what this really was all about. Perhaps the city of Havre de Grace or the State of Maryland was offering enticements to attract new businesses and Fox saw it as a way of reducing costs. More likely, though, it was the result of some internecine tempest arising out of Ansley Fox's willful nature. He was, beyond question, a difficult man to work with, probably even more difficult to work for, and all indications are that the company was in a fairly constant state of turmoil. General manager George Mosher threw in the towel

A Grade 12-gauge, 1908 WILLIAM W. HEADRICK

A. H. Fox Gun Company A Grade, No. 2 ROBERT LINTHOUT

sometime in 1908, and Ansley Fox hired his old friend Adolph R. Roll to oversee the company sales program in the East and Midwest.

Roll was an old-timer in the shooting world and was a well-known pigeon shot around the turn of the century. He and Ansley Fox likely had struck up an acquaintance during Fox's tournament-shooting years, and some evidence suggests that the two became close friends. At any rate, hiring Ad Roll was a wise move. Not that he exerted any great influence over Ansley Fox—no one did—but the older man certainly lent some stability and considerable professional talent to a company clearly in need of both. Indeed, Roll remained with the A.H. Fox Gun Company long after Ansley Fox was gone, serving as sales manager for many years.

The summer of 1908 came to a close amid portents of both misery and hope. A cholera epidemic raged across Russia, more than 15,500 cases reported during the first three weeks of September alone. Orville Wright became the first man to stay airborne for more than an hour, and on another flight twelve days later, his passenger Lieutenant Thomas Selfridge of the U.S. Army Signal Corps became the first man to die in a plane crash. The United States claimed eighteen first-place medals in the Olympic Games, held in London.

Billy Durant organized General Motors, Winston Churchill married Clementine Hozier, and on September 2, the Ithaca Gun Company filed a brief in U.S. Circuit Court seeking to restrain the Syracuse, New York, sporting-goods retail firm of Burhans & Black from selling A.H. Fox guns.

Ithaca claimed the guns violated a patent for "certain improvements in cocking and safety mechanism" awarded to Emile Flues in 1895 and subsequently transferred to Ithaca Gun Company. Although the Fox Company wasn't specified in the suit, not even the most delicate-handed journalists could help but observe that "the real defendant is said to be the maker of the Fox gun." Someone, presumably counsel to Burhans & Black, denied that any patent infringement existed, and the news report concludes that "a lively contest over the question of ownership will result."

Maybe it did, but apparently no one bothered to cover the story, and in any event, Fox guns were neither changed nor removed from the market. The court most likely dismissed the whole thing. Older patents often were so broadly worded that virtually any similar item could be the target of a suit, and by 1908 the courts were inclined to take a narrower view. In any case, the U.S. Patent

An early A Grade, No. 154   ROBERT LINTHOUT

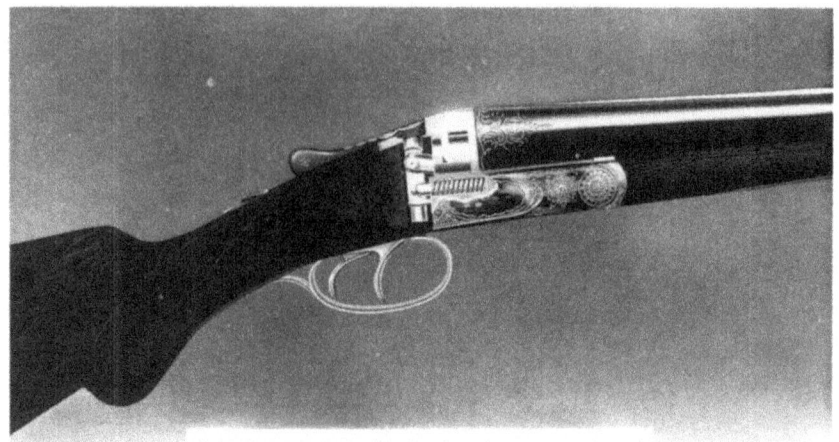

The Fox Gun Company's rotary fastener, illustrated in the 1907 catalogue.

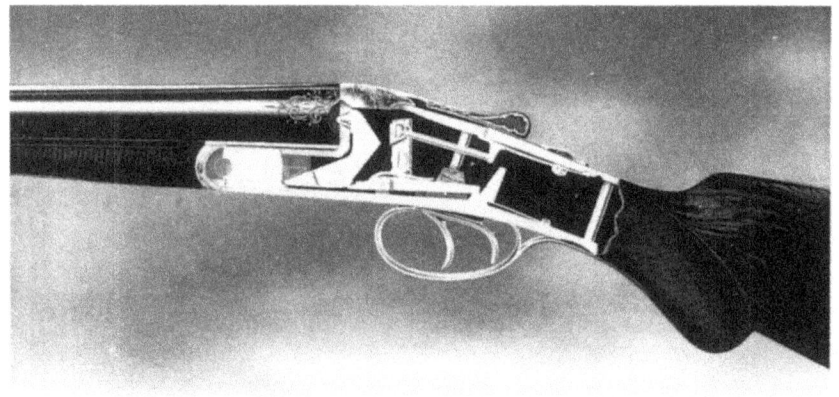

Safety system, 1907 catalogue

Office had in 1905 accepted the Fox cocking system as patentable, so the Ithaca case really had little merit.

At some point in 1908, the Fox Gun Company reorganized, probably in an effort to secure a financial infusion. At year's end, Ansley Fox was president, Frank Barthmaier secretary and treasurer. Louis H. Eisenlohr, G. Brinton Roberts, H.A. Poth, Walter E. Hunt, Frank Reily, Frank Barthmaier, J.H. Eyster, and Ansley Fox were directors. Subscribed capital totaled $400,000.

True to a promise he had made in 1904, Theodore Roosevelt did not seek reelection in 1908. William Howard Taft, who was TR's choice as a successor, became the twenty-seventh president. In the eight years since McKinley's assassination, Roosevelt had become the most popular President since Abraham Lincoln and had improved the federal government immeasurably, but he was tired of politics and public life. What he most wanted to do was head off to Africa and do some hunting. It would become the most famous safari of the twentieth century, and the Fox gun would share in the glory.

FE Grade 12-gauge, built for exhibition at the 1909 Grand American Handicap

WILLIAM W. HEADRICK

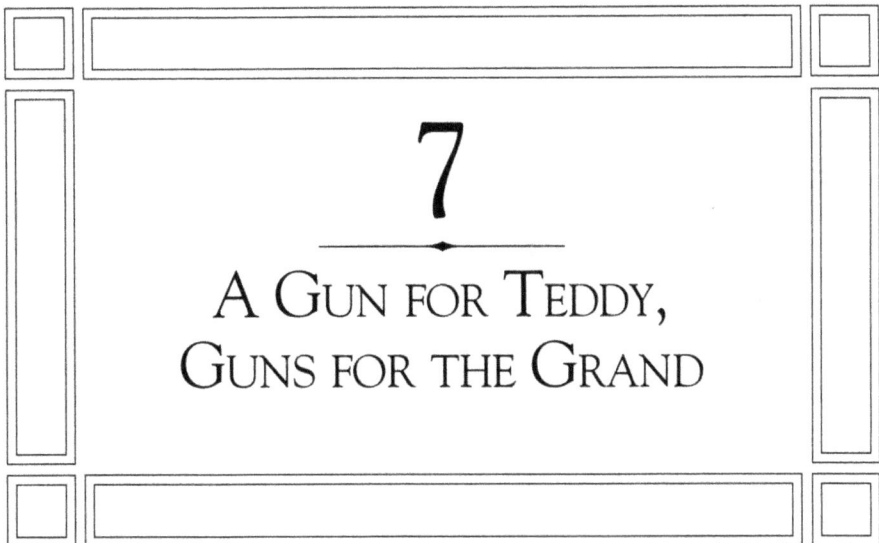

7

A Gun for Teddy, Guns for the Grand

Ansley Fox knew exactly where to find the greatest concentration of shooting men anywhere in the country. He'd been there as a shooting man himself.

As I said in an earlier chapter, one of the most valuable things Ansley Fox gained from his career as a pigeon shot and professional gunner was an appreciation for the marketing opportunities available in the formal target-shooting world. Although certainly a minority compared with hunters, target shooters, in terms of interest and buying power, made up the hard core, the elite, the key population upon which a gunmaker could focus, and in those days, the one time and place to find most of them together was at the Grand American.

The A.H. Fox Gun Company was the first American gunmaker to mount a full-scale display at the Grand, and although the idea of doing so has been attributed to A.W. Connor, the evidence suggests that the notion originated with Ansley Fox himself.

Connor, whom we'll meet shortly, unquestionably was the most successful gun salesman of the time, and he greatly influenced the course of Fox Gun Company during his brief tenure. But plans for the first A.H. Fox display at the Grand American were underway months before Connor arrived on the scene.

The evidence rests with two guns built during the winter of 1908. The first is No. 13292, the order entered on September 18. It was to be an F Grade fitted with 30-inch barrels choked modified and full, stocked to a fourteen-inch pull with 1 5/8 inches bend at the comb and 2 1/2 inches at the heel. The work-order

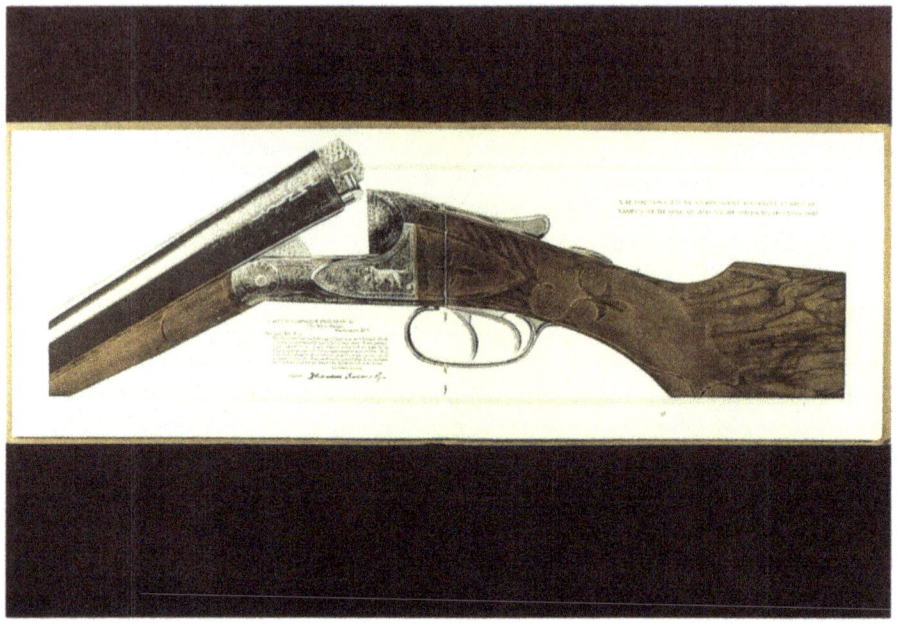

Several Fox catalogues of the mid-1910s featured an FE Grade gun and Theodore Roosevelt's letter to Ansley Fox – although the gun shown is not the gun that Teddy owned.

MICHAEL McINTOSH

card calls for an automatic safety, trigger pulls of five pounds on the right and six pounds on the left, and a total weight of seven pounds, eight ounces. The card was stamped "EJECTORS," but this was crossed off.

Notations are as follows: "This gun is for exhibition purposes and must be as perfect as skill can make it." "Thin comb" (underlined boldly). "Shop records simply say Exhibition gun." "Mr. Fox will select stock, frame & bbls."

Less than a month later, on October 6, the production people received a second order, this time for a Grade FE. At A.H. Fox—and every other gun factory in America—numerical sequence and production sequence kept only casual company together, and this second gun bears a lower number: 13291. Again, the card calls for 30-inch barrels, chokes of modified and full, a stock of fourteen-inch pull with $1\,^{5}/_{8}$- and $2\,^{1}/_{2}$-inch bends, trigger-pulls of five and six pounds, automatic safety, and a total weight of $7\,^{1}/_{2}$ pounds. This one was to have a half-pistol grip. The notation reads simply "Exhibition."

The following August, a couple of months after the 1909 Grand American, *The Sporting Goods Dealer* ran a short news item that begins, "One of the features of the Grand American Handicap at Chicago, Ill., this year, was the exhibit made by the A.H. Fox Gun Company, of Philadelphia, Pa..." The accompanying photo shows a peak-roofed wall-tent blazoned "Buy an A.H. Fox Gun. 'The Finest Gun in the World.' Ask the Man who Shoots One."

Clearly, the two F Grade guns were meant to be part of the display, and No. 13291 undoubtedly was in the tent when the photo was made. No. 13292, however, was at the time somewhere in East Africa with Teddy Roosevelt.

Exactly how this came to be is unclear. The story in the collectors' community is that Edith Carow Roosevelt ordered the gun as a gift for her husband. There may be some truth in it; she may have ordered a gun, but nothing in the records indicates that construction of No. 13292 was begun with Roosevelt in mind. The back of the work-order card bears only a single notation—"Pres. Roosevelt"—but it was not written by the same hand that filled in the other side. If the First Lady did contact Fox Gun Company, the company filled the order simply by diverting No. 13292 from its intended use as an exhibition gun.

Or perhaps—and this seems more likely—the whole idea originated at Fox Gun. Roosevelt's plans to make an African safari following his departure from the White House certainly were no secret. He'd made the decision in 1908, at the urging of the famous white hunters Frederick Selous and Edward Buxton, and the expedition was supported by grants from the Smithsonian Institution, by private

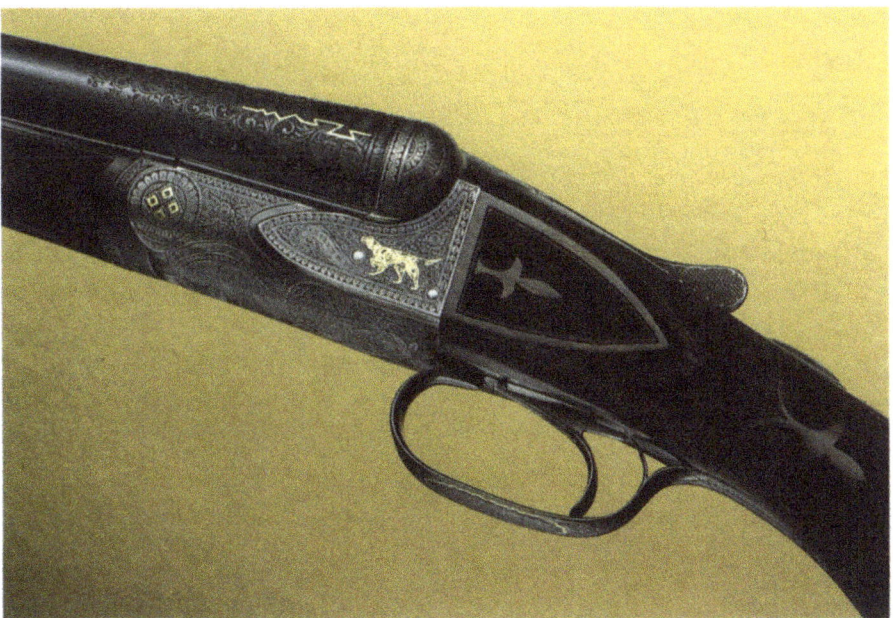

FE Grade No. 13291, a companion to the Roosevelt gun, No. 13292. No. 13291 is more richly engraved than TR's F, and the Fox Company used it as an exhibition gun for several years.

WILLIAM W. HEADRICK

subscriptions, and by Charles Scribner's Sons in the form of a $50,000 guarantee against royalties for a book on the trip. Given the public's level of anticipation to learn of Teddy's Great Adventure, it isn't difficult to imagine that someone at Fox Gun Company—Ad Roll, perhaps, or Ansley Fox himself—saw an opportunity to share the limelight and decided that one F Grade on display at the Grand would be enough, especially if the other went to Africa with the President.

Whatever the scenario, Roosevelt ended up with the gun and Ansley Fox with a letter of thanks.

My dear Mr. Fox:

The double-barreled shotgun has come, and I really think it is the most beautiful gun I have ever seen. I am exceedingly proud of it. I am almost ashamed to take it to Africa and expose it to the rough usage it will receive. But now that I have it, I could not possibly make up my mind to leave it behind. I am extremely proud that I am to have such a beautiful bit of American workmanship with me.

Sincerely yours,
Theodore Roosevelt

If giving a gun to the President was the company's idea, it certainly would have been a high grade, and since we know that two F Grades were in the works at the time, logic suggests that Fox would have chosen the gun most nearly complete, which would have been No. 13292. In fact, Ansley Fox may have been in such a swivet to act before some other maker beat him to the punch that he ordered the gun sent before it truly was complete. No. 13292 is somewhat less-extensively engraved than other F Grades of the period; the barrels aren't engraved at all, nor are they treated with the gold lightning bolts typical of the F. Considering that as of September 1908, the gun was meant to be "as perfect as skill can make it," it seems clear that someone changed his mind somewhere along the way.

Of the two, No. 13291 is by far closer to perfection. You can see as much in the photos here, although good as they are, mere film cannot truly do this gun justice. It's exquisite in every detail of materials and craftsmanship and decora-

PLANT OF THE A. H. FOX GUN COMPANY, PHILADELPHIA

tion. I have to tell you, it is not only the finest Fox but truly the single finest American gun I've ever seen.

Exactly how long it remained an exhibition gun is unknown, but eventually it was sold. Prior to taking delivery, the purchaser asked that the stock be bent to less drop—1 1/2 inches at the comb and 2 1/4 inches at the heel—and that a single trigger be installed. The work-order card shows these changes but no final shipment date. The single trigger suggests it was after 1914.

Although No. 13291 no doubt served the company well as an exhibition piece, No. 13292 predictably became the more famous. Theodore Roosevelt left office as President on March 4, 1909, in the midst of a blinding snowstorm, and on the 23rd, he and his son Kermit steamed out of New York harbor. They landed at Mombasa, British East Africa, on April 21, boarded the Uganda Railway—the Lunatic Express of the Tsavo man-eating lions fame—and met their safari at Kapiti Plains.

They would not emerge from the African wilderness until eleven months later, but during that time, Roosevelt wrote monthly essays for *Scribner's Magazine*, dispatching the manuscripts from camp to Nairobi by runner. In one of these,

WHAT THIS MARK MEANS TO THE USERS OF SHOT GUNS

THE A. H. Fox Gun Company has always tested every gun built in their factory with charges equal to proof required by the European Governments.

Tremendous overcharge is fired from every gun, which guarantees to the shooter that no defect can exist in either the barrels, frames or any other part of the gun, that must stand the strain of continuous shooting.

It further means that you take no chances of personal injury with the "Fox proved and tested gun."

Every gun we have made has been tested as above, and certificates of proof (see copy below) will be furnished upon request.

CERTIFICATE OF PROOF

This is to certify that Barrels, and all parts of A. H. Fox Gun Serial No._____ have been tested and shot with excessive overcharges in accordance with the abnormal test required by European Government Proof Houses.

The "Fox Proof" is another evidence of the great care we take to insure our patrons guns that are absolutely safe and perfect in material and workmanship.

Signed A. H. FOX GUN CO.,

Ansley H. Fox

President.

The Fox Company began using the "Fox Proof" stamp about 1908. Since the United States has never had a national proof house, each American gunmaker has devised its own proofing system to ensure that guns are sufficiently strong.

published in October 1909, he said: "I had a Fox No. 12 shotgun; no better gun was ever made."

Fox never used testimonial advertising to the extent that some other American gunmakers did, but this was too good to pass up. The company played Roosevelt's comment for all it was worth, and then some.

A.W. Connor no doubt masterminded the whole affair, as only A.W. Connor could.

Albert Connor was three years older than Ansley Fox. He entered the gun business at the age of fourteen, as a clerk at the Powell & Clement Company of Cincinnati, at the time one of the largest and best-known gun dealers in the country. Over the next nine years, Connor learned the business thoroughly and well, and in 1895 joined the Simmons Hardware Company of St. Louis as a traveling gun and sporting goods salesman. In 1903, having risen to become head buyer in Simmons' sporting goods department, he accepted the position of sales manager with Savage Arms Company. Ironically, the company that would one day own the Fox gun was itself in danger of going under.

Connor clearly was a creative, gifted executive. He reorganized the Savage sales department and implemented a marketing program that vastly improved the company's standing. Six years later, he was widely regarded as the preeminent sales executive in the American industry, and when the Fox Gun Company in April 1909 offered a vice-presidency, charge of the sales program and a directorship, A.W. Connor went to Philadelphia.

If Ansley Fox already had a notion of displaying his guns at the Grand American, as I believe he did, the idea sat well with his new sales manager. Connor had visited the great annual English shooting matches at Bisley in 1905 and noticed that manufacturers' displays got great attention from the spectators. Whatever his contribution may have been at the 1909 Grand American (he had, after all, been on board for only a couple of months), there's no question that he took the idea as far as he could. Over the next several years, the Fox company's appearances at the Grand grew more and more elaborate, heralded by pre-tournament announcements and newspaper ads. Indeed, as we shall presently see, the company used the Grand as the main venue for introducing its small-bore guns.

In the mean time, however, A.W. Connor launched a remarkably aggressive campaign to market Fox guns. By early 1909, the American economy was showing signs of recovery. As it turned out, the signs were more apparent than real, prompted by a belief that President William Howard Taft would continue the progressive policies established by Roosevelt. Taft's failure to do so would not be fully appreciated until 1910, so American industry was in a hopeful mood when Connor arrived at Fox and found the company thinking expansion.

A trade-journal item of May 1909 says Fox was contemplating "extensions to its present buildings so as to enable it to take care of about 60 per cent additional business. Considerable new machinery will be required, which has not yet been fully decided upon." This may have been mostly puffery designed to create a band-wagon effect on sales, but there is no question that Connor's efforts bore considerable fruit. In a letter of July 1, 1910, independent accountant and auditor Henry G. Cornell certified that the Fox Company's net sales for the first six months of the year were 106 percent higher and that specified orders on hand were 133 percent higher than those of the same period in 1909. A month later, sales were up 113 percent and orders up 135 percent. If the production figures of 2000 guns per year from 1907 through 1909 are accurate, even a hundred-odd-percent annual increase certainly would not set the shooting world awash in Foxes, but twice as much business is still twice as much, and 1910 appears to have been the company's first truly successful year.

AE Grade 12-gauge, 1910. Catalogues of 1907-1912 featured the "campfire" cover illustration.

WILLIAM W. HEADRICK

Among other things, Connor capitalized on Teddy Roosevelt's endorsement, losing no time in seeing that the former President's opinion on Fox guns was quoted in all the trade journals. Despite Roosevelt's immense popularity, the whole thing would have burned brightly for a time and then faded out, but then the vagaries of politics and chance handed Connor a matchless opportunity.

Roosevelt returned from Africa in June 1909 to a welcome that bordered on hysteria—and to a political party seething with rebellious rage. Progressive Republicans viewed Taft as a traitor to the progressive cause and implored Roosevelt to return to politics. At first, wishing only to retire to his home at Sagamore Hill and pursue other interests, he attempted to reconcile the growing polarity between the progressive and conservative elements within the party, and failed. Within a few months, prompted by extraordinary public demand, he began a series of speaking engagements around the country, and by 1910 his speeches resounded with the political implications of what he called the "New Nationalism," which in turn became the Progressive Republicans' cause celebre.

Ultimately, it all would lead to the presidential election of 1912, with Roosevelt running as the Progressive or "Bull Moose" Party candidate against Taft and Woodrow Wilson, a race in which Roosevelt's presence, by dividing the Republican vote, virtually assured a Democratic victory.

But that remained in the future. In 1909 and 1910, Teddy's speaking schedule of public appearances grew heavier and heavier, and after the Republicans lost their majority in the House of Representatives in the elections of 1910, the old Rough Rider seemed to be everywhere at once.

Often as not, A.W. Connor got there first, working with retailers in the cities where Teddy was scheduled to appear, setting up displays of Fox guns in which Roosevelt's name held a prominent place. As *The Sporting Goods Dealer* of December 1910, in a story obviously planted by Connor, put it: "The wide awake sporting goods dealer in the cities visited by Colonel Roosevelt in his present 'New Nationalism' rambles has an opportunity of a lifetime in boosting the sales or arousing interest in the Fox guns, and many supply houses who are so fortunate as to handle 'the finest gun in the world' have taken advantage of such visits."

The story goes on to describe a display mounted at the Philip Gross Hardware Company in Milwaukee, in which nearly the whole front window was given over to Fox guns and the Roosevelt safari. "It seemed," the item concludes on a breathless note, "that the passers never would get tired of looking at the 'gun

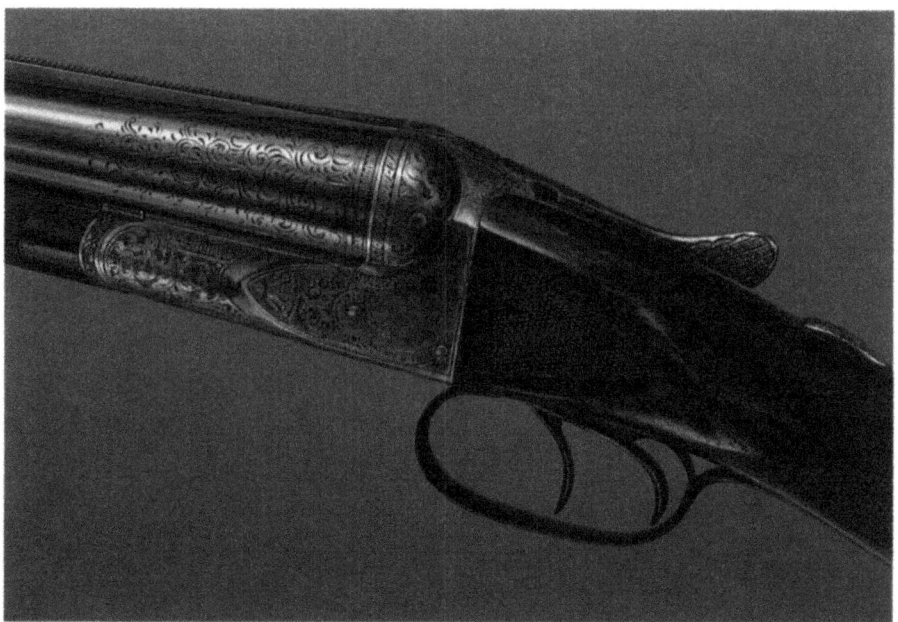

DE Grade 12-gauge, 1909, showing first-generation engraving style.   WILLIAM W. HEADRICK

like Teddy shot,' and the Gross Company found that the exploitation actually sold the guns."

If retailers in the industry were surprised by this last observation, A.W. Connor surely wasn't.

Fox continued pounding the Roosevelt drum for years, even including the text of his letter to Ansley Fox in the 1915 catalogue, along with a center spread illustration of an FE Grade gun—which is not the one that belonged to Teddy, although the catalogue copy invites you to think it is.

By 1915, though, many things had changed at the Fox Gun Company, and the most important changes began in 1910. It was, as I said earlier, a banner year for Fox, and one good reason why A.W. Connor was able to pull off his dramatic surge in sales is that he had a new gun to place before the market.

Sterlingworth Company 12-gauge, 1910 WILLIAM W. HEADRICK

8

NEW GUNS, NEW MEN

In its early years, the Fox Gun Company's approach to the market was a mirror-image of Ansley Fox himself—sharply focused within relatively narrow limits. Of itself, the Fox gun was a paragon of merit, but like an animal thoroughly adapted to a single niche, it was scarcely able to survive in a larger, more varied environment. Any shooter could get the best of all American guns from Fox—provided he wanted a 12-bore; and he could choose among five grades—provided he was willing to begin at a relatively pricey level and go up from there. If he wanted anything else, a smaller or larger bore or an inexpensive but sturdy utility gun, he must perforce look to another maker.

When he arrived at Fox, A.W. Connor already knew full well the limitations inherent to what sales people now call a vertical approach. Doing one thing better than anyone else can be a firm cornerstone of success, provided you're willing to start small and allow excellent performance or an excellent product to be the source of its own growth. This, of course, was not Ansley Fox's way. Ansley Fox started big, leapt immediately for the top, and clung to an absolute conviction that intrinsic excellence would always be both readily apparent and self-sustaining. It's a basic characteristic of those who find their keenest fulfillment in defying gravity; look inside every truly gifted rock-climber or aerial acrobat, and you'll find a simple, unshakable faith: They *will not* fall. Some don't, through a combination of flawless technique and sheer good fortune. But when the wire breaks or the mountain simply sheds a sliver of rock at the wrong moment, the risk-taker rides the weight of his faith all the way down.

As we've seen, gravity was working mischief with the American economy. In the first ten years of the century, the cost of food alone increased by thirty percent while the wages of the vast American working class rose scarcely at all. With real earnings in decline, discretionary money, money available to buy such things as guns, naturally declined as well. The barrier of price had effectively walled the Fox gun into an increasingly narrow and crowded niche, and Connor knew the company could never hope to reach a broader share of the market without a less-expensive product.

Beginning in 1911, Sterlingworth guns were no longer stamped with the Sterlingworth Company *name.*

WILLIAM W. HEADRICK

No one knows what Ansley Fox thought about that, but we have some clues. Certainly he could not have failed to recognize the advantages of offering a low-priced gun, and he apparently had the good sense to take Connor's advice seriously. No doubt Ad Roll was also a voice in favor of giving less attention to the shrinking top end of the market and more to the bottom. In any case, Ansley Fox gave in to better judgement sometime during 1909 and agreed to break out of the graded-gun mold that had been his stock in trade since Baltimore days.

But he drew the line at having his name associated with low-priced guns, at least in the beginning. So, when the new field-grade Fox was announced to the retail trade in March 1910, it appeared not as a Fox but rather as a product of The Sterlingworth Company of Philadelphia.

You have to wonder if Ansley Fox really believed he was fooling anyone. For one thing, the advertising describes the Sterlingworth as "The Finest $25 Hammerless Shotgun in the World." For another, both the advertising and the hang-tag attached to the guns indicate that they were manufactured under patents No. 714,688, No. 767,557, No. 796,119, No. 801,862, and No. 810046—the same patents, in other words, you'll find on Fox guns dating back to Philadelphia Arms.

Sterlingworth Company news releases, also published in March 1910, say the gun is the result of "...the investment of over a quarter of million [sic] dollars in the most modern gunmaking machinery and tools..."; that "...every dollar spent in its manufacture goes into real gun value. It is 'all gun,' without any useless embellishments... standardized in every detail, for the parts are made to fit maximum and minimum limit gauge [sic] and are interchangeable."

The price was protected by patent license, so that any sale at less than retail was unauthorized and could be construed as infringement of patents. This was part of Connor's strategy to prevent discounting and thereby bolster his dealer network. It was a shrewd move on the company's part, and besides, even at full

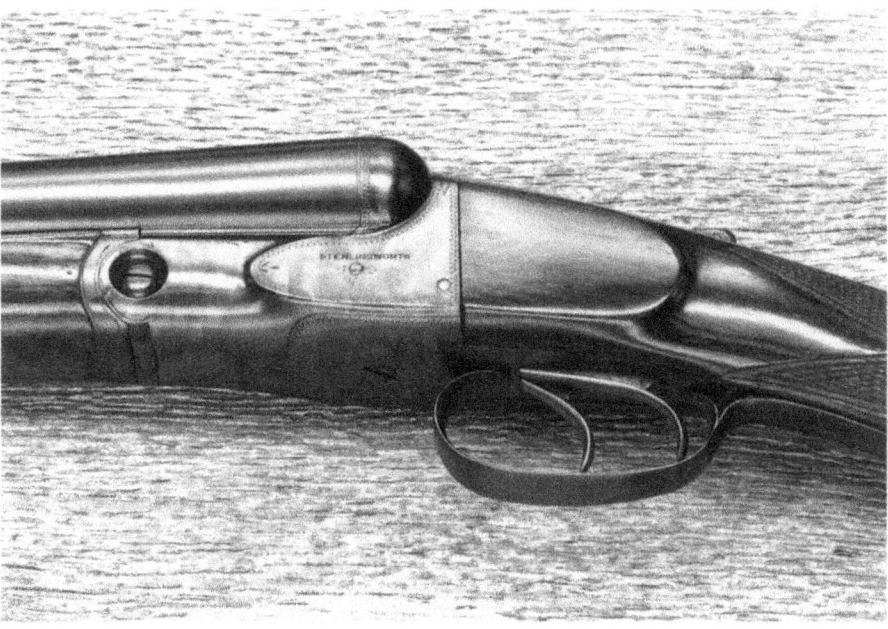

A Sterlingworth "pin" gun. The dished sculpting around the hinge pin was a brief carry-over from Philadelphia Arms Days; it appears on 12-gauge Sterlingworths built in 1911 and 1912 and on a very few graded 12-bores of the same period.

WILLIAM W. HEADRICK

retail of $25, the Sterlingworth represents the greatest value ever offered on the American gun market before or since.

"Sterlingworth" is a lovely, evocative name for a gun, although where it came from is anyone's guess. Philadelphia city directories from 1904 through 1911 list a Sterlingworth Railway Supply Company, but I've found no evidence that Ansley Fox was in any way associated with it. Predictably, The Sterlingworth Company does not appear in any city directory, nor did the name survive in advertising for long.

It does appear, however, on roughly the first 3000 guns. Twelve-gauge Sterlingworth serial numbers begin at No. 50000. The lowest-numbered gun I have information on is No. 50044, which is the forty-fourth built (in its serial-number blocks, Fox typically numbered the first gun 1, so the first Sterlingworth was No. 50001). No. 50044 shows "The Sterlingworth Co." engraved—not roll-stamped—on the sides of its frame. The right barrel is marked "Sterlingworth Fluid Compressed Steel," the left "Made by The Sterlingworth Co., Wayne Junc. Pa. U.S.A."

The earliest advertising lists the Sterlingworth Company address as simply Philadelphia, but the earliest guns show it as Wayne Junction, which was a railway-junction area in Germantown, not far from the Fox factory. By the time gun No. 50471 was built (which was shipped to Marshall Wells Hardware Company of Duluth, Minnesota, on March 24, 1910), the address on the guns was changed to Philadelphia, and all marks were roll-stamped. I don't know at exactly what number the dies were changed, but "Wayne Junction" guns clearly were built very early on and in small number—no more than 400-odd, probably fewer.

The "Sterlingworth Company" marque lasted somewhat longer, although certainly not beyond the end of 1910. It appears, for instance, on guns No. 50280 and No. 51600. The highest-numbered Sterlingworth Company gun I know is No. 52088.

"Made by the A.H. Fox Gun Company" began appearing in Sterlingworth advertising in the fall of 1910—although the ads are illustrated with a gun stamped "The Sterlingworth Co." By 1911, the frame stamp simply read "Sterlingworth," and the Fox Gun Company name appeared on the barrels.

The early Sterlingworths are remarkable for more than just their name and addresses. They look for all the world like a hybrid between A.H. Fox and Philadelphia Arms. The cocking and fastening systems clearly are those used by Fox Gun Company, but their frames are shaped like those of Philadelphia Arms vintage—side-panels rounded rather than pointed in the distinctive Fox style, and the same dished sculpting around the ends of the hinge pin that helped Philadelphia Arms guns look like Parkers. Among the second-phase guns—those stamped "The Sterlingworth Company" with the Philadelphia address—some have rounded frame panels and some are pointed. The rounded panels ceased to appear about the same time as the Sterlingworth Company stamping, but the hinge-pin sculpting continued to appear for some time after.

Fox collectors call these "pin guns." A very few graded guns were made the same way, but the majority by far are Sterlingworths. Nearly all of them date from 1911 and 1912, although as with other Foxes, a few no doubt got lost in the factory, either as numbered frames or finished guns, and weren't shipped until several years later.

Regardless of the occasional anomaly, however, most of the pin guns I'm aware of are numbered in the 56000-range or lower. I do know some exceptions: No. 57729, shipped July 19, 1911; No. 58657, shipped September 15, 1911; No. 60026, date unknown; No. 60507, shipped August 9, 1912; No. 61412, date unknown, No. 60726, shipped July 22, 1912; and No. 62244, date unknown. The highest-numbered pin gun I've ever heard of is No. 62262, which was shipped September 27, 1912.

The most compelling question about the pin guns is *why*? The sculpting certainly is an elegant feature, but if "every dollar" of production cost was directed toward "real gun value," then why sculpt the frames in a purely decorative way? Does this not qualify as "useless embellishment," which, as company literature asserts, was to be avoided in the Sterlingworth?

The most compelling answer is the simplest one: The early Sterlingworths were built on frames already partly machined and therefore already sculpted— which is to say they were built on frames left over from Philadelphia Arms.

I cannot track down absolute documentation for this, so I may be wrong. But I don't think so. The guns themselves certainly bear out the conclusion. I have found no evidence at all of a Fox pin gun, whether Sterlingworth or graded, in any gauge but 12—even though small-bores and pin guns were manufactured at the same time. The small-bores were built on frames reduced in scale inside and out; a 12-gauge frame wouldn't work. But an inventory of left-over Philadelphia Arms frames would be ideal for 12-gauge guns meant to be manufactured at minimal cost and sold at very low price, and the early Sterlingworths were exactly that.

The Sterlingworth is mechanically identical to graded Fox guns— using the same cocking and fastening systems and the same three-piece lockwork—but its fore-end latch is different. Instead of the Deeley-type latch standard on graded guns, the Sterlingworths always had snap-on fore-ends. In the earliest guns—essentially those built in 1910—the mechanism includes a

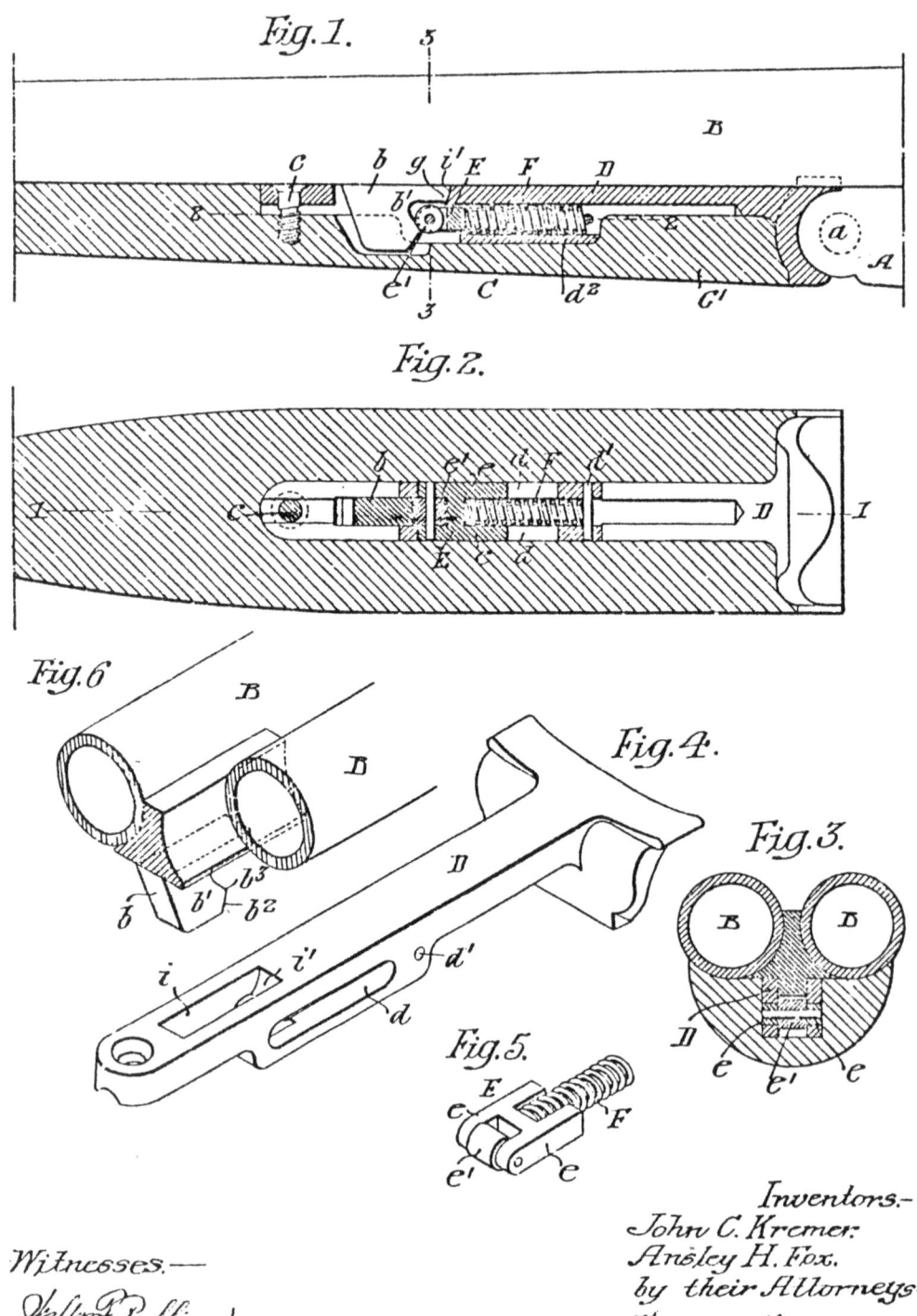

curved, leaf-type tension-spring similar to that of a number of other American guns. By the end of 1910, however, Fox had devised a new, coil-spring fastener for Sterlingworth fore-ends. The actual design appears to have been principally the work of John C. Kremer, who probably was a company engineer, but he and Ansley Fox jointly filed application for a patent on December 23, 1910. Although they requested protection on only two points, the patent—No. 1,029,374—was not issued until June 11, 1912. The system went into production early in 1911, and guns built over the following eighteen months carry a "Patent Applied For" stamp on the fore-end iron.

Mechanically, it's as good as any snap-on arrangement and decidedly better than most. The latch itself is simply an H-shaped bolt driven by a coil spring; its bearing surface is a steel roller pinned to the front end of the bolt. This roller, by reducing friction as the bolt rides over the hook in the barrel loop, makes the fore-end easy to snap off and on, even though the spring is strong enough to hold it firmly in place.

Kremer's latch has several advantages over the traditional Deeley design. For one thing, the spring-tension holds the fore-end iron firmly against the frame, which helps compensate wear in the action joint. For another, it significantly simplified the process of assembling the gun. In nearly every break-open gun, a close-fitting fore-end is essential. The fore-end literally holds the gun together, plays a key role in cocking the locks, and by its tension helps keep the action joint tight and working smoothly. The Deeley latch works fine so long as the barrel loop, or lug, is properly positioned, but getting the loop in the right place is a painstaking job that calls for skillful, precise hand-work. Set it a few thousandths too close to the breech, and the latch has to be hand-filed to fit; set it a few thousandths too far forward, and the fore-end is soon loose. Most of the world's great gunmakers, including the London trade, prefer the Anson-type push-rod fastener, because its spring-tension automatically compensates minor variations in position of the loop. Kremer's latch accomplishes the same thing. With it, barrel loops can simply be positioned within certain tolerances, by less-skilled workers, and still produce a close fit between barrels and frame. It's a good way of reducing production time and cost. Parker, which also used the Deeley latch for graded guns, would take a similar approach a few years later and develop a snap-on fore-end for the Trojan. The Parker latch isn't as good as the Fox-Kremer version, but it works.

Nearly everything about the Sterlingworths was standardized, from barrel length and chokes to stock dimensions. In 1910, it was available in two styles, designated Standard and Field—both, of course, in 12-gauge only and representing minor variations on a single theme.

Sterlingworth ad, late 1910. Other ads describe the Sterlingworth as "Not a Cheap Gun – but a Good Gun Cheap."

The Standard gun had thirty-inch barrels and a fourteen-inch, pistol-grip stock of about 2 $\frac{3}{4}$ inches bend. Chokes customarily were full and full, but the right barrel would be bored out to modified upon request. The Field gun differed only in having twenty-eight-inch barrels and about a quarter-inch more drop in the stock. Standard boring was modified and full, with cylinder and modified as an option.

The Brush version was introduced in 1911. It was stocked like the Field gun and came with twenty-six-inch barrels bored cylinder and modified.

Any departure from the basic specifications incurred additional cost: $15 more for ejectors (which were made available for the Sterlingworth in August, 1911), $10 for different stock dimensions, $2 for having thirty-two-inch barrels on a Standard gun or thirty-inch tubes on a Field gun, $5 for a Silver's recoil pad, and $15 per pair for extra sets of barrels. By then, the retail price was up to $35, but still it was a splendid value.

That Sterlingworths are numbered in a sequence of their own no doubt originated from Ansley Fox's initial reluctance to identify them with the Fox Gun Company. Later, with introduction of the small-bores, the company would adopt serial-number blocks as a matter of policy, always keeping Sterlingworths and graded guns separate and assigning specific blocks of numbers to each gauge. Therefore, graded 20-bores begin with No. 200001, 20-gauge Sterlingworths at No. 250001. Graded 16s are numbered from 300001, Sterlingworth 16s from No. 350001. Later still, single trap guns would be assigned the 400000-range, beginning with No. 400001. Yet other guns are numbered in a 450000 series; for those, see Chapter 20.

With Sterlingworths making a satisfying impact on the market, Connor began implementing other aspects of his plans for improving the Fox Company's standing. Plant superintendent and chief engineer Frederick T. Russell was already working on a better ejector system, and his design team was developing blueprints of a scaled-down Fox frame and lockwork that could be used for 16- and 20-gauge guns.

Besides pressing for new products, Connor also kept an eye out for ways of making old ones more economical to produce, and that inevitably led to a hard look at decoration. To understand Ansley Fox's inclinations in that regard, one need only look at the guns. Up to about 1911, Fox engraving follows essentially English motifs. Even the early A Grades show this in their delicate line-and-border work. British influence is even more apparent in B Grades, with their minimal though fine-line scroll, and it reaches full bloom in grades C and above, where the scrollwork grows progressively smaller and the coverage more extensive.

You can get an idea of how far Ansley Fox hoped to go in decoration, at least early on, from the fact that A.H. Fox gun No. 2, which is an A Grade, has some engraving on the barrels and even on the screw-heads in the fore-end—this on a gun meant to turn a profit at $50.

From a gunmaker's point of view, elaborate engraving is desirable so long as it enhances a gun's appeal in the buyer's eye and therefore fetches a price accordingly higher. But good engraving takes time, and it wasn't cheap even at the turn of the century. Connor probably pointed this out, and Ansley Fox probably replied that his motto was quality first and cost second—at which Mr. Connor must surely have reminded Mr. Fox that neither quality nor cost could be anything more than academic notions to a company that failed to stay in business.

Whether exactly such an exchange ever took place, I have no idea, but something much like it certainly did, because in late 1910 or early 1911, William H. Gough moved to Philadelphia and took charge of the engraving department at the Fox Gun Company.

William Gough was three months older than Ansley Fox, born at Birmingham, England, in March 1875. His father was an engraver in the Birmingham gun trade, and young Gough apprenticed to learn the craft as well. He emigrated to the United States sometime before the turn of the century, and ended up in Meriden, Connecticut, working at the International Silver Company under the tutelage of engraver and designer Frank Sporrns. From there, he went to work for Parker, where I believe he designed and executed the engraving of the prototype A-1 Special (for more on this, see the chapter on Fox single trap guns).

From Parker, Gough went to Hartford and worked at Colt, and then on to Philadelphia. At first, he lived at 4445 North Uber, moved to 4524 North Carlisle in 1913, and in 1918 to 4530 North Sixteenth, where he remained until moving to Utica, New York, following Savage Arms' purchase of Fox. Throughout the Philadelphia years—indeed, throughout the remainder of his life—Gough did freelance engraving in addition to his work at Fox. Much of it, in fact, was done in the engraving room at the Fox factory. The freelance jobs often came from other gunmakers, such as Winchester, Colt, and Hollenbeck. William Gough even engraved some of the A.J. Aubrey guns manufactured for Sears Roebuck. At Utica, where he lived until his death in the mid-1950s, the freelance business grew so brisk that by the beginning of World War II, he employed a staff of twenty engravers. Whether because of the volume of work or because Savage Arms wasn't as amiable as the Fox company had been about allowing work for other makers to be done on the premises, Gough rented separate quarters for freelancing—in the Gardner Block from 1937 to 1952, thereafter in the McLoughlin Building on Genesee Street.

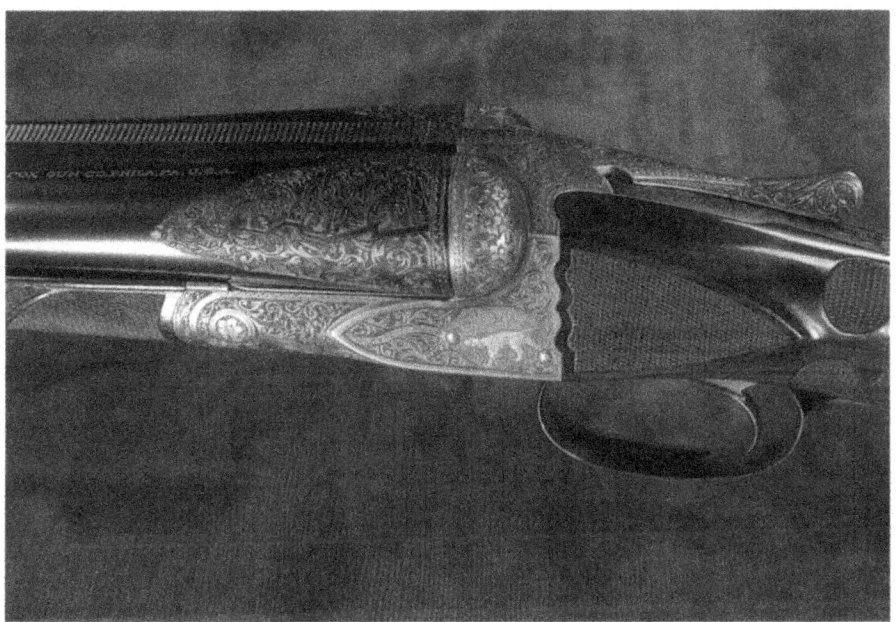

Second-generation FE Grade engraving is bolder and more open than the fine, tight scroll of earlier years. MICHAEL McINTOSH

Although vegetable gardening was his favorite pastime in later years, he appears to have been a target shooter as well. A William H. Gough, presumably the same one, founded the Philadelphia Shooting Academy, which was a trap shooting club. According to an item in the April 1, 1916, issue of *The American Shooter*, his sixteen-year-old daughter, Miss Leaphy C. Gough, assisted in running the club and was herself a trap shot of some skill.

At Fox Gun Company, Gough was assigned to redesign the standard engraving patterns for the various grades, with an eye toward a more economical approach. The transition from the scrollwork of first-generation Fox engraving to the second generation's bolder floral patterns began about 1912 or 1913 and appears first among the high grades. Decoration of D and F grade guns already had become somewhat bolder and less detailed—this is readily apparent on F Grade guns built after about 1909—but Gough took the changes farther still. The engraving became deeper, the interior patterns larger, and by 1914, the second-generation styles were in place for all grades.

In some cases, notably grades A and B, second-generation engraving is more extensive than it was before. The second-style B Grade is especially gussied-up, probably as an attempt to increase its sales, which apparently never were very brisk. (Quite a few B Grades also were stocked with wood more highly figured than

Second-generation FE engraving MICHAEL McINTOSH

seems appropriate for the grade, likely for the same reason.) Even so, the most salient characteristic of the new decoration is that second-generation patterns required less time and labor to execute. You can see this most clearly of all in the D and F grades.

Only the C Grade remained relatively unchanged. The scrollwork became a bit bolder and often was not as smoothly cut as before, but the pattern itself remained essentially the same. There are three possible explanations for this. The C Grade always was popular, much more so than Grade B, for instance, and the company might have decided not to tinker with a gun that already was selling well.

Or they may have left the C as it was in order to keep at least one grade with a decidedly English flavor. English guns had long been the world standard of quality and elegance, and English influence, strong throughout the American trade, was a subtle but powerful part of many guns' appeal.

It also is possible that Gough could not come up with a bolder pattern for the C Grade that was noticeably more elaborate than the second-generation B and yet noticeably less than the X Grade. I'll treat the X in more detail in another chapter, but it's important to note here that X Grade guns were built and shipped in 1912 and 1913, even though they weren't advertised as X Grade in the Fox catalogue until 1914. The point is, the engraving patterns of the second-style B

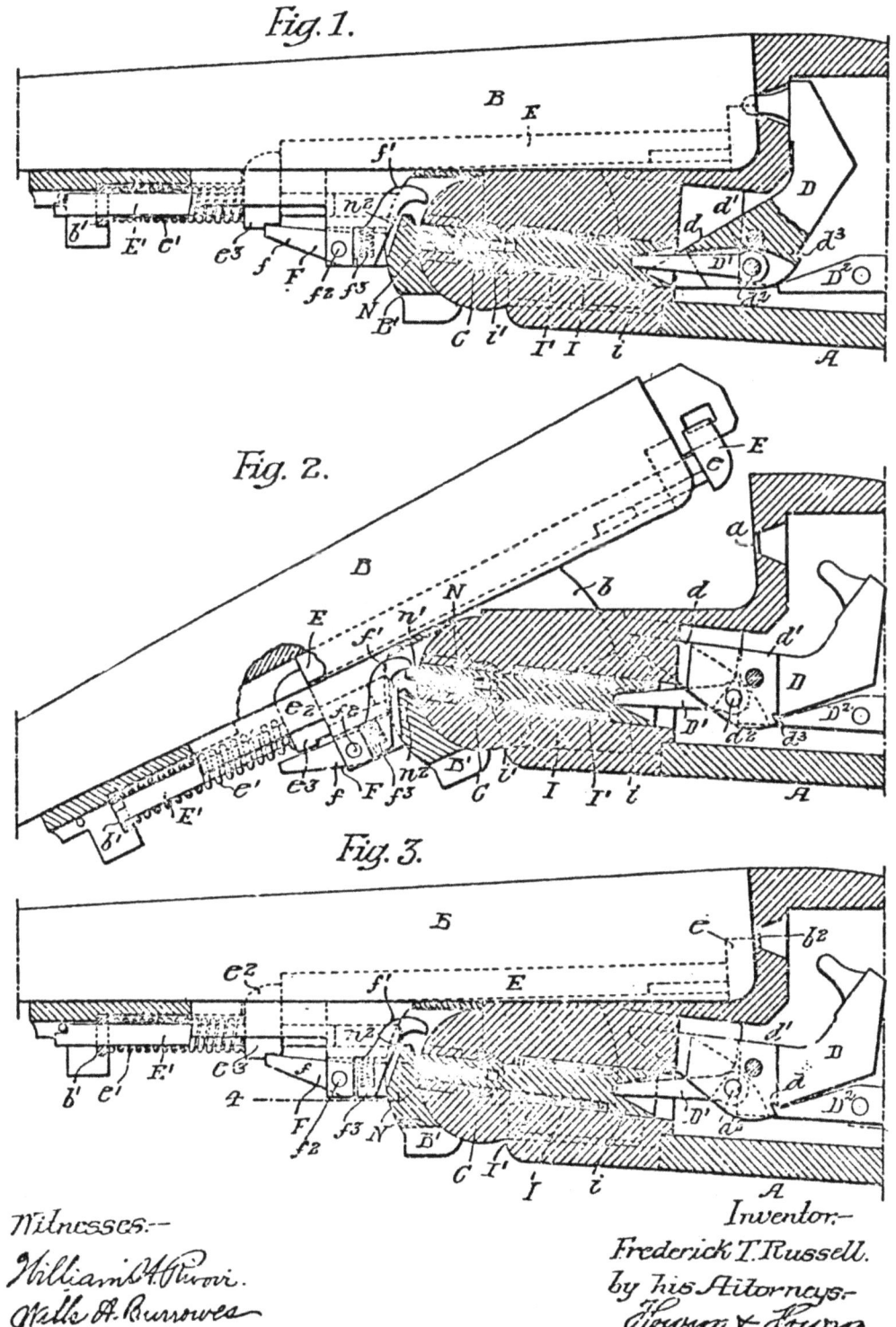

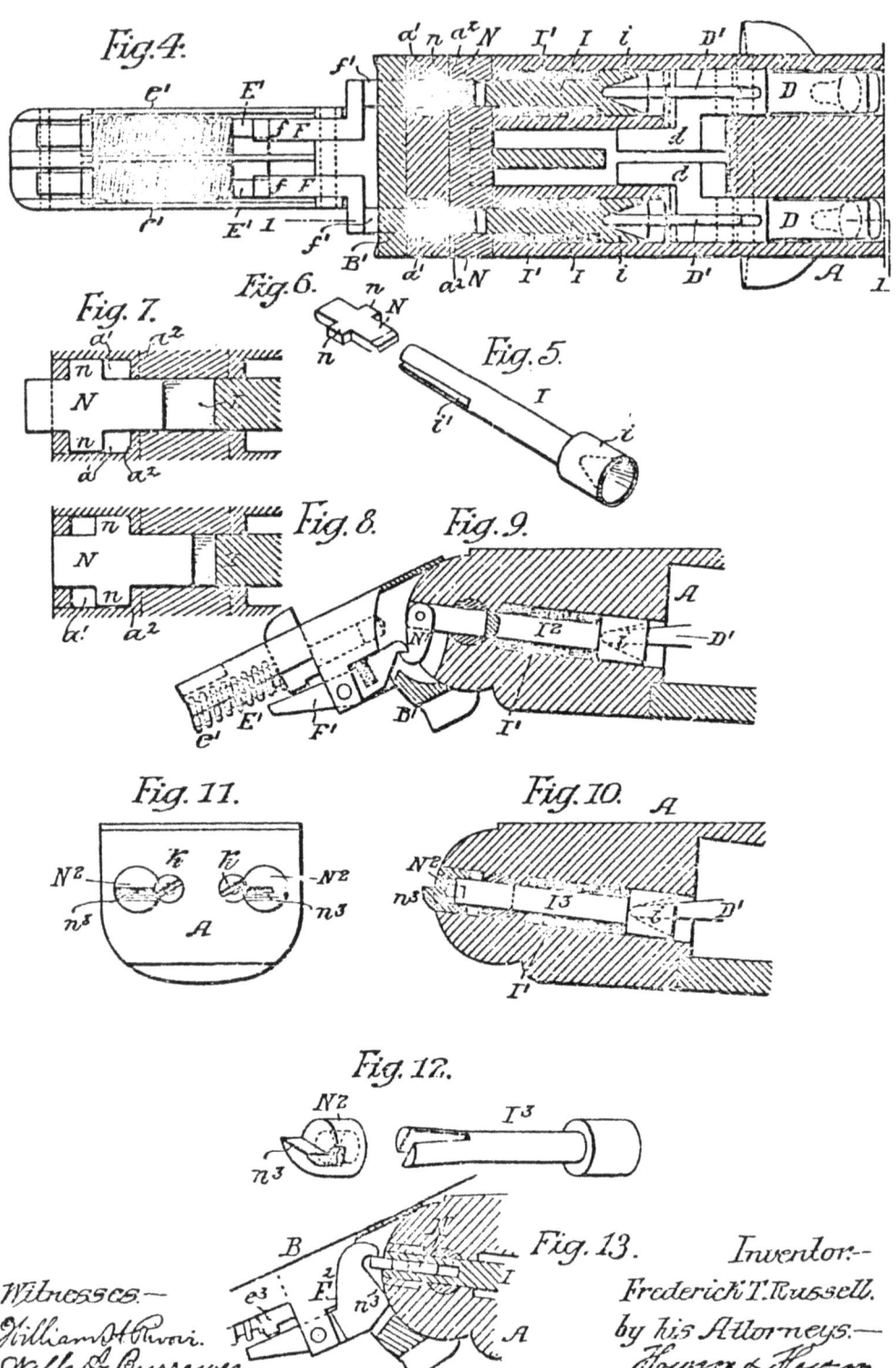

and the X grades are distinctively different but not so different that you could easily come up with a third, equally distinctive pattern in between, and that may be why the C Grade never changed much.

At any rate, William Gough appears to have been successful in accomplishing the goal of more economical decoration. Whether he was equally successful artistically is largely a question of taste. I prefer the elegant subtlety of the older-style engraving, myself—though I cannot fully agree with E.C. Crossman when he describes the second-generation look as "the grand and glorious Acorn stove type of gun decoration in the cheaper grades, the huge sprawls and whirls and general wall paper ornamentation, appearing at close range as if done by pushing the frame carelessly against a revolving buzz-saw, and adapted to making the yokel think that for his $75, he's getting a veritable Corot cut in a gun frame." Post-1914 Fox engraving may be overly gaudy in some cases, but the actual craftsmanship ranges from good in the lower grades to excellent in the highest ones.

William Gough himself only worked on very high-grade guns, presentation and exhibition pieces, and guns otherwise requiring special attention. The factory engraving staff, a group comprising both men and women, did the rest, following the designs Gough had created. The procedure at Fox was much the same as in engraving shops worldwide. Once he had the standard patterns worked out, Gough engraved them on brass plates about six inches square. To duplicate the designs, the staff engravers inked the plates, laid on sheets of transfer paper, and ran them through a pair of rollers under pressure. The paper was then laid onto a gun frame, polished and in the white, and rubbed to transfer the pattern to the steel.

Another technique used at Fox for duplicating a gun already decorated involved rubbing a compound of wax and red pigment into the engraving and pulling an impression directly onto transfer paper. In either case, the result was a clearly detailed, standardized guide that the staffer could simply trace over with his gravers.

By the end of 1910, the design for a new ejector system was complete, designs for the small-bores nearly so, and Fox announced its plans for the new year in a double-truck ad in the January 1911 issue of *The Sporting Goods Dealer*. The company would offer a "more complete" product line, admitting that the Sterlingworth "has always been made by the A.H. Fox Gun Company' and promising that in 1911 all Sterlingworths would be branded with the Fox Company name. The ad refers to Fox guns as "Model 1911" and speaks of such forthcoming improvements as "Model 1911 ejectors" and "chrome-nickel and vanadium steel." Fox had already flirted with the business of using model-something-or-other names, and a few graded 12-bore guns are stamped "Model

1910." Actually, the "Model 1911" designation was most closely associated with Sterlingworths, but after the new ejectors went into production, quite a few graded 12-bores were stamped "Model 1911" on the fore-end iron; this presumably was meant to identify the ejectors rather than the whole gun.

The ad also says, in a somewhat confused but certainly well-intentioned statement, "While we are not yet ready to accept orders for 16 and 20 gauge guns, we announce that we are now preparing to furnish Fox Guns in these gauges and we suggest that the trade keep this in mind in placing orders."

Announcement of the new ejector system may have been a bit premature, since Frederick Russell didn't apply for the patent until February 18, but the design was a good one, showing considerable creativity and mechanical skill, and the Patent Office accepted it quickly and without amendment as patent No. 991,375, issued May 2.

The small-bore announcement may seem premature as well, considering that the company was not prepared to accept orders. But Fox knew it was onto something with its exhibits at the Grand American Handicap, and A.W. Connor had plans to make the 1911 Grand the grandest yet.

It was scheduled for June 20-23 at Columbus, Ohio. More than 400 shooters would enter the handicap-championship event. Thousands would come to watch. A great many would make their way to the A.H. Fox Gun Company tent to have a look at the only real 20-gauge gun ever built in America.

A.W. Connor and Ansley Fox devised the lure and trolled in through the Columbus newspapers for more than a week prior to the Grand—a boxed item headed "Special Notice to All Shooters."

"Every trap shooter and sportsman," the notice reads, "is especially requested to visit The Columbus Gun Club June 21 and 22 and inspect the complete exhibit of Fox Guns, 'THE FINEST GUNS IN THE WORLD,' including FOX NEW 20-GAUGE—the only real 20-gauge gun ever built in America. We mean it is a 20-gauge from butt to muzzle. Also a new 16-gauge in the same class." It goes on to mention that every other grade of Fox gun would be on display, from the new Fox-Sterlingworth Ejector to "a duplicate of [the] FE Grade Gun used by Colonel Roosevelt in Africa," but the small-bores were the centerpiece.

Actually, the 20-gauge was meant to be the belle of the ball, clearly the innovation upon which the company pinned its deepest hopes. In most of its early promotion, as in this instance, the company treated the 16 almost as an incidental, a tag-along.

It was a canny move on Fox's part. The 16-bore's day was far from over, but good 16s had been on the market for a long time, from all of the best makers.

The 20-gauge, however, was just beginning its ascendancy. Although both Lefever and Parker were building 20s in the 1890s or before, neither shooters nor other gunmakers gave the gauge much thought until after the turn of the century. Ithaca adopted the 20-bore in 1904, L.C. Smith in 1907. By 1910, the little guns were truly catching on, largely owing to steady improvements in ammunition. With good cartridges available, 20s rapidly evolved from a status not much above toys to guns that bird hunters could take seriously. They were lightweight, compared with the typical American 12-bore, and seemed to promise something new and delightful on the shooting scene.

Size alone is a major part of their appeal. Shooters have always seemed to go warm and fuzzy over little guns—and not always wisely. I had a friend years ago who stood six-foot-seven in his socks; a basketball in his hand looked like softball in mine. He was a bird shooter of great enthusiasm, and the gun he cherished above all else was a wispy little 28-gauge, scarcely longer than his arm, that weighed roughly the same as one of his shoes. He looked like a man shooting a swizzle-stick. He couldn't hit a damn thing with it, of course, but he really didn't care. So far as he was concerned, that gun was the niftiest thing since canned beer—mainly, I think, because he was fascinated that something so small could truly go bang. (And it was an honest infatuation; he fell for and married a sweet lady who barely topped five feet in high heels and weighed about as much as the gun, probably for the same reason.)

Fox's claim that its version was the first "real" 20-gauge ever made in America is typically outrageous but not altogether lacking merit. More than a few gunmakers built their 20-bores using 12-gauge lockwork and therefore found reducing frame size in all dimensions impossible. A 20-gauge Parker, for instance, is just as deep in the frame as a 12. This is not true of a 20-gauge Fox, with its scaled-down locks inside a scaled-down frame.

Fox used the same frame for both 16- and 20-gauge guns. My eye tells me it's scaled just a wee bit closer to 16 than 20, but Fox small-bores are so exquisitely proportioned that it's hard to tell a 16 from a 20 at first, or even second, glance. No other American gunmaker ever achieved such proportional harmony.

It's impossible to say exactly how many small-bore guns Fox had on display at the Grand American, or at the Eastern Handicap Tournament in Wilmington, Delaware, the following month. They must have shown at least one of each gauge, possibly two. The work-order cards for the first two 20-bores—No. 200001 and 200002—are missing, but I've seen photographs of No. 200001, and it has the look of a gun meant for exhibition. It's a C Grade, high enough to display well and low enough to have been completed in a relatively short time, but all the water-table markings—patents, number, grade, and such—are engraved rather than roll-stamped, which means this was a C Grade that got special attention. It would be interesting to see No. 200002; if it's finished the same way, then there probably were two 20s in the Fox tent in Columbus.

Sixteen-gauge No. 300001 probably was there, too. It's a DE Grade, which certainly suggests a gun meant for exhibition, and it would later be the first 16-bore sold and shipped.

The DE Grade 12-bore No. 17060 may also have been part of the Grand American display. It was ordered with two sets of barrels—one set thirty inches with extra-full chokes, the other twenty-eight inches and choked cylinder and full. It also was ordered with no safety, which makes virtually certain that it was meant as a pigeon or trap gun, or both. A Silver's pad and rather high stock ($1\,^1/_2$ inches bend at comb and $2\,^1/_4$ inches at heel) suggest this as well. The work-order card shows instructions to select extra-fine wood and to deliver the finished gun to A.H. Fox. There is no delivery date, but if the gun was built in standard sequence, the number would date to 1911. It's unlikely that a shooter placed the order—in that event, the card would show more detailed specs for trigger-pulls and such—so it either was meant for display or was a gun that Ansley Fox intended giving to someone as a gift.

We'll never know which, for sure, but either way, it suggests that Fox was willing to pull out all the stops for its 1911 campaign.

The company's advertising shows this even more clearly. Connor bought a full page in *The Sporting Goods Dealer* every month and went whole-hog with eight pages in the March issue. Other ads appeared in virtually every magazine a potential gun-buyer might see: *National Sportsman*, *The American Field*, *Scribner's*, *The Saturday Evening Post*, *Cosmopolitan* (which obviously was of an altogether different format from today), *Outer's Book*, *Outlook*, *Field & Stream*, *Recreation*, *Everybody's Magazine*, *Outdoor Life*, *The Outing Magazine*, and many others.

Many of the trade-journal ads mention a wall-hanger display item promoting the FE Grade gun, a $13\,^1/_2$- by 22-inch poster on "heavy card, bearing an actual sized picture of the Grade FE gun in natural colors." The text, of course exploits the Roosevelt connection. Copies were available free to gun dealers: "We will be glad to send it to you free of cost, securely wrapped, all charges prepaid by us. All that you have to do is drop us a postal card and the picture will follow in the next mail." Sets of display cards for shop windows, illustrating the complete Fox line, also were available free to the trade.

Other ads touted the Sterlingworth with the catch-phrase "Not a Cheap Gun—but a Good Gun cheap."

The second-generation ejector system, 1913 catalogue.

By November, Fox claimed to have produced more high-grade guns during 1911 than any other maker. Sales in September, the company said, had been sixty-percent greater than those of September 1910.

In January and February 1912, Fox announced that delivery of 16- and 20-gauge guns to the trade would commence by September 1. Taking one last crack at the "model-so-and-so" marketing approach, the company called the small-bores the "Fox 1912 Models." The first guns delivered, the advertising promises, would be higher grades.

Sterlingworth guns with ejectors, announced several months earlier, had met with such "unprecedented demand" that the company apparently had been caught short: "We will be equipped this year to fill orders promptly, at least all the early orders."

But then again, maybe not. There's no question that Fox made considerable headway in the market during 1911, but it wasn't enough. Despite everyone's best efforts, sales income could not provide cash-flow at levels compatible with production spending, and Ansley Fox reportedly was borrowing money regularly just to meet operating costs. By the end of February, it all came crashing down.

In March, Spencer K. Lewis published the following letter to the trade:

> *In order to protect the interests of the stockholders, creditors and trade in general of the A.H. Fox Gun Company, the undersigned has been appointed receiver by the United States district court, and an immediate effort will be made to reorganize the business. During the receivership*

> *the same restricted prices, both to the dealer, jobber and consumer, which are now in effect, will remain operative, and we do not have the slightest intention of placing any Fox Guns upon the market, or permitting anyone else to do so, at less than the regular schedule prices. The sales department will remain in charge of Mr. Connor, the same as in the past, and you can count upon the same loyal co-operation as you have always received from him. It is hoped that the receivership will be of short duration, and that the business will again at an early date be continued as formerly.*

Happily, the receivership did prove a short one. On March 21, 1912, even before Lewis's letter appeared in print, Edward H. Godshalk took over the company. Godshalk had already made his fortune in textiles, and was heavily invested in Fox Gun Company at the time it went bust.

The speed with which the transfer of ownership occurred suggests that Ansley Fox and Godshalk may have struck a deal in advance, providing Fox with a financial stake for the future and allowing Godshalk to buy the company out of bankruptcy at a much-reduced level of creditor liability. It wouldn't be the first time, nor the last.

Whatever the maneuvers, though, by the time the *Titanic* went down in the North Atlantic on April 15, 1912, bearing 1595 people to an ice-water grave, Edward Godshalk was in and Ansley Fox was out. He was thirty-six years old, his life almost exactly half over. He would never again be a gunmaker.

XE 16-gauge, vintage 1920s　　　　　　　　　　　WILLIAM W. HEADRICK

9

MATTERS OF THE HEART: ELLEN

She was a poised, graceful young woman with striking eyes. Her family called her Ella.

Ellen L. Gerou was born September 23, 1885, in Philadelphia. Her father, William H. Gerou, was born in New Hampshire and possibly was of French-Canadian descent, for there is some evidence that the family name originally was spelled *Giroux*. Her mother, Mary Bella Frazier, was born in Kentucky in 1859. The Gerous bore a second child, William, Jr., in 1887, and sometime later the family broke up. By 1914, Ellen no longer knew her father's whereabouts.

In 1910, Ellen lived at 244 Berkley Street in Germantown. Her brother William lived a few blocks away, on North 19th Street, and worked as a machinist at the A.H. Fox Gun Company. Young William had struck up what would be a lifelong friendship with his employer and at some point introduced his older sister to Ansley Fox.

One of the essential and regrettable differences between history and art is that history seldom records emotion. We'll never know just what spark was struck between Ellen Gerou and Ansley Fox, nor when nor how it grew nor exactly how they felt about it, but the emotion clearly was powerful. Ansley Fox had some reputation as a womanizer, but this was different. Meeting Ellen Gerou altered the course of his life.

He was married; she was not. What agonies or recriminations came between Ansley and Fentress Fox is something else we'll never know, but it ended in the Philadelphia County Court of Common Pleas in the March term of 1913. Fentress, represented by attorney Henry J. Scott, petitioned for divorce on grounds of adultery.

For an entire year following the court hearing, no address for Ansley Fox appears in any public document. It's possible—and my romantic bent would have it so—that he and Ellen lived together on Berkley Street, forging the closeness that would endure for nearly thirty years, but this is scarcely more than speculation, for there isn't much solid evidence to support it.

Still, their intentions were clear enough. On March 23, 1914, Judge J.M. Patterson issued a decree of divorce for cause of adultery in the case of Fentress DeVere and Ansley Herman Fox. (In the court papers, his middle name is misspelled as *Hermon*.) The co-respondent in the matter is not named, which undoubtedly was a condition of the settlement, but that person obviously was Ellen Gerou. On March 25, Ansley Fox and Ellen Gerou applied to the Clerk of the Orphans' Court of Philadelphia County for a license to marry. The following day, March 26, 1914, they were married at All Saints' Lutheran Church by Pastor F.A. Bowers.

They lived at 244 Berkley Street, the address both of them listed on the marriage-license application, until 1923, when they moved to 5044 Erringer Place, also in Germantown—a block-long street between Fernhill Park and the lawns of the Germantown Cricket Club. Family recollection has it that they also lived on Laurel Avenue, down the block from the Woolworth family, and on Queen Lane, although these addresses do not appear in Philadelphia city directories. They lived somewhat formally, in spacious houses, attended by a small staff of servants.

Ellen was fond of keeping pace with the latest fashion and is said to have been generous in sharing her wardrobe with her brother's wife, Millie. She remained close to her brother and her mother, who at some point remarried and became Mary Cunningham. Ellen and Ansley Fox produced no children. Their marriage endured for the remainder of Ellen's life, which, from her wedding day, was one day short of twenty-eight years and nine months.

CE Grade 20-gauge WILLIAM W. HEADRICK

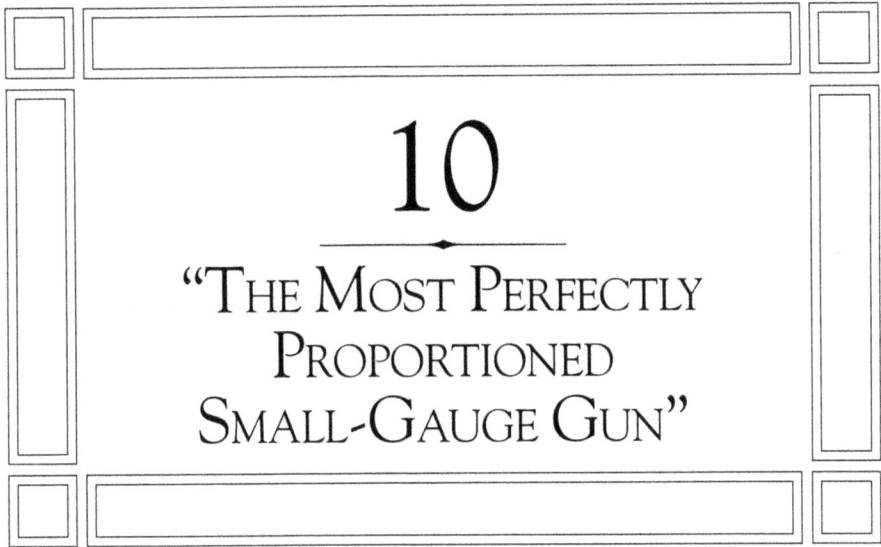

10

"THE MOST PERFECTLY PROPORTIONED SMALL-GAUGE GUN"

In the reorganization that followed the new ownership, Edward Godshalk became president of Fox Gun Company. J. Lyle Peden served as vice-president and general manager, Spencer K. Lewis as secretary and treasurer. Within a year, Clarence A. Godshalk, Edward's son, would be named treasurer. He would become vice-president in 1915 and would succeed his father as company president in 1920.

Despite the receiver's promise that A.W. Connor would remain in charge of sales and distribution, scarcely a month passed before Connor left for New York City to become associated with the advertising agency Street & Finney, Inc. He would later work for the Parker Pen Company.

It's impossible to say what circumstances prevailed in Connor's departure, whether he left by choice or whether Godshalk served walking papers. The only clue is that the *Sporting Goods Dealer* item announcing the move to Street & Finney does not mention the Fox Gun Company by name, saying only that he had previously served as sales manager of "a prominent Eastern firm." But this, unfortunately, is no clue at all, since not mentioning a company so recently bankrupt may have been nothing more than a delicacy on the copywriter's part.

In any event, Godshalk does not appear to have made any major changes in the sales policies and marketing strategy that Connor had put in place. Indeed, it probably was at this point when Ad Roll succeeded Connor as sales manager.

Getting the small-bore guns into circulation was the first order of business. Besides a vigorous campaign of magazine advertising, the company

A trio of small-bores: top, CE Grade 20-gauge, 1916; center, CE Grade 20-gauge, 1917; bottom, XE Grade 20-bore, 1918.

ROBERT LINTHOUT

published an eight-page brochure dedicated to the small-bores. Exactly when is impossible to say, since it isn't dated, but indications in the text would place its appearance sometime in the autumn or winter of 1911.

Titled "Complete Description of the A.H. Fox 16 and 20 Gauge Guns/ 1912 Model/The Most Perfectly Proportioned Small-Gauge Gun Ever Built," this is an interesting little document, for several reasons, not the least of which is sheer scarcity. None of the truly advanced Fox collectors I've talked with have seen more than one original copy; most have never seen an original at all.

Clearly, the brochure never was widely distributed, probably because the brave plans that Ansley Fox and A.W. Connor had made a year earlier were no longer feasible by the beginning of 1912. In many ways, therefore, the small-gauge brochure is a testament to dashed hopes, an outline of intentions that didn't quite come off as planned.

For one thing, it contains the earliest use of the trade-name "Chromox steel" that I've been able to find. Since the beginning—indeed, since Philadelphia Arms days—Fox had used Krupp barrels exclusively. No one has ever found much quarrel with the quality of Krupp tubes, but they were expensive, and Fox appears to have begun seeking an alternative as early as 1910. Throughout the Philadelphia years and for a few years after the Savage takeover, Sterlingworths were barreled with what the company called Sterlingworth Fluid Compressed Steel; who actually made the tubes is anyone's guess, but I have a notion it was the same Belgian foundry that supplied the barrels and frame forgings that Fox trade-named Chromox. The "chrome-nickel and vanadium steel" mentioned in connection with the Sterlingworth in January 1911 certainly suggests this.

At any rate, the small-bore brochure has this to say: "With the assistance of the best steel experts in the world, we have been able to have created specially for us an entirely new steel, known as 'Chromox' High Pressure Fluid Steel, which will be used exclusively by us in both 16 and 20 gauge *barrels* and *frames*." The italics are theirs.

The appearance of Chromox did not, however, bring the use of Krupp barrels to an end. Twelve-gauge guns were built with Krupp tubes until World War I effectively shut off the supply, and even then, enough sets remained in inventory that the factory sent out a few Krupp-barreled guns in the 1920s. Nor, despite the brochure's promise, were all of the early small-bores made of Chromox. Between 1912 and about 1918, about as many 16s and 20s were built with Krupp barrels as with Chromox, and while some were made on Chromox frames, the majority built before the end of World War I were not. (You can tell the difference between Chromox frames and those made of the earlier standard steel by the color

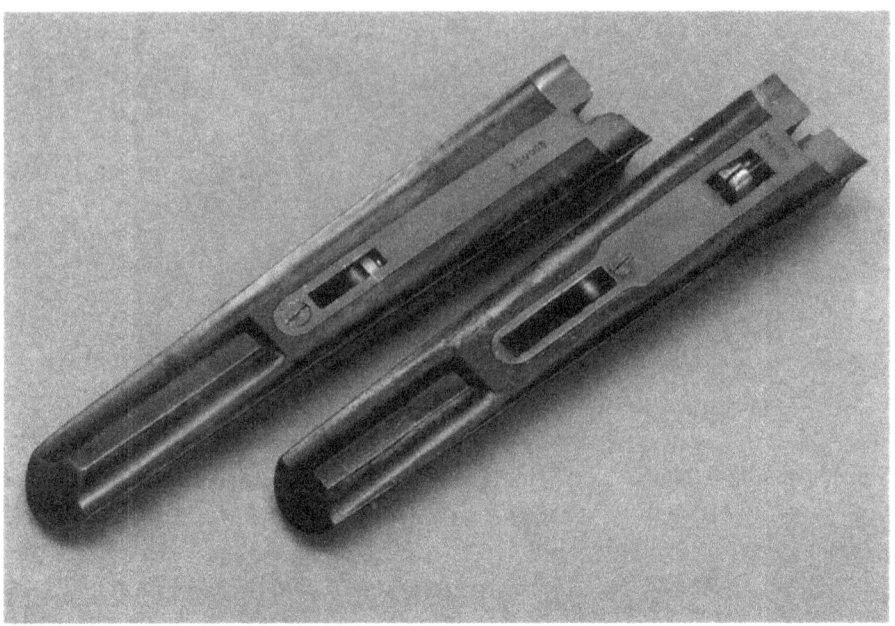

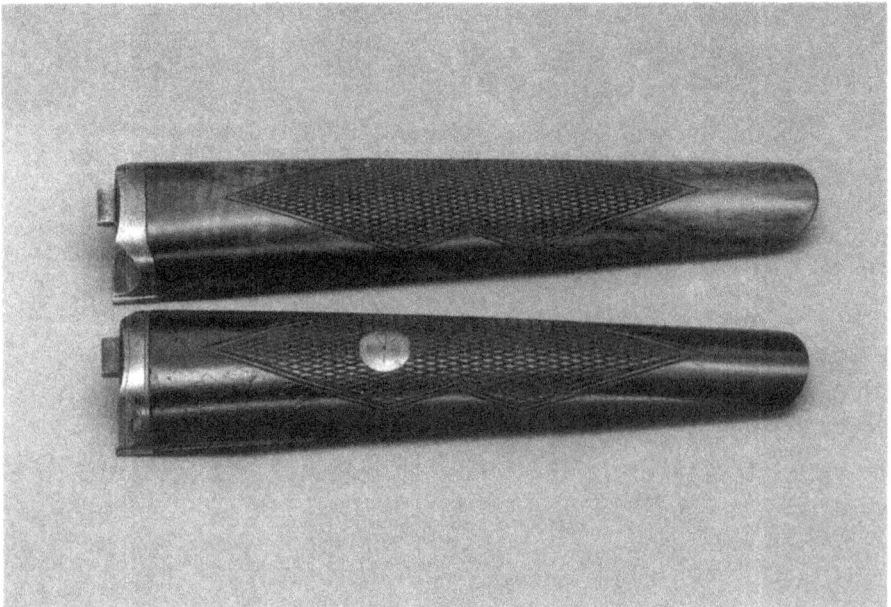

WILLIAM W. HEADRICK

The earliest graded small-bores featured snap-on fore-ends of the same design used on Sterlingworth guns (left and top). After about 1915, however, graded small-bores were given the same Deeley latch used on 12-gauges, and the Sterlingworth fore-end fastener was changed to an altogether different design (right and bottom). Note the metal anchor used on ejector guns.

and patina they take on as the case-hardening colors fade. When the case colors disappear, either through wear or exposure to sunlight, the older steel turns a soft, dull gray; Chromox, on the other hand, goes as bright and silvery and shiny as a new nickel.)

In another point of interest, the brochure describes the 20-bore only as the "*perfect* 20 gauge gun," (italics theirs) but says the 16 is "built on [a] specially designed 16 gauge frame." As I said earlier, I consider Fox's small frame to be a bit more of a 16 than a 20, and the language here makes me wonder if the factory didn't think so, too. Not all Fox men agree with me on this point of proportionality, and it certainly is arguable that the brochure's wording is mainly an attempt to promote both gauges without saying they're actually built on the same frame.

Basic specifications call for Circassian walnut stocks of half-hand design, $13 \frac{1}{2}$ to $14 \frac{1}{2}$ inches in length, pistol-grip and straight-hand versions available on special order. The standard lightweight guns would be bored with $2 \frac{1}{2}$-inch chambers; heavier ones could have $2 \frac{3}{4}$- or 3-inch chambers upon request. Barrels could be twenty-six, twenty-eight, thirty, or thirty-two inches. The shorter barrels, twenty-six and twenty-eight inches, naturally proved by far the more popular; small-bore Foxes with thirty-inch tubes show up now and then, but thirty-two-inch guns are quite scarce. Even so, as I'll discuss in more detail later on, Fox would accommodate any reasonable request, and I know of one A Grade 20-bore that was fitted with thirty-four-inch barrels. I imagine a few others were made the same way.

The brochure refers to a "new Fox Coil Spring Compensating Type" fore-end for the small-bores, which in fact is the John Kremer design used for Model 1911 Sterlingworths. The snap-on fore-end appears on roughly the first 700 graded small-bores, but it was discarded about 1915 and replaced with the same Deeley-type latch used on the graded 12-bores.

The reason for this change isn't clear. As I discussed earlier, the Kremer latch is both mechanically and economically superior to the Deeley, so the change really wasn't an improvement. Possibly the market perceived a snap-on fore-end as a low-grade feature; it was, after all, standard fare for Sterlingworths and field-grade guns by other makers. If a man had to spend the same money for a small-bore as for a 12-gauge of the same grade, he might well expect the gun to be the same in all respects.

The reason may also have been mechanical. Dismounting a Kremer-latch fore-end requires some muscle, and it's not an easy job for a youth or a woman or a man with small hands—all of whom were prime potential customers for small-gauge guns. Perhaps customer complaints prompted the change.

The small-bore booklet, produced in 1911, is one of the rarest of all Fox publications.

WILLIAM W. HEADRICK

Indeed, complaints may have prompted an even more far-reaching change, for a new fore-end latch began to appear on Sterlingworths about the same time or even a bit earlier. In this one, the coil-spring tensioner is fastened to the barrel loop rather than to the fore-end iron. All that's in the iron is a cross-pin, usually fitted with a roller, for the barrel-hook to latch onto. As in Kremer's version, the fore-ends of ejector guns are fitted with a steel cylinder that acts as an anchor for the screw holding the fore-end iron to the wood. It's about ⅝-inch in diameter and is inlet to the wood from the outside, so any Sterlingworth ejector gun (or graded small-bore with a snap-on fore-end) is easy to identify from a distance.

This third—and final—Sterlingworth latch apparently never was patented, which is a curious thing but by no means unique during the Godshalk years. All told, the design isn't quite as good mechanically as the Kremer latch, but it still is better than the Deeley. In fact, the work-order records of later years show several instances in which graded guns were specifically ordered with Sterlingworth fore-ends. These guns often are of a configuration likely to be used for high-volume shooting—trap guns and such—and they presumably were ordered by people who recognized the Sterlingworth latch's durability and wear-compensating virtues.

As Fox had indicated in other advertising, the brochure says the small-bores would be ready for delivery "between September first and December, 1912," in grades C, CE, D, DE, F, and FE, "and higher grades only." Another interesting point, this last. Later Fox advertising indicated a willingness to build guns of higher grade than F, but that came much later than the small-bore brochure. Perhaps ultra-high grades were another idea from former days that the Godshalks put on hold, or perhaps the "higher grades" comment refers to the X Grade—which, as we shall see, actually did exist about the time the small-bore brochure was made up.

The first small-bores were indeed shipped in the fall of 1912 (beginning with No. 200011, a CE Grade 20 that left the factory September 17), but as it turned out, the Godshalks also changed the plan for making the first small-bores in Grade C and above. Of the first fifty 20-bores shipped, nine were C or CE Grade, one (No. 200047) was a B, two were unrecorded, and the rest were A Grade (three of these, Nos. 200004, 200005 and 200009, were AE). Obviously, the Godshalks were more inclined to be conservative in production cost than Ansley Fox had been.

A few work-order cards are missing, but surviving records show a total of eighty-three 20-bore guns shipped during 1912 and 144 the following year. The first DE Grade 20, No. 200108, was shipped January 10, 1913, but no one ordered

The sixty-first Fox 20-bore, A Grade, 1912 WILLIAM W. HEADRICK

At $67.50, this 1919 Sterlingworth Ejector was one of the all-time great bargains in American guns.

WILLIAM W. HEADRICK

Despite Fox's earlier promise that the first small-bores would be high grades, the majority were A and B grades, like this A shipped in 1912. WILLIAM W. HEADRICK

an FE 20-bore until the halcyon days of the 1920s; the first was No. 202027, shipped April 4, 1921.

On the other hand, the first 16-gauge (or more properly, the first production 16, lest we forget gun No. 17), truly was a high grade. This is No. 300001, the DE Grade that probably was built for display at the 1911 Grand American. It was shipped October 21, 1912.

A few of the earliest 16-gauge work orders are missing, but all grades from A through DE are represented among the guns shipped in the last weeks of 1912. No. 300003 is a CE Grade shipped November 11, No. 300005 a B Grade shipped November 16, and No. 300006 an A Grade shipped December 11.

The earliest small-bores were decorated with first-generation engraving patterns, but second-generation styles begin to appear rather soon. For instance, 20-bore gun No. 200061, shipped November 15, 1912, has old-style engraving (it also has Krupp barrels), but I know of a B Grade of late-1913 or early-1914 vintage that's decorated with the deep chiseling of the second style; it has Chromox barrels. A slightly later A Grade—No. 300380, shipped March 8, 1914—has second-generation engraving and Krupp tubes.

If, as I believe, the company began implementing the change of engraving style in the latter part of 1913, then all of the old-style-engraved 20s should be A and B grades. (The C Grade pattern, remember, didn't change.) The only certain exception is the first DE 20, which also has old-style decoration. The second and third DE 20-gauges, Nos. 200157 and 200173, were shipped September 23 and October 15, 1913, respectively; these may have old-style engraving, but I've never seen either one.

As you'll see in Chapter 15, the attempt at devising a 16-gauge version of the Super-Fox was unsuccessful. Catalogues of the 1930s always listed Trap/Skeeter Grade as available in 12, 16, and 20 gauges, but no evidence has yet turned up to indicate that any were made in 16-gauge. Otherwise, small-bores are

---

COMPLETE DESCRIPTION OF THE

A. H. FOX
16 AND 20 GAUGE GUNS
1912 MODEL

THE MOST PERFECTLY PROPORTIONED SMALL-GAUGE
GUN EVER BUILT

---

represented in all Fox grades—precious few, in some cases, but represented nonetheless.

Roe Clark provided the following gauge/grade breakdowns, gathered directly from existing work-order cards, for all grades except Sterlingworth.

16-GAUGE

Grade	Made in Philadelphia	Made in Utica	Total
A	1580	1132	2712
B	186	0	186
C	202	103	305
X	79	11	90
D	29	2	31
F	3	0	3
*SP/SPE	0	164	164
Trap/Skeeter	0	0	0
"Special"	15	6	21
Unknown	3	6	9
	2097	1424	3521

*These figures may include a few SP Skeet & Upland Grade guns.

Add 354 missing cards to the final figure, and the total number of graded 16-bores comes to 3875.

The 20-gauges are fewer still.

20-GAUGE

Grade	Made in Philadelphia	Made in Utica	Total
A	2034	345	2379
B	177	0	177
C	366	47	413
H	50	10	60
X	150	2	152
D	49	5	54
F	3	3	6
SP/SPE	0	146	146
SP Skeet & Upland	0	34	34
Trap/Skeeter	0	3	3
"Special"	10	0	10
	2839	595	3434

About 575 of the 20-gauge work-orders are missing, including an entire block from No. 203241 through No. 203500; I rather suspect Savage Arms simply skipped those numbers for one reason or another and never assigned them at all. If this is true, then total production of graded 20-bores would have been only about 3751 guns.

Add everything up, and the number of graded Fox small-bores, 16s and 20s alike, amounts to roughly 7580 guns. That isn't many, compared with the output at Parker—nor even compared with the production of Sterlingworths, which Roe Clark estimates at about 28,000 in 16-gauge and about 21,000 in 20-bore.

Considering that the remaining Fox records are incomplete, you shouldn't take these totals as absolute gospel, although the subtotals for the highest-grade guns are quite accurate. Even allowing for some variance, though, it's clear that graded Fox small-bores are by no means overly plentiful. That 16-bores should outnumber 20s should come as no surprise, for the enormous popularity the 20-gauge enjoys nowadays didn't really begin until after World War II. In the first half of the century, the 16 was the queen of small-gauge guns.

This also goes some way toward explaining why 20s outnumber 16s in the highest grades: X, D, and F. In the 1910s and '20s—and certainly in the '30s—most of those who owned 20-gauge guns owned several other guns besides, which means they were sportsmen of some economic clout and therefore both more able and more likely to pop for high-grades.

No doubt everyone involved, from Fox Gun Company to Savage Arms, wished the demand were greater and the numbers higher overall, and a lot of gun fanciers nowadays would certainly agree. But it's no use being rueful of spilt milk or unmade guns; considering what sleek and lovely things they are, we're fortunate that small-bore Foxes were built at all.

XE Grade 20- (top) and 16-gauge — WILLIAM W. HEADRICK

11

OVER HERE, OVER THERE

E ven apart from the bankruptcy, receivership, and subsequent change of ownership, 1912 was a pivotal year for Fox Gun Company. The small-bores promised to extend the company's reach in the gun market; the second-generation engraving styles offered a new look, while new materials such as Chromox helped make production more economical.

The company might also have simplified the product line and offered guns in fewer, more standardized forms—might have, in other words, sought to avoid Ansley Fox's particular weakness for offering too much at too low a price by reducing the number of grades, by ceasing to offer special-order features at no additional charge, and so on. This, however, would have impaired Fox's ability to compete with Parker and Smith and the others and would have further eroded its already-minimal share of the market. The alternative was to lower production costs, through less-expensive materials or more efficient manufacturing methods or a combination of both, and this was the direction the company chose.

Both Ansley Fox and the Godshalks clearly recognized the value of using machine work to the maximum extent possible while at the same time holding hand-work to the least amount compatible with satisfactory levels of quality. The change in engraving style is evidence of this, and so is the system of segregating barrels by weight in the rough-machined stage.

Virtually all modern guns begin as a chunk of steel forged (or in some current instances, investment-cast) to the approximate shape of a frame and a pair of tubes that can be brazed or soldered together to form the barrel assembly.

XE 12-gauge, Philadelphia vintage WILLIAM W. HEADRICK

In a shop where guns are made largely by hand, the forgings may all be the same size, regardless of what size and weight the finished piece might be, but for production guns there is an obvious advantage in having components machined to several sizes. The nearer the components are to finished size, the less hand-work is required.

That Fox only used two frames—at least until the early 1920s, when the Super-Fox was developed—helped simplify that end of things. But just as frames take time to file and finish, so do barrels, and the hand-work needed to strike a set of heavy tubes into a pair of lightweight barrels could eat up a sizeable chunk of company profit.

To avoid this, Fox established standard weights and dimensions for rough-machined barrels in all three gauges, ranging from heavy to light. Thus a given tube could be matched to one of similar weight, and the two, when assembled, could then be selected according to how little hand-work would be required for a finished gun of predetermined weight.

The grading apparently was done in the barrel shop when the blanks were put through the first stages of machining, and the tubes were then stamped with a numerical code indicating their weight class. The stamps were applied to each tube just ahead of the water table and often remained visible when the gun was finished. Since there is nothing on the guns to indicate what these numbers mean, they naturally have invited all sorts of speculation and have been interpreted as everything from indications of choke (Ithaca identified chokes by number, but Fox didn't) to the "personal numbers" of certain factory gunsmiths. All they really indicate is the weight class to which the rough tubes originally belonged.

No one knows exactly when Fox initiated the system, but the following charts come from factory blueprints dated 1912. For some reason, 20-gauge barrels were given a slightly different numbering sequence—0-2-3-4, as opposed to the 1-2-3-4 sequence used for 12s and 16s. And about 1922, the factory added a fifth 12-gauge class, No. 0, for the Super-Fox. Otherwise, the system is quite consistent for all gauges, and in every case, the higher the number, the lighter the barrels. According to factory standards, barrels could not vary more than one ounce per pair from the weights specified.

12-GAUGE

Code	Barrel Length	Weight
No. 1	26 inches	3 pounds, 14 ounces
No. 1	28 inches	4 pounds, 0 ounces
No. 1	30 inches	4 pounds, 2 ounces
No. 1	32 inches	4 pounds, 4 ounces
No. 2	26 inches	3 pounds, 10 ounces
No. 2	28 inches	3 pounds, 12 ounces
No. 2	30 inches	3 pounds, 14 ounces
No. 2	32 inches	4 pounds, 0 ounces
No. 3	26 inches	3 pounds, 6 ounces
No. 3	28 inches	3 pounds, 8 ounces
No. 3	30 inches	3 pounds, 10 ounces
No. 3	32 inches	3 pounds, 12 ounces
No. 4	26 inches	3 pounds, 2 ounces
No. 4	28 inches	3 pounds, 4 ounces
No. 4	30 inches	3 pounds, 6 ounces
No. 4	32 inches	3 pounds, 8 ounces

16-GAUGE

Code	Barrel Length	Weight
No. 1	26 inches	3 pounds, 15 ounces
No. 1	28 inches	4 pounds, 1 ounce
No. 1	30 inches	4 pounds, 3 ounces
No. 1	32 inches	4 pounds, 5 ounces
No. 2	26 inches	3 pounds, 10 ounces
No. 2	28 inches	3 pounds, 12 ounces
No. 2	30 inches	3 pounds, 14 ounces
No. 2	32 inches	4 pounds, 0 ounces
No. 3	26 inches	3 pounds, 4 ounces
No. 3	28 inches	3 pounds, 6 ounces
No. 3	30 inches	3 pounds, 8 ounces
No. 3	32 inches	3 pounds, 10 ounces
No. 4	26 inches	2 pounds, 15 ounces
No. 4	28 inches	3 pounds, 1 ounce
No. 4	30 inches	3 pounds, 3 ounces
No. 4	32 inches	3 pounds, 5 ounces

20-GAUGE

Code	Barrel Length	Weight
No. 0	26 inches	3 pounds, 14 ounces
No. 0	28 inches	4 pounds, 0 ounces
No. 0	30 inches	4 pounds, 2 ounces
No. 0	32 inches	4 pounds, 4 ounces
No. 2	26 inches	3 pounds, 7 ounces
No. 2	28 inches	3 pounds, 9 ounces
No. 2	30 inches	3 pounds, 11 ounces
No. 2	32 inches	3 pounds, 13 ounces
No. 3	26 inches	3 pounds, 0 ounces
No. 3	28 inches	3 pounds, 2 ounces
No. 3	30 inches	3 pounds, 4 ounces
No. 3	32 inches	3 pounds, 6 ounces
No. 4	26 inches	2 pounds, 10 ounces
No. 4	28 inches	2 pounds, 12 ounces
No. 4	30 inches	2 pounds, 14 ounces
No. 4	32 inches	3 pounds, 0 ounces

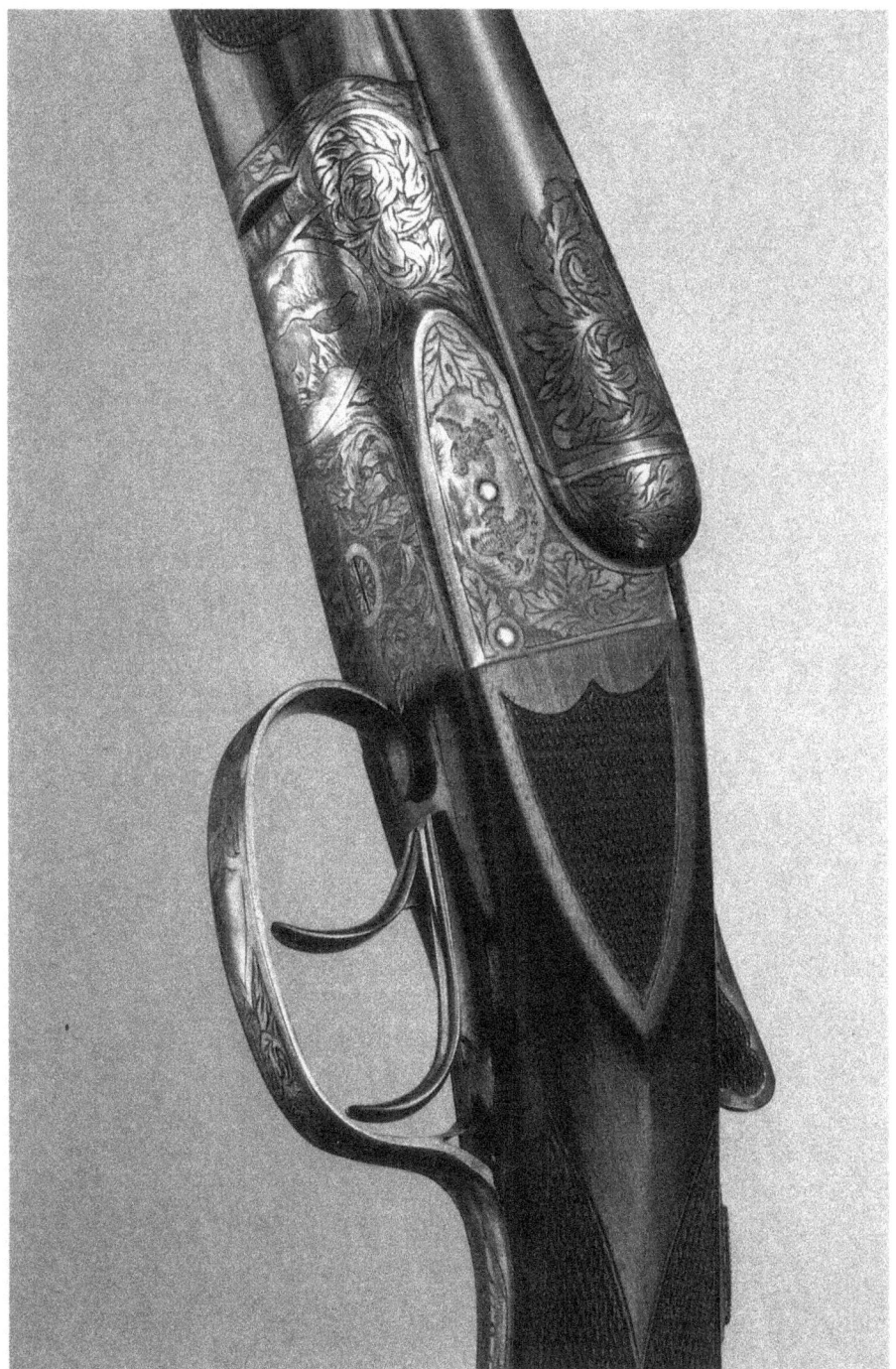

XE engraving is one of the handsomest of the second-generation patterns, as on this 16-gauge.

WILLIAM W. HEADRICK

If you look at a lot of Foxes, you'll notice that the weight stamps are nearly always clear and crisp on heavy guns, decidedly faint and blurry on lighter ones, and often missing altogether from the lightest. The reason is simple: the heavier the gun, the less steel is struck from the barrels in shaping and finishing. By the same token, so much is removed to make very light barrels that the weight mark often gets struck off completely.

Ansley Fox and the Godshalks clearly were of a mind on quite a number of things—among them the willingness to take on special-order projects. One of these, begun during Ansley Fox's tenure, eventually led to an entirely new grade of gun.

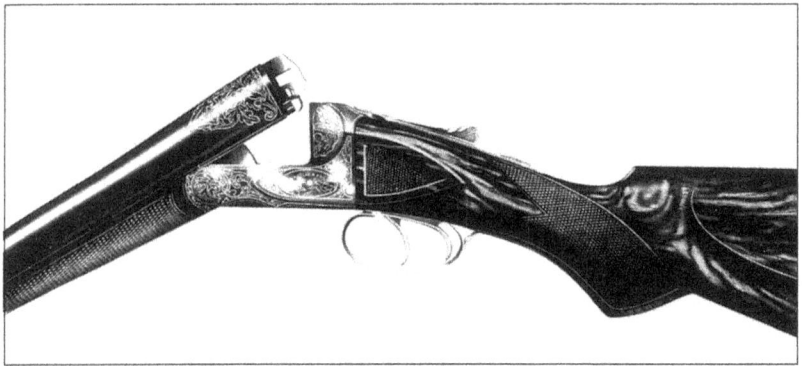

When the XE Grade first appeared, in the catalogue of 1913, it was called the "Special Trap Gun".

Exactly when the X Grade was conceived is impossible to say, but it was first illustrated in the 1913 Fox catalogue as the Special Trap Gun—built to order, the text says, for "one of Philadelphia's well known trap shots" according to "his own ideas in regard to engraving, checkering, finish and shape of stock, etc., and was put out by the A.H. Fox Gun Company at a very moderate price... This Special Fox Gun has given its owner absolute satisfaction. (Name will be furnished upon request.)"

No doubt someone did enquire to know who the gentleman was, but unfortunately he left no record of what the company told him—or at least, he left it no place where I can find it.

A year later, the 1914 catalogue features the same illustration, but now it's called the X Grade and is described as "the result of the increasing demand for a trap gun which shall be as nearly perfect for the purpose as it is possible to be made."

The barrels are of Krupp steel, "polished and tested until the pattern not only gives the choke desired with standard loads, but an exceedingly even pattern as well. No such careful workmanship as is used on this and our D Grade has ever before been put into an American gun." Stocks are Circassian walnut, available in pistol, half, or straight hand, "or in the Monte Carlo type, as desired." The illustration, which appeared in Fox catalogues for many years after, shows a gun with a half-hand stock, the bottom of the grip flat rather than round, and a cheekpiece. You can't tell from the catalogues whether the stock is a true Monte Carlo of the rifle type or whether the cheekpiece alone served to define a Monte Carlo stock so far as Fox was concerned. The catalogues mention "Monte Carlo" as an extra-cost option right from the start, and the factory did turn out a few guns so stocked, but you'll look a long time to find one.

At any rate, the 1914 catalogue goes on to describe the engraving as a "new design, conforms to the artistic standard of the other high grade Fox guns." This much, at least, is indisputable; X Grade decoration is William Gough second-generation Fox engraving at full stretch—bold, busy, showy, and yet still possessed of a certain elegance.

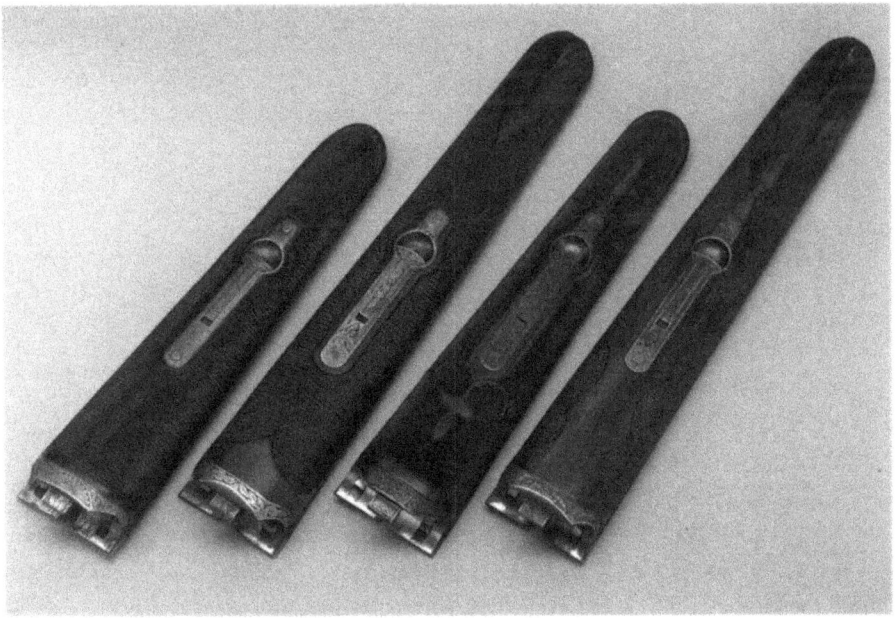

In the first years, all Fox fore-ends were the same length; after about 1914, longer fore-ends with schnabel-shaped horn tips were used for XE, DE, and FE grades. From left: early CE, XE, early FE, later DE.

WILLIAM W. HEADRICK

Finally, the catalogue says the X is always furnished with ejectors, a Silver's recoil pad, and Lyman available in any gauge or barrel length; net price $100.

This is all straightforward enough and, on the face, seems the result of a carefully planned campaign to devise and introduce a new grade. Not so. X Grade guns were built, and identified as X Grades, at least two years before they appeared as even Special Trap Guns.

I have a notion—and some veteran Fox men agree—that the well-known Philadelphia trap shot was William Gough himself, chief engraver at Fox Gun Company, who for a time ran the Philadelphia Shooting Academy. There is something decidedly English about the XE, nothing overwhelming but there nonetheless. For one thing, the fore-ends of XE Grades, like those of DE and FE grades built after about 1914, are noticeably longer than the fore-ends of grades A through C—about 9 $^3/_8$ inches, as opposed to about 8 $^1/_4$ inches for the lower grades. And like the D and F grades built after about 1913, XE fore-ends are inlaid with a narrow wedge of buffalo horn and shaped to a slight schnabel.

The engraving pattern certainly has an English look—more so, actually, than any grade other than C. If an Englishman with a fine aesthetic sense were to create an American gun, bound by American parameters of machine manufacture, he'd create the XE Fox. I say it was Bill Gough, but I'll never know for sure.

Nor will I know exactly when, but I do know it was well before 1913. The earliest XE I've found reference to is gun No. 19225. According to the work order, it has thirty-inch barrels, full chokes, a half-hand stock with diamond grip, D Grade checkering and "Special X grade engraving." It was shipped on February 22, 1912, to Marshall-Wells in Canada, intended for Mr. W.R. Rosebrugh, whose name is inlaid in gold on the trigger guard.

Fox seems to have had some difficulty deciding exactly what to name the XE. Some very early specimens show up in the records as "X Special," "Special X," and simply "X." As late as September 1914, a Fox ad in *Field & Stream* calls it the "New $100 Trap Gun" and never mentions X Grade at all. And why X, anyway, rather than some other letter? "G" obviously wouldn't work, since it would imply a grade higher than F, which the X isn't. I have a notion that the Fox people started using X simply because it's an easy mark to make on the work-order sheets, especially since in the very beginning they probably had no intention of building more than one such gun anyway. By the time they decided to standardize the grade, the X had simply stuck. One thing is clear: The XE was not the product of careful planning but rather, like Topsy, just grew.

Since the Rosebrugh gun obviously is not the original XE, the first one surely dates at least as early as 1911, possibly even before. The earliest 20-gauge

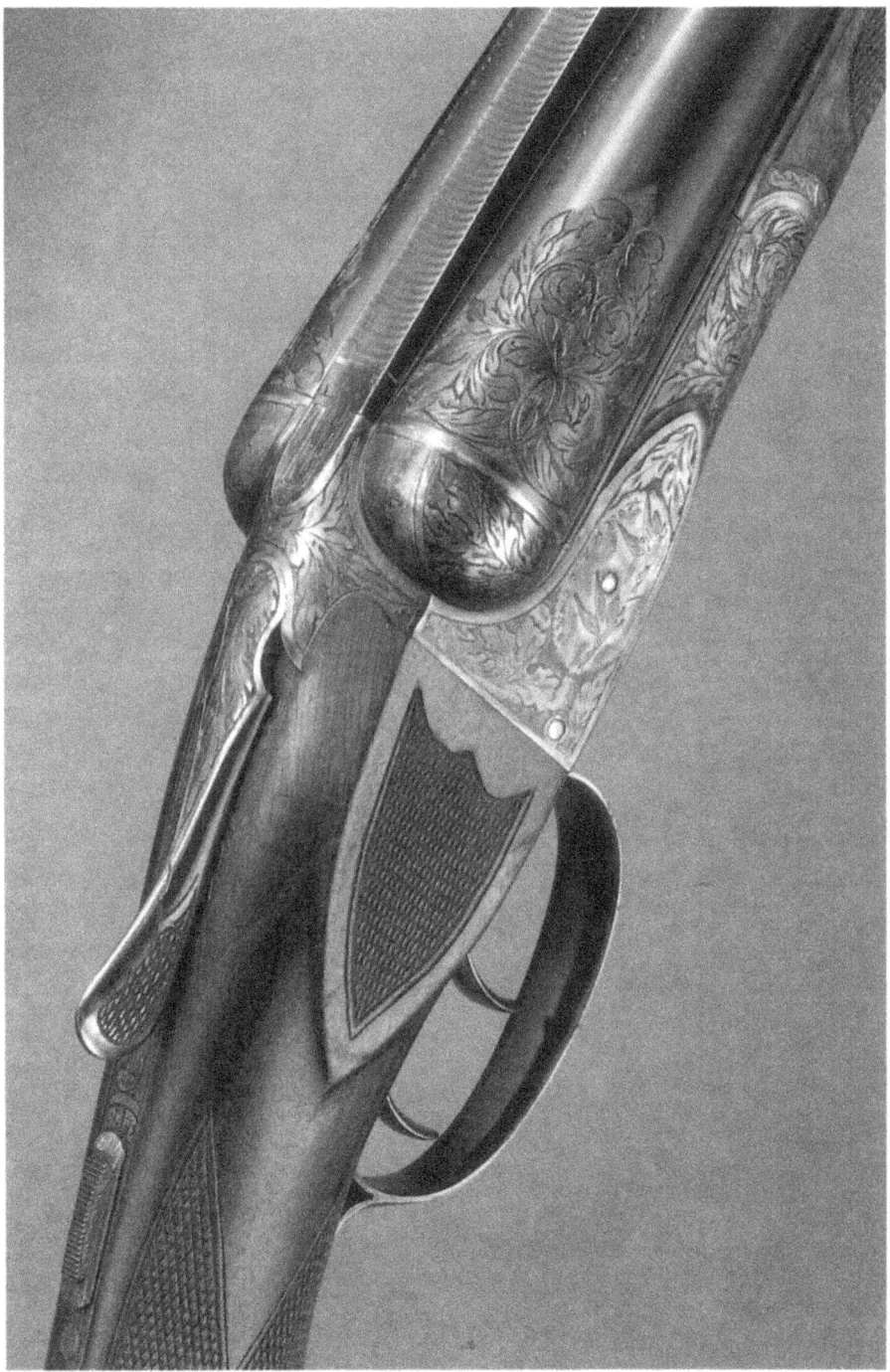

Like the DE and FE grades of the second generation, XE frames were filed with rebates at the top and bottom tangs, and the top of the standing breech was filed to match the curve of the barrels.

WILLIAM W. HEADRICK

XE 20-gauge; notice the frame rebate just above the trigger-guard.   WILLIAM W. HEADRICK

versions—and they're identified in the records as X Grade—left the factory in the fall of 1913; the first three were all in sequence: No. 200184, shipped September 26; No. 200185, shipped October 15; and No. 200186, shipped October 2. Two others were shipped before the end of the year—No. 200260, on October 22, and No. 200292, on December 6.

Although its origins are perhaps not as clear-cut as a historian would like, there's no denying that the XE is one of the handsomest of all Fox guns—although about the time the XE first appeared as a catalogue item, the other high grades began to receive some aesthetic touches that made their already lovely appearance lovelier still. Even as the factory abandoned its old-style engraving patterns, the frame-filers began adding subtle, elegant details to XE, DE, and FE grade guns. Where the top and bottom tangs fair into the frame, they began filing graceful little rebates (which may or may not have pleased the stockmakers), and in the same grades, they started filing the top of the standing breech to match the arcs of the barrels as they curve in to meet the rib. In addition, a lot of second-generation FE Grades were filed with scallops at the rear edges of the frame, a touch English gunmakers call a "fancy-back." Among American guns, only the old-style, pre-1912 L.C. Smith frame is as gracefully sculpted as the Fox's.

To further enhance the desirability of the higher-grade guns, the Godshalks decided early on to make ejectors standard features in C, X, D, and F grades, so from 1913 they were therefore officially called CE, XE, DE, and FE.

Not all aspects of the Fox's transition were in place by the end of 1913, but with eighteen months behind them, the Godshalks must have looked toward the coming year with a measure of hope. And indeed, the opening days of 1914 brought intimations of prosperity. On January 1, the State of New Jersey enacted legislation establishing a minimum wage for women of $9 per week. Four days later, Henry Ford announced that Ford Motor Company would guarantee every employee a minimum $5 per day, would employ several thousand more people by expanding its previous schedule of two nine-hour shifts per day to three shifts of eight hours each, and would share more than $10 million of 1913's profits with the workers. The Panama Canal, a shortcut trade route between the coasts of the Western Hemisphere dreamed of since the 16th century, was nearing completion.

The gun business apparently showed promise as well. An item in the February issue of *The Sporting Goods Dealer* announced that Fox Gun Company was thinking of adding a two-story, thirty- by fifty-foot addition to its premises.

Part of the world was titillated when on March 16, the wife of the Finance Minister of France shot Gaston Calmette, editor of the newspaper *Figaro*, because of editorial attacks upon her husband... and because M. Calmette allegedly refused to return letters she had written to her husband years before.

In some ways, the Calmette case was a synecdoche of Europe itself. Conflicts fueled by nationalism and war cults and expansionist dreams, complicated by an intricate and at times contradictory system of military alliances, made Europe a powder keg waiting for a match.

A nineteen-year-old student named Gavrilo Princip lit the fuse on the 28th of June, in Sarajevo, capital of the Austrian province of Bosnia, by assassinating Archduke Francis Ferdinand and his wife, the Duchess of Hohenberg. The Archduke was heir to the throne of Austria-Hungary, and Princip was a member of a Serbian secret society seeking a terrorist solution to a long-standing dispute between Serbia and Austria-Hungary over ownership of the provinces of Bosnia and Hercegovina.

Now, it makes events in Yugoslavia during the spring and summer of 1992 seem eerily familiar. Then, it was the spark that blew up half the world. A month after the Archduke's murder, Austria-Hungary declared war against Serbia. In turn, Germany declared war against Russia and France; Britain against Germany; Austria against Russia; Serbia and Montenegro against Russia; France against

> All guns shown in catalog are carried in stock and are made in specifications that conform to a standard weight, length of barrel, drop and length of stock as indicated under each gun. Orders calling for other than these standard measurements must be built to order and cannot be furnished in less than 8 to 10 weeks time. There is no extra cost for special specifications on any grade except the FOX STERLINGWORTH. See page 4 for details.
>
> All our guns are chambered for standard length shells. 12 ga. for $2\frac{3}{4}$ in. shells—16 ga. for $2\frac{9}{16}$ in. shells and 20 ga. for $2\frac{1}{2}$ in. shells. We will put any chambering in our guns that a customer wants without extra charge on any grade gun.
>
> There are Twenty Reasons Why the FOX is "The Finest Gun in the World."
>
> 1. Made of the best known gun materials.
> 2. Most skilled and highest paid workmanship.
> 3. Acknowledged the best balanced American gun and peer of any foreign make.
> 4. Stocks so fitted and joined that strain is evenly distributed at head—no splitting, no light joints.
> 5. Barrel Construction is positively scientific—weight only where it is necessary.
> 6. Choke—The FOX Created Method of boring has made the FOX famous.
> 7. Coil Mainspring guaranteed forever.
> 8. Exclusive Top-lever Action with coil spring.
> 9. Rotary Bolt—effective against shooting loose.
> 10. Simplest and strongest and only genuine three-piece lock in the world.
> 11. Fastest Hammer ever put on a gun.
> 12. Safety—can be made either independent or automatic, insuring real safety—in other words, "fool proof."
> 13. Forend holds tight forever—latest word in compensating device.
> 14. Frame Construction prevents dirt and gases from backing into locks.
> 15. Triggers are positive—no creep whatever. Trap shooters can appreciate this point.
> 16. Top Rib Constructed so that the eye has proper line of sight.
> 17. Easiest Cocking Device. On account of its extremely short water table it has greater leverage under the hammers, hence ease in opening gun.
> 18. Every FOX Gun is guaranteed—it is the strongest guarantee given with a gun—and we stand behind it.
> 19. The "FOX PROOF" mark is on every gun—this means safe and sound.
> 20. It also means that this safe and sound test has been backed by an *inspection* more thorough and painstaking than is given any other gun made.
>
> The unusual demand for all our guns assures us that our work is appreciated by men who love a good gun. There is nothing we will not do to please the FOX owner. This matter of gun making is a life's work with us. We are proud of the success the FOX has made. And the owner of a FOX has reason to be as proud as we are. To possess a genuine FOX is to possess "The Finest Gun in the World."

Twenty reasons why Fox was "The Finest Gun in the World," from the 1913 catalogue. Despite the promise that 12-gauge guns would be bored with 2 3/4-inch chambers, most of the Foxes built in Philadelphia – and a great many made by Savage – were chambered at 2 5/8 inches.

Austria; Austria against Belgium; Russia against Turkey; France and Britain against Turkey. By the end of August, the shooting was well under way.

The United States declared neutrality but with more hope than conviction. Sympathies—toward the Allied cause, toward Germany, toward neutrality—began to divide the country immediately, and young men by the dozen left colleges and rushed to enlist in the armies of Canada, Britain, and France, and to set up an ambulance service in the Allies' aid. The majority of working people, on the other hand, remained steadfastly in favor of staying out of the conflict altogether. Sentiments would continue to simmer and seethe for nearly three years before the United States ultimately found neutrality impossible.

In the mean time, in the midst of it all, the country attempted to carry on business as usual. Teddy Roosevelt had been off on another expedition, this time into the wilderness of Brazil, and as A.W. Connor had before, Ad Roll and the Godshalks saw an opportunity to associate the old Rough Rider and the Fox gun. The company placed a brief piece in the June 1914 issue of *The Sporting Goods Dealer*, remarking on the firearms that Teddy and his colleagues took to South America: "a Springfield rifle, two Winchesters, two revolvers—a Colt and a Smith & Wesson—and a Fox 12-gauge gun. This is the same Fox gun which Col.

Roosevelt carried with him on his African trip and which he says gave him such satisfactory service. It is interesting to note that this Fox gun has never been returned to the factory for repairing or overhauling of any sort—a striking tribute to the serviceability and reliability of Fox guns."

Whether the Roosevelt connection still carried enough clout to affect sales is hard to tell eighty years after the fact, but the Godshalks clearly were determined to spare no effort in the gun's behalf. And, although they couldn't have known it at the time, those efforts would reap an exceptional reward before the country could no longer resist the dark tide of war.

DE Grade 12-gauge, with second-generation engraving and Fox-Kautzky single trigger

WILLIAM W. HEADRICK

12

Triggers, Accolades & Flare Guns

By the time the Great War began, single triggers were nothing new among American guns. Dan Lefever was the first of the great makers to offer one, as early as 1898. Hunter Arms adopted Allen Lard's patent trigger for the L.C. Smith in 1904 as the Hunter One-Trigger. Ithaca adopted the Infallible single trigger, made by Lancaster Arms Company, in 1914. Parker would not offer a similar option until 1922, although a great many shooters had Fulford triggers, designed and patented just after the turn of the century by Elijah Fulford of Utica, New York, installed in Parkers as aftermarket conversions.

Fox no doubt received enquiries and requests for single triggers from the beginning, but the response was that no such gizmo would be installed on a Fox gun until someone came up with one that proved sufficiently reliable. It was a wise decision. All of the early American single triggers suffered from being too complicated and delicate to withstand much use before going out of whack and were extremely difficult to put right thereafter. Even so, the company couldn't hold out forever; the market was going to demand a single trigger, good or bad, from every maker. The Godshalks certainly realized this, so they must have been especially pleased when Fortune conspired to bring the best single trigger of the time within their reach. And it came, of all unlikely places, from Iowa.

Joseph Kautzky was born at Rokitnitz, Austria, in 1862, as the fourth generation of a gunmaking family. At thirteen, he apprenticed in Vienna and when his time was up, returned to Rokitnitz to work in his father's shop. In the 1880s, Kautzky's siblings, three brothers and two sisters, joined the growing flood of Europeans emigrating to America. They ended up on the great tallgrass prairie near Des Moines and their letters home presently began to extol the virtues of the New World. In 1893, married and the father of three children, Joseph Kautzky packed his tools, sold the remainder of his possessions, and brought his own family to join them.

The Fox Company published this brochure in 1914, announcing the new Fox-Kautzky trigger; it was inserted in some 1914 catalogues.

> **THE FOX-KAUTZKY SINGLE TRIGGER**
>
> THIS latest "added attraction" to *Fox Superior Features* is acknowledged to be the Premier of Single Triggers. It stands the Fox test. It is recommended and guaranteed by the A. H. Fox Gun Company.
>
> Like all good things it is exceedingly simple. Mechanically it is perfect. It is operated by the locks of the gun. There is no part that can wear or break. Your locks being in order, the trigger will always operate perfectly.
>
> **IT WILL NEVER BALK**
>
> And being absolutely independent of recoil—*no matter how heavy the recoil*—the trigger will not engage the locks of the second barrel until you release it. In other words—
>
> **IT CANNOT DOUBLE**
>
> The simple shifter gives you perfect control of *right* barrel to *left* barrel, *left to right, all right or all left.*
>
> Just relax the trigger finger and you engage the trigger for the second shot. The *snap* "telephones"—even through a thick glove—that all is ready to "let her go." Then add to this advantage the fact that with the *Fox-Kautzky* Trigger there is
> **NO CREEP POSSIBLE**
>
> **CANNOT DOUBLE** **NEVER BALKS**
> **NO CREEP POSSIBLE**
>
> No cutting away of stock is required to fit this trigger. Any position of trigger (a little ahead of rear position has proven the most desirable) will be made if specified in your order.
>
> **We guarantee the Fox-Kautzky Trigger** to be perfect in all points demanded of a single trigger.
>
> We will fit this trigger to your Fox Gun for $20. The entire gun must be sent, shipping charges prepaid. Or we will equip new Fox Guns of any grade with the *Fox-Kautzky Single Trigger* at a cost of $20, in addition to the regular price of the gun.
>
> **A GUN TO BE PROUD OF**
>
> This trigger with the Fox Automatic Ejector makes the Fox Gun (with its many superior points) not only the true sportsman's *ideal*, but a gun that will meet all his *practical* needs. Colonel Roosevelt said: "No better gun was ever made."
>
> **THE A. H. FOX GUN COMPANY.**
> PHILADELPHIA, PA.

He first set up shop in Perry, Iowa, and spent the next four years eking out a living doing repair work and building at least four guns—three 16-bore hammer guns and a 12-gauge hammerless. In 1897, he moved fifty-odd miles north to the larger city of Ft. Dodge and opened a gun and sporting-goods shop.

In the economic hard times at the turn of the twentieth century, success came slowly to Joseph Kautzky, but through the combination of repair work, retailing, and building a few more guns of his own, he managed. He was a man of inventive mind as well as excellent craft, and in June 1905, he filed application for patent protection on a selective single trigger for double guns. The application was approved the following year as Patent No. 827,242.

Like Ansley Fox, Joseph Kautzky recognized potential in the still-new sport of clay-target trapshooting. About 1908, he organized the Ft. Dodge Gun Club and over the next few years earned considerable prominence, both local and national, as a shooter. This naturally accrued similar recognition to his ability as a gunsmith, particularly for his single trigger, which was vastly superior to its only real rival, the Hunter One-Trigger.

Good as it was, Kautzky saw room for improvement, and in September 1910 applied for patent on yet a second design. That one became the cornerstone of his success. Even before the patent, No. 990,562, was issued on April 25, 1911, the Kautzky trigger was gathering a cult following in the trapshooting world. By 1913, he had made and installed more than 600 of them—including several for the

The Fox-Kautzky Single Trigger

Single triggers grow more popular every day, and the latest edition to Fox Superior Features is acknowledged to be "the Premier of Single Triggers,"

It stands the Fox test. It will never balk; it cannot double, and no creep is possible. **It is guaranteed by the A. H. Fox Gun Company.**

On the other side of this sheet a space is left where you may specify the equipment of your gun with this single trigger.

The price of the Fox Kautzky Single Trigger is $20, in addition to the regular price of the gun.

In ordering, bear in mind these facts:

1st. The length of stock is taken from actual position of the trigger.

2nd. If single trigger is ordered in rear position, it will make the stock actually longer than if ordered in intermediate or front position. Therefore, it is better to order the stock a little shorter when single trigger is ordered in intermediate or rear position, than would be ordered if the gun were equipped with double triggers.

For example, a double trigger with 14 inch stock would show a stock measurement of but 13¾ inches if equipped with a single trigger in rear position.

This is important. [Over]

Fox order blank, 1916

great bandmaster and amateur trap shot John Philip Sousa, who by then was entrusting all his gunsmithing work to Joseph Kautzky.

All single triggers must somehow deal with the involuntary pull, the phenomenon by which the shooter pulls the trigger without meaning to (or even knowing he does it) while the gun is recoiling from the first shot. If the mechanism isn't designed to accommodate this, the gun fires its second barrel during the involuntary pull, which naturally makes shooters sore both of shoulder and humor. Early on, single-trigger designers used one of three basic approaches for solving the problem. The British favored the three-pull system, in which three distinct pulls are required to fire two shots. Fulford used the delay system, in which a pistonlike mechanism simply slows down the shift from one sear to the involuntary pull.

Otherwise, though, Kautzky's trigger shares little mechanically with Lard's or Parker's. Firing is accomplished by a small steel rocker that engages cams formed in the ends of the sears. It rocks backward to fire the right barrel and forward to fire the left, which makes tripping both sears at once mechanically impossible. A single-trigger Fox can only double if recoil jars the second sear out of its notch—and that will only happen if the sear is badly worn, broken, or improperly shaped.

Shaping and adjustment are critical, however, and if the cams aren't accurately filed and spaced, the Kautzky trigger can go just as badly on the blink

Subject-to-Inspection Order Blank

So that you can get a Fox Gun right before you and examine it carefully, we accept your order on this blank with the understanding that if, after receiving the gun, you wish to return it for any reason, we will refund whatever you have paid for it.

How to Order

All guns shipped by us are sent C. O. D., and 25 per cent of the cost of the gun must accompany the order, but with the above understanding that the entire cost will be refunded if you wish to return the gun after examination. All prices quoted by us are F. O. B. Philadelphia, U. S. A.

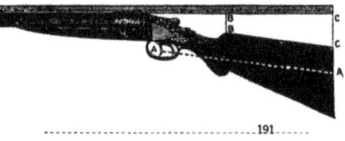

A. H. FOX GUN COMPANY
Philadelphia

....191......

With the above described inspection privilege, please enter my order for the Fox Gun specified below :...........................

Grade......................... Gauge................... Length of Barrels..................................
Weight............. Automatic Ejector ....
Bore, Right Barrel............. Left Barrel.................................
Length of Stock from A to A .... Drop of Stock from B to B.........................
Drop of Stock from C to C.......................
Remarks ....

| SINGLE TRIGGER ORDER BLANK |
| (See back of this sheet) |
| Please equip my gun with the Fox Kautzky Single Trigger .... |
| Place it in .... position |
| (Rear; Intermediate; Front) |
| The extra cost to be $20.00 |

Name ....
St. Address...........................
City............................. State...................

TEAR OFF ALONG THIS LINE

Service Information Blank

If you have not made up your mind sufficiently to use the above order blank, we can help you a great deal in selecting the best type of gun for your purpose, and if you will answer the few questions listed below, tear off and return this part of the sheet.
We want you to feel that using this blank does not place you under the slightest obligation. It is simply a part of our service which you can use unhesitatingly.

1. What kind of shooting do you expect to use your gun for? ....
2. Do you know what loads you will use?..................................
3. What grade of gun are you considering?.................................
4. Have you any particular gauge in mind?..............................
5. Have you any particular weight in mind?...........................
6. Have you any particular barrel-boring in mind?.....................
7. Do you wish any special information regarding stock dimensions?................
8. Are you considering an ejector?....................................
9. Are you considering a single trigger?..............................
10. Would you like information about our specially designed stock for women? ....
11. What other information can we give you?..........................

Name"...........................
Post Office Address ....
City................................. State.........................
[Over]

as any. If you have a single-trigger Fox that needs attention, don't give it to anyone but a first-class trigger man.

No one knows exactly when the Kautzky-Fox relationship began, but it apparently started well before the company adopted the Kautzky trigger. A Fox ad in a 1909 issue of *The Sportsmen's Review* reads thus: "'253 Unfinished' was the remarkable world's amateur record of an A.H. Fox Gun in the hands of Jos. Kautzky, an amateur, at Jewell, Ia., on November 27th and 28th last. The same man, with his 'Fox,' also won the 'Smith Cup,' making 50 straight at 18 yards, and shot through the second day's program without a miss."

We'll never know, of course, but it's tempting to wonder if Joseph Kautzky didn't develop his trigger with the Fox gun specifically in mind. It's equally tempting to wonder if Ansley Fox didn't have some plan for the Kautzky trigger all along.

We do know, however, that Kautzky revised the sear block mechanism, for which he received Patent No. 1,109,632 on September 1, 1914, and sold manufacturing rights to the Fox Gun Company that same year. He spent several months in Philadelphia, teaching the factory gunsmiths to build, install, and repair the Kautzky trigger.

To reap the benefits of the trigger's already substantial reputation, Fox wisely chose to keep Kautzky's name associated with it, so references to the Fox-Kautzky trigger presently began to appear in the advertising. The 1914 catalogue was already printed and in the dealers' hands, so the company worked up a one-page flyer as a catalogue insert. Surprisingly, it's described as "The Premier of Single Triggers" rather than The Finest Single Trigger in the World, but the text

Second-generation BE engraving   WILLIAM W. HEADRICK

The 1916 catalogue bore a reproduction of the blue ribbon the Fox Company won at the Panama-Pacific International Exposition in 1915.

WILLIAM W. HEADRICK

makes some claims that are grand enough otherwise—such as the line that reads "There is no part that can wear or break." On the whole, though, the Kautzky trigger is about as good as the company said it was, and at $20 it was a bargain besides. The price, moreover, was the same whether you wanted a Fox-Kautzky trigger fitted to your old gun or added to a new one.

On August 15, 1914, a passenger-cargo ship named the S.S. *Ancon* made the first complete trip through the Panama Canal, marking the realization of an idea that began with Balboa in 1517. The United States had spent more than ten years and $380 million to create the canal and understandably was in a mood to celebrate the accomplishment. As it turned out, the celebration was a bit premature, since a massive landslide in the Gaillard Cut blocked passage for several months in 1915 and 1916 (and since President Wilson didn't declare the canal officially open until July 1920), but it was a grand affair nonetheless.

Planning for the Panama-Pacific International Exposition had been under way since 1910, and the site in San Francisco had been under construction since 1911—and when it opened in February 1915, no one failed to grasp the irony of holding a world fair while much of the world was locked in the bloodiest, most savage war in history. Even so, the Exposition must have been a wonder to behold—180-odd acres of buildings and displays meant to demonstrate the finest achievements in manufacturing and agriculture, mining and transportation, arts and sciences and education.

For its part, Fox Gun Company went all-out with a magnificent pavilion displaying sixty-six guns, ranging from Sterlingworths to FE Grades to gold-inlaid guns now referred to in the collector's community as "Gough specials" or "raised-gold specials." (All of which are decorated with bold, open chisel-work that is neither particularly graceful nor even particularly well-executed, and the gold work, at least what I've seen of it, borders on being downright crude.) Fox employee Harry Overbaugh was in charge of the exhibit, which included a display of each step in the manufacturing process. The Fox-Kautzky trigger was prominently featured, and a report in the June 1915 issue of *The Sporting Goods Dealer* mentions "two new models [of guns] fitted with specially designed stocks for ladies' use."

What the ladies' stocks were all about is a mystery to me, since I haven't found any other reference to them anywhere, but the Exposition ultimately proved to be a major feather in the Fox cap. When the judging was over, the International Jury of Awards gave A.H. Fox Gun Company the Gold Medal for the best double shotguns and single trigger.

No doubt this pleased the Godshalks and other Fox people no end; naturally, the awards were mentioned in the gun ads and catalogues for some time

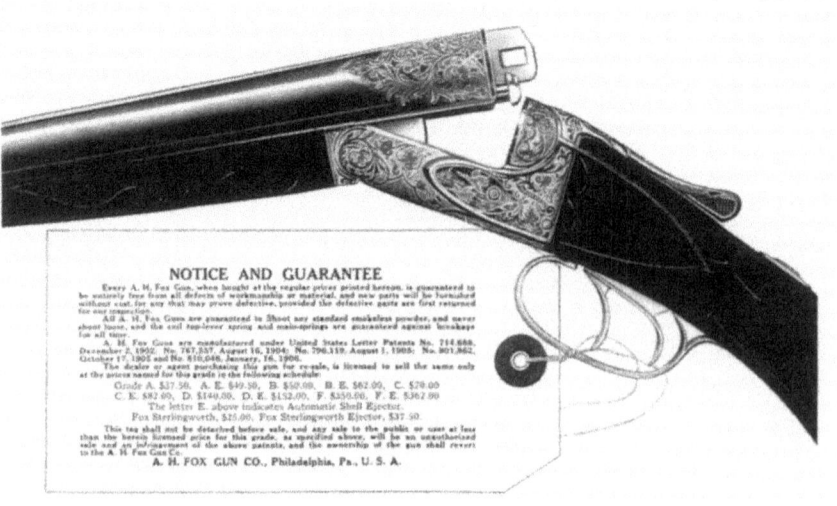

Fox guns always were covered by a broad guarantee of materials and workmanship. This illustration is from the 1915 catalogue.

after, which probably didn't harm sales a bit. Neither, I suspect, did the brief association between the Fox gun and the Georgia Peach.

By 1915, Ty Cobb was indisputably the greatest player in baseball. He had batted better than .300 every year since 1907—and in fact, except for the 1916 season, would lead the American League in batting every year until 1919. When the 1915 season was over, he would lead the league in batting, with a .369 average; in hits, with 208; runs, with 144; and establish a record of ninety-six stolen bases that would stand until 1962, the year after Cobb died.

He was an enthusiastic hunter, both of big game and birds, and owned a number of champion-class dogs. Early in 1915, members of the Mystic Shrine in Philadelphia decided to honor their fellow Mason with an appropriate gift and placed an order with the Fox Gun Company. I haven't been able to learn any details of the gun itself, not even the grade, though it probably was an XE or DE, but the presentation took place in July, during a game at Philadelphia's Shibe Park. According to *The Sporting Goods Dealer*, Cobb had just come up to bat when a committee of Shriners approached home plate and in a short ceremony bestowed a copy of the Finest Gun in the World upon "The Greatest Ball Player in the World... an .800 hitter in the field; a gunner of no mean ability who can give any hunter a good run for the best average."

The Fox people no doubt hoped for an endorsement, and Cobb, who endorsed everything from cigars and chewing gum to suspenders and underwear, was happy to oblige—at least to the extent of allowing the company to use a

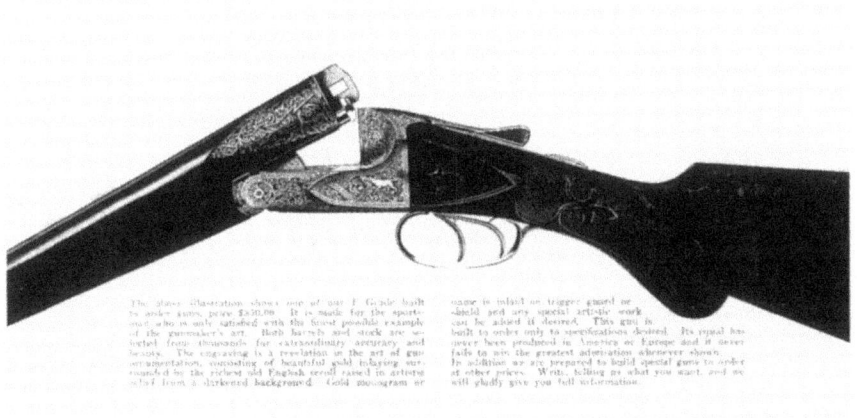

In the 1914 catalogue, Fox began referring to the FE Grade as a "built to order" gun.

During the last few months of World War I, the Fox Company manufactured Very flare pistols under government contract.   WILLIAM W. HEADRICK

photograph of him and his new gun in a couple of magazine ads. This was enough to suit the Godshalks, who probably had some mixed feelings about having the Fox name associated with that of a man whose reputation for brawling both on and off the ballfield was almost as great as his reputation as an athlete. (Three years earlier, in May 1912, Cobb was given a ten-day suspension for climbing into the stands during a game in New York and pounding the snot out of a man named Claude Lueker, who'd been heckling him—which in turn set off the first players' strike in the history of baseball.) The fans and opposing players in Philadelphia probably had some mixed feelings that day as well, seeing the belligerent Georgia Peach standing at home plate with a shotgun in his hands.

Despite President Wilson's determination that the United States should stay out of the European conflict, American industry was becoming more and more involved. Early in 1915, the British offered the Fox Company a contract to produce Serbian Mauser rifle barrels at the rate of 2500 units per day. Before any could be shipped, however, German, Austrian and Bulgarian armies invaded Serbia in October, and the Central Powers were in complete control of the country by the end of November.

Then New England Westinghouse offered Fox a subcontract to produce barrels and magazines for Russian Moisin-Nagant rifles, a venture ultimately

From 1913 through 1917, Fox published a series of large-format catlogues with cover illustration featuring a larcenous-minded red fox and the slogan "A Fox Gets the Game." The stock shows the quality of wood typically used for DE Grade guns of the period.   WILLIAM W. HEADRICK

brought to an end by the collapse of the czarist government and Russia's subsequent withdrawal from the war. While the job lasted, Fox turned out about 400,000 magazines. After the war, the left-over barrel blanks would be turned into shotgun tubes. (I assume the blanks were Chromox and that they were so marked when subsequently used as shotgun barrels—since I've never seen a late 1910s Fox with barrels stamped "Russianox" or anything similar; if you have, let me know.)

At the end of 1916, Fox was making brave plans for the future. Ad Roll issued a press release declaring that the company was "making preparations to put out more guns during 1917 than has ever been turned out in one year in the history of the business." Business, he says, showed a "tremendous increase" in 1916 "...because of the inability of the sportsmen to buy their favorite imports."

This surely was true, for 1916 was the most prosperous year the American economy had yet known, and everyone predicted that 1917 would be at least as good. But things didn't work out quite according to plan. At the end of January, the German government announced an intention to abrogate its former position of restraint in U-boat attacks on supply ships approaching the British Isles, and President Wilson broke off diplomatic relations with Germany. Two weeks later, the famous "Zimmerman Note" came to light, revealing that Germany had been attempting to persuade Mexico to join in a military alliance against the United States. When Congress convened on April 2, Wilson addressed a joint session and asked for a declaration of war, arguing that "the world must be made safe for democracy." The Senate approved the declaration on April 4, the House on April 6, and when President Wilson signed it later that afternoon, the United States entered the Great War.

And with that, the Fox Company's plan to make 1917 a banner year went out the window. As the country mobilized for war, production and sales of sporting arms took a sharp drop—although Fox advertising continued to show the price range of $25 to $1000 that had first appeared in mid-1915. The Sterlingworth represented the low end, of course, while the high end no doubt reflects the company's willingness, or perhaps simply its hope, to build a few more of the "Gough specials" that served so well at the Panama-Pacific Exposition. Since the FE Grade of the 1910s sold for $350, one has to wonder just how serious their expectations were. What Fox turned out most during the next twenty months were parts for Colt .45 military pistols.

In August 1918, the U.S. military awarded Fox a contract to produce Very flare pistols. These make up an interesting footnote in the Fox story—brass-framed break-action handguns with short barrels of about 10 bore, marked with the A.H. Fox name. Of the few I've seen, no two are exactly alike. Apparently, most were single-shot, although I know of one three-barrel—side by side by side. It's a massive thing, naturally, fitted with a grip safety like a Colt autoloader. If Ansley Fox had been involved, I imagine they would have been called The Finest Flare Gun in the World—and that might not have been too great an exaggeration. Every one I've seen shows remarkably high levels of craftsmanship.

The factory was turning out 500 flare guns per day—and preparing to double the production rate—when the November 11 Armistice brought the war to a close. With so many produced, you might imagine that Fox flare pistols would be plentiful, but that doesn't seem to be the case. Nonetheless, I suppose no serious Fox collector could feel completely fulfilled without one, as a conversation piece if nothing else. A friend of mine owns two, which in keeping with his rather fey sense of humor he has cased like a set of dueling pistols, and he sometimes refers to them as The Finest Big-Bore Dueling Pistols.... you know the rest.

For Fox as for the rest of the country and much of the world, the best thing about World War I is that it came to an end. Unlike some American gunmakers that had greatly expanded their physical plants during the war (Winchester is a prime example), Fox had not, and that put the company in a relatively good position to resume making sporting guns economically. Changes in production methods helped as well. Not long before the United States entered the war—in

BE Grade 20-gauge, 1917, showing second-generation engraving style WILLIAM W. HEADRICK

1915 or 1916—Fox had abandoned its old bone-charcoal method of case-hardening and adopted instead the simpler, cheaper cyanide process.

Production perked up considerably in 1919; in fact, the 1300-odd Fox guns built that year just about equaled the output of 1917 and 1918 combined. At some point in 1918, the Godshalks had decided that the B Grade was no longer holding up its share of sales. Or maybe it never had; B Grade guns of any era seem to me relatively scarce. At any rate, the B Grade does not appear in catalogues or price lists after 1918.

Which isn't to say that the Fox line was thereby diminished. On the contrary, 1919 saw the birth of something entirely new.

L Grade single trap gun　　　　　　　　　　WILLIAM W. HEADRICK

13

SINGULAR GUNS

The transition from live birds to clay targets not only altered the nature of trapshooting as a game but eventually altered the nature of the gun as well.

The rules of pigeon shooting have always allowed two shots at each bird, but it became clear early on that clay-target trap should essentially be a one-shot game. This made the two-barreled trap gun something of an anomaly, although certainly a persistent one, and thus prompted creation of the most specialized of all target guns.

Dan Lefever built the first single trap gun to appear on the American market and introduced it in the 1905 D.M. Lefever Company catalogue. Unfortunately, the company folded early in 1907, so Uncle Dan's single made no impact at all on either trapshooting or the arms trade. The Baker single, announced in 1909, was the first to achieve any real success, and other gunmakers soon introduced their own versions—Ithaca in 1914, Parker and L.C. Smith in 1917.

I don't know whether Ansley Fox had any notion of making a single trap gun, but the Godshalks clearly did, almost from the beginning. Some of the early design drawings are dated 1914 and 1915. In November 1914, Clarence Godshalk applied for a patent on a ventilated rib, and the drawing shows the rib as it would be applied to a single-barrel gun.

Specifically, the patent—No. 1,137,477, issued April 27, 1915—covers means by which the rib is attached to the barrel to allow "longitudinal movement between the parts." It is, in other words, a floating rib, and it was developed

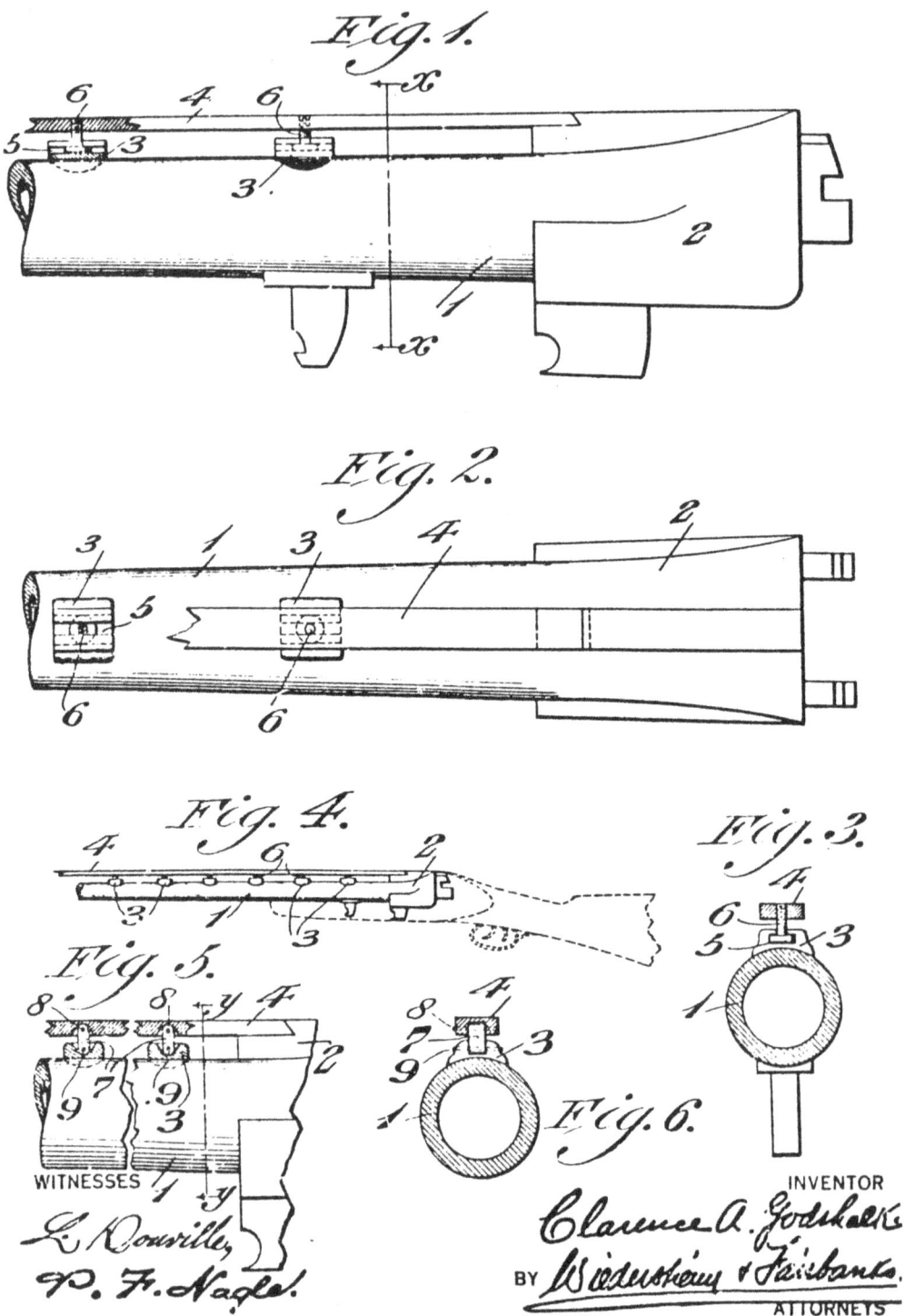

because in testing the first prototype guns the company discovered that a ventilated rib does not expand the way the barrel does as it heats up, and if it's made with top strip and posts all of a piece, it can actually bend the barrel enough to change the shot swarm's point of impact—or else rib and barrel part company altogether. Predictably, neither of these make trapshooters happy.

The rib described in the Godshalk patent is not, by the way, the same vent rib that became available for double guns in the mid-1920s. The double-gun version is not a floating rib.

Unlike L.C. Smith, Fox chose not to adapt the double gun's rotary fastener to the single trap. Instead, the designers borrowed once again from Greener and used a crossbolt that bears against lugs on either side of the chamber. In addition to being considerably simpler to machine and fit, the crossbolt fastener also takes up less space, thereby promoting a shallower frame.

And unlike any other maker, Fox designed the single with the top-lever trip on the outside of the frame, where it can be operated by hand. It's the little button you see on the left side of the frame, just below the fastening bolt. A thoughtful touch.

If performance is any indication, the factory also appears to have taken special pains in boring and polishing single trap barrels, for I haven't shot a one that didn't pattern beautifully.

Design-wise, it's difficult to trace exactly how the gun evolved: I have never seen a Fox single that bears patent stamps, not even one for the ventilated rib, and several searches through the patent records have all drawn a blank where the single is concerned. Apparently, the Godshalks felt the double-gun patents were protection enough, even though the fastening system is completely different.

At any rate, the earliest advertising for the single trap appeared in September 1919, and it mentions three grades: J, K, and L. The highest grade, M, appears in both the advertising and the factory price lists from 1920 on but not in the catalogues until about 1922—which suggests that the company used the same catalogue, printed before the M Grade was decided upon, in 1919, 1920, and 1921.

The four grades essentially correspond to the CE, XE, DE, and FE grades of double guns in price and in some other ways as well. The checkering patterns of grades K and L, for instance, are the same as those of XE and DE, respectively. There also is some similarity in engraving styles; like the CE, Grade J is decorated with scroll, although the actual pattern is quite different.

The most interesting exception to all this is Grade L, which, the catalogue copy says, features "elaborate original engraving." This is true, on both counts. In fact, *elaborate* scarcely describes the intricate tangle of vines, leaves, flowers, and foliage the L Grade wears—a style of decoration that does not appear on any other Fox gun of any type. (While the style is unique among Foxes, it isn't unique among guns. If you'll have a look at Larry Baer's book on Parker, at the photos of the prototype A-1 Special on pages 20-24, you'll see an engraving design virtually identical to the Fox L Grade—which as I mentioned in an earlier chapter, leads me to believe that William Gough designed and executed the decoration of the first A-1 Special. Anything else is just too much coincidence.)

Gun for gun, the single traps are much more elaborately decorated than the doubles. Bill Headrick describes them as the best buy in American gun art ever, and I can't argue with that.

Naturally, the singles were built only in 12-gauge, and they came with the option of 30- or 32-inch barrel. Thirty-two inches is the standard; the records show only twenty-three guns built with 30-inch barrels, although there may have been a few more. As with the double guns, single stocks could be straight-hand, half-hand, or full-pistol. They could also be straight-comb or Monte Carlo, and quite a few shooters did choose the Monte Carlo—proportionately more, I believe, than chose it for Fox doubles. (Savage Arms would later make the Monte Carlo standard fare.) Custom dimensions and other features were of course available upon request, and trapshooters being trapshooters, quite a few singles indeed show evidence of custom work. I know of several, for example, that were ordered with oversized, deeply curved pistol grips of the sort that Rudy Etchen made famous among trapsmen.

The first singles left the factory in July 1919, beginning with J Grade No. 400006, shipped July 19. The first K Grade shipped was No. 400023, September 15; the first L, No. 400083, August 29. The first M Grade didn't go out until April 5, 1921—No. 400346, which happens to be the gun you see pictured here. It originally went to E.K. Tryon sporting-goods company in Philadelphia and later was returned to the factory, possibly because Tryon couldn't find anyone willing to pay $500 for a trap gun. It was shipped again on April 19, 1922, to a Mr. Charles N. Stiger, location unknown.

Because it was the last of the classic American singles to appear on the market, the Fox never quite achieved the popularity it deserved. E.C. Crossman in 1920 predicted that someone eventually would win the Grand American Handicap with a Fox single, but so far as I know, no one did. Which is not to say it didn't win its share of tournaments. William C. Letterman used a Fox to win the Pennsylvania amateur championship on June 20, 1923, and in the process established a new tournament record of 198 x 200 with 168 straight. Dr. J.D. Griffith won the B Class at the same shoot with 193 x 200, and he, too, shot a Fox. Bunny Sanders won the 1934 Ladies Clay Target Championship of North America with her Fox single and a score of 191 x 200.

J Grade, lowest of the four grades of Fox single-barrel trap guns WILLIAM W. HEADRICK

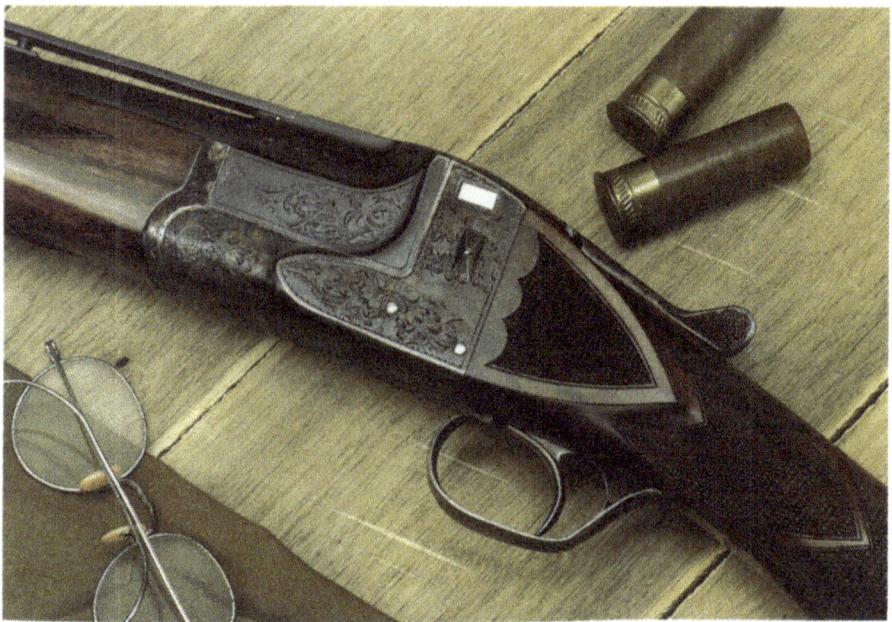

K Grade single trap WILLIAM W. HEADRICK

Although the singles are by no means the scarcest models of Fox gun, they certainly aren't the most numerous, either. In the course of his work with the factory records, Roe Clark summarized the entire production and has been kind enough to share the results with me. As was Fox's practice, the singles are numbered in a series of their own, beginning with No. 400001. The highest number listed is No. 400568. Assuming every number was used—which I believe is a perfectly safe assumption—that makes a total production of 568 guns. Add the fact that in three instances two guns were given the same number, and the total goes to 571. (No. 400115 was used for an L Grade shipped December 31, 1924 and for a J Grade shipped June 10, 1931; No. 400354 refers both to a K Grade shipped March 7, 1921, and to a J Grade shipped January 8, 1927; No. 400498 appears on a J Grade shipped December 4, 1925 and a K Grade shipped September 14th of an unknown year. Roe tells me he's run across a few cases in which two double guns also were given the same number; see the Specials & Oddments chapter.)

Like all of the Fox records, those for the single trap guns are somewhat incomplete, but we still can get a good overall picture. The grades break down this way: J Grade-410; K Grade-75; L Grade-25; M Grade-9; Unknown-52. One gun, which is described in Chapter 16, was called a Trap Grade Special.

Of the 482 guns for which I can identify the year of shipment, the numbers fall this way:

Year	Guns Shipped	Year	Guns Shipped
1919	59	1928	17
1920	13	1929	19
1921	55	1930	6
1922	31	1931	14
1923	71	1932	6
1924	35	1933	1
1925	30	1934	4
1926	20	1935	4
1927	42	1936	1

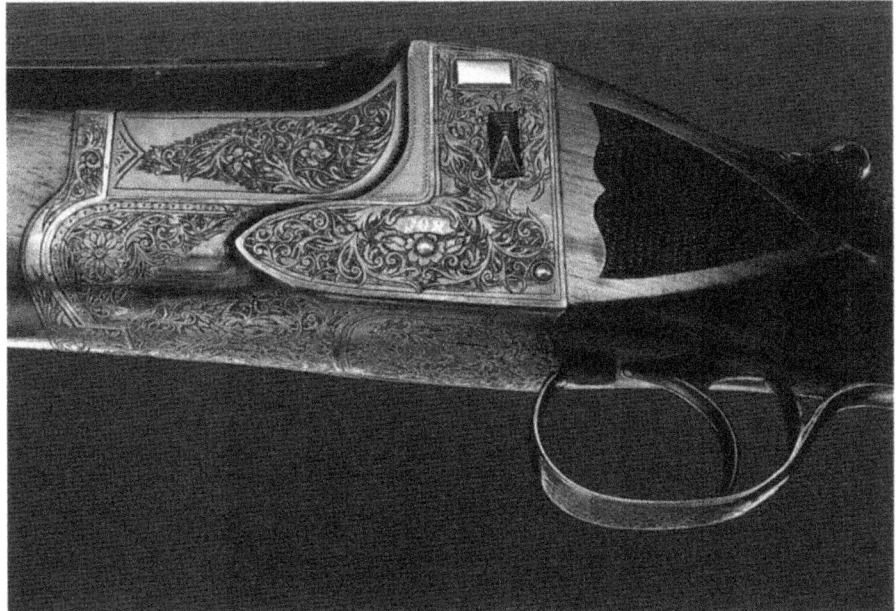

The engraving pattern William Gough designed for the L Grade Fox single is remarkably similar to the pattern he developed years earlier for the prototype Parker A-1 Special.

WILLIAM W. HEADRICK

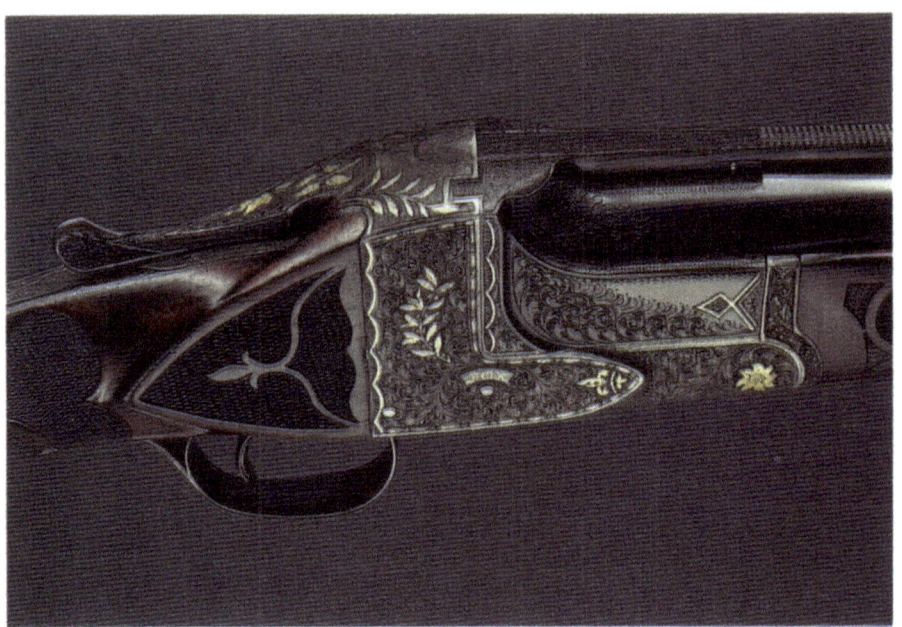

The first M Grade single, No. 400346, shipped in April 1921. Only nine M Grade trap guns were ever built.

WILLIAM W. HEADRICK

    This shows only when a given gun was shipped the first time. Some were shipped more than once; most of these had been returned for repair or alteration, but I also suspect that some simply refused to stay sold. One M Grade gun, No. 400370, holds the record of having been shipped four times altogether: on March 9, 1925, December 8, 1926, September 17, 1929, and November 19, 1929.

    The Great Depression was no kinder to the single traps than to other Fox guns. As we'll see in a later chapter, Savage Arms made a valiant attempt to pitch the target-shooting market, and part of the company's effort appears to have gone toward improving the single trap gun—or at least toward improving its marketability. A little two-fold, three-panel brochure, issued about 1931, announced the "New Fox Trap Guns," and says of the single: "The frame of the new Fox Single Barrel Trap Gun has been redesigned to a form which extends the top rib line back across the frame to the shooter's eyes, insuring perfect alignment in sighting. The standard stock is full pistol grip, Monte Carlo style..."

    This "redesigned" frame business is a bit misleading; what Savage actually did was form a matted line of rib-width across the top of the frame. It does extend the rib *line*, but that's the extent of it.

Like the Super-Fox, the single was simply too specialized and too much a luxury item to find a market during hard times. Savage Arms didn't offer K and L grades after 1934 or M Grade after 1936, but by then, taking them out of the catalogues was no more than a formality. The last of the middle grades were shipped in December 1931—the last L, No. 400566, on the 11th, and the last K, No. 400372, the day after Christmas. The last M Grade to go was No. 400476, shipped June 16, 1932.

Although Savage kept the J Grade as a catalogue item until 1939, the actual end came much earlier. The last one—which also was the last Fox single shipped from inventory—went out on January 31, 1936.

As I said, the Fox never did make a great impression on the trapshooting world, never was as popular as Ithaca or Parker or L.C. Smith, and eventually all of the old-style singles lost their standing as serious competitors amid the high-tech trends of the 1960s and '70s. Which is a pity, because the Fox singles are a particular delight to shoot, beautifully balanced, crisp of trigger—a singular achievement any way you look at it.

While Ansley Fox was preparing to introduce the Fox automobile, Fox Gun Company was turning out guns like this AE Grade 20-gauge.

WILLIAM W. HEADRICK

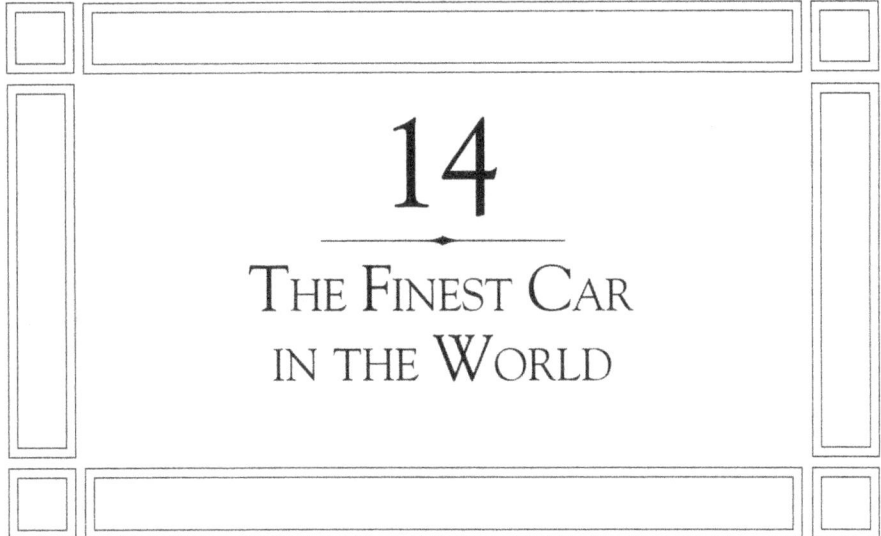

14

THE FINEST CAR IN THE WORLD

Of all the agents of change at work during Ansley Fox's lifetime, none was more pervasive, nor ultimately more profound, than the automobile. And in this, as in so many things, time and events conspired to place him on a watershed of history.

The automobile as we know it did not exist when Ansley Fox was born, but he was less than a year old when N.A. Otto invented the gasoline engine and scarcely seventeen when Rudolf Diesel came up with his version of an engine using the principle of internal combustion. By the time Ansley Fox died, the automobile had literally reshaped the world.

Certainly, it had reshaped life in America. At the turn of the century, motor cars were far more numerous in other parts of the world—France, for instance—and until about 1910, they were little more than playthings of the wealthy in the United States, and rather suspicious toys at that. They belched out a terrible stink, and the noise scared horses witless. More than a few farmers wouldn't allow an automobile on their land, and even some villages banned them from within town limits.

In 1905, Theodore Roosevelt said that he had ridden in horseless carriages only twice during his presidency and refused to do so again because on the second one he'd suffered the embarrassment of having his driver stopped for speeding. In 1907, Woodrow Wilson, then president of Princeton University and shortly to be President of the United States, urged his students to eschew motoring, which he described as "the picture of the arrogance of wealth." Nothing, he said, has done more to "spread socialistic feelings in this country."

But Americans didn't buy it. Instead, we embraced the automobile with a passion unheard-of before, a fervor that would not be repeated until we began buying television sets in the 1950s. Henry Ford's Model T, brought onto the market in 1908, was the seminal item. Americans bought more than a half-million tin lizzies in 1916, nearly four times as many in 1923. When Ford replaced it with the Model A in 1927, the total manufacturing run of Model Ts amounted to an astonishing fifteen million units.

THE FOX AIR-COOLED CAR
This wonderful car will go from 18 to 25 miles on a single gallon of gasoline. It will travel from 700 to 1000 miles on one gallon of lubricating oil, and it will go over 10,000 miles to a set of tires. It is a big, roomy car with 128" wheel-base.

By 1916, motorists' complaints about poor roads, which had been the major obstacle to the proliferation of automobiles, finally prompted Congress to institute a program of matching state road-building funds dollar for dollar. What happened after that, as they say, is history.

The automobile affected every older form of transportation. It destroyed the economic environment that had grown around the use of horses and in its place created an even larger economy devoted to motoring. It created suburban living, penetrated the isolation of the countryside, literally changed the nature of life in America. Considering that the gasoline engine, perfected in the motor car, eventually was used for everything from bulldozers to aircraft, its implications and influences are truly staggering.

In the first thirty years of the century, the country teemed with would-be automakers. In all, about 2400 different marques have existed in America. Many enjoyed only brief lives, never to be heard from again; others were absorbed by larger companies. The point, however, is that the United States went on a frenzy

This Amazing Air-Cooled Car Hurdles a Decade of Motor Progress

AT a time when the interest of other manufacturers seems centered on the development of minor refinements, this dynamic air-cooled car makes its historic debut.

The attractive lines and ample power, typical of water-cooled construction, have been combined with the outstanding economy of the air-cooled motor. The advantage of both types of cooling have been merged into a truly beautiful, supremely competent car.

Never, at any price, has a more graceful and beautiful car been built. Every line of the low-hung body is in exquisite taste.

In flexibility, acceleration, hill-climbing ability, power and versatility, the Fox, with its fifty horsepower, can be compared only to the most highly developed types of water-cooled cars.

The Fox has developed roadability and comfort to an unexampled degree. Terrific road impacts are transmuted into gentlest ripples by five-foot springs, stabilizers and perfect balance.

While nothing in the appearance or performance of the Fox suggests air-cooled construction, it is important to remember that it is the basic secret of light weight, great tire mileage and extraordinarily low consumption of gasoline and oil, as well as freedom from operating annoyances.

Think of commanding the power and ability of the Fox, with its 132" wheelbase, yet consistently securing *18 to 20 miles to the gallon of gasoline,* and other operating economies in proportion! The constant annoyance of freezing or overheating is completely abolished.

Everywhere in the car is evidenced advanced construction and patented features of design, deserving extended comment. But it is not fitting to single out special points, because *every* detail contributes to a harmonious whole.

The Fox will be exhibited during the New York, Chicago, Philadelphia and Boston Shows. At New York, in the lobby of the Hotel Commodore. At Chicago, in the lobby of the Auditorium Hotel.

At all shows it will be undoubtedly a veritable sensation. Not to have seen the Fox is to be unfamiliar with the decade's greatest advance in automobile construction.

FOX MOTOR CAR COMPANY, PHILADELPHIA

FOX
A Powerful-Beautiful AIR-COOLED CAR

The first unit of the Fox factory in Philadelphia is a model of advanced construction and modern appliances. The Fox Motor Car Company is owned by more than 3,000 individuals, all of whom are motor car owners

PRICES
(including five cord tires and wire, wood or disc wheels, motometer, stabilizers, backing and automatic signal lamps and other unusual equipment)

Open Models—Thirty-nine Hundred Dollars
Closed Models—Forty-nine Hundred Dollars
F. O. B. Factory

Advertisement, *Automobile Trade Journal*, January 1, 1922

of auto manufacturing, and it was just the sort of environment that appealed to Ansley Fox.

Apparently, the horseless carriage had caught his fancy early on, for he was awarded a patent for a car-brake on February 11, 1896—the same year Henry Ford, Ransom Olds, Charles Brady King, and Alexander Winton all put their first gasoline-powered motor cars on the road. What came of it, if anything, is lost in the shadows of time, and there is no evidence that Ansley Fox did anything further in the automotive world for nearly twenty years.

Once out of the gun business, however, his interest in cars surfaced almost immediately, beginning with a patent issued August 4, 1914, covering a vehicle spring. Ownership of the patent was assigned to what's listed as "Automobile Development Company."

But the first shots of what later would be called the Great War had been fired three days earlier, and within a few weeks half the world was involved. For the first time in history, the motor vehicle was used as an implement of war, and though the United States was not yet a party to the conflict, the burgeoning industry seized the opportunity to supply vehicles and parts to the Allied armies.

Although he clearly planned to become an automaker himself, Ansley Fox realized there was money to be made in manufacturing components, which could be put into production more quickly. And he had no trouble deciding which component, since he had already filed application for a patent on a shock-absorber (December 18, 1913). By the time the patent was granted on August 24, 1915, Ansley Fox was president of the Fox Pneumatic Shock-Absorber Company, 704 Abbott Boulevard, Philadelphia. William S. Furst was vice-president and E.W. Wrigley treasurer. The company was incorporated in Delaware.

He was granted yet another shock-absorber patent on February 22, 1916, and it, too, was assigned to the company. Four days later, on February 26, 280,000 of Kaiser Wilhelm's troops launched an attack on the French fortresses at Verdun, setting off a series of battles that would continue until the middle of December and leave 700,000 French and German soldiers dead. This obviously was not destined to be a brief war, and despite President Wilson's sincere, almost heroic efforts for peace, it was increasingly clear that the United States could not remain off the battlefield for long.

And this gave Ansley Fox yet another idea. He had been a gunmaker, after all, and a nation at war would be a nation in need of arms. Thus, sometime in 1916, he organized the Ansley H. Fox Company, incorporated in Delaware, with offices at 1600 Land Title Building in Philadelphia—officers Ansley Fox,

FOX THREE-PASSENGER COUPE
A beautiful closed car with artistic body lines and appointments to please the most critical. Price $4900 F. O. B. Factory, Philadelphia

FOX FIVE-PASSENGER TOURING CAR
Showing the pleasing long and low-hung body effect. Price $3900 F. O. B. Factory, Philadelphia

FOX AIR-COOLED CAR—FIVE-PASSENGER TOURING MODEL
Courtesy of the Fox Motors Company

president, and H.N. Williams, treasurer. Its business, according to the Philadelphia city directory, was "machine guns."

Whether Fox actually manufactured any is highly doubtful—although he later made a point of what he called his "intimate experience" with machine guns. He did, however, obtain three patents, the first on February 4, 1919. This covered a gas-operated gun, as did the second, issued jointly to Ansley Fox and Walter J. Rice on February 18. A year later—March 30, 1920—Fox and Rice earned yet another patent for a machine-gun cartridge-feeding device.

By then, of course, it scarcely mattered. The war had been over since November 1918, and because it was thought to be the war that would end all wars, weapons manufacture instantly went into a slump that would continue for twenty years. The Ansley H. Fox Company charter was repealed January 27, 1923.

Ansley Fox had contributed to the American war effort, however. In 1917, with Walter J. Rice as secretary-treasurer, he converted the shock-absorber company into the Fox Motor Company, 2545 North Broad Street. (The shock-absorber company charter was repealed January 28, 1920.) The nature of the motor company business is listed as "machinists;" actually, it manufactured air-cooled engines.

As one of the odd bits of paperwork that sometimes come a researcher's way, I have a copy of a letter written September 12, 1919, by Lieutenant-Colonel P.J. O'Shaughnessy of the Frankford Arsenal, Philadelphia. It's addressed to Mr. Frank H. Schrenck of Philadelphia (who I suspect was doing some background enquiries before deciding whether to join up in yet another of Ansley Fox's ventures), and it goes this way:

> *In reply to your inquiry of the 11th instant relative to the Fox Motor Company of Philadelphia, you are advised that they completed contracts with this arsenal for the manufacture of gauges, tools, etc., during the period of the War amounting to considerably over $100,000.00. The work which they did for us required a very high degree of mechanical skill, the dimensions frequently being as close as 1/10,000 of an inch. It was extremely difficult to get manufacturers to understand and appreciate our requirements, and this arsenal considered itself fortunate in being able to interest the Fox Motor Company in the manufacture of gauges, tools and instruments of precision. We have no hesitancy in saying that they saved the Government a very great many thousand dollars. The work which they performed was entirely satisfactory. Their deliveries were prompt, the percentage of rejections was almost nil, considerably lower than any of their competitors, and we cannot speak too highly of their fair and honorable business dealings.*

The good colonel's response apparently satisfied Mr. Schrenk, because about a year later his name appears on the stationery of the Fox Motor Car Company as a director, along with the names of Sheldon Potter, F.J. Germane, Budd G. Nice, M.A. Sherritt, Ansley H. Fox, Walter J. Rice, and A. Roy Robson. And there is no question of what the company intended to do, for the letterhead also reads "Manufacturers of Automobiles." Corporate offices were at Seventh Street & Grange Avenue.

As I said earlier, it was inevitable that Ansley Fox should try his hand as an automaker. Components are one thing, and even by 1920, the industry had spawned a thriving trade in the manufacture of parts. But as in the gun trades, the name on the final product is the name of the man who puts it together, not of those who made the parts. Ansley Fox's pride, driven both to create and to be recognized for it, would tolerate no less. And of course, what the Fox Motor Car Company offered was beautiful and luxurious and exotic.

By the end of the 1910s, the typical American automobile was a mass-produced affair powered by a huge, inefficient, water-cooled engine of about 4.3-liter displacement. Nonetheless, it was relatively dependable on the standard diet of notoriously low-grade fuel, and this, along with a low price, was its chief virtue.

THE DEMAND FOR AIR-COOLED AUTOMOBILES IS PRACTICALLY UNLIMITED

THERE ARE NOW OVER 100 DIFFERENT MAKES OF PASSENGER CARS ON THE MARKET, BUT ONLY 2 OF THEM ARE AIR COOLED.

IT MUST BE PLAIN THEN THAT THE MANUFACTURE OF AIR-COOLED CARS IS IN ITS INFANCY. WE ALL KNOW THAT AIR-COOLED CARS ARE IN SUCCESSFUL OPERATION EVERYWHERE, EVERY DAY, AND IN CONSTANTLY INCREASING NUMBERS. TENS OF THOUSANDS OF THEM ARE IN DAILY OPERATION ALL OVER THIS COUNTRY. PEOPLE ARE BEGINNING TO REALIZE THAT AUTOMOBILES RUN SUCCESSFULLY WITHOUT WATER. SOME OF THE SHREWDEST AND MOST SUCCESSFUL DEALERS AND ENGINEERS IN THE AUTOMOBILE BUSINESS NOW ADMIT THAT THE ULTIMATE CAR WILL BE AN AIR-COOLED CAR. AND IT WILL BE. IN THE LAST FOUR YEARS THE INCREASE IN THE NUMBER OF WATER-COOLED CARS HAS BEEN LESS THAN 47 PER CENT., WHILE AIR-COOLED CARS INCREASED OVER 250 PER CENT.

FOX MOTOR CAR COMPANY
MANUFACTURERS
PHILADELPHIA, PA.

PHOTOGRAPHIC VIEW OF THE FIRST UNIT OF OUR NEW PLANT, PHILADELPHIA, PA.

Ansley Fox used direct mail as a means of securing investors for his automobile. The mailing comprised a letter and a card bearing a photo of the Fox auto factory. The reverse side (opposite) is a post card potential investors could use to obtain more information.

THE FOX AIR-COOLED CAR
This wonderful car will go from 18 to 25 miles on a single gallon of gasoline. It will travel from 700 to 1000 miles on one gallon of lubricating oil, and it will go over 10,000 miles to a set of tires. It is a big, roomy car with 128" wheel-base.

TEAR APART ON ABOVE LINE AND MAIL THIS CARD

POST CARD

PUT A TWO CENT STAMP HERE

GENTLEMEN:

WITHOUT OBLIGATION TO MYSELF I WILL LOOK OVER THE INFORMATION REFERRED TO IN YOUR LETTER.

NAME

ADDRESS

CITY AND STATE

FOX MOTOR CAR CO.

SEVENTH STREET & GRANGE AVENUE

PHILADELPHIA

PENNA.

Luxury and sporting cars catered to a different market, one more demanding of performance and technical innovations. Only these—the likes of Duesenberg, Wills-St. Claire, Stutz, Marmon, and Mercer—used overhead cams and valves. Even fewer makers, notably Franklin, used the more sophisticated system of air-cooling. Ansley Fox decided to use both. As T.R. Nicholson puts its in *The Antique Car: 1919-1930*: "People who bought a Franklin or a Fox could afford to be eccentric."

The Fox Motor Car Company was formally organized in Delaware on November 21, 1919, and had a prototype vehicle finished by the following month, but before Ansley Fox could actually supply automobiles to the eccentrics of America, or anyone else, he needed money to build them. To get it, he chose direct mail. For at least a year, perhaps longer, the company sent out packets comprising a photo of the Fox air-cooled car, a printed post card for requesting further information, and a cover letter that makes the pitch. I have copies of three, one from December 1920 and two from April 1921. They are virtually but not exactly identical. The earlier version reads:

> This Corporation will put the new Fox Air Cooled Car on the market in the near future. We believe it is the only car in the world that possesses all the many advantages of air cooling, and is equal to the best water cooled cars in power, general performance and handsome appearance. It sets an entirely new standard for air cooled motor cars, and has wonderful commercial possibilities.
>
> An opportunity to secure a limited investment (one $500 Stock Ownership) in this Company is being extended to certain Owners of motor cars in each State. Not more than one Ownership is sold to any one person. While a substantial number of invitations to subscribe will be sent out, the average number of Ownerships allotted will be less than 50 for each State. A total of 2,000 ownerships will be distributed among the various States of the Union, thus creating a wide diffusion of interest in this Company, and in the Fox Car, and we extend you an opportunity to subscribe for one of them. If desired, these Ownerships may be paid for in installments covering eight months. Within a few months, over 1900 motor car Owners in various States have subscribed over $950,000. for Ownerships in this Company. This opportunity is not being offered to the general public.

Will you be good enough to inform us by the enclosed card, if you will look over some very interesting information which we will be glad to send you, without the slightest cost or obligation to yourself?

Yours very truly,
FOX MOTOR CAR COMPANY.
Ansley H. Fox
President.

P.S. We invite investigation.
REFERENCES: *Girard National Bank of Phila., Chelten Trust Company of Phila., Philadelphia Chamber of Commerce.*

The number of these sent must truly have been substantial, since this one went to a man in Kalispell, Montana, which in 1920 probably was not a hotbed of motor car Owners.

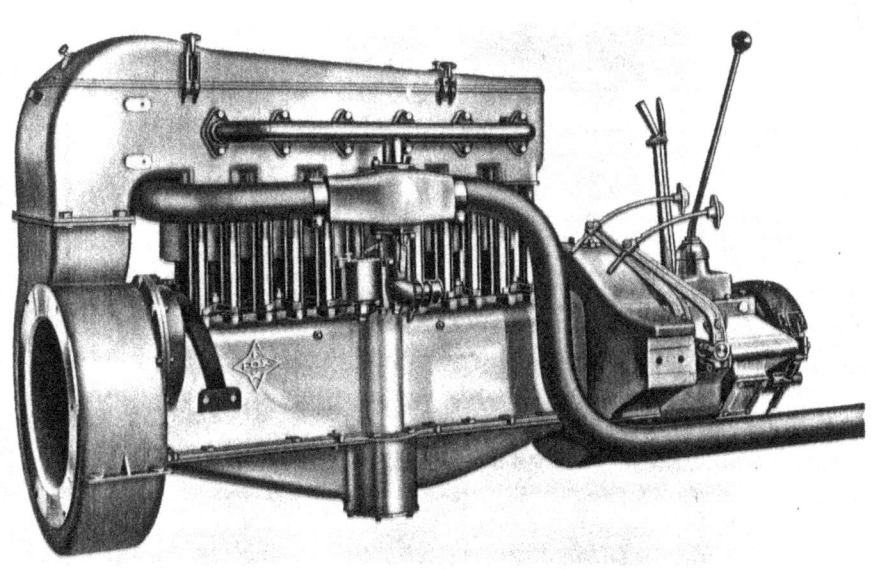

THE FOX AIR-COOLED ENGINE

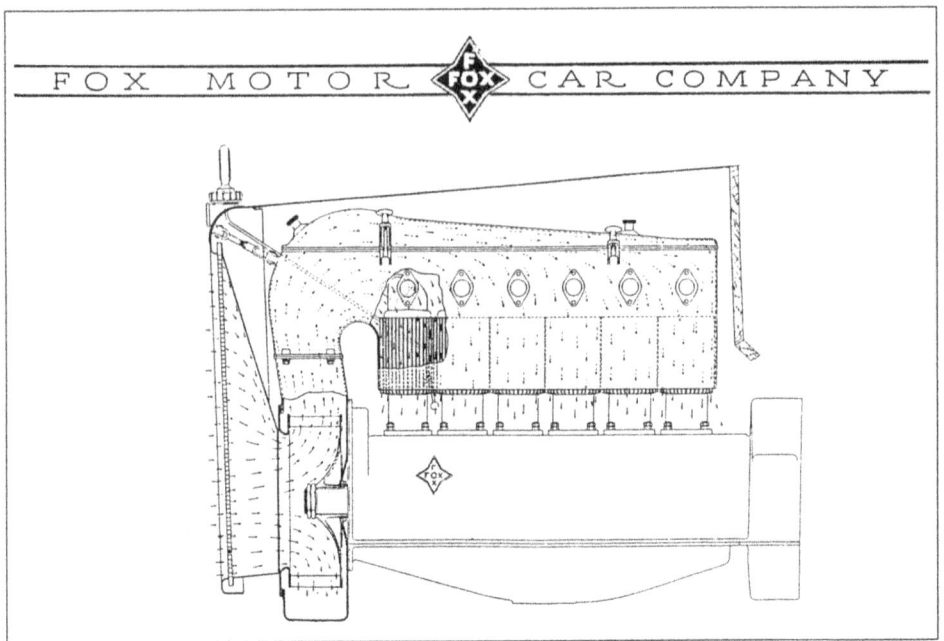

The Fox air-cooling system, illustrated in the 1922 Fox Motor Car catalogue.

In April 1921, the tune was much the same, but the harmony was a bit different. By then, according to the letter, "over 2400 motorists" had bought in for "a total of $1,200,000." (By my calculator, that's *exactly* 2400 times $500, but let's grant the author of it some poetic license.)

The letter now additionally says "Our fine new concrete and steel factory... is now completed and being equipped with modern automobile making machinery. There is not a dollar of mortgage against it." The number of Ownerships to be allotted is also different, raised to 6000, and "the average number of Ownerships allotted will be less than 125 for each State."

All of this suggests to me that Ansley Fox and his colleagues were finding auto manufacture to be an expensive business. No record remains to show what it cost to build the factory at North Seventh Street and Grange Avenue (which, incidentally, wasn't completed until July 1921), but the company later said it had spent "almost one hundred thousand dollars" developing the car itself.

Whatever the cost, it would have been higher yet if the company had set out to manufacture an entire car, but Fox actually built only the engine, transmission, and chassis and relied on the supply industry for everything else. The magneto came from Bosch, the carburetor from Zenith, the vacuum system from Stewart, the generator and starter from Westinghouse, the clutch from Borg & Beck, open-body coachwork by Fleetwood, closed-car coachwork by Derham, and so on. Nonetheless, what the Fox company actually did manufacture—and the way it used the components it bought—was notable enough.

All told, Ansley Fox earned seven patents for automobile engines and features thereof. The earliest was issued February 8, 1921, and covered an "air cooling system for internal combustion engines"—as did the second, issued August 7, 1923. The next three were all granted in 1925, two for an internal-combustion engines, issued October 6 and December 1, and the third, also issued December 1, covering "means for air-cooling engines." He received two additional patents for engines—one issued April 6, 1926 and the other May 7, 1929. Ironically, only the first two were granted during Ansley Fox's actual tenure as an automaker, and none during the lifetime of the Fox Motor Company, which was absorbed by the Fox Motor Car Company in 1920.

Engines obviously were his main interest, and as so often was the case, what he created was an item ahead of its time. It was a V-6 with $3\,^1/_2$-inch bore and five-inch stroke. The cylinders were separately cast, with integral fins milled quite thin, and mounted on an aluminum crankcase. A Sirocco fan fastened to the crankshaft forced air over and around the cylinders inside an aluminum housing designed to ensure even distribution to all six.

Each cylinder had its own detachable head, fitted over a shoulder on the cylinder itself so it needed no gasket, and the heads were larger at the top than at the bottom to accommodate oversized valves.

The American auto industry certainly was not rife with air-cooling technology and engineering know-how, and Fox managed to lure personnel from other makers into the company fold. Early in 1921, H.O. Swanson left the engineering department at H.H. Franklin of Syracuse, New York, to become chief engineer at Fox. At about the same time, Frank H. Golding resigned as general manager of the Holmes Automobile Company, Canton, Ohio, to hire on as treasurer and general manager.

In March 1921, Fox announced that its automobile would be on the market by fall, available as a touring car that would sell for $3500. The company also said it would build no fewer than 2000 units over the first year. A further announcement in July promised four body styles—touring, sedan, roadster, and coupe.

Production apparently went slower than planned, for the Fox car was not put to test on Philadelphia streets until December, and it was not officially presented to the public until January 1922.

The unveiling came at the annual New York Auto Show in New York City, with the entire line of the Fox Motor Car Company on display in the main lobby of the Hotel Commodore: a touring car and sedan, built for five passengers each, and a three-passenger coupe. Not all of the promises made the previous year came true; the roadster had been scuttled altogether, and the touring car now sold for $3900, the sedan and coupe for $4900. Decidedly pricey, but then the Fox was not just any automobile.

According to the 1922 catalogue—titled, not surprisingly, "The Finest Car in the World"—the Fox was a first-class item in every detail, from the "molybdenum pressed steel" frame to the solid-brass, nickel-plated headlamps. The instrument board was Circassian walnut, as was the curtain compartment behind the front seat. The open models were upholstered in leather, hand-buffed and "stuffed with real hair," the closed cars in "plush velour."

All told, it was a big (132-inch wheelbase), heavy (nearly 4000 pounds), handsome automobile, and the company made brave claims for its quality and performance. "Tests have proven," the catalogue says, "that a Fox Car will accelerate from ten to forty miles per hour on high gear in $12\,^1/_2$ seconds" and "will climb the steepest hills on high gear without 'rushing' the hill at the bottom. In a recent demonstration on a very steep hill near Philadelphia, a well known make of air-cooled car rushed the hill at forty miles per hour at the bottom but died down to eleven miles per hour at the top, while the Fox Car started at ten miles per hour at the bottom and finished at over thirty miles per hour at the top, accelerating all the way up."

For the most part, the performance claims were true. In a test report published in January 1922, *Motor* magazine found that the Fox developed "50 horsepower at 2200 revolutions per minute, and the torque curve is fairly flat." The car, the editors said, "has a road speed in excess of sixty miles per hour and it handles with a degree of flexibility which we have never before associated with an air-cooled vehicle."

The "well known make" the catalogue refers to obviously was a Franklin, which was by far the most successful of the air-cooled automobiles built in America and clearly Fox's most important competitor. This posed some fairly tricky marketing problems. Like Franklin, Fox had to sell the merits of air-cooling, but Fox had to do so without allowing the praises to spill over to Franklin's benefit. The approach Fox chose, which is a continuing motif in nearly all its advertising, was to promote its success with air-cooling while at the same time implying failure on Franklin's part. A typical example comes from a full-page ad in the January 1923 issue of *Motor*, bannered "The Beautiful, Powerful, Air-Cooled Fox," in which part of the copy reads: "FOX perfected air-cooling is a heritage of the war—the result of ANSLEY H. FOX'S intimate experience with air-cooled machine-guns, applied *successfully* to the automobile."

THE AIR-COOLED
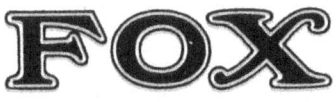
SPECIFICATIONS

Unit power plant, 3 point suspension; engine, clutch and transmission form a single compact unit. Fully enclosed as to working parts, and unusually clean-cut in appearance.

Ultra-sized (2½") crankshaft in aluminum alloy crank case, stiffened by seven heavy-ribbed webs supporting shaft.

FOX exclusive design engine. Six cylinders cast separately, valve-in-head type 3⅜" bore, 5" stroke. Dynamometer test, 50 h.p. at 2200 r.p.m. Valves operated by overhead camshaft, *entirely eliminating over 250 parts*, including push rods, rocker arms, valve lifters, etc.

Camshaft spiral bevel gear-drive, exceedingly quiet. Cylinders, fine-grain, hard cast iron, accurately ground, heads removable for removing carbon and grinding valves.

Brown-Lipe multiple disc clutch, with Brown-Lipe special 30-A transmission. Pressure-feed, circulating oil system, with FOX gear pump feeding all bearing surfaces under positive pressure.

Chassis lubrication, Alemite oil fittings, with high-pressure oil gun.

Scintilla magneto, delivering current direct to spark plugs without coils. Westinghouse generator and starter (Bendix drive to flywheel). Exide 6 volt, 120 ampere battery, latest type Zenith carburetor, especially adapted. Fuel tank in rear holds 18 gallons, with 3 in reserve, hinged filler cap to prevent losing.

FRAME—pressed steel, ⁵⁄₃₂" thick with channel 6½" deep.

Springs of silico-manganese, semi-elliptic, underslung; front, 45 x 2¼"; rear, 60¼ x 2½".

Ross steering gear. Timken axles and Timken roller bearings throughout.

Tires, 32 x 4½", Goodyear or Goodrich Cord. Wheels; wire, wood or disc optional. 132" wheelbase.

Most Complete Accessory Equipment. Write for Fuller Details

MODELS AND PRICES

5 Passenger Phaeton, $3900, List, F.O.B. Factory
5 Passenger Sedan,   4900, List, F.O.B. Factory
3 Passenger Coupe   4900, List, F.O.B. Factory

War Tax is Not Included in List Prices

FOX MOTOR CAR COMPANY
OF PHILADELPHIA

THIS SYMBOL IN ANY ADVERTISEMENT MEANS: SEE "CHILTON AUTOMOBILE DIRECTORY" FOR COMPLETE BUYING INFORMATION

Advertisement, Automobile Trade Journal, August 1, 1922

Again and again, Fox drummed its message: that air-cooling was the automotive concept of the future, that the demand for air-cooled cars was "practically unlimited," and that Fox had tomorrow's car today. To support its contention that "the manufacture of air-cooled cars is in its infancy," the company pointed out that of more than a hundred makes available at the time, only two were air-cooled.

Although this wasn't strictly true, it was close enough. The problem was that Fox misinterpreted the facts. The vast majority of American automobiles were water-cooled because the vast majority of American motorists wanted them that way. Water-cooled engines certainly were far from perfect, but their problems, as T.R. Nicholson puts it, "were familiar and straightforward." Dr. Ferdinand Porsche would one day vindicate Ansley Fox and the others who recognized the potential of air-cooling, but by then the Fox car would be only a memory.

Regular production began in May 1922, and throughout the year, the Fox got enthusiastic receptions in the motoring press and on the auto-show circuit in New York, Boston, Chicago, Pittsburgh, Atlanta, and Philadelphia. The company announced plans to build an air-cooled truck. It sought distributors for the cars through ads in the automotive trade magazines. (Coolbaugh-Macklin Motor Company, 3723 Walnut Street, was the Fox distributor in Philadelphia.)

Sales, however, never got off the ground—except among bootleggers, who appreciated the Fox's luxury and power and its lack of problems with overheating. In fact, the rum-runners liked the Fox almost as much as the Pierce-Arrow. The pity was, from Fox's point of view, anyway, that there weren't more of them.

The average car-buyer never took to the Fox at all. Price no doubt was one reason. A business recession that sent tremors through the economy in 1920 and '21 still wasn't fully past by 1922, and the Fox was simply too expensive. A widespread view of the automobile as a symbol of financial and social status was about to blossom and ultimately would make the 1920s the truly great age of luxury cars—but there the Fox probably was hindered by being mechanically exotic.

The company made some minor changes for the 1923 models and lowered the prices, to $3975 for the coupe and sedan and $2975 for the touring car. It didn't help. Receivers were given charge of the Fox Motor Car Company on November 7, 1923. A reorganization plan failed, and production was halted in January 1924. "Impaired finances" were cited as the reason—liabilities of $213,000 against total assets (including equipment, machinery, and real estate) of $529,920. On January

"Not just another car"

Three Models
Five-Passenger Touring.......$2975
Five-Passenger Sedan......... 3975
Three-Passenger Coupe....... 3975
at Philadelphia

A Car With a Reason for Being

The FOX meets the long-standing demand for a car with the beauty and power of the best water-cooled types, plus the admitted advantages of air cooling. In all truth, the FOX is "not just another car."

A noted designer of noted cars, D. McCall White, predicted overhead camshafts and overhead valves for the cars of the *future*. He further prophesied an increase in the number of air-cooled cars. FOX is air cooled and it has overhead valves, operated by an overhead camshaft now—*today!*

The FOX cannot overheat and it cannot freeze! FOX perfected air cooling is the result of Mr. Fox's war experience with the air-cooled machine gun. He applied the principle to the automobile with marked success. Compare the FOX with ANY car!

FOX MOTOR CAR COMPANY
PHILADELPHIA

THIS SYMBOL IN ANY ADVERTISEMENT MEANS: SEE "CHILTON AUTOMOBILE DIRECTORY" FOR COMPLETE BUYING INFORMATION

Advertisement, *Automobile Trade Journal*, February 1, 1923

31, the U.S. District court ordered that the company and its assets be sold at auction. Its Delaware charter was repealed January 24, 1927.

No one seems to know exactly how many cars Fox actually built. Some estimates run as high as 3000; other auto historians insist that about 1000 is closer to the mark. All things considered, I suspect the lower figure probably is more nearly correct. Even at that, the Fox is by no means the rarest of American antique

Advertisement, 1923. Despite brave claims, the Fox Motor Company was foundering by mid-1923 and was in receivership before the year was out.

cars, but it's scarce nonetheless. And it's still pricey as well. According to the latest edition of Kimes & Clark's *Standard Catalogue of American Cars*, a 1922 touring car of museum quality (Condition 1, in car-buff lingo) should fetch about $23,000 and a sedan about $15,000. Condition-1 specimens of the 1923 models are valued at $15,000 for the sedan, $17,000 for the coupe, and $35,000 for the touring car.

On April 5, 1924, Ansley Fox organized the Fox Holding Company with himself as president and Melvin E. Southard as secretary and treasurer. As usual, it was incorporated in Delaware. Two addresses are listed: 2545 North Broad Street (the address of the old Fox Motor Company) and 1212 Franklin Tower Building. The holding company bought all of the Fox Motor Car Company patents at the receivers' sale. Perhaps he had some plans for them, or perhaps he wanted to retain ownership just in case. The 1926 Philadelphia directory shows that J.H. Sayles had replaced Melvin Southard as secretary-treasurer, but the company never operated actively and, as the Atlantic City Chamber of Commerce said in a March 6, 1928, letter to the Philadelphia Better Business Bureau, was "doing nothing but holding their purchases." Which, I suppose, is why Ansley Fox named it the Fox Holding Company. The charter finally was repealed on April 1, 1930.

Apart from the holding company, it isn't clear what his business connections were in the years immediately following the demise of Fox Motor Car Company. An A.H. Fox is listed in the 1927, '28, and '29 city directories as manager (in 1929, secretary) of the Craveroiler Company of Philadelphia, 1604 Fairmount Avenue; nature of business, "auto supplies."

Whether this is our A.H. Fox or one who just happened to have the same initials, I don't know. That a man of this name should be involved in the automobile industry at just that time does tempt speculation. On the other hand, certain evidence suggests that Ansley Fox left Philadelphia about 1926, and there's no question that he was living in New Jersey in 1928. The Craveroiler Fox's residence is listed as 5029 North Ninth. This may simply have been an apartment for use during business trips to the city; Ansley Fox did have business interests in Philadelphia virtually throughout the remainder of his life, and he did keep apartments there.

In any event, it's an academic question, for by the late 1920s, Ansley Fox's life had taken yet one more turn. In some ways, it would be the last.

HE-XE Super-Fox, 1925 WILLIAM W. HEADRICK

15

Super-Fox

It's impossible to know now just whose idea the Super-Fox was. For a while, it seemed that everyone but Gandhi and Calvin Coolidge claimed to have had a hand in inventing it. Ironically, the one man who had nothing at all to do with the finest waterfowl gun of its time—or of any time—was Ansley Fox himself.

Actually, the Super-Fox was the product of several minds, all focused on the remarkably complex problems involved in getting a shotgun to reliably deliver a high percentage of its shot to roughly the same place at any distance much beyond forty yards. It also was the product of technologies unknown before and of splendid talents brought together at precisely the right time.

By the end of World War I, the search for a truly long-range shotgun had been underway for nearly two generations. Often it was more a process of discovery than of solution, as each new advance uncovered more problems yet to be solved. Choke-boring had been an almost universal practice since the turn of the century, but gunmakers were learning that there's more critical territory in a shotgun barrel than the few inches of muzzle taken up by choke. They began to understand that the relationship between chamber and bore, and even the bore itself, influenced the behavior of a shot charge in important ways. Exactly how these influences came to bear and exactly what to do about them loomed as questions yet unanswered.

Cartridges, too, came in for a share of attention. By then, the limitations endemic to the older generation of shotshells were becoming clearer. Smokeless powders, still relatively new, showed possibilities not yet explored.

Smaller-gauge guns were showing potential unthought-of only a few years before. Eight-bores had been legislated out of existence, and the 10-gauge was a moribund graybeard of a gun, tottering along, but only just. In those days, the standard 10-gauge load carried a maximum 1 1/4 ounces of shot, and the 12-gauge already had proven capable of digesting at least that much in a lighter, better-handling gun. The trick was to make it do so at distances useful to the wildfowler, for the once-vast flocks of waterfowl were nearly gone. What chances the average gunner got at game came more and more often at the ragged edge of his shotgun's reach or beyond.

Onto the stage thus set, enter E.M. Sweeley and Charles Askins, Sr. Sweeley was a lawyer in Twin Falls, Idaho, a University of Michigan football star from the days of Coach Harry Fielding Yost, and a shotgunner keenly interested in ballistics. He also was an intelligent, hardheaded experimenter determined to find some answers to the old problems of extending shotgun's range. Askins was the best-known and most authoritative gun writer in the country, a superb game shot, and also preoccupied with learning why a shotgun behaves the way it does.

One of Sweeley's more fruitful notions was that overboring would improve a gun barrel's performance. It wasn't an original idea, but Sweeley demonstrated to his own and Askins' satisfaction that it worked, using a gun reportedly custom-bored by Ithaca. He experimented with ammunition as well, at one point using thin, flexible copper over-powder wads that he believed would somehow promote tighter patterns.

Perhaps they did, but a real breakthrough in shotshell design was already on the way. By 1920, John Olin, owner of the Western Cartridge Company, was nearing the end of a project that would have a profound effect upon shotgunning worldwide. For several reasons, a shot swarm traveling through the air spreads in length as well as diameter. Some stringing seems to be inevitable, but from even the best shells of those days, pellets at the tail-end of the swarm might lag thirty feet or more behind those at the front. Olin correctly saw such extreme stringing as a major weakness in shotgun performance even at relatively close ranges, and he also recognized it as a problem caused mainly by deformed pellets. His solution was to use harder shot and to develop a progressive-burning powder that pushed rather than blasted them down the bore.

Charles Askins did a great deal of field-test work with Olin's experimental shells, and as he, Sweeley, and the Western ballisticians studied what they were learning, it became clear that a combination of specially designed barrels and Western's remarkable new cartridges was the key they'd all been looking for.

There remained only the task of finding a gun-maker to wrap all the pieces together. The Fox Gun Company already was deeply interested in Olin's

A promotional booklet accompanied the Super-Fox's introduction in 1923. It was revised in 1925 to include the 20-gauge Super. WILLIAM W. HEADRICK

project—and had access to the best barrel man in the country, besides. So in June 1922, Askins headed for Philadelphia to meet with Fox executives and with Burt Becker.

Burt Becker was born in 1871 in the village of Phoenix, Oswego County, New York. He left school at fourteen and traveled a few miles south to Syracuse, where he signed on for a four-year apprenticeship with Dan Lefever. Under Uncle Dan's tutelage, Becker became a gunsmith in the best European tradition. By the end of his long career, he was an engineer, a machinist, a barrel-maker, an actioner, a stockmaker, and even a competent engraver.

Becker left the Lefever shop in 1889 to hire on at the Batavia Gun Works, Batavia, New York. In 1900, he went to work for Remington Arms, where he built six fine double guns for display at the Louisiana Purchase Exposition, held at St. Louis in 1904.

Exactly when Burt Becker moved to Philadelphia isn't clear, but it probably was 1908, since he first appears in the 1909 city directory. His occupation is listed as "gunmaker" and his home address 4538 N. Bouvier. According to papers in the Nash Buckingham archives, hand-written by Becker in 1956, he first worked at A.H. Fox Gun Company in 1915. As no evidence exists to indicate that Becker ever was formally employed at Fox, I suspect his work for the company was done as an independent gunsmith under contract.

The 1913 city directory lists his address as 4549 N. 17th Street, near the Fox factory. In 1917, his home address appears as 4523 Gratz; this changes to 4531 Gratz in 1923 (most likely, the block was renumbered in 1922), and he remained there until after 1950. In the Buckingham-archive papers, Becker says he worked for Savage Arms less than a year, presumably on the same basis as he had worked for Fox, and spent fifteen years in business for himself.

For all his talents, boring barrels seems to have been Burt Becker's particular gift. Of the guns that John Olin had used to test his new cartridges, the best was a Becker-bored Fox 12-gauge with barrels carefully overbored ahead of three-inch chambers. In 1921, Olin sent the gun and eight unmarked boxes of shells to an old friend in Memphis, asking that he try them on ducks and geese and report back with an opinion. With that, Olin delivered Burt Becker, and eventually the Super-Fox, into the hands of history.

Nash Buckingham was not yet the most famous sporting writer in America, but he was well on the way. He was, though, certainly the finest long-range wingshot of the last generation to know first-hand a truly enormous wealth of American game. He was just the man to test the limits of any gun and ammunition. Buckingham was so impressed by the performance of the gun and the shells that he immediately abandoned his thirty-four-inch Parker and whatever cartridges he'd been using. By the time Askins arrived in Philadelphia, Buckingham had a Becker-bored Fox of his own, and Olin's cartridges were beginning to appear in sporting-goods stores around the Midwest, under the trade-name Super-X

Fox had already assigned Becker the task of developing a gun that would realize all the potential the new ammunition had to offer. Through the summer of 1922, Becker and Askins bored and tested barrel after barrel, refining both the design and the manufacturing techniques. At this stage, they used a single trap gun to minimize the expense of scrapping barrels. By October, they had the technique well enough in hand that they switched to double guns, and the Super-Fox was born.

Appropriately, John Olin got one of the first, gun No. 28069, fitted with a single trigger and thirty-two-inch barrels choked full and full. Olin ordered a straight-hand stock of 13 3/4-inch pull, 1 1/2 inches bend at the comb, 2 1/4 inches at the heel. The gun weighs nine pounds, and it was shipped to Olin at the Western Cartridge Company address on December 28, 1922.

Fox announced the gun with a full-page ad in the January 1923 issue of *The Sporting Goods Dealer*, billing it, with modesty that Ansley Fox would certainly have approved, as "the outstanding shot-gun achievement of the past twenty

One of the first Super-Foxes built went to John M. Olin, owner of the Western Cartridge Company and later owner of Winchester. The Super-Fox was designed specifically for Olin's then-new Super-X line of cartridges.   ROBERT LINTHOUT

years." The text declares the Super-Fox proven to kill single ducks "with the greatest certainty at sixty yards, perfectly capable of killing singles up to seventy yards, with ability to take birds out of flocks at much longer range." The copywriter, whoever he was, earned his pay, despite his tacit encouragement of flock-shooting. In an excess of enthusiasm it would later regret, the Fox Company guaranteed that every Super-Fox would deliver minimum full-choke patterns of eighty percent. Behind the hype was a gun that for the most part would do exactly what they said it would.

  Even though Fox assigned the gun grade status as the HE Grade, the Super-Fox actually is a separate model. It is mechanically identical to other Fox guns and made from the same materials, but it is significantly different in execution. The frame is massive, about one-sixteenth-inch larger all around than the standard Fox 12-bore frame and, like the barrels, milled from Chromox steel. A Super-Fox could weigh as much as $9\,^3/_4$ pounds. Only 30- and 32-inch barrels were available; if the buyer wished, the barrels would be regulated for a specific load and shot size.

The HE Grade engraving pattern is almost identical to that of the first-generation Fox A Grade.   WILLIAM W. HEADRICK

Ejectors and doubles triggers came as standard equipment, with the Fox-Kautzky single trigger available as an option. All other Fox options could be had as well—vent rib, beavertail fore-end, rubber recoil pad, skeleton steel buttplate, and Lyman ivory bead sights.

The guns were stoutly stocked with fairly plain, straight-grain English walnut and made to standard dimensions of 14 $^{1}/_{8}$-inch pull, 1 $^{5}/_{8}$ inches drop at the comb, and 2 $^{5}/_{8}$ inches at the heel. Grips could be straight-hand, half-hand, or full-pistol, all at the same price. Fancier wood and custom dimensions were available upon request. There is some evidence that William Naracom, head stockmaker at the Fox factory, personally headed and shaped all Super-Fox wood.

The standard Super-Fox is a plain gun, treated only to simple line engraving around the contours of the color-case-hardened frame. The pattern is almost identical to that of the standard A Grade Fox of about 1910.

In *Modern Shotguns and Loads*, published in 1929, Captain Askins reports that Fox attempted to create a 16-gauge Super as well but failed. "The reason," he says, "was always a mystery to me, and I was there trying out chamber, bore, choke and cone changes until I got tired, never being able to produce an average pattern of 80% with factory cartridges."

The 20-gauge, however, was another story. Twenty-bore Super-Foxes are not mentioned in Fox catalogues or price lists until about 1925, but factory records suggest they were available from the start. The first one shipped was No. 202099, which left the factory December 14, 1922.

Like the 12-bores, Super 20s also are built on frames all their own—the same width as the Super 12 frame but the same length ($3^1/4$ inches) as the standard smallbore frame. I doubt the 20-bore Super frame was a completely separate forging; it's more likely they were made from standard 12-gauge frame forgings.

Super 20s can weigh as much as $8\ ^1/4$ pounds. Like the big-bores, they came with 30- or 32-inch barrels, which are proportionately even thicker-walled than the 12s.

In 1923, when it first appeared in the factory price lists, the Super-Fox cost $100, $25 more than the A Grade and only $15 less than the much more elaborately engraved C Grade. The buyer got plenty of gun for his money. What the Super-Fox lacked in cosmetic appeal was more than made up by the meticulous craftsmanship of its fit and finish and by its startling performance. The heart of that came from the special wizardry of Burt Becker.

Getting a breechloading gun to pattern as efficiently as a muzzle-loader was a nettlesome and certainly ironic problem for gunmakers at the turn of the century. It must have seemed at times as though the improved firepower and convenience of the self-contained cartridge had come at the expense of good performance. The problem is that the inside diameter of the shell case has to be the same size as the bore, which in turn means that the chamber must be larger than bore size. It took gunmakers a while to discover that the forcing cone—the tapered section of barrel between the chamber and the bore—is a critical point. Short, steep-angled cones batter the shot charge as it passes from the case to the bore, deforming the pellets on the outside of the column and bashing the inner ones together. Once free of the muzzle, these misshapen pellets either fly wide of the main swarm or lag far behind, contributing nothing to pattern efficiency. Muzzle-loaders don't have that problem because they have neither chambers nor cones.

Becker clearly understood the advantages of keeping a gunbarrel free from abrupt changes in diameter, and his solution involves a three-fold approach. First, Super-Fox chambers are bored to extremely close tolerances, and most will not accept a cartridge that is even slightly oversized. There also is a bit more taper in Super-Fox chambers than in the average gun's. Becker's forcing cones are $^3/4$ -inch long and obliquely angled, so that shot columns are eased rather than squeezed into the bores. Finally, to reduce the difference between chamber and bore diameters even further, Becker overbored the barrels. A 12-gauge Super-Fox has nearly 11-gauge bores. The 20s are similarly treated.

Overboring has been in and out of vogue several times over the past 150 years or so. At the moment, it's in again, mostly for finely tuned target guns. (But it's not strictly a custom-shop affair; in the 1930s and perhaps before, Remington Arms offered overbored barrels for all of its shotguns, and in 1988, Remington began overboring the barrels of all its Model 870 TC trap guns.) Besides ameliorating the problems of diameter change, overboring shortens shot columns and reduces friction, both of which help improve pattern density. In practice, it is at best an inexact science, as much a matter of instinct as prescription, and like most such things, it has its share of detractors. But there is no question that overboring works when properly done and certainly no question that Burt Becker knew how to do it.

Early on, Becker and Askins overbored their 12-gauge Super-Fox barrels by .020-inch, from the standard .730-inch to .750-inch, and applied .050-inch constriction at the muzzle. By experimenting with choke cones from 3 $\frac{1}{2}$ inches up to six inches, they settled on 4 $\frac{1}{2}$ inches as optimum, bored to parallel configuration, with a straight, untapered section of bore for the last inch or so at the muzzles. Eventually, in order to accommodate the widest possible range of ammunition, they established .740-inch as the standard Super-Fox bore and .048-inch as standard constriction in a 4 $\frac{1}{2}$-inch choke cone. The Super 20's choke cone is 3 $\frac{1}{2}$ inches and standard constriction .033-inch.

Becker gave his bores a high polish to reduce leading and to minimize the inevitable abrasion between the barrel walls and the outer layer of shot pellets. At the time, thirty years before ammunition-makers began wrapping shot columns with protective plastic collars, polishing was about all a gunmaker could do.

The same attention that went into making Super-Fox barrels efficient also went into making them strong. For one thing, 12-gauge barrels struck for an oversized frame naturally will have unusually thick walls. Moreover, all tubes were proved twice, first in the rough with an English proof load of 7 $\frac{1}{2}$ drams of black powder behind 1 $\frac{7}{8}$ ounces of shot, and again as finished barrels with a 1 $\frac{3}{4}$-ounce shot charge and enough smokeless powder to generate about 14,000 pounds of pressure.

Because it was built specifically with Olin's new Super-X ammunition in mind, the standard Super-Fox was chambered for 2 $\frac{3}{4}$-inch shells, unlike most

The Super-Fox's "Barrels Not Guaranteed" stamp has been a perennial source of confusion. It refers to pattern density, not barrel quality. MICHAEL McINTOSH

other Foxes made in Philadelphia. Three-inch chambers were available in the Super-Fox upon request.

It's wise to check the chamber length of any Super-Fox before you stuff it full of three-inch Roman candles and whale away. The tight, tapered chambers are very difficult to accurately measure with the typical drop-in gauge, and factory-bored three-inch Super-Fox chambers can appear to be 2 3/4 inches or even shorter.

As yet another misleading feature, many Supers have a stamping on the barrel flats that reads "Barrels Not Guaranteed - See Tag." This refers to the ill-advised guarantee of minimum eighty-percent full-choke patterns that Fox tossed around during the first few months of the Super's life. Some very early guns are stamped "Barrels Guaranteed - See Tag."

Whoever came up with the whole idea of guarantees and stampings and tags apparently didn't know that a shotgun can be as fickle as a high-school beauty queen, or at least failed to realize that the company had no control over the shells that might be stuffed into one of its guns. Even though Fox hedged its bet by qualifying the guarantee with such phrases as "with the proper loads" or "with shells recommended," they no doubt had to replace or at least rework some guns that didn't perform as promised. They should have known better in the first place.

Incredibly, a Savage Arms Super-Fox ad in the July 1930 issue of *The Sporting Goods Dealer* also guarantees eighty- to eighty-five-percent full-choke patterns. No doubt it was only a momentary lapse, perhaps a fit of frugality in trying to get one more use out of an already-engraved printer's block. The same guarantee appears in the 1934 Savage catalogue, probably for the same reasons.

At any rate, the "Barrels Not Guaranteed" mark first appeared on Super-Foxes as early as 1924 and probably was applied to all of them built thereafter. Presumably, a hang-tag of some sort was attached at the factory, explaining the stamp's meaning, but such things inevitably get tossed away. Anyone buying the gun second-hand would have no way of knowing that the stamp refers to pattern density, not barrel quality. Consequently, you're apt to see Super-Foxes with the word *Not* obliterated—obviously done by some bozo who wanted to sell the gun, didn't know what the stamp meant, and figured nobody would notice if he chiseled off a word here and there.

Yet another explanation for these stampings, which has circulated through the collectors' community, has it that only Supers with three-inch chambers were marked "not guaranteed." There's a certain logic to this—on the face of it, anyway—but it doesn't wash. I know of several Super-Foxes, stamped "not guaranteed," whose original 2 3/4-inch boring is factory documented. Moreover, standard 12-bore Foxes could be ordered with three-inch chambers, and some were, and I've never heard of a standard Fox with a "guaranteed" or "not guaranteed" barrel stamp. The whole matter of guarantees, as I said before, refers only to pattern density.

At least one early gun goes the "barrels guaranteed" idea one better and actually has pattern percentages stamped on the barrel flats. This is No. 28069, the one built for John Olin. The right barrel flat is stamped "87%" and the left "88%."

Guaranteed or not, a Super-Fox on a diet of Super-X cartridges was—and still is—a formidable tool for any wildfowler. E.C. Crossman, at the time firearms editor of *The Sporting Goods Dealer*, pattern-tested Super-Fox No. 27822 in the fall of 1922. He was unimpressed with the results, which he said were "far, far from 80 per cent." A second attempt, with gun No. 28304, had a happier result. (No. 27822 apparently was returned to the factory for reworking; Abercrombie & Fitch eventually bought and resold it.) Crossman found much to praise in the design and workmanship of No. 28304 and, after some pattern work and field experience, concluded that he was "inclined to think the Western and gun making people are pretty much correct in their claims of eighty yard range."

The Super-Fox soon caught other gunmakers' attention, and within a couple of years, Ithaca, L.C. Smith, and Parker all went a-courting in the wildfowler's market. None took the pains that Fox did to create a long-range gun from scratch. In 1924, Ithaca simply lengthened its 10-gauge chambers from 2 $^3/_4$ inches to 2 $^7/_8$ inches and called the results the Super 10. That same year, L.C. Smith brought out its Long Range Wild Fowl Gun, which for the most part was a standard 12-gauge with three-inch chambers and a reinforced splinter between the barrels behind the fore-end lug. Parker in 1925 offered a 12-gauge waterfowl gun built on a No. 3 frame and fitted with thirty-four-inch barrels chambered for three-inch cartridges.

Crossman compared the Super-Fox and the Smith Wild Fowl in yet another series of pattern tests. The Smith performed well enough, but Crossman, who generally seemed more comfortable doling out criticism than praise, was moved to write: "I should characterize this 2 $^3/_4$-inch Beckerized Fox as the best shooting twelve-bore I have ever tried, and the most useful."

High praise, indeed, but the best was yet to come. In 1926, Nash Buckingham contacted Ad Roll and commissioned a 12-gauge Super-Fox waterfowl gun for work on what Nash liked to call "the tall ones." He specified that the barrels be bored by Burt Becker, which was easily accommodated, since Becker bored or at least supervised the boring of all Supers. This time, though, the results would make Becker the undisputed guru of long-range shooters. The gun itself would become the most famous shotgun ever built in America.

Becker built the gun himself, from start to finish. According to Buckingham, in a letter written in the 1950s, it was Fox No. 31108 – either a case of faulty memory or an instance when the same number got stamped on two guns (which happened a few times); the only work-order card for No. 31108 describes an A Grade 12-gauge with 30-inch barrels and a half-hand stock, shipped to Supplee Biddle Hardware Company in Philadelphia July 16, 1926 – definitely not a Super-Fox.

Whatever the number, Becker made Buckingham a Super with 32-inch barrels chambered for three-inch shells and regulated for Nash's favorite Super-X load of 4 drams, 1 $^3/_8$ ounces of No. 4 coppered shot. It has a straight-hand stock, which both Buckingham and Becker preferred, a rubber recoil pad and, at Nash's order, no safety. The finished gun weighed just under ten pounds, and when it left Philadelphia, both barrels would put ninety percent of the shot charge into a thirty-inch circle at forty yards.

Becker engraved Buckingham's name on the left barrel and probably put his own name on the gun as well. But soon it had a name of its own – *Bo Whoop*, coined by writer Harold Sheldon after the characteristic hollow roar of the big gun's report. Of such stuff legends are made.

Buckingham was so pleased with the gun that he did everything but canonize Burt Becker. Soon, all of the gunners in the little coterie that gathered around Buckingham had Becker-bored Super-Foxes of their own. Nash and Bo Whoop were virtually inseparable, both in literature and in fact, for more than twenty years, until they came to a regrettable parting on December 1, 1948, after a morning duck shoot at the Section 16 Club near Clarendon, Arkansas. A careless game warden laid the gun on a car fender after examining game bags and guns, and two equally careless hunters—Buckingham and Cliff Green—drove off without remembering it was there. The resulting hue and cry stopped just short of mobilizing the National Guard, but it did include radio announcements and highway roadblocks. For some time after, the following appeared in the classified-ad section of the local paper:

> LOST—*Becker double-barrel shotgun in canvas case. Name Nash Buckingham on case and gun. Liberal reward. No questions asked. Call Russell, 8-0346; after 6 p.m. 4-3145.*

In spite of it all, Bo Whoop was gone for good.

In July 1950, Nash's old friend Berry Brooks and a Corps of Engineers captain named George Warner—a fan who had never actually met Nash Buckingham—hatched a plan to replace Bo Whoop. Becker was retired by then, but he agreed to build one last gun for Mr. Nash. There is some evidence that Becker bored the barrels and subcontracted the rest of the work. Discussing the gun in a letter to his, and Buckingham's, old friend Henry Bartholomew, dated September 27, 1950, Becker says: "Mr. B. let me tell you. i could not make a Gun like it for less then 750.00 the Wood thats in the stock and Forend. i would not be able to get at this time."

The gun bears serial number 121, clearly numbered in Becker's own sequence (although not all Becker Foxes are). The old master was nearly eighty by then, and his eyes were beginning to fail; when he put his number dies into their holder to stamp the barrel flats, he got both "1" dies upside down.

Except for the engraving and a pistol-grip stock, which reportedly was the result of Becker misunderstanding the specifications, the second Bo Whoop is identical to the first. Buckingham used the gun until 1968, his eighty-eighth year,

Nash Buckingham's second Bo Whoop. Like the original Bo Whoop, it was largely the work of the great gunsmith Burt Becker. DONALD RUTT

when age finally made it impossible for him to shoot well with a heavy, high-combed gun, and then sold it to his old friend Dr. William Andrews of Memphis.

From the beginning, the Super-Fox could be ordered with high-grade engraving and figured wood. Of the handful of such guns I know about, the first, shipped April 1, 1924, is No. 29090; it's a nine-pound, four-ounce 12-gauge with 30-inch barrels and pistol-grip stock. The order specifies dark, figured wood and B Grade engraving—a curious choice since Fox had discontinued the B Grade six years before. Perhaps someone wanted a Super-Fox to match an old favorite gun he already owned.

After testing some factory loaners, E.C. Crossman decided to have a Super-Fox of his own. He ordered 32-inch barrels, three-inch chambers, full chokes, checkered triggers, and a pistol-grip stock made to his prescription. The gun itself, No. 30017, is a curious thing. It appears in the records as an "XHE" Grade, but in fact, it's a hybrid that's more nearly C Grade than X. The frame is filed up like that of an X, D, or F grade—it has the little rebates beside the top and

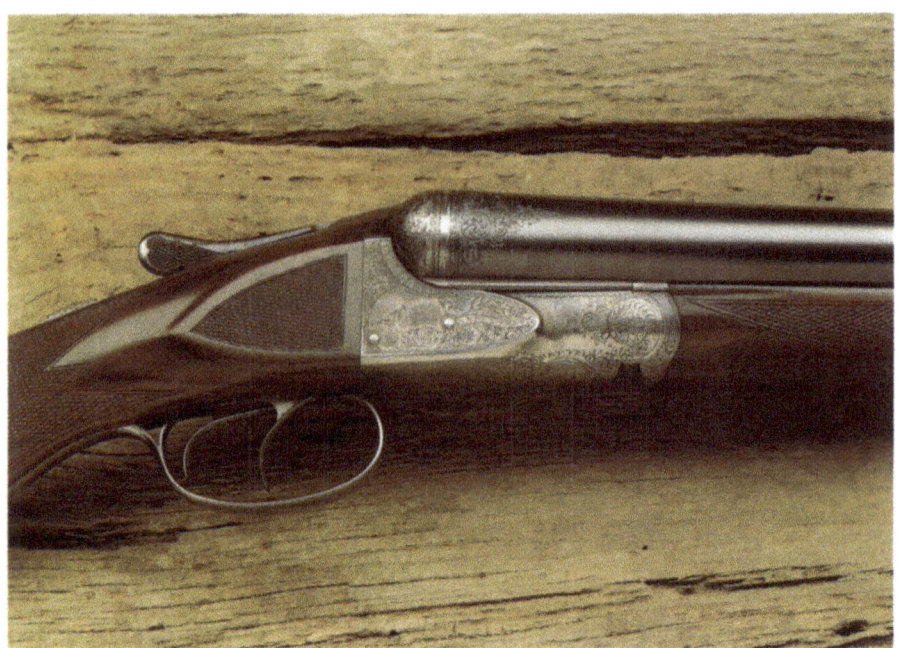

Writer E.C. Crossman's Super-Fox, completed in 1925. A highly unusual gun, it combines certain characteristics of XE, DE, and FE grades with an essentially CE Grade engraving pattern.

ROBERT LINTHOUT

bottom tangs, and the tops of the fences are rounded to follow the contour of the barrels. The top lever is checkered on both sides, which is typical of guns X Grade and higher. In other respects, however, the gun is essentially C Grade. The fore-end is the short splinter typical of C Grade or below, not the long version with the schnabel tip and buffalo-horn wedge that Fox put on the XE and the second-generation D and F grades. The checkering is exactly the standard C Grade pattern—although the pistol-grip cap is the one you'd find on a Grade X or higher.

The engraving is basically the C Grade pattern, with some minor variation.

All in all, this is one of those instances when you wish you could have been a fly on the wall at the Fox factory, to learn why the gun came out the way it did. The frame filing suggests that it was started as an XE, but why it was changed to something more like a C, we'll probably never know. Perhaps Crossman decided in mid-production that he didn't want to pay the extra price for a true XE, or maybe there was some other reason altogether. The lower edge of the work-order card bears the notation "C" along with some stock dimensions that are slightly different from those noted on the main body

The finest high-grade Super-Fox of all, an XE Grade completed in June 1925.

WILLIAM W. HEADRICK

198 South McLean
October 16th 59

Mr. Edgar B. Caldwell,
5225 Dee Road
Memphis 17, Tenn.
Dear Mr. Caldwell-:,

    In my opinion, your Ansley H. Fox 12 bore H E grade Magnum #30069, is undoubtedly Burt Becker bored and finished. He worked ONLY on the top-grade guns, Magnum field. In 1923-24 when these Askins-Sweely (Fox) guns first appeared, I was in the sporting goods business, in Memphis and owned two; before Capt Roll, Fox's sales manager had the HE made for me with special Becker boring, 1927.31108. So Burt undoubtedly turned out your fine weapon, in 1925. When Fox later consolidated or sold out, Becker didn't go with the new firm but opened his own shop in Philadelphia. I have the last 12 Ga. Magnum he turned out-in '50. In the opinion of the late Col. H.P. Sheldon, in my opinion the country's finest gun-editor and critic, in his Saga of Bo-Whoop(my original Becker) speaks of Becker as "unquestionably the finest gun-borer that ever lived." You are exceedingly fortunate to have such a fine weapon by so fine a master of his trade. We'll have to turn it loose this season with some of my favorite 4--1 3.8th #4's-coppered. You'll see mention of my gun in Lucian Cary's current article in True magazine "How Far Will A Shotgun Kill." Keep in touch with me as reports filter in from the mallard front.

    With every good wish and best regards

    Nash Buckingham.

Letter from Nash Buckingham, signed in pencil, to a former owner of XE Grade Super-Fox No. 30069. Buckingham played a key role in popularizing both the Super-Fox and Burt Becker.

of the card, but that's the only reference. (A number of work-order cards show similar variations in stock dimensions or gun weight or some other detail; in these, the body of the card shows what was ordered and the marginal notations indicate how the gun actually ended up.)

Regardless of why the Crossman gun was changed, it came out a handsome piece, shipped on March 2, 1925. Crossman used it, presumably with pleasure, for the remainder of his life.

The finest Super-Fox of all was completed in June 1925. It's No. 30069—a nine-pound 12-gauge with 32-inch barrels, ordered with X Grade engraving and dark, X Grade wood for both butt and fore-end. Both barrels are bored full choke and are factory-regulated for No. 4 shot. Chambers originally were $2\ ^3/_4$ inches, rebored to three inches sometime later. It has double triggers, ivory bead sights, Silver's recoil pad, and a pistol-grip stock. Whoever ordered it wanted the finest.

He also bought it to use. The old gun has seen service on the Carolina coast, in the Texas Gulf, and at Buckingham's old Beaver Dam Club—for by some chance in the late 1950s, it ended up in the possession of one of Nash's acquaintances. He queried Buckingham on the Becker connection, and Nash's reply, a paean to Saint Becker, concludes, "You are exceedingly fortunate to have such a fine weapon by so fine a master of his trade." The current owner naturally feels much the same way.

Another high-grade Super left the factory February 3, 1926, another 30-inch 12-gauge, No. 31019. This one was ordered with C Grade engraving and XE Grade wood made to standard dimensions, with a half-hand grip. It weighs just under nine pounds.

No. 32051 was ordered with CE Grade engraving, 30-inch barrels choked full and full, and a pistol-grip stock with Hawkins pad. It's chambered for three-inch cartridges, fitted with a single trigger, twin Lyman ivory beads, and independent safety. A note on the work-order card says, "gun to be as heavy as possible," and it weighs just under nine pounds—actually fairly light for a Super-Fox. It was shipped to the New York Sporting Goods Company on February 13, 1928.

And in 1928, Nash Buckingham ordered a high-grade Super in 20-gauge, probably for his shooting chum Hal Bowen. The order specified C Grade engraving and checkering, a high-combed stock with cheekpiece, and two sets of barrels. One set is thirty inches long, choked improved-modified and full, the other twenty-eight inches long with both tubes choked improved-cylinder. This is gun No. 202651, shipped June 1, 1928, listed in factory records as a CHE Grade. Nash mentions it again and again in his stories, usually as "the big 20-gauge."

One curious footnote to these guns: Even though the standard engraving patterns of B, C, and X grade Foxes includes some engraving on the barrels, I know

Savage Arms announced the Fox Sterlingworth Wildfowl Grade in 1934; it was built on the Super-Fox action and barrels.

WILLIAM W. HEADRICK

of only one high-grade Super that has any barrel engraving. Why is anyone's guess. The only explanation that makes any sense, bizarre though it seems, is that Fox chose not to weaken the breeches by cutting sharp, though shallow, engraving into them. Realistically, it would be pretty damn tough to blow out a Super-Fox barrel, but the absent engraving, if that's really why it's absent, would suggest that Fox paid great attention to detail in the Super.

The Super-Fox appears in A.H. Fox Gun Company catalogues and price lists from 1923 through 1929 and in every Savage Fox catalogue from 1930 to 1942, but not many actually were built during the Depression. The great droughts of the early '30s devastated North American waterfowl populations to the point where even the few who could afford a Super-Fox couldn't find much opportunity to use it. Except in its 1934 catalogue—an anomalous document in a number of ways—Savage didn't advertise the 20-gauge version after 1931, although seven Super 20s were shipped between 1932 and 1940.

Still, there was an inventory of Super-Fox frames and barrels taking up warehouse space, and in 1934 Savage announced the Fox Sterlingworth Wildfowl Grade—a 12-gauge of about nine pounds heft, fitted with ejectors and 30- or 32-inch barrels chambered for either $2\,^3/_4$- or 3-inch shells. It was, in fact, the Super-Fox without the standard HE Grade engraving, stocked in plain American walnut. Everything else was the same, down to the Deeley-type fore-end latch, which the standard Sterlingworth never had. At $62.50 in 1934, the Wildfowl cost $23 more than the standard Sterlingworth and only $9.50 less than the HE Grade.

As the Depression dragged on, the Wildfowl found a few takers but only a few. It does not appear in the catalogues after 1940.

Even in its best years, from 1923 to about 1928, the Super-Fox was simply too specialized an item to sell in great numbers. Though it was available for twenty years, total production probably was no more than about 300 guns, all but a handful of them 12-gauges.

Factory records show sixty Supers built in 20-bore—fifty-nine HE Grades and the Buckingham/Bowen CHE. All but nine, possibly eleven, were shipped prior to Savage ownership. As is often the case among Fox guns, some 20-gauge Supers were assigned a block of serial numbers; others are scattered throughout the 20-gauge numbers. Known Super 20s are as follows:

A.H. FOX

Number	Date Shipped
202099	December 14, 1922
202118	January 30, 1924
202124	June 9, 1924
202125	July 10, 1924
202166	unknown
202169	August 21, 1925
202172	September 15, 1925
202277	January 28, 1924
202278	September 17, 1925
202279	December 24, 1925
202280	November 5, 1925
202281	September 11, 1925
202282	May 27, 1925
202283	June 2, 1925
202285	November 6, 1925
202286	July 31, 1929
202287	unknown
202288	September 9, 1926
202289	December 15, 1930
202290	July 9, 1925
202291	August 8, 1926
202292	August 14, 1925
202293	March 29, 1926
202294	February 26, 1931
202295	October 11, 1927
202296	November 26, 1925
202405	August 20, 1928
202406	June 3, 1926
202407	June 3, 1926
202408	June 16, 1926
202409	May 20, 1927
202410	October 5, 1927
202411	unknown
202412	unknown
202413	December 31, 1928
202414	July 31, 1928
202415	unknown

202416	July 31, 1928
202417	unknown
202418	January 4, 1932
202419	September 8, 1929
202420	May 12, 1927
202499	May 31, 1929
202500	July 13, 1928
202615	May 4, 1927
202620	March 28, 1927
202651 (CHE)	June 1, 1928
202676	August 10, 1928
202677	September 11, 1928
202694	August 3, 1929
202775	February 12, 1940
203006	October 24, 1929
203007	October 14, 1929
203017	June 15, 1939
203629	October 15, 1931
203685	May 22, 1934
203688	unknown
203727	unknown
203775	March 17, 1936
203875	December 21, 1939

For the August 1923 issue of **National Sportsman**, editor and artist William Harnden Foster painted a wrap-around cover featuring the Super-Fox.

WILLIAM W. HEADRICK

WILLIAM W. HEADRICK

Standard Super-Fox chambering was 2 ¾ inches, with three-inch chambers available on request. A number of standard Supers were later rebored to three inches.

WILLIAM W. HEADRICK

As we've frequently seen, there seldom is much consistency between the sequence of Fox serial numbers and the order in which guns actually were assembled and shipped. The work-order card for the last Super 20 to be shipped, No. 202775, is marked "Office Sample;" exactly what Savage executives had in mind for the Super 20 in 1940 is anyone's guess.

Judging from the ones I've seen, and in talking with the most advanced Fox collectors, Super-Fox 12-bore guns with 30- and 32-inch barrels seem to exist in about equal numbers. Records suggest the majority were bored with 2 ¾-inch chambers, though many apparently were later rebored to three inches.

A completely original, mint-condition Super-Fox will fetch a good price on the current collector's market, but don't hold your breath till you find one. They were guns meant to be used, and nearly all of them have been, often under conditions that are as hostile to guns as they are attractive to ducks.

Steel shot has all but killed the market for the old, heavy, long-nosed doubles—but if I were going to use any of them as a fowler these days, it would be a good Super fitted with a pair of Jess Briley's stainless-steel choke tubes. Even if you're not a waterfowler, or if you don't care to have your gun screw-choked, the Super-Fox still has some good uses.

My pal Steve West, who from time to time enjoys beating himself senseless firing heavy loads at patterning boards in search of the ultimate turkey gun, has thoroughly tested all of the old long-range doubles, and although he'll give you a fishy-eyed look if you bring up Crossman's comments on eighty-yard performance, he has demonstrated clearly that the Super-Fox has an edge on the others. "With the right loads, the Smith Wild Fowl and the Parkers are good to fifty yards," he tells me, "but the Super will go fully ten yards more. It's the only genuine sixty-yard gun I've ever found."

Bill Headrick, who is the best long-range wingshot I know, retired his Supers from wildfowling with the advent of steel shot and now uses them with upland loads to smoke mourning doves at distances where they look the size of mosquitoes.

I imagine any Super-Fox would perform splendidly as a turkey gun, but you might have to look a bit to find the right one for doves. Even with careful attention, it's not easy to build a nine-pound gun that handles gracefully, and some Super-Foxes have all the snappy dynamics of a bridge timber. Others, though, are simply astonishing, both in the hands and on target—just as they were meant to be.

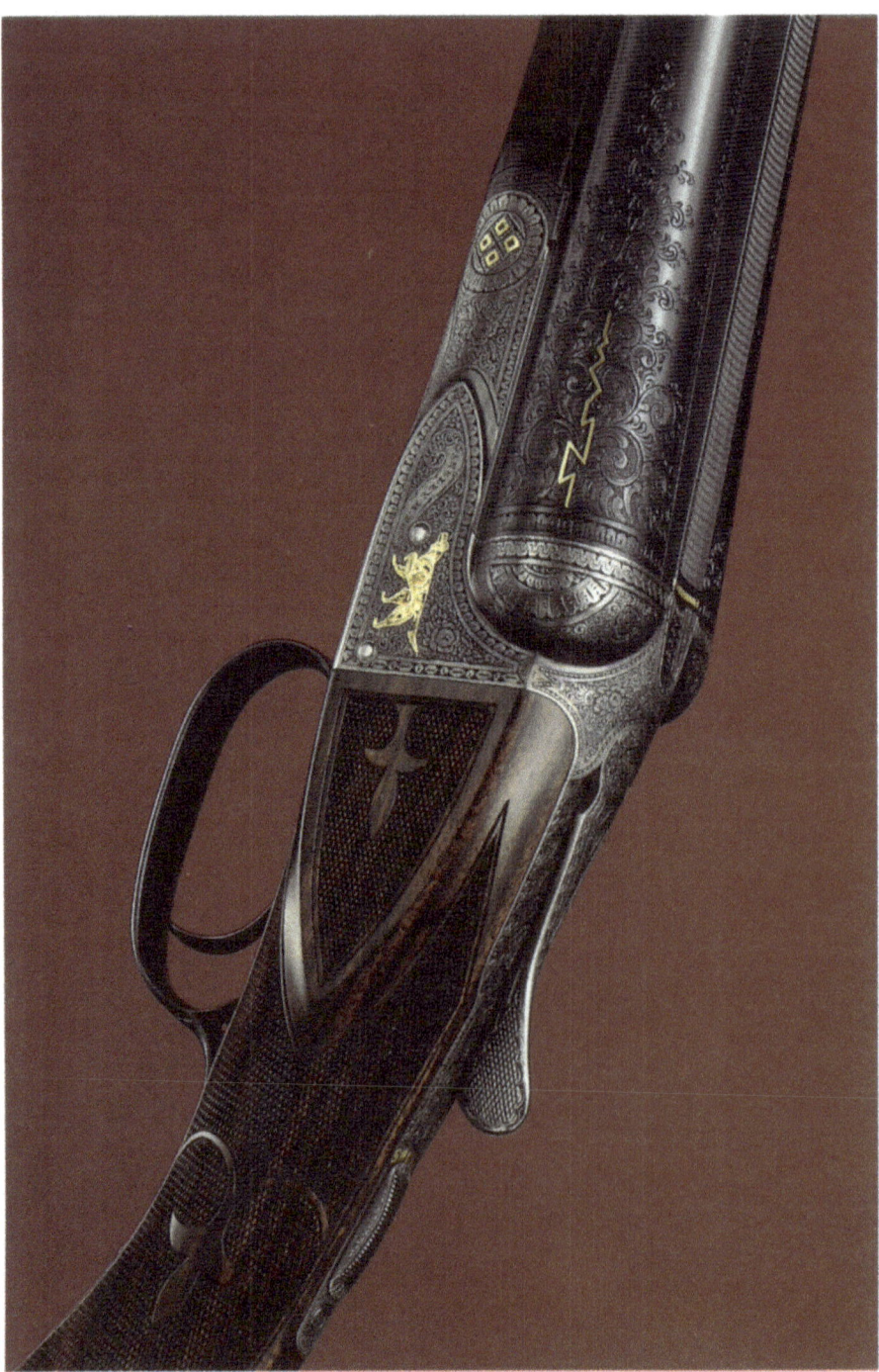

Despite the fact that the GE Grade appeared in factory price lists for eight years, there is little evidence that Fox actually built any guns of that grade. The FE Grade, like this 1908 12-gauge, was the highest standard grade built.

WILLIAM W. HEADRICK

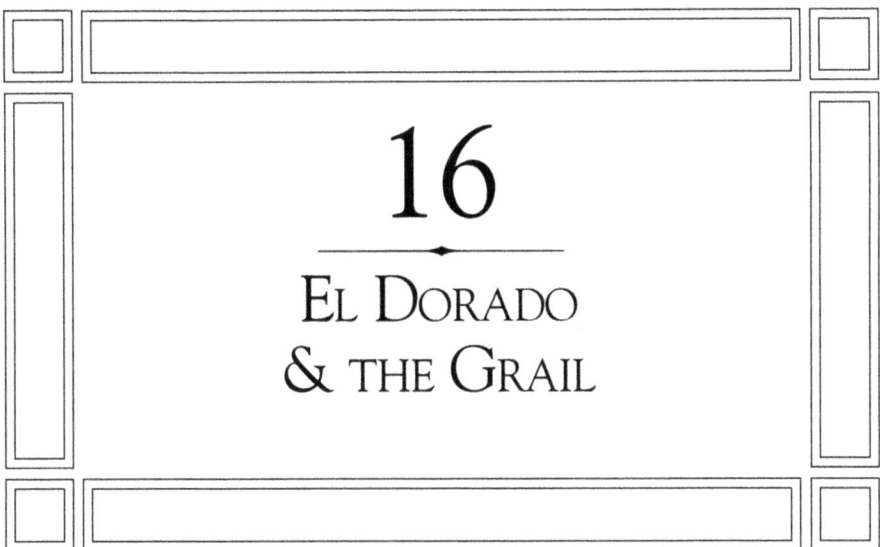

16

El Dorado & the Grail

The GE Grade first appears in the Fox Gun Company price list issued January 1, 1922. It came with none of the fanfare that would accompany the Super-Fox a year later—no trade-journal advertising, no news items, not even a photoengraving, nothing but a single line in the price list:

"GE Grade.......$1100."

Surprisingly, the GE Grade is not mentioned in any Fox catalogue I've seen, nor has any special factory brochure come to light. But for the price lists, which were printed separately from the catalogues, you'd never know it existed.

Fox clearly seems to have been testing the water at the high-ticket end of the gun market, just as Parker did at about the same time with its Invincible Grade. The national economy was improving, and both companies probably decided to toss out the lure of an ultra-high-grade gun and see if anyone would bite. That neither did so with a flourish suggests that it was a fishing trip begun with few expectations.

Parker built at least two Invincibles. One, No. 200000, is pictured in both the 1926 and 1930 Parker catalogues; its fate still is a mystery. It simply disappeared. Mr. A.C. Middleton of Moorestown, New Jersey, bought the other, No. 230329, late in 1929, just before the American economy went down for the long count. That one surfaced a few years ago and now is the centerpiece in someone's collection.

The GE Grade Fox is more problematic. If any were built during the 1920s, the company apparently did not use them for advertising, and no work-order cards for GE Grade guns have yet turned up.

Still, the GE continued to appear in Fox price lists through 1930, and magazine advertising mentions a price range of up to $1000 as late as the fall of 1931. The retail price of $1100 remained until 1925 or 1926; from then on, it's listed at $1026. After 1930, the GE Grade predictably does not appear at all.

Several highly ornate Fox guns described as GE Grades have shown up on the market over the past few years, all of them more elaborately decorated than even the fanciest FE and all problematic to some extent. One, No. 2728, is marked "Special" on the water table, and since the work-order does not exist, there's no factory documentation to justify calling it a GE.

Some other lavish guns were built well after all Fox production had ceased. The best-known of these actually are a pair—a double and a single trap. Shortly after World War II, Savage Arms executive vice-president Herbert A. Stewart asked for a pair of Foxes of the finest quality. As the story goes, Wilfred

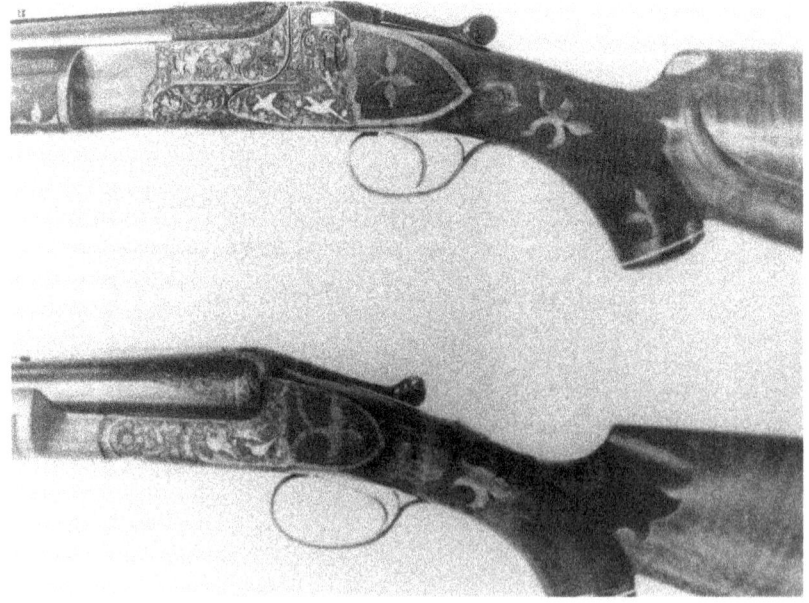

Factory photos of two guns built for Savage Arms executive Herbert A. Stewart in the late 1940s and early 1950s. The engraving and gold inlay was done in Germany. Some Savage records refer to the double as a G Grade Skeet and to the single as a Trap Grade Special.

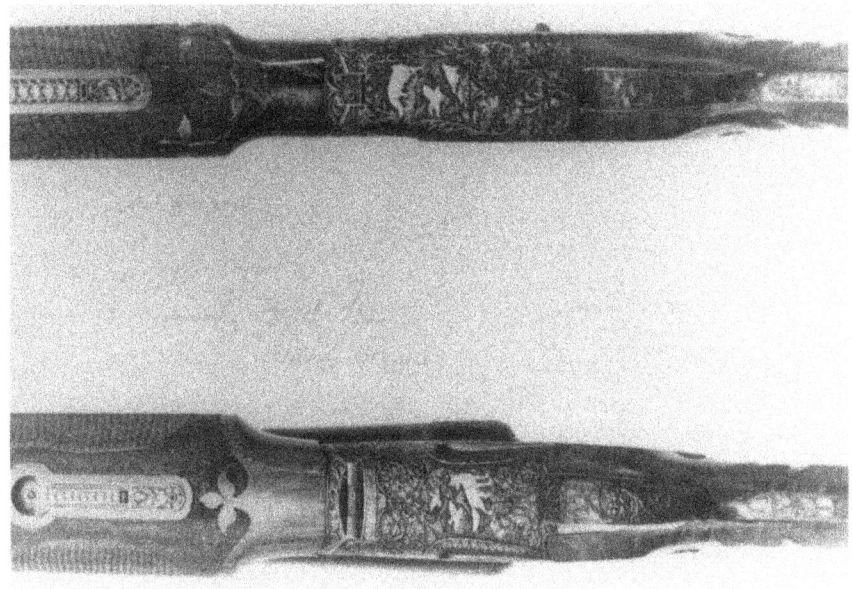

Wright, an expatriate English gunmaker who worked for Savage at the time, began building the guns about 1947.

The double, a 12-gauge, No. 35031, was made up with two sets of barrels, one of 26 inches choked improved-cylinder in both tubes, the other 28 inches long with modified and full chokes. Both sets have vent ribs. Not surprisingly, the gun was given virtually every available option—beavertail fore-ends on both sets of barrels, single trigger, pistol-grip stock, and skeleton steel buttplate. The ejectors are gold-plated.

The companion single trap gun, No. 400539, is somewhat more conventional as Fox singles go, largely because there were fewer options available. It has a thirty-two-inch barrel with the standard vent rib, beavertail fore-end, and pistol-grip Monte Carlo stock. The most unusual feature is a cheek-piece on the buttstock, an option long available (but apparently seldom chosen) for any Fox gun.

The frames of both guns are scalloped in the Burt Becker style, but there is no evidence that Becker had any part in building them. He was retired by the early '50s, anyway. The trap gun's frame is otherwise typical, but the side panels of the double's frame are rounded like the old Philadelphia Arms guns, not pointed in the distinctive Fox Gun Company style.

The guns were built at the Savage plant, which by then was in Chicopee

Falls, Massachusetts, and then shipped to Germany for engraving by a firm called *Waffen Bock*, or Bock Gun Works. As is clear in the photographs, the style is typical Germanic deep-relief chiseling. The double was given nine gold inlays, the trap gun seven.

Records do not indicate whether the stock decoration was done in Germany or at Savage. In any case, it's unusual work in that surprisingly large areas around the carved fleur-de-lis designs are stippled rather than checkered, much on the order of some later Grand American Grade Model 21 Winchesters.

Exactly who owned these guns—Savage Arms or Mr. Stewart personally—is hazy, but they were sold in the fall of 1967. Both went to the same buyer at that time, but sometime later the set apparently was split. A California gun dealer put the double up for sale in December 1986, at an asking price of $125,000.

By then, it was in an oak-and-leather case with a complement of accessories, none of which is factory-original. The accessories are, predictably perhaps, gold-plated—snap caps, patch box, oil bottle, and two anonymous containers with gold caps. There also are two ivory-handled screwdrivers, one scrimshawed with a quail, the other with a woodcock. The gun has changed hands several times since.

In a letter accompanying the gun, Mr. Stewart explains that the decision to have the guns engraved in Germany stemmed from his, or Savage Arms', conviction that no contemporary American engraver was capable of either the style or the quality of work being sought.

Such pious declarations were made fairly frequently by the American arms industry and by gun dealers during the post-war years. At best they are misleading and at worst are pure hogwash. The fact is, some of the best engravers in the world were working in the United States at the time; Alvin White, Josep Fugger, E.C. Prudhomme, and Arnold Griebel name only a few. But none of them worked cheaply, and that's the crux of it. Amid the shambles of post-war Germany and well after, there were gunsmiths and artisans of all kinds willing to do splendid work for very little money, and a lot of thrifty Americans bought a lot of German engraving at bargain prices between 1946 and the late 1950s. Unfortunately, a great many of them saw fit to disguise penny-pinching as a deep regard for quality.

There's nothing wrong with saving a few bucks, but neither was there any good reason to denigrate American craftsmanship. American craftsmen, after all, were good enough to build Fox guns in the first place, and they certainly were not all wartime casualties.

Actually, these guns wouldn't swell any Deutscher's chest with nationalistic pride. They do not display well. It's impossible to truly appreciate the quality of a gun from a photograph, but on the other hand, poor craftsmanship shows up very well in even a fuzzy picture. The double gun has now been restocked at least twice, but the photos here show what the guns looked like when they were built. Wood-to-metal fit around the frames and tangs seems almost inept, and some of the checkering appears very poorly done. Even the stippling appears flawed with runovers. Had either of these guns been built during the 1920s, when the GE Grade presumably was available from Philadelphia, would they have justified a price more than twice that of an FE Grade? I doubt it.

And there is an even more basic question: Are these truly GE Grade Foxes? The fact that the engraving and inlay is not factory work, even though they were factory-authorized, arguably places them in a gray zone. Even Savage Arms apparently was not entirely certain what to call them. Some factory records call the trap gun a Trap Grade Special and the double a G Grade Skeet.

Fox No. 500000 is yet another possibility, although it's marked "Exhibition" and not, to my knowledge, GE. The gun reportedly was built for Wilfred Wright, and his name is inlaid in gold on the trigger guard. Like the Stewart double's, the frame panels are rounded, but this one has considerably more gold, and the workmanship, both in fit and decoration, appears to be substantially better.

I asked Roe Clark's opinion on this one, and he answered, "I doubt very much if the gun was made for him; I'd sooner believe that he made it for himself and got the serial number out of the hat." This seems reasonable to me, since Wright was both a skillful gunsmith and an engraver.

So still we come full circle, back to yet another question: Did Fox build any GE Grade guns, during the '20s or at any other time? Considering the absence of factory documentation, I can only say that I've seen no indisputable evidence that there ever was a bona fide, factory-righteous GE Grade built. But there's one axiom that a Fox researcher would do well to keep in mind: Never say never.

"The Finest Play Gun in the World," 1920s WILLIAM W. HEADRICK

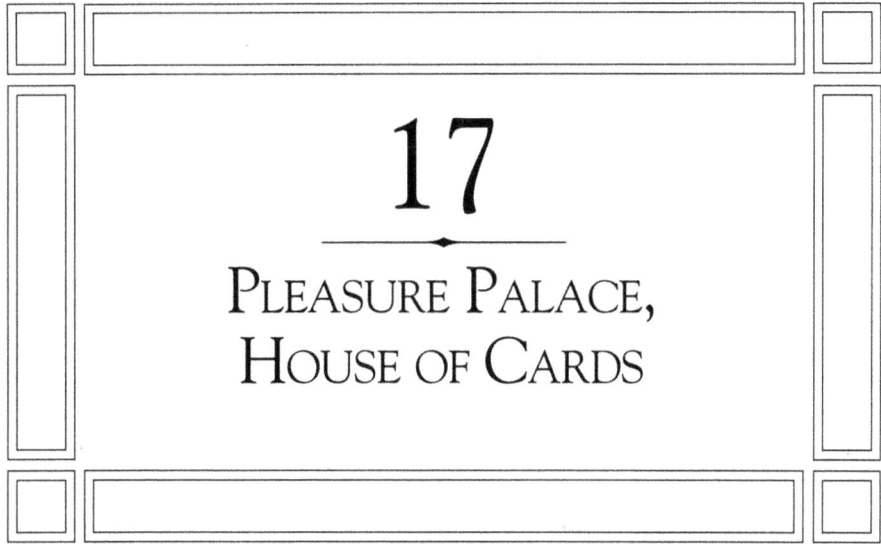

17

Pleasure Palace, House of Cards

In the aftermath of World War I, the American economy slid into a recession that lasted until the end of 1921. The Godshalks had managed the Fox Company's war-time development intelligently, and when the demand for materiel shut down, they chose to diversify rather than reconvert the entire factory back to gun production. It was a wise decision, for despite the promise of such new items as the single trap gun and the Super-Fox, the market for sporting guns showed every indication of remaining a very small pond populated with just as many big frogs as ever. But the demand for other kinds of consumer goods was growing apace, and like Ansley Fox himself, the Godshalks recognized the automobile as the thing of the future.

Unlike Ansley Fox, however, they took a path of lesser risk. In a 1920 press release, the company put it this way:

> *Upon the cessation of hostilities this war plant with its splendid modern equipment and its great force of men highly trained to the Fox ideal of quality production was devoted to the manufacture of quality Auto accessories. Careful analysis of many patents, processes of manufacture and materials ensured before these accessories were selected. The almost instant acclaim accorded them by the American motoring public and accessory dealers indicates clearly how Fox*

individualized quality is appreciated in these days of careless quantity production.

By way of illustration, the release cites three such items—a steering-wheel lock designed for Fords, a theft-proof spare-tire carrier, and an emergency gas tank and gauge, also designed for Fords. Unlike Winchester Repeating Arms, which attempted to survive the 1920s by manufacturing everything from roller skates and radiators to flashlights and diaper-washing machines, the Godshalks kept their focus relatively narrow, concentrating on the automotive industry and branching slowly toward the electrical devices that would be the company's manufacturing base during the Depression. Between 1924 and 1928, Fox Gun Company obtained a total of sixteen patents on items unrelated to guns: steering-wheel locks, auto lamps, a tilting steering wheel, circuit breakers, switches, lock-nuts, gear cases, gear-case caps, tire locks, vehicle signaling devices, and so on.

It was an age of diversity and contrast, experience and experiment, in which America reveled. The country seemed bent on creating every possible contradiction. We amended the Constitution to prohibit the manufacture, sale, import, and export of alcoholic beverages and then instantly set about finding ways of circumventing the ban. The Great War had offered the first opportunity ever for great numbers of Americans to experience European cultures, and afterwards they found their own culture, still doggedly clinging to its Puritan roots, too restrictive. Fueled by the revelations of Freud and Jung and Havelock Ellis; by the new, immensely emotional music called jazz (which the Reverend Henry Van Dyke described as "a sensual teasing of the strings of sensual passion"); by bathtub gin, all the more exciting for being forbidden—fueled by these and more, an entire generation set out to rid itself of every inhibition, to express every natural impulse that high-minded America sought to repress. They did not, as some insisted at the time, turn the country into a reprise of Sodom and Gomorrah, but they did change the course of American culture forever.

Predictably, the changes touched the gun world as well. In the years following World War I, Americans enjoyed a steadily increasing amount of leisure time, and this in turn led to a tremendous surge of interest in sports. Team sports, both collegiate and professional, flourished, as did boxing and horse racing. Tennis and golf, once viewed as belonging solely to the ultra-wealthy leisure class, became enormously popular in virtually every social stratum. Hunting and shooting remained as popular as ever, bolstered by a whole generation of former doughboys who transferred their military experience with firearms to sport. From the mid-'20s on, the new game of skeet attracted target shooters in huge numbers.

AE Grade 12-gauge, mid-1920s WILLIAM W. HEADRICK

A.H. FOX

As I discussed in previous chapters, Fox sought to capitalize on the sporting wave by bringing out the Super-Fox and also made a play for the country's increasing wealth by advertising the GE Grade. The efforts, however, began slowly and with a measure of caution. To maintain a competitive position in the market, the company announced early in 1922 that prices for the entire line would be reduced, a move Fox would make a number of times in the coming years. In the fall of 1923, Fox hired the Ed. W. Simon Company of New York City as the exclusive representative for Fox guns in the South and Southwest. A year later, the company announced plans to erect a new three-story factory building at Eighteenth Street and Wagner Avenue in Philadelphia, but this apparently was meant to house the auto-accessories and electrical end of the business, since advertising continued to show the gun works at the North Eighteenth Street address.

By mid-decade, the party was in full swing. In November 1926, Secretary of Commerce Herbert Hoover declared the American standard of living to be the highest in the nation's history, pointing out that production and consumption had risen to unprecedented levels. Americans owned thirty-nine percent of the world's automobiles. At the end of 1927, General Motors paid its shareholders the

Fox used at least two different fastening systems for the break-action play guns; one operated by the top lever and the other, shown here, comprised a simple metal stud and a friction-spring.

WILLIAM W. HEADRICK

largest single stock dividend in history—more than $65 million. Three months later, Wall Street set a new record for a single day's trading, with nearly five million shares changing hands. Where Fox guns themselves are concerned, the 1920s were relatively stagnant years. Except for the Super-Fox and the single trap guns and the elusive GE—all of which were in place by 1922—no new models or grades were introduced, and designs were not changed in any significant way. Beginning around 1927, a few double guns were built with vent rib and beavertail fore-ends, but for the most part, the Fox's evolution slowed almost to a standstill.

Which was not the case with the Fox company. In 1925, Clarence Godshalk decided that the sons and daughters of sportsmen represented a previously untapped market and assigned engineer Walter Paxson the task of designing a toy version of the Fox gun. This Paxson did, and filed application for a patent on September 25. The Patent Office apparently found some problems with it and did not issue the patent, No. 1,671,541, until May 1928. Undaunted in the face of the coming delay, Godshalk turned the matter over to Frederick Henke, who applied for protection on a design of his own on September 21, 1926. This one went through fairly quickly, resulting in patent No. 1,644,058, issued October 4, 1927.

Among other things, Henke sought, according to the patent papers, to create "a toy gun, small in size, simulating in almost exact detail the outward appearance and the manner of manipulating a real shot gun..." In fact, it does indeed resemble a double shotgun, at least insofar as it has two barrels, two triggers, and breaks open to load. Whether this constitutes "exact detail" I'll leave for you to decide.

Essentially, the whole thing is made of sheet-metal—barrels, fore-end, and frame—with a buttstock cut from some plain wood, perhaps gum or poplar, its edges slightly rounded. The standard piece is about twenty-nine inches long overall, and there was a shorter-barreled version that may have been used for promotional purposes. Some play guns even come apart the way a real double does; in these the hinge pin is spring-loaded and you simply press on it to dismount the barrels/fore-end assembly. This presumably was for the lad who wanted to store his toy gun in a trunk or leg-o'-mutton case, just like his Dad stored his Fox.

So far as I know, all of the double-barrel play guns were break-action, but there were at least two variations on the fastener. Some are held shut by a stud under the barrels that fits into a friction-spring recess in the water table. Others, however, have a loop under the barrels, a slot in the water table, and an actual fastening hook that's operated by the top lever.

Before Godshalk sold the gun works to Savage, the play guns were stamped *A.H. Fox Gun Co., Phila. Pa. U.S.A., Pats. Pend. on Gun and Shell* on

Only three working parts — the simplest gun made

The lock mechanism of the Fox Gun is the simplest and strongest known. The hammer strikes the primer direct, eliminating the usual delicate, troublesome firing pin. Made heavier where the greatest strain comes—unbreakable.

The mainspring is made of the finest spring wire, carefully tempered and tested. It is permanently guaranteed against breakage.

The sear is made of special drop-forged steel. It will withstand long, hard service, always giving uniform results. All parts are guaranteed; should a defect be found at any time, replacement will be made gratis.

—"and this is my first year of gunning!"

WHEN November brings the lure of the open—when you can hear the call of migrant ducks above the city's din—

Do you gratify that age-old instinct to go a-hunting? Or do you stifle it and deny yourself the pleasure and benefit of a few wholesome days in the open—days of relaxation in which care has no place, nights of genuine rest under the stars? Probably you have been on the point of going several times—then make your start this year.

Much of the enjoyment and success of your trip will depend upon your gun. It must be hard-hitting, smooth in action, dependable, a gun to justify your pride and others' admiration, and above all it must be perfectly suited to you individually. Fox Guns combine every desirable feature with the very best of materials and workmanship—"The Finest Gun in the World." To help you in your choice, ask for our little booklet on "How to Choose a Gun."

A. H. FOX GUN COMPANY
4658 NORTH 18TH STREET
PHILADELPHIA

Magazine ad, 1920

the bottom of the frames. Those built in the 1930s are identified as products of the Fox Manufacturing Company by a decal applied to the stock.

All told, the play gun is a cute little thing and rather fun to fool with. The most clever aspect is the "cartridge" it's designed to use, which fires a wooden ball by means of a spring-loaded piston. The spring-release is in the base of the cartridge, where the primer of a real cartridge is, and it's activated by the toy gun's firing pin. This, too, was covered by patent—two of them, actually, both issued November 12, 1929. No. 1,735,079 went to Frederick Henke, and the other, No. 1,735,086, to Walter Paxson.

The company apparently had no easier time deciding what to call its new product than it had deciding what to call the XE Grade. Some factory literature has it the Fox Play Gun, and some has it the Fox Toy Gun. In all cases, though, it's predictably described as the "Finest Toy [or Play] Gun in the World."

It ultimately earned the *Child Life Magazine* seal of approval and actually proved quite a popular item, neatly packaged and accompanied by targets of various kinds (one of which was an image of Santa Claus; imagine putting *that* on the market in the Year of Grace 19 and 90-something). A trade-journal piece published in October 1927 announced that "about 150 jobbers in all parts of the country are now handling the 'Fox' play gun, newest product of the A.H. Fox Gun Company..." The advertising campaign was fairly extensive, in such magazines as *Child Life*, *Junior Home*, *The Saturday Evening Post*, *The Parents' Magazine*, and others—even *The Sporting Goods Dealer*.

Sometime later, the company brought out a single-barrel version, which now is much rarer than the double, and a couple of multi-shot repeaters of fairly high magazine capacity. These, too, are quite scarce nowadays. In the 1930s, the Fox Ranger Repeating Cannon was introduced, described thus: "A repeating toy cannon that shoots six pellets at one loading. The iron cannon is mounted on wheels, so that it can be moved about easily. When a lever at the side is pulled back it releases a spring which allows the cannon balls to shoot out. The ammunition consists of hard rubber balls about $1/2$" in diameter. Sturdily built and an *ideal gift*. Price $2.25."

Some toy-gun ads that appeared in the sportsman's magazines ran under the headline "Start Your Boy Out Right," and in at least one case, it worked just that way. My friend Dick Wolters, best known as Richard A. Wolters of dog-training book fame, lived in Philadelphia as a child, just a few blocks from the Fox Gun Company plant, and he told me a wonderful story. Afternoons, it seems, usually found young Dick, age five or six, on the front steps of his family's house at about the time Fox workmen were headed home. One man always offered a

Fox fishing reels built before 1930 are stamped "A.H. Fox Gun Company." The reel catalogue shown here dates from the early 1930s, after Savage Arms bought the Fox gun works.

WILLIAM W. HEADRICK

A. H. Fox Gun Company surf reels. Fox sold the reel business to Ocean City in 1932.

WILLIAM W. HEADRICK

All FOX REELS have "LONG LIFE" Bearings Throughout

SALT WATER REELS

MODEL DC-250:
250-Yard Capacity

High quality, beautiful reel combining special features. Free spool, star drag. Genuine moulded end-plates with reinforcing metal ring inside. All outside metal parts chromium plated; non-rusting mechanism; steel pivots; convenient improved throw off lever; adjustable Fox long life bearings and new special bronze gears; one piece lightweight reel seat; click drag.

DC-250—Each, $5.50
Amber DC-250—Each, $7.25

Star Drag—Free Spool—All Chromium Finish
Models DC 250 and DC 300

Star drag reels are easy to operate, smooth in action. Automatic handle lock, when fish is on line it pulls only against the drag. Handle will not turn backwards—thus it prevents the skinning of knuckles and cutting of fingers when big fish runs with line.

MODEL DC-300: Same as above except 300 yard capacity. Each, $6.75

MODEL Amber DC-300.   Each, $8.50

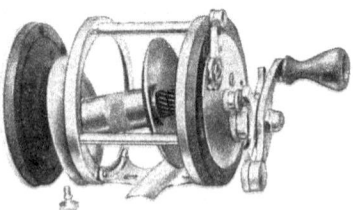

A beautiful high-grade reel with free spool—star drag—Bakelite moulded end plates with polished chrome plated reinforcing plate—special bronze gears and a new take-apart feature. By loosening one small hand screw the reel may be instantly dissembled for cleaning and oiling. Star drag has same special features found on DC Models. For the fisherman who wishes the best in reels, this model will make a great appeal.

Models GC 250 and GC 300

	Each
Model GC250—250 yards capacity	$10.00
Model GC300—300 yards capacity	12.00
Model Amber GC250—Same, with Amber color end plates	11.75
Model Amber GC300—Same with Amber color end plates	13.75
Model KC250—Same as GC250, but without star drag	9.00
Model KC300—Same as GC300, but without star drag	11.00
Model Amber KC250—Same with Amber color end plates	10.75
Model Amber KC300—Same with Amber color end plates	12.75

250-yd. surf reels—Diameter of end-plates 3¼", width over end-plates 2¾". Spools—Diameter 2 9/16", length 2". Approximate weight 1 lb. 1 oz. Star Drag Models, 1 lb. 4 oz.
300-yd. surf reels—Diameter of end-plates 3 9/16", width over end-plates 2 13/16". Spools—Diameter 2⅞", width 2". Approximate weight 1 lb. 4 oz. Star Drag Models 1 lb. 7 oz.

From the reel catalogue, 1930–1932

Fox used small-format "Fox Gets the Game" catalogues from 1918 till 1925.   WILLIAM W. HEADRICK

greeting as he walked past and eventually made it a point to stop and exchange a few words with the boy.

One afternoon, he came carrying a cardboard carton and asked to speak to Dick's mother. When Mrs. Wolters came to the door, he asked her permission to give the boy a gift. Inside the box was a Fox play gun. Owning it, Dick says, was a high point of his childhood. He never learned the man's name.

For Fox, the toy gun was only the beginning. Sometime in 1926, Clarence Godshalk decided to expand the company's presence in the sporting-goods industry by edging into golf, so the Fox Gun Company began manufacturing and marketing the Kumbak Putting Green, designed to let a golfer practice putting indoors. It amounts to a metal plate braced to stand on a slant; a hole in the middle is the aiming-spot. A ball that misses the hole simply rolls back down the plate and, presumably, back to the putter. A ball that drops into the hole is also fed back, via a side-delivery chute underneath. The device is pictured in a great many Fox gun ads from mid-1926 through 1927 and after, usually accompanied by the advertising slogan "There's room in any room for a KUMBAK."

At about the same time the Kumbak appeared on the scene, the fishing market caught Godshalk's eye, and in the fall of 1927, Fox bought the John Lauterbach Company of Philadelphia, manufacturer of fishing reels. A press

A.H. FOX

release on the acquisition reads, "It is the intention of the Fox company to extend and broaden the line of reels already being made, and to make this line a worthy companion product of the well-known 'Fox' shot gun." A catalogue published not long after shows twenty different models altogether, reels for bait-casting, for fly rods, for surf fishing, and more. The line expanded even further in the early 1930s. Typically for Fox, the reels are high-quality, well-made items.

Like the play gun, Godshalk kept the fishing reels when he sold the Fox gun, and by 1932, the company was able to report an increase in sales over the previous year. To keep the momentum, the designs were revised somewhat in 1932, making a great many parts interchangeable among models of similar type. Some models were thereafter fitted with side-panels of a material called "lumarith" instead of the black bakelite used previously. Lumarith, the company said, "is an attractive amber-colored material, strong but light in weight, and is semi-transparent, permitting the shadow of the reel mechanism to be seen through the side plates."

The reels earned an excellent reputation for quality, and that in turn, attracted interest within the industry. In November 1932, the trade was informed that the Ocean City Manufacturing Company of Philadelphia had purchased the

The "wood-grain" catalogue cover was introduced in 1925. It was used in the small format until 1927 and in the larger format during 1928 and 1929.

WILLIAM W. HEADRICK

Brochure advertising Fox guns, 1928

reel business from Fox. The dies, machinery, stock, and employees were moved to the Ocean City plant 1341-47 Noble Street and set up as the Fox Division.

Ocean City revised the Fox line yet again in 1933 and for a year or more used the Fox name prominently in its advertising. By then, however, the Depression was at its depths, and Ocean City either scuttled Fox altogether or simply absorbed the products under the parent-company name. In any event, Fox reels do not appear in the advertising after 1934.

Even as the Roaring Twenties seemed to roar the loudest, some of the flash and glitter was wearing thin. Along with paeans of prosperity, Secretary Hoover's 1926 report conceded to some unemployment, primarily in coal mining and the textiles industry. By 1928, the Commerce and Labor departments were at odds over just how extensive unemployment really was. Commerce said that two million Americans had no jobs; Labor put the figure at four million, which was an even ten percent of the work force. The pleasure palace was on its way to becoming a house of cards.

In December 1927, Walter Paxson sent out a press release for the A.H. Fox Gun Company that begins and ends this way: "In looking forward to the prospects for next year, we cannot help feeling very optimistic, as our product has met with a ready demand throughout 1927...Everything considered, we feel that next year should be a very satisfactory one, if we can judge by appearances so far."

The same appearances brought Herbert Hoover to the White House in 1928, driven by a fifty-eight-percent majority of the popular vote and an electoral college total of 357. Since 1926, the same sort of optimism had fueled a wild orgy of financial speculation, stock-pooling, ill-conceived lending on the part of banks, and all manner of shenanigans virtually unregulated by law. It all came crashing down in October 1929.

In January 1930, *The Sporting Goods Dealer* reported that Savage Arms Corporation had acquired the shotgun business of the A.H. Fox Gun Company. Exactly what the situation at Fox may have been earlier in the year is not clear, but the sale, which took place in November, probably was not prompted by the stock-market crash; acquisitions among major manufacturing companies just don't happen that quickly. Most likely, the gun market failed to reward the optimism Fox felt at the beginning of 1928. The fact is, despite Paxson's comment about a "ready market," sales of graded guns had dropped to fewer than 1000 per year, and The Finest Gun in the World had become an albatross. The company's other operations—auto parts, reels, even the toy gun—no doubt returned higher profit margins at lower production cost, and future projections for the gun business probably were bleaker still.

Although quality of workmanship showed an overall decline in the late 1920s, Fox still turned out some lovely guns during the period – like this DE Grade 12-gauge.

WILLIAM W. HEADRICK

CE Grade 20-gauge, 1928   WILLIAM W. HEADRICK

CE Grade 12-gauge, mid-1920s WILLIAM W. HEADRICK

"Certainly can't blame you for being proud of this gun, Bob."

Only three working parts — the simplest gun made

The lock mechanism of the Fox Gun is the simplest and strongest known. The hammer strikes the primer direct, eliminating the usual delicate, trouble-some firing pin. Made heavier where the greatest strain comes—unbreakable.

The mainspring is made of the finest steel, carefully tempered and tested. It is permanently guaranteed against breakage.

The sear is made of special drop-forged steel. It will withstand long, hard service, always giving uniform results. All parts are guaranteed; should a defect be found of any kind, repairs thereto will be made gratis.

THE crisp tang of autumn, brown fields, sleek pointers trembling with eagerness, the thrill of a flushed covey, the sharp report awakening wide echoes, the triumph of a successful shot—

The thread of memory—and anticipation—is interwoven with the look and feel of "The Finest Gun in the World"—your Fox. And respect for your judgment is deepened when friends examine your choice.

No wonder the sportsman has a strong feeling of affection for his Fox—a tie, a bond, something closer and deeper than he feels for most of his other possessions; for he knows that it is a true friend, the companion of many days of wholesome pleasure.

Make certain that you get the fullest measure of satisfaction, the keenest possible enjoyment from your shooting this year—see that your gun is a Fox.

A. H. FOX GUN COMPANY
4658 NORTH 18th STREET
PHILADELPHIA

FOX GUNS

Magazine ad, early 1920s

Whatever the scenario, Savage announced in January that "arrangements will be made for the immediate transfer to Utica, N.Y., of the entire shotgun manufacturing equipment of the Fox plant, and the A.H. Fox Gun Company will operate as a unit, utilizing space in the Savage Arms Corporation's buildings.

"The transfer of most of the Fox manufacturing personnel to Utica insures the maintenance of the same high standard of quality which has given the Fox double gun its eminent position in the high-grade gun field."

Clarence Godshalk and his successors, operating as Fox Manufacturing Company, Fox Automotive Products Company, and eventually as simply Fox Products Company, spent the next fifty years turning out myriad light-industry items, from battery chargers and aircraft parts to locks, electrical outlets, switches, and the like. They remained in business until 1980.

But as of 1930, it was no longer the A.H. Fox Gun Company, and the Fox gun was no longer in Philadelphia, and the country was in dire trouble. In more ways than one, the future would be measured in savage years.

DE Grade 12-gauge WILLIAM W. HEADRICK

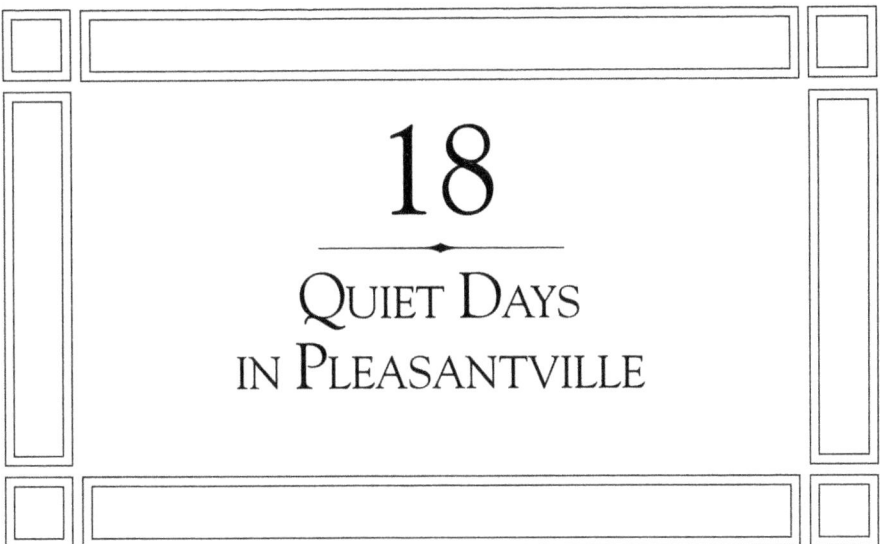

18

QUIET DAYS IN PLEASANTVILLE

Ansley Fox's name first appears in the Atlantic City directory of 1927, which means he was living there in 1926. He is listed as president of the Seaboard Development Corporation, 303 Union National Bank Building, with a Pleasantville office at 350 South Main Street. C.H. Landsettel was secretary-treasurer, E. Hildebrand assistant secretary-treasurer.

The business was land-development and real estate. Ansley Fox set about buying land in the Pleasantville section of West Atlantic City, with an eye toward creating a suburban residential community known as Ansley Park—in which Ansley Boulevard naturally was a main thoroughfare. In 1927, he founded the Ansley Park Construction Company, office at 350 South Main, Pleasantville, and appointed William Gerou, his brother-in-law and confidante, superintendent.

Exactly where Ansley and Ellen Fox lived in the first few years is not clear. The 1927 directory shows his residence as 214 Palmer Avenue; in 1928, it's simply Ansley Park; in 1930, Ansley Boulevard and Prospect Street; in 1931, 214 Palermo Avenue. These may all be different ways of identifying the same house, especially since "214 Palmer" could be a typo for "214 Palermo." In any event, 214 Palermo Avenue would be Ansley Fox's home for the remainder of his life. William Gerou and his wife Millie lived at 8 East Oakland Avenue in 1926 and in 1927 moved to 114 Genoa Avenue, where they lived for many years after.

Ansley Fox was not much in the public eye during the Pleasantville years—certainly not to the extent he had been from the turn of the century

Dec. 15, 1931.   A. H. FOX   1,836,312
CIGARETTE LIGHTER
Filed April 21, 1930

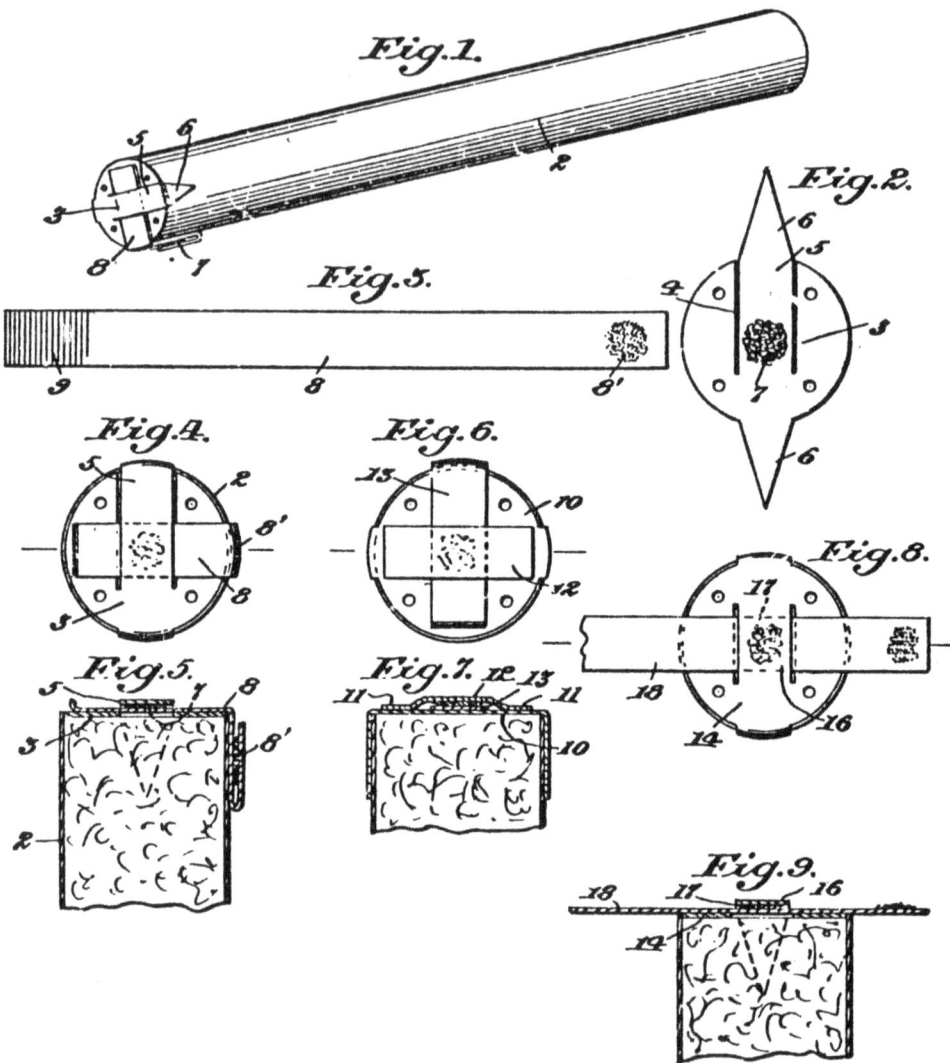

Inventor:
Ansley H. Fox,
By Jas. L. Skidmore
Att'y.

through the demise of the motor-car company. There were, however, two notable exceptions.

In the spring of 1931, with the national economy sliding toward the nadir of the Great Depression, controversy raged on the power trust issue, a widespread debate over whether utilities should be publicly owned or should remain in private hands. Early in May, the Atlantic City Electric Company sent a pamphlet to all its customers, claiming that private ownership best served the public good, and Ansley Fox disagreed. On May 13, the *Atlantic City Press* ran a news story headlined "Fox Attacks Electric Co. Rates Here," in which Ansley Fox is quoted at some length, concluding with the statement that the enormous profits shown by privately owned utilities are "conclusive evidence to my mind that the people are being mercilessly exploited, and that all attempts at fair rate regulation on these necessities of life which are monopolized by privately owned utility companies, has completely failed."

In the next day's issue, the *Press* published a letter to the editor dated May 1, 1931, and signed by Ansley Fox. His subject was the relationship of government to private business and the public weal, and for a man who had spent his entire life in private enterprise, his rhetoric is as fiery as any Depression-era Democrat's:

...In the final analysis it appears that business is trying to place itself in the false position of being superior to government. It is beyond all question that the first duty of government is to protect its citizens either in time of war or in time of depression and we should always keep in mind the important fact that business and capital are merely instruments to serve the people and if they attempt to sacrifice the welfare and happiness of any nation through action motivated from private profit then the government must act to protect its citizens.

...I am quite sure the government will compel business to provide unemployment insurance as a most practical humane means of preventing the intolerable conditions from which our millions of unemployed are now suffering. ...History...records the fact that whenever a highly organized and selfish minority of the people make living conditions intolerable for the majority, the masses of the people will demand relief.

Most remarkable in all this is a single sentence that reads, "Individualism is a necessary incentive to ambition, but if that ambition happens to be detrimental to the public good then individualism may become a menace." This from one of the great individualists of modern time—though he was right, of course, as

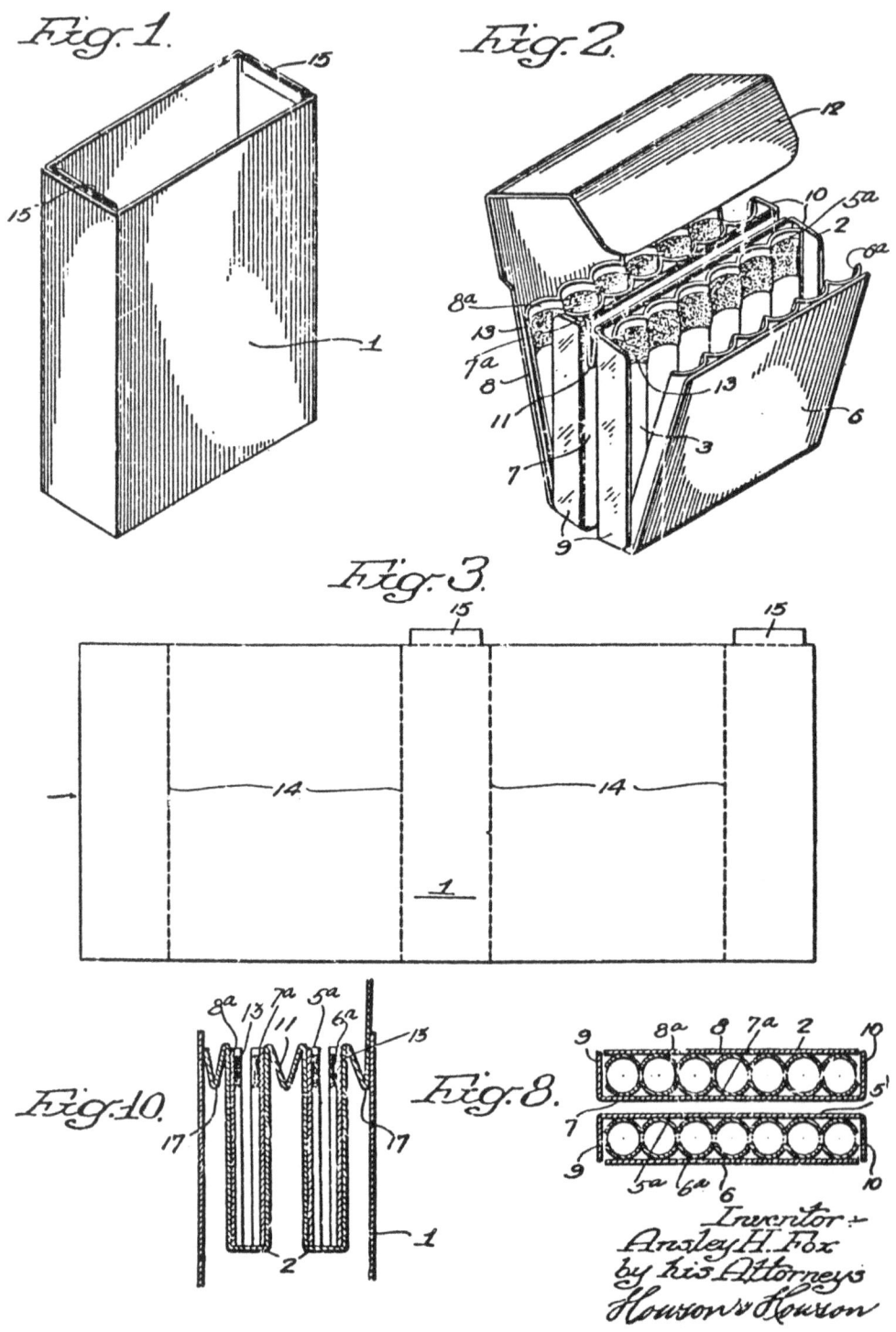

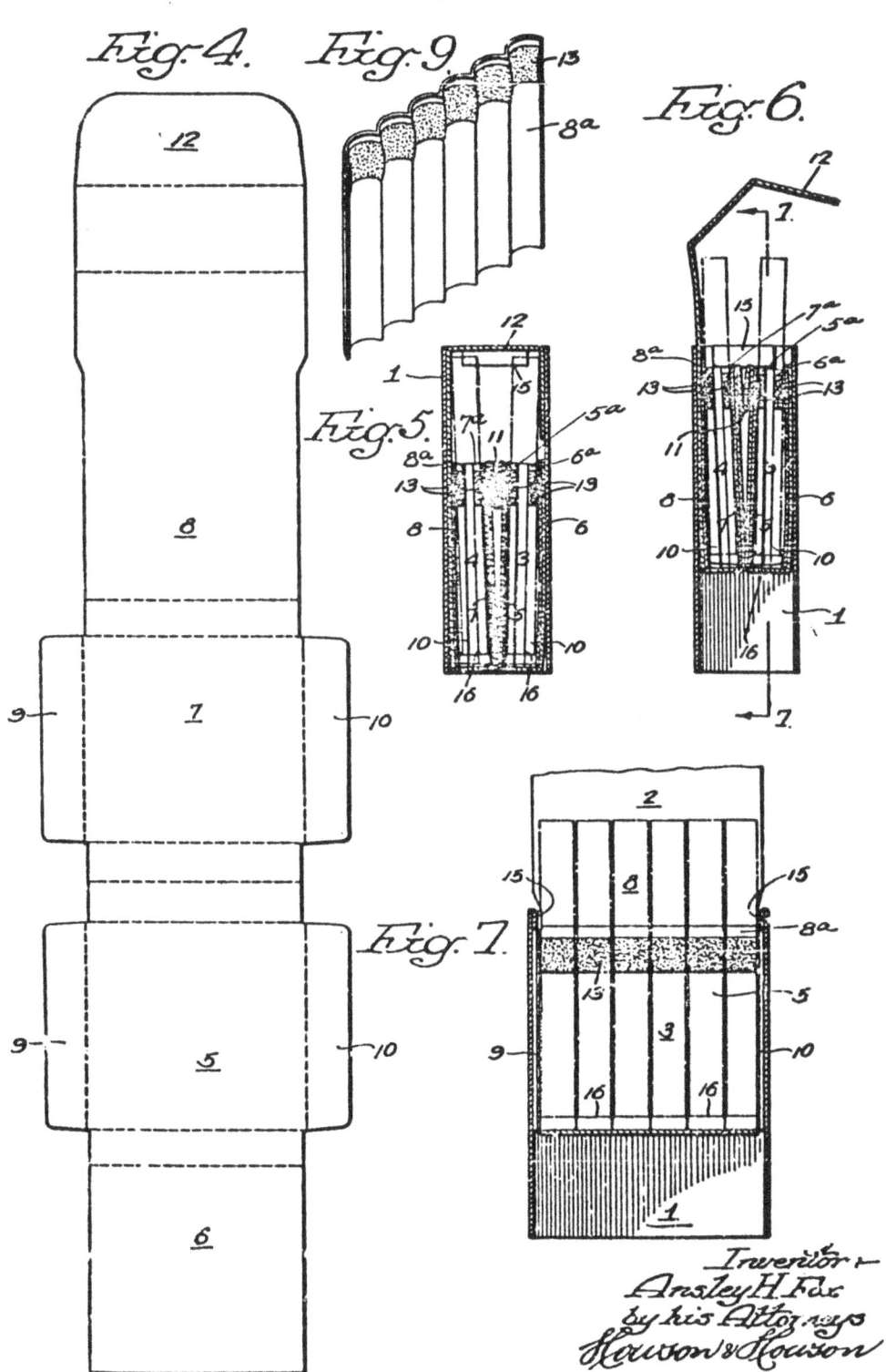

May 12, 1936. A. H. FOX 2,040,733

IGNITION ELEMENT FOR SELF LIGHTING CIGARETTES AND THE LIKE

Filed April 13, 1933

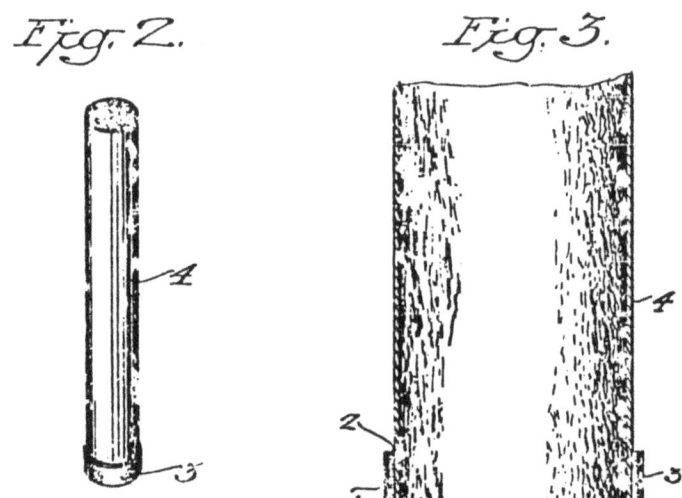

Inventor:
Ansley H. Fox
By his Attorneys
Howson & Howson

history would make horrifyingly clear just two years later when an Austrian housepainter named Hitler became Chancellor of Germany.

The Eighteenth Amendment to the Constitution of the United States, the Prohibition amendment, was repealed on December 5, 1933. We don't know how Ansley Fox felt about that, but in July 1936 he was one of several local citizens to protest when Roy Walsh, owner of a clam stand on Pleasantville Boulevard, announced that he would petition the Egg Harbor Township Committee for a license to sell liquor. According to a July 23 story in the *Press*, "Ansley H. Fox, famous firearms inventor...assailed the move yesterday stating: 'West Atlantic City is a place for men, their wives and children—not saloons. If persons living in West Atlantic City want to buy a drink, and I am not condemning them, they can go to Pleasantville, a drive of two or three minutes, or to Atlantic City. I am wholeheartedly against saloons in this beautiful residential section.'"

Thanks to the kindness of two people, I have an unusually good picture of Ansley Fox as he was in the mid-1930s. One is Millie Gerou's younger sister, who lived with the Gerous as a young girl of thirteen or fourteen and to whom Ellen Fox seems to have taken a particular shine. She remembers Ansley Fox as a friendly, soft-spoken man who wore a hearing aid, a man who dressed well and exhibited a refined demeanor. The Foxes, she told me, kept a dog and a cat as pets, both of whom were quite fond of Ansley Fox.

James Kelly's college roommate introduced him to Ansley Fox about 1935. "Fox was a dead ringer for the old movie star Guy Kibbee," Mr. Kelly wrote to me, "a sight to see as he climbed into his air-cooled Fox car.

"He was an unquenchable enthusiast who had done his homework, with a feeling of youth about him despite white-rimmed baldness and comfortable paunch. He had an endless supply of anecdotes, was always good company as he leaned back in his rubicundness, cigar in hand, always verging on laughter. Fox looked like the sort of successful executive for whom life has been a thoroughly enjoyable experience, exactly the mellow prototype of people one used to see behind the plate glass windows of the New York University Club on Fifth Avenue. Born promoters, all."

A promoter, indeed, and neither the gun nor the automobile nor the auto parts nor real estate were the whole of it. In July 1930, the U.S. Department of Internal Revenue, as it was then called, announced that Americans had bought and smoked one billion more cigarettes than they had the previous year, noting that cigarettes had become the most popular way of smoking tobacco since the rolling machine was invented in 1881. That struck Ansley Fox as an opportunity of some sort, and presently his busy mind zeroed in on just what sort.

May 14, 1940.   A. H. FOX   2,200,420
MACHINE FOR ATTACHING IGNITION BANDS TO CIGARETTES
Filed Oct. 27, 1936   3 Sheets-Sheet 1

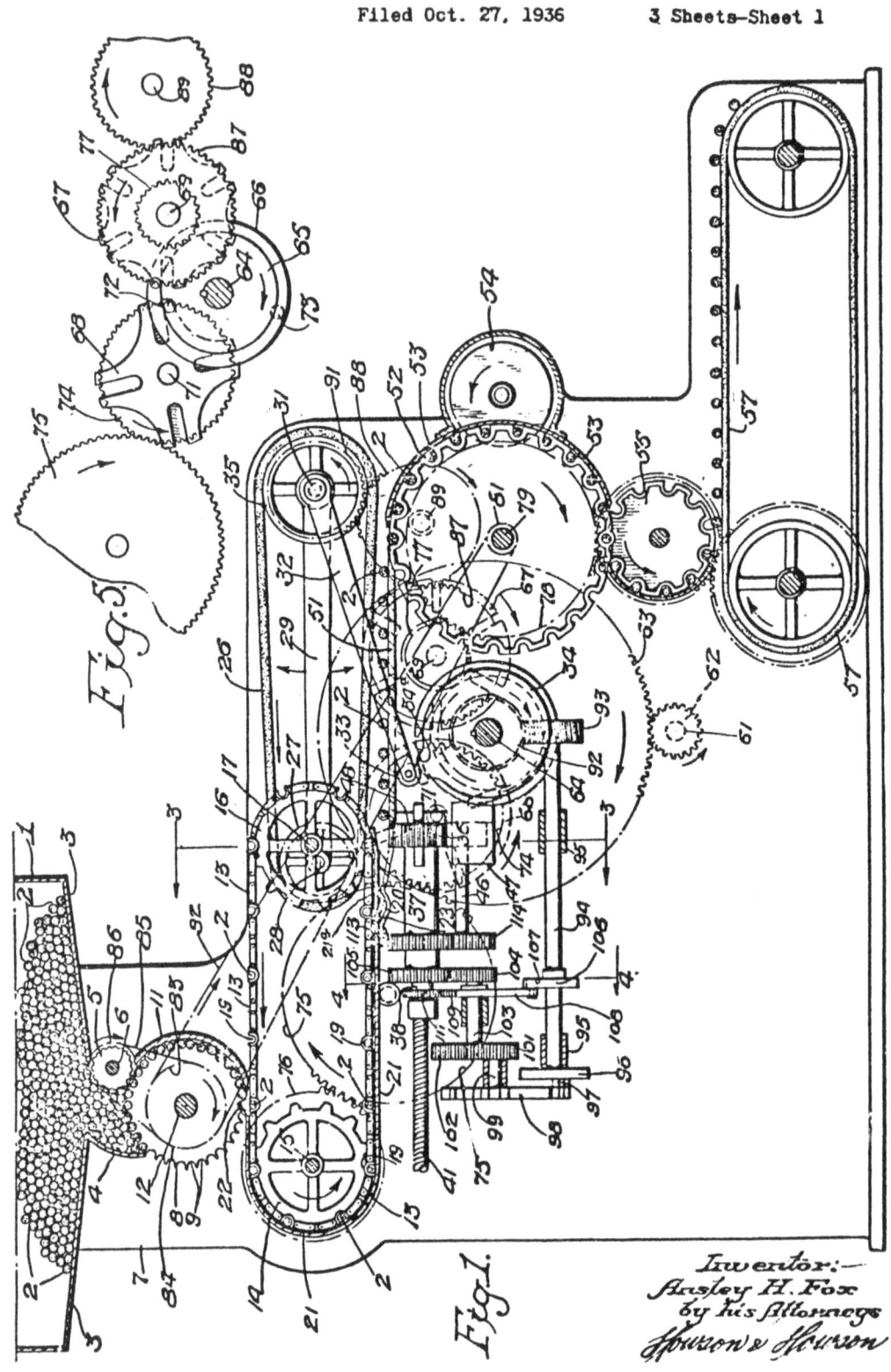

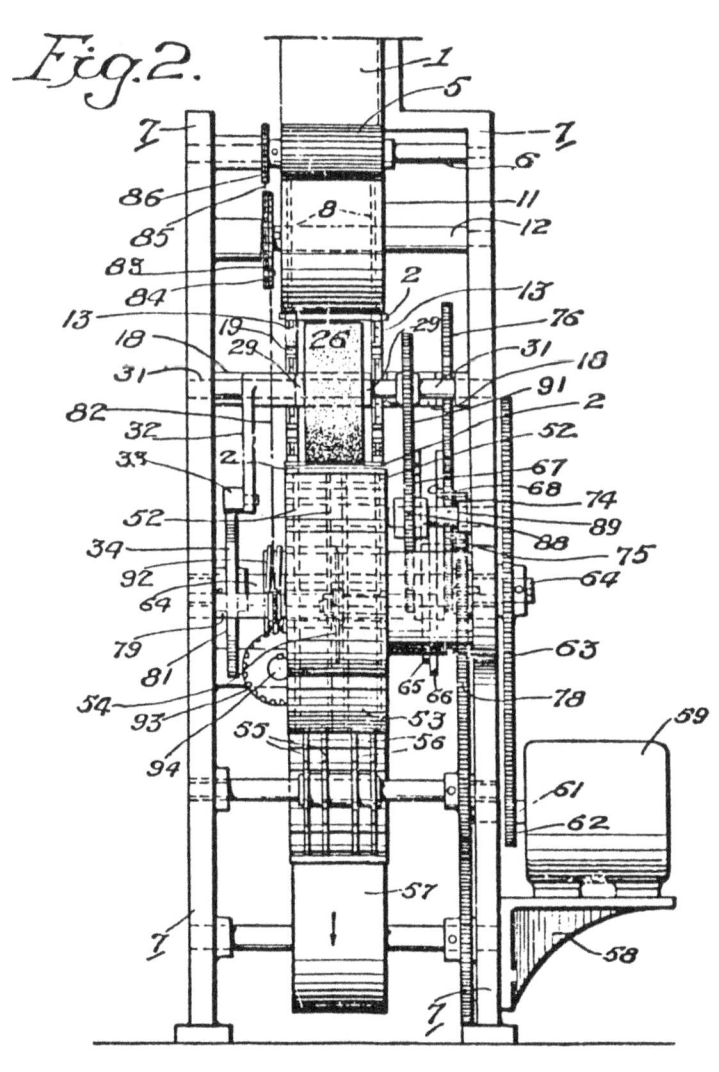

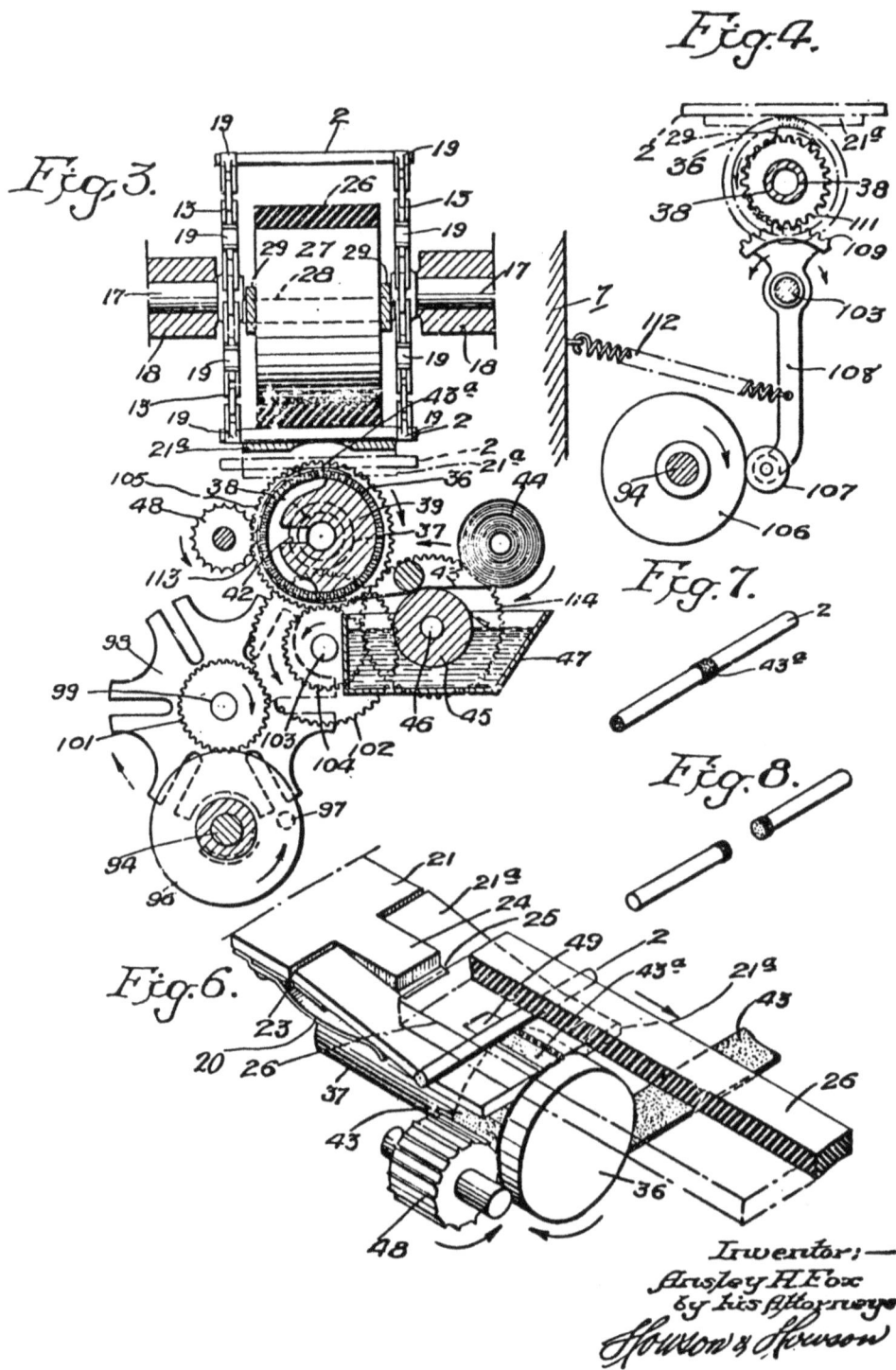

The cigarette itself didn't leave much room for improvement, but what about means of lighting it? George Blaisdell would have a similar notion in 1932, and his solution was the Zippo lighter. Ansley Fox's was a cigarette with its own lighter attached. Naturally, he sought to patent the idea, with an application filed April 21, 1930; the U.S. government agreed that it was indeed a novel idea and awarded patent No. 1,836,312 on December 15, 1931. Fox assigned it to the Self Lighting Cigarette Corporation of America.

The patent papers describe a cap that could be fastened to the tip of cigarette. Across the top of the cap is "an integral bridge piece carrying a coating on its underside of any suitable combustible or inflammable material, such as is commonly used in the head of a safety match," and this is fitted with a paper pull-strip coated with some "frictional material." Pull the strip, the combustible chemical ignites, and all the smoker has to do is drag away. It was, he thought, the perfect item for smoking on a windy day, at an outdoor sporting event, or while motoring in an open car.

William Gerou, ever faithful, was one of Fox's chief testers during the R&D phase, and the word in his family has it that getting the cigarettes to ignite was one thing but keeping them lit quite another. Considering that the first drag would be full of sulfur fumes, I'm not really surprised.

The more Ansley Fox thought it over, the more convinced he was that he could do better. On April 13, 1933, he applied for patent protection on a whole new approach. In this one the tip of a cigarette is wrapped with a "fuse band" comprising a mixture of powdered glass, dichromate of potash, manganese dioxide, chlorate of potash, sulfur, and powdered hickory wood. Then he designed a container to hold each cigarette with a slight pressure on the fuse-band end and filed patent application for that on May 24, 1933.

The Patent Office took a bit longer to digest these, first issuing a patent for the container (No. 2,006,591) on July 2, 1935, and finally for the fuse band itself (No. 2,040,733) on May 12, 1936.

As the final step, Ansley Fox designed a machine to attach the bands to the cigarettes. He applied for the patent October 27, 1936, but protection was not awarded until May 14, 1940, as patent No. 2,200,420.

All three patents were assigned to the Inventions Holding Corporation.

To capitalize, promote, and market the product, Fox proposed that he, Carl Dellmuth, and a third party set up a company called the Triune Corporation. Carl Dellmuth brought in James Kelly. "We all had stock," Mr. Kelly wrote, "and a supply of the product for demonstration in cigar-store display windows. The big tobacco and match companies were watching our experiments, we needing only one percent of tobacco grown in the U.S. to enjoy untold wealth.

WAR DEPARTMENT
OFFICE OF THE CHIEF OF ORDNANCE
WASHINGTON, D. C.

13 September 1945

Mr. Denis McCormack, President
Fox Munitions Corp.
21st Street and Arch
Philadelphia, Pa.

Dear Mr. McCormack:

    At this time of final victory it is my desire to express my sincere appreciation to you and all of your associates and employees for the part which you played in producing Ordnance equipment for our fighting men.

    The production record which you achieved throughout the war was, I am sure, only the result of the extra effort put forth for many months by your entire organization.

    The armed forces thank you for helping to keep them supplied with the very best weapons and equipment. May I personally thank you for a job well done, for your fine cooperation with us, as a member of our Industry-Ordnance team, and your contribution to our great victory.

Sincerely yours,

L. H. CAMPBELL, JR.
Lieutenant General, Chief of Ordnance

"I wish," he concluded, "I had saved one of the hand-made boxes with the self-lighting cigarettes and a handsome stock certificate to go with it, but alas, they never made it beyond the arrival of World War II." I wish so, too, just so I could look to see if "The Finest Cigarette in the World" is mentioned anywhere.

When Europe once again erupted in war, Ansley Fox responded by organizing the Fox Munitions Company, offices at 21st Street and Arch, Philadelphia. I don't know exactly what sort of ordnance equipment the company supplied; the pertinent correspondence is scattered throughout the Ordnance Office's records in the National Archives, and since the whole matter is at best peripheral to the interest of this book, I'll leave that for some other researcher to tackle. Whatever the Fox Munitions contribution was, it apparently was brought off well, for the company earned a letter of citation, dated September 13, 1945, from Lieutenant General L.H. Campbell, Jr., Chief of Ordnance, thanking Fox Munitions president Denis McCormack for "your fine co-operation...and your contribution to our great victory."

It was well that the last company to bear his name should be so recognized. For Ansley Fox, not many victories remained ahead.

SPE Skeet & Upland Game, 20-gauge WILLIAM W. HEADRICK

19

SAVAGE YEARS

By the last days of 1929, the American economy was crumbling. The paper markets—stocks, bonds, and the like—were a shambles, and the aftershocks of the collapse were only beginning. Ultimately, no commercial endeavor would remain unaffected.

The gun industry kept its balance for a while and then took a dreadful beating. Between 1931 and 1933, the total value of all its products declined by thirteen percent, or about $1.4 million. The market for double guns collapsed almost altogether, and the number of doubles built in the United States fell from nearly 40,000 in 1931 to fewer than 8000 in 1933.

In announcing the acquisition of Fox, Savage promotional sales manager W.D. Higgins said, "By including the Fox gun in the products of the Savage Arms Corporation, it is now in a position, directly and through its subsidiaries, to supply a sporting arm for every purpose." True to its word, the company almost immediately set about adapting the Fox to every possible niche in the market and promoting the guns with great vigor. Its first Fox retail catalogue is a strikingly handsome thing, with a full-color Lynn Bogue Hunt duck-shooting scene appliqued on black cover stock; Savage would use the same format, with a few changes inside, through 1934. (Savage was not, however, inclined to waste money, and you'll sometimes run across a 1928-1929 A.H. Fox Gun Company catalogue that was overstamped with the Savage Arms name and address or with a Savage sticker applied over the Philadelphia address on the front cover.)

Savage Arms issued its first Fox catalogue in 1930, featuring cover art by Lynn Bogue Hunt, and used the same design until 1935.

WILLIAM W. HEADRICK

The Sterlingworth remained the best-selling Fox gun throughout the Depression

Savage clearly started off with the intention of preserving—and enhancing—all the prestige the Fox gun had earned over the previous twenty-odd years, and deciding how best to express its own role in regard to the Fox evidently took some time. This, I suspect, explains the barrel stamp that appears on a few guns built during the transition period, most likely in the last few weeks of 1929 or very early in 1930: "BUILT FOR SAVAGE ARMS CORP BY A.H. FOX GUN CO." These guns probably were either the last built in Philadelphia or the first in Utica. Savage presently settled on billing itself as the manufacturer of A.H. Fox guns, and from the beginning of 1930 on, language to that effect is used in the advertising and other printed matter.

Savage issued a price list of its own in 1930, dated January 2, and with one exception, it is identical to the list Fox Gun Company put out the year before. All prices are the same, including the GE Grade at $1026. It would be the GE's last appearance. The exception is that the 1930 list marks the first appearance of the Sterlingworth DeLuxe, which is simply the standard Sterlingworth with a rubber recoil pad and two Lyman ivory beads. At $39.50, it sold for $3 more than the standard model. Whether it was a change that Fox Gun Company had planned before the sale or whether the DeLuxe was solely a Savage idea is impossible to tell, but it was soon evident that Savage had more than a few new ideas for the Fox gun.

In 1930, the company made two additions to the Fox line, which appear for the first time in the catalogue of 1931. The Sterlingworth DeLuxe Ejector simply adds the DeLuxe features to the Sterlingworth Ejector, which had been part of the line for twenty years. At $51.50, it was the most expensive of the four Sterlingworth models, whose prices began at $36.50 for the basic gun.

A short digression here, for the sake of clarity: Even to a greater extent than A.H. Fox Gun Company had done, Savage Arms took pains to present the various Fox guns as separate entities, which is sound marketing and good salesmanship. But it also tends to blur the distinction between model and grade. Strictly speaking, finish and decoration, not accessory-type features, are primarily what distinguish one grade from another. All the various Sterlingworths—the Brush, Trap, Ejector and others from early days, as well as the DeLuxe and those that followed—really are models of the same grade. They're all Sterlingworths, just as the SPE and SPR are different models of SP Grade—even though they appear in the catalogues and price lists as SPE Grade and SPR Grade. For a quick reference to which are the grades and which the models, see Appendix III.

Now, with that said, we come to the Skeeter, which Savage introduced in the 1931 catalogue and which truly was a new grade of Fox. It was an appeal to the growing interest in the still relatively new game of skeet. As the 1931 catalogue puts it: "To the famous Fox Double has been added a scientifically

A. H. FOX GUNS

THE FOX VENTILATED RIB

FURNISHED as an "Extra" on any Fox Double Gun except Sterlingworth and Sterlingworth DeLuxe Grades. The Fox ventilated rib is the latest development in the double gun field. It provides a perfect sighting plane and eliminates glare and heat waves.

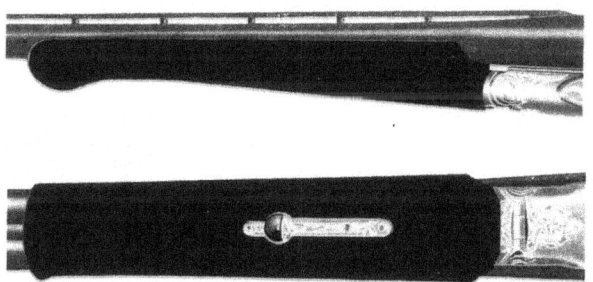

THE FOX ENGLISH TYPE BEAVERTAIL FOREND

FURNISHED as an "Extra" on any Fox Double Gun except Sterlingworth and Sterlingworth DeLuxe Grades. The Fox English Type Beavertail Forend is perfectly proportioned, fits the grip and affords absolute protection to the hand. It is particularly adapted to skeet shooting and to field use.

THE FOX TRAP STYLE BEAVERTAIL FOREND

THE Fox Trap Style Beavertail Forend is built on somewhat fuller proportions than the English type forend and is particularly adapted to trapshooting.

Vent rib and beavertail fore-ends for Fox doubles first appeared in catalogues in 1930.

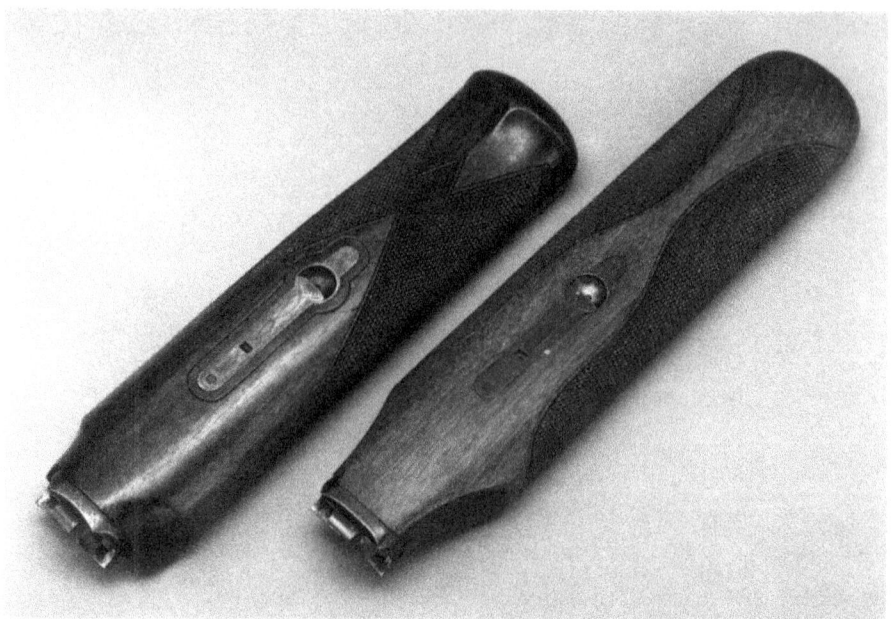
Two of the various Fox beavertail designs – trap (left) and skeet. WILLIAM W. HEADRICK

correct ventilated rib which gives a perfect sighting plane and eliminates glare and heat waves. Regularly equipped with a beaver-tail forend, soft rubber recoil pad and ivory bead sights." Since the second shot in skeet doubles is the incoming target and therefore taken at closer range than the first, the Skeeter was bored improved-modified in the right barrel and improved-cylinder in the left. It sold for $108 in 1931, available in 12- and 20-gauge only and only with 28-inch barrels.

As I mentioned in a previous chapter, the vent rib on the double guns is not the same as the one on the single trap. Although the Fox Gun Company reportedly built some vent-rib doubles in the late 1920s, the rib did not become a catalogue item until the beginning of Savage ownership. Thereafter, it was available as an extra on any grade of gun except the various Sterlingworths, the SP, and SPE. (Savage briefly offered an SP with a vent rib and called it SPR, but I'll come to that presently.)

Like the rib, the beavertail fore-end reportedly existed in the late '20s, but it wasn't listed in catalogues until Savage took over. All told, the Fox beavertails came in at least five different designs, from scarcely larger than a fat splinter-type to some that are very wide indeed. A couple were made with a distinct, rather bulbous schnabel tip. The Skeeter version is what Savage called the "English type" beavertail, fairly flat, wide at the rear, and schnabel'ed at the front. The Trap style is a somewhat larger version of the "English-type" skeet. The Field version is slimmer.

From 1930 through 1933, the beavertail was available on graded guns only. It was added as an option for the SP and SPE in 1934, and for the SP Skeet and Sterlingworth Skeet in 1935. From 1937 on, you could have a beavertail on any Fox gun from Sterlingworth to FE.

By the early 1930s, the 2 $^3/_4$-inch cartridge case was standard throughout the ammunition industry. In the Philadelphia years, standard chambering for Fox guns was a nominal 2 $^5/_8$ inches—although according to Mitzie Bielin, a former Savage Arms employee who until his death in 1992 specialized in repairing Foxes and in supplying factory-original parts, the reamers actually were 2 $^9/_{16}$ inches. The 1913 and 1914 Fox catalogues say all 12-bore guns would be bored 2 $^3/_4$ inches, but this never came to pass as a factory standard.

This of course does not mean that every Philadelphia Fox was so bored, because any chambering from 2 $^1/_2$ to three inches was available upon request, and 2 $^3/_4$-inch chambers always were standard for the Super-Fox. Nonetheless, the typical Philadelphia Fox did leave the factory with chambers 2 $^5/_8$ inches.

I've been told that Savage Arms began boring new Fox guns to 2 $^3/_4$ inches immediately, but there is evidence to suggest that this may not be true. Quite a few work-order cards from the 1930s specify 2 $^3/_4$-inch chambers, but a great many do not. So I have to wonder: If the longer chambers were standard, why mention

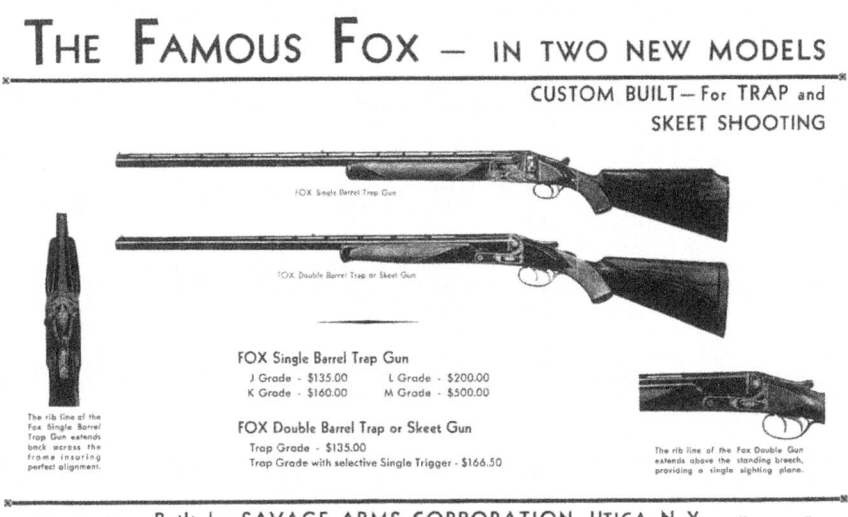

Savage Arms trap guns brochure, 1932

them? I have a notion they didn't actually become factory-standard until mid-decade or thereabouts.

Eventually, Philadelphia Foxes received at Savage for repair were rebored to 2 3/4 inches as a matter of course and were stamped accordingly. I don't know exactly when this policy was inaugurated, but I suspect it wasn't until the early 1960s. A factory-issued list of repair prices from 1956 simply offers rechambering as an option. By 1965, however, it was Savage's policy to put every Philadelphia Fox through a barrel-wall-thickness test and, if it passed, to rebore the chambers if they hadn't been already and proof-test the gun (at owner's risk, of course). From these and earlier days, you'll see some older Foxes with 2 3/4" heavily stamped on them—and not always on the barrel flats nor even under the fore-end.

That a lot of Philadelphia guns are still out there digesting 2 3/4-inch cartridges through 2 5/8-inch chambers is no cause for alarm. Even in the old days of thick paper cases and rough felt wads, an eighth-inch difference did not promote any great spike in chamber pressure, and now, with thin-mouthed plastic cases and slick poly wads, the rise in pressure is scarcely noticeable. If your Fox shooter still has short chambers, any good gunsmith can deepen them in just a few minutes; except in very lightweight pieces or guns whose barrels have been restruck or rebored, there should be plenty of steel to accommodate 2 3/4-inch

The only Trap Grade Fox ever built in 20-gauge. It was used for exhibition at the 1932 Grand American.

WILLIAM W. HEADRICK

Trap grade 20-bore   WILLIAM W. HEADRICK

The SUPER-FOX GUN

Made in 12 and 20 Gauge

Design—Description   Ballistics and Pattern
Range and Power
Grade, Measurements and Price

A. H. FOX GUNS
Manufactured by
Savage Arms Corporation
Utica. N. Y., U. S. A.

Savage Arms Super-Fox brochure, published in the early 1930s, an extremely rare publication

A. H. FOX GUNS

THE FOX SELECTIVE SINGLE TRIGGER

THE simplest and strongest single trigger ever built. Because of new patent sear block, it Cannot Double. There is no part that can wear or break and it will always operate as intended and will never Balk. There is no creep possible. It has forced release properly timed for second shot which can be felt even through a heavy glove. It is perfectly selective at all times and when one barrel only is fired and gun reloaded, trigger returns to original barrel without attention from the shooter. The only single trigger with Automatic Safety. Fitted to any Fox gun, new or old.

THE FOX GUN BUILT TO ORDER

MANY sportsmen prefer to have their guns built to order, so that they may obtain a more perfect "fit." We have always built guns to order on all grades except the Sterlingworth, at no extra charge. In the higher grades, however, we build guns to numerous specifications to enable us as far as possible to fill orders promptly, but whenever the purchaser will allow us the necessary time (7 to 12 weeks) on an order we are always glad to build a gun to his own requirements and take special pride in filling the most exacting specifications. Any jobber or dealer handling Fox Guns, submitting their order to us in detail, will be promptly advised as to whether we can fill it from our large stock, or if it will have to be built to order and just when it can be delivered. Bear this in mind when ordering a Fox and allow for the time which will probably be necessary to build the gun. Don't forget that you are doing the factory a kindness and avoiding a chance of being disappointed if you get your order in early.

From the beginning, Savage Arms Fox catalogues mention the single trigger's redesigned sear block and offer guns built to customer specifications.

Announcing—
the New FOX Double
With single trigger...

"FOX SPECIAL" SP Grade

Retail Price $50

FOR a generation, purchasers of fine sporting arms have chosen Savage and Fox products because they are "extra value." This extra value was never more pronounced than now, never better exemplified than in these three NEW Savage-Fox models.

Fox Shotguns and Savage Rifles are bridging the wide gap between the best custom-built sporting arms and the modest purse... each year are widening your range of customers, and securing for you added profits.

In the new "FOX SPECIAL" double, Fox gun builders have realized their ideal and fulfilled the wants of *your* customers for a Fox Grade Double Barrel Shotgun *equipped with single trigger* to sell at a moderate price. This new model justifies the title "Priceless, but not high priced."

Specifications:
"Fox Special" SP Grade

High quality fluid steel barrels, proof-tested and guaranteed for shooting qualities.

Forged ordnance steel frame—streamline—black gun-metal finish.

Oil finished stock of selected walnut. Nicely checkered. Special fore-end.

Non-selective single trigger—simple in design and positive in operation.

Built in 12, 16, and 20 gauges—all standard barrel lengths and borings.

SP Grade without single trigger—$45.00 Retail.

A. H. FOX SHOTGUNS *Manufactured by*
SAVAGE ARMS CORPORATION, UTICA, NEW YORK

Announcement of the "Fox Special" or SP Grade, 1932

chambers without creating a thin spot in the barrel walls. A competent gunsmith will measure the walls before he reams, anyway.

In its original form and under its original name, the Skeeter Grade was short-lived, appearing in the wholesale catalogue and price lists only in 1931. In fact, none of the factory literature I've seen shows a true Skeeter engraving style at all. For some reason, Savage chose gun No. 450001 as the catalogue illustration—but No. 450001 is an A Grade with vent rib and beavertail. The true Skeeter's engraving is completely different from any of the A Grade designs. The Skeeter is done up in scroll that's a sort of hybrid between what you'll see on a first-generation B Grade and what's on a J Grade single trap. As my pal Headrick says, it's "scroll with lots of hairy tails on it."

No one knows exactly how many were built—and so far as I know, none was actually marked "Skeeter"—but the number undoubtedly is very small. Most of them presumably were 12-bores, since only two 20s have shown up in the records: No. 203622, shipped June 15, 1939, and No. 203623, shipped September 28, 1933. Yet a third, No. 203625, was begun on August 6, 1931, but by the time it was finished, it was no longer a skeet gun at all—and therein lies a tale.

A brief wave of interest in a 20-gauge event rippled through the trapshooting world in the early 1930s, and the gun trade responded by bringing out guns set up in the traditional trap-style configurations—high-combed stocks,

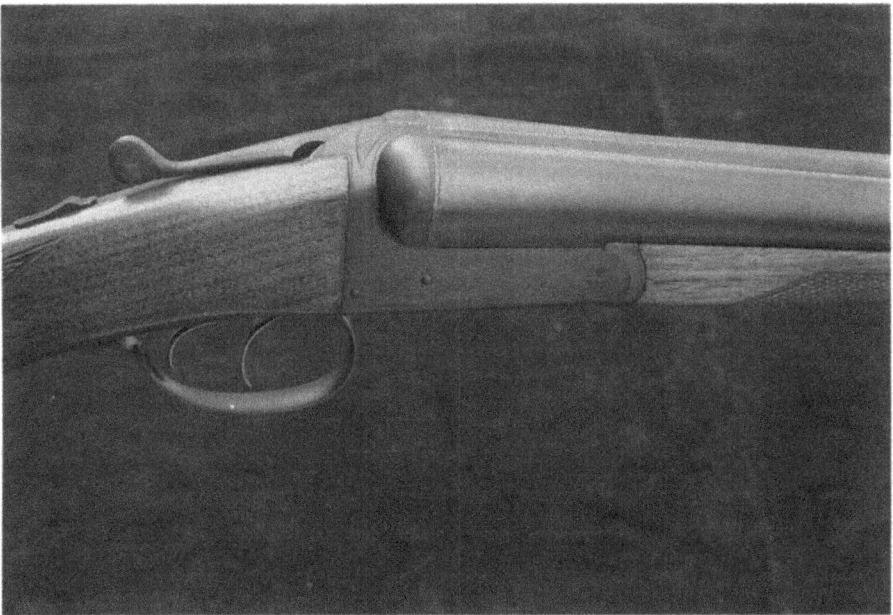

Fox SP Grade   MICHAEL McINTOSH

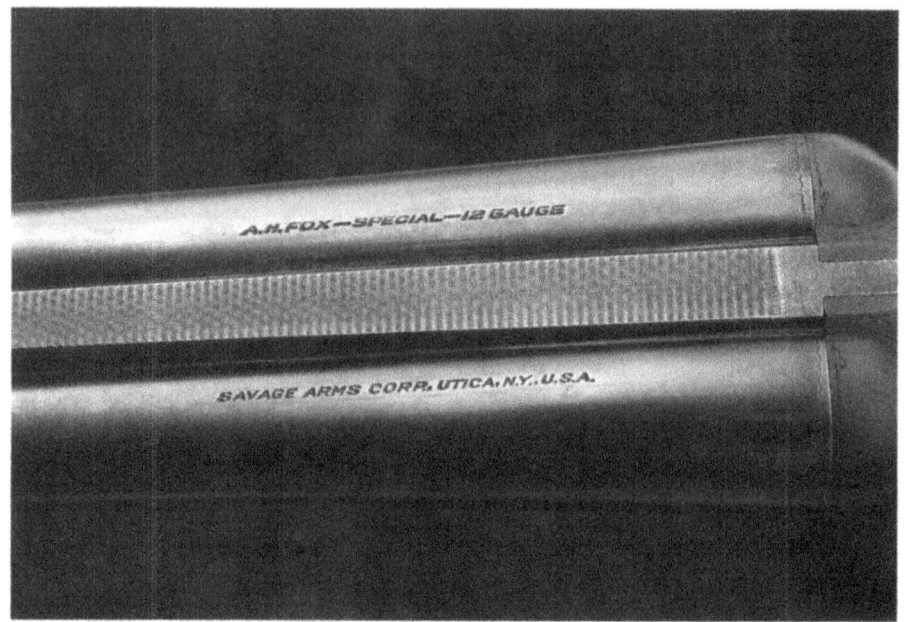

SP Grade barrel stamp. Don't confuse the SP Grade with the Specials discussed in the next chapter.

MICHAEL McINTOSH

vent ribs, beavertail fore-ends, and the like. Toward the end of 1931, Savage executives must have decided that trapshooters offered a larger market, so when the 1932 catalogues appeared, the Skeeter was out and the Trap Grade was in.

Actually, the Trap Grade is the Skeeter under a different name, meant to cover the whole target-shooting market, designed, the wholesale catalogue says, "especially for Trap and Skeet shooting." Now, however, it was available in all three gauges and with four different barrel lengths. Twenty-six- and 28-inch barrels were choked improved-modified and improved-cylinder for skeet, 30- and 32-inch tubes full and full for trap. The skeet guns were stocked to field-gun dimensions and given the skeet-type beavertail. The trap-version stocks are thicker, have higher combs, and the beavertails are the fuller, trap-style designs. Retail price $125 with double triggers, $153.90 with Fox-Kautzky single trigger. (The prices for all grades went up a few dollars in 1932.)

It seems contradictory to speak of a "Trap Grade skeet gun," and perhaps Target Grade would have been a more accurate name. Nonetheless, Trap Grade it was, and it stayed that way for some time, because the Trap Grade remained a catalogue item through 1936.

Trap versions outnumber the skeet guns but not by much, and even at that, Trap Grade Foxes of any sort are mighty scarce. (And as with the Skeeter, none were actually marked with a grade-stamp.) I don't know of any in 16-gauge, and only one 20-bore was built as a trap gun.

Which brings us back to No. 203625, the Trap Grade you see pictured here. As I mentioned earlier, it was planned as a skeet gun for office-sample use, and the work-order is so marked. Presently, however, Savage hatched the Trap Grade notion and changed the specs on 203625 to make it a trap gun that W.D. Higgins would take to the 1932 Grand American for display. So, it was stocked to trap dimensions with a thick, straight hand, given a trap-style beavertail, fitted with a selective single trigger and all the other Trap Grade bells and whistles, and its 28-inch barrels bored modified and full. (Either it had already been actioned with the 28-inch barrels before the change order came through or else Savage didn't settle on using 30- and 32-inch barrels for trap guns until a bit later.)

Like most of the Skeeter and Trap Grade work orders, the card specifies the engraving as "same as HE," even though the actual pattern isn't much like the HE's at all.

SP Grade advertisement, mid-1930s

The little gun was finished and consigned as an office sample on April 29, 1932. It went off to the Grand with Higgins on August 18, was returned to the factory August 29, and remained as an office sample until it was shipped out July 6, 1933, presumably sold. Whoever bought it couldn't have known that it would be the only 20-gauge Trap Grade trap gun ever built.

SPE Skeet & Upland Game Gun, 20-gauge. Fewer than thirty-five SPE Skeet & Upland guns were built as 20-bores.

WILLIAM W. HEADRICK

The Trap Grade's debut wasn't the only change in the Fox line for 1932, nor indeed was it the most far-reaching. By 1931, the economy was still plummeting, and no one knew how deep the bottom would prove to be. Savage had already begun experimenting to see what could be done with the Fox to reduce production cost and still offer a gun the market would find attractive; these experimental pieces were the guns of the fabled 450000 serial-number range, and they probably proved that substantial cost-savings would require some basic changes in the gun itself. The shooting world perceived the Fox gun as having a certain distinctive shape to its frame, as being color-hardened, fitted with Chromox barrels—all the things, in other words, that gave the gun its particular identity.

These things also establish a certain bottom-line level for production cost. Simply devising a new grade of the same basic gun could not, the Savage people saw, change that base-level cost—but a new model could. Taking a cue from Winchester, which advertised the Model 21 for the first time in January 1931, Savage changed its focus from merely tinkering with grades to rethinking the Fox gun itself—not with an eye to scrapping the original design altogether, which would have been counter-productive where the market was concerned, but

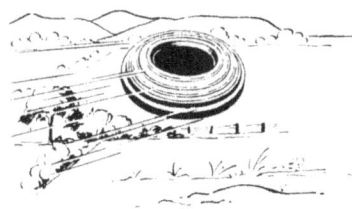

A. H. FOX GUNS

A. H. FOX HAMMERLESS DOUBLE GUNS
12 GAUGE   16 GAUGE   20 GAUGE

FOX SP GRADE SKEET AND UPLAND GAME GUN

THE FOX SP GRADE Skeet and Upland Game Gun is an arm with black gun-metal finish frame, handsomely engraved; imported walnut stock and forearm with fine mesh checkering.

The length and boring of barrels are correct for use on quail, partridges, woodcock and other upland game birds at ranges up to 35 yards. These specifications are also correct for skeet shooting.

BARRELS—Chromox fluid steel, 26″. Bored: right barrel, skeet cyl., left barrel quarter choke. Two ivory bead sights.
FRAME—Forged ordnance steel. Stream line. Black gun-metal finish.
ENGRAVING—Scroll work on frame and barrels.
ACTION—Two trigger, extractor type.
STOCK—Selected walnut in hand rubbed oil finish. Straight grip. handsomely checkered. Length 14″, drop at comb 1½″, at heel 2½″. Checkered walnut butt.
FOREND—Semi-beavertail, handsomely checkered.
WEIGHT—12 gauge, about 7 lbs. 16 gauge, about 6 lbs. 20 gauge, about 5¾ lbs.

The following "Extras" are furnished to order on the Fox SP Grade: Automatic Ejectors, Fox-Kautzky Selective Single Trigger, Full Beavertail Forend, Recoil Pad, Ivory Bead Sights.

From the 1935 catalogue

A rare 20-gauge SPE Skeet & Upland Game Gun WILLIAM W. HEADRICK

rather to come up with something more economical to produce while still essentially, recognizeably Fox.

The Fox Special or SP was the answer. Savage described it as:

> A double gun of Fox quality down to the minutest detail. The smooth action, uniform patterns, ease of handling you naturally associate with every Fox Gun—and in addition a non-selective single trigger that means faster, more accurate shooting—all this in the "Fox Special" SP Grade Double, setting a new standard of value.

The 1932 wholesale catalogue shows the SP available in 12, 16, and 20 gauges with "high quality fluid steel" barrels 26 to 32 inches. The frame is "forged ordanance steel. Stream line. Black gun-metal finish." The stock is American walnut with a capped pistol grip and the fore-end of "special design." It sold for $45 with two triggers, for $50 with a non-selective single. The same gun with ejectors, designated SPE Grade, cost $57 and $62, depending upon the trigger arrangement you chose.

Mechanically, the SP is no different from the classic Fox. The frame, however, is squarer, boxier—not as graceful as the original but not unhandsome, either. Surely, though, it was simpler to machine, and economy is the key to all the SP differences—American-made barrels rather than the more expensive Chromox (and the supply of Chromox blanks was about to run out, anyway), American walnut instead of European, the frame blacked rather than case-colored.

The SP's single trigger is the standard Fox-Kautzky with the selector mechanism removed, and it cost less than half as much as the selective version. In 1933 and 1934, Savage offered the non-selective trigger as an option for any grade of Fox. It did not, however, prove very popular, and you can look a very long time before you find a graded gun that has one. It's rare enough even on an SP.

All told, the SP Fox was one of the best gun values available at the time. With ejectors and single trigger, it cost $66.50, which was $15 less than a similarly set-up Model 21. In February 1933, *The National Sportsman* called the SP "a 'British' double gun for $50," remarking that "the Fox-Savage Co. has slipped something over on the gun trade with this double gun of theirs at $50 for the single trigger model, by offering to the shooter a gun built on the beautiful lines of the highest grade British guns such as the Westley Richards."

A bit extreme, this (and the $50 price was for the double-trigger version, not the single), but not altogether unjustified; the typical English boxlock is even more square-framed than the SP Fox, and while never so well-finished as a British

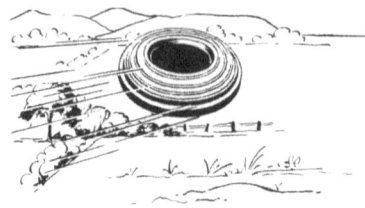

A. H. FOX HAMMERLESS DOUBLE GUNS
12 GAUGE   16 GAUGE   20 GAUGE

STERLINGWORTH SKEET AND UPLAND GAME GUN

TO meet the demand for a moderately priced skeet and upland game double gun we have produced the famous Fox-Sterlingworth gun in this new straight grip model with 26″ barrels bored: right, skeet cyl., left quarter choke. This is a standard stock model possessing the features of skeet boring and stock design heretofore available only in custom-built guns.

BARRELS—Fluid compressed steel, 26″ length; boring, right barrel, skeet cyl.; left barrel quarter choke.

STOCK—American walnut, straight grip. Length 14″, drop at comb 1½″, drop at heel 2½″.

ENGRAVING—Ornamented with line engraving on frame and guard.

ACTION—Two trigger, extractor type.

WEIGHT—12 gauge about 7 lbs., 16 gauge about 6 lbs., 20 gauge about 5¾ lbs.

The following "Extras" are furnished to order on the Sterlingworth Skeet and Upland Game Gun: Automatic Ejectors, Fox-Kautzky Selective Single Trigger, Beavertail Forend, Recoil Pad, Ivory Bead Sights.

From the 1935 catalogue

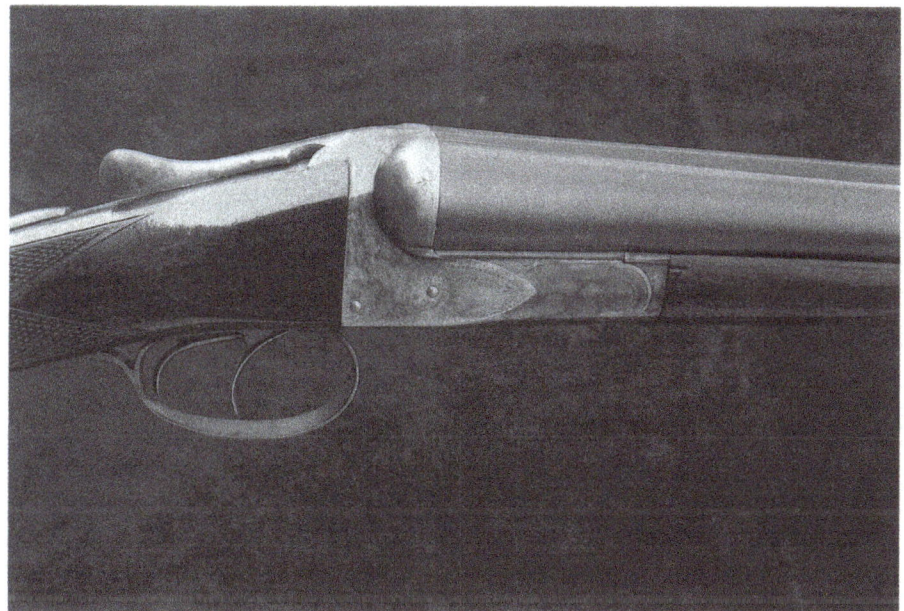

Sterlingworth Skeet & Upland Game Gun, 12-gauge MICHAEL McINTOSH

Art Deco catalogues of the mid-1930s; 1936 edition on top, 1935 underneath. WILLIAM W. HEADRICK

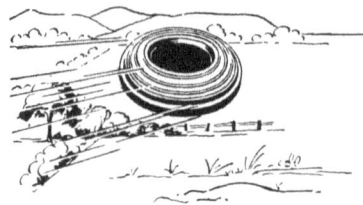

THE FOX MODEL B
12 GAUGE   16 GAUGE   20 GAUGE :: .410 BORE

THE new Fox Model B has the features of light weight, stream-line design, perfect balance and superior shooting qualities which distinguish our other Fox models. Large-volume production, simplification in design and construction and the elimination of costly hand operations enable us to supply this new Fox model at an astonishingly low price.

ACTION—Two trigger, extractor type. Lightning-fast coil spring, hammer and sear design.

BARRELS—Alloy forged steel, proof tested. Chambered for 2¾″ shells, except .410 bore which is chambered for 3″ shells. 12 gauge 26″, 28″ and 30″ barrels; 16 gauge 26″ and 28″ barrels; 20 gauge 26″ and 28″ barrels; .410 bore, 26″ barrels. 26″ barrels are bored cylinder and modified, 28″ and 30″ barrels are bored modified and full, and .410 bore, are both full choke. Other standard borings furnished to order at no extra charge.

STOCK—American walnut, stream-line design. Checkered pistol grip. Fluted comb. Length about 14″; drop at heel about 2¾″. Hard rubber butt plate.

FORE-END—American walnut, checkered.

FRAME—Black gun-metal finish. Shock-proof bolting mechanism which provides positive lock-up.

WEIGHT—12 gauge, 7¼ to 7½ lbs.
          16 gauge, 6¼ to 6½ lbs.
          20 gauge, 6 to 6¼ lbs.
          .410 bore, 5¾ to 6 lbs.

From the 1940 catalogue

best, it was considerably more graceful overall than the early versions of its rival Winchester 21.

The stock has much to do with this, and virtually every gun writer of the period remarked upon the decidedly English appearance of the SP's woodwork. It has that look, E.C. Crossman wrote, because "the Fox-Savage Co. merely hired some high class British gunstockers."

Crossman was right, actually. Savage did hire some English craftsmen in the early '30s. I don't know how many, but I know something about one of them, whose name was Wilfred Wright. None of the Savage old-timers still living are old enough to remember whether he worked at Fox before the acquisition, but they do remember that he was a World War I veteran who was a gunsmith, engraver, and designer and that he worked at Savage for many years. By the end of his career, he was head of the Savage model shop and, as I discussed in Chapter 16, was the man who built the so-called GE grade guns for Herb Stewart. Wright died in the early 1950s.

Actually, the SP stock design does show some British influence in its trim lines, while the fore-end is a sort of hybrid between a splinter and an English beavertail (British English, that is, not the Fox "English-type").

For Savage Arms, the SP idea came along just in the nick of time. As if to top off the effects of a ruined economy, nature seemed to turn against the country as well. Across an enormous swath in the center of the continent, from the Missouri River to the Rockies, from Montana and North Dakota south to the Rio Grande, the rains simply did not come in the early 1930s. Much of the land had been planted to wheat during World War I, and wheat-farming as it was performed in those days left the soil exposed to the mercy of sun, wind, and drought. By 1934, soil from the Great Plains was blowing off the Atlantic coast in huge, dense clouds.

The worst of the Dust Bowl centered in the area where Kansas, Oklahoma, Texas, New Mexico, and Colorado meet, but agriculture and wildlife on the northern Plains suffered as well. Waterfowl could not breed on the desiccated prairies, nor could upland game sustain the numbers it once knew. Over much of the country, the 1930s were not good years in which to be a hunter, to say nothing of a gunmaker.

Although Savage brought out the Sterlingworth Wildfowl model (which, as I discussed more fully in Chapter 15, is the Super-Fox under a different name), target-shooting seemed the only market to offer a measure of salvation, and a target version of the SP Grade was a natural step. It first appears in the factory price list effective March 1, 1934, identified as the "Fox Special" Skeet Grade, available for $92 with two triggers and $115 with a selective single. Unfortunately, the gun does not appear in the text of the 1934 retail catalogue, so I'm not sure what the original specifications were. (The 1934 retail catalogue is a strange piece of goods for several reasons; the Trap Grade is not included, but the Skeeter is, and the Super-Fox page mentions the old guarantee of eighty-percent patterns. On the whole, the 1934 catalogue is seriously at variance with the price lists and some other factory literature, and it is therefore not a reliable historical document.)

In 1934, Savage refined the SP Skeet even further and gave it a new name—SP Grade Skeet and Upland Game Gun—and from that point until the beginning of World War II, it truly did amount to a separate grade, distinct from the standard SP. This was not the case, however, with the Sterlingworth Skeet and Upland Game gun, which also first appeared in the wholesale catalogue and price lists of 1935; it simply was the standard Sterlingworth built with 26-inch barrels of "skeet cylinder" and quarter-choke. It was, however, the only Sterlingworth model available with a straight-hand stock.

The Fox workshops at the Savage Arms factory in Utica, New York   PHOTO COURTESY ROE S. CLARK

According to the catalogue, the SP Skeet and Upland Game was fitted with 26-inch Chromox barrels, bored with the same chokes as the Sterlingworth version. (Twenty-eight-inch barrels were added as an option in 1936.) The Chromox tubes were a good selling point, and Savage may actually have built a few SP Skeet and Uplands with them, but there couldn't have been many. Most of the guns you find now have the standard Savage barrels marked "Special Alloy."

Nonetheless, the SP Skeet and Upland is quite a handsome little gun. It's built on the standard SP frame but treated to a modest amount of nicely cut scroll engraving. A straight-hand stock with checkered butt and a slim beavertail, both shaped from European walnut, were standard, with pistol grip and recoil pad available on request. It was offered in all three gauges, and at a retail price of $70 for the basic, double-trigger extractor version, it was a tremendous value.

By mid-decade, the supply of Chromox barrels was all but gone, and in fact, very few guns were fitted with Chromox tubes after about 1933. The 1936 jobber's catalogue lists all Fox guns, from SP Skeet and Upland Game to FE Grade, as barreled with "special alloy steel."

Savage clearly was not finished experimenting with the SP Skeet and Upland, for the same catalogue lists the SPR Grade Skeet and Upland as a variation. This one came with a vent rib (which I take to be the "R" portion of the grade designation), ejectors, and a selective single trigger—all for $140 retail. Since the 1936 jobber's catalogue and retail price list are the only factory-published documents I've ever seen that even mention the SPR, I can only conclude that the market found it decidedly underwhelming. Among 20-bores, for instance, only four have turned up in the records: No. 203774, shipped March 5, 1936; No. 203826, shipped August 6, 1936; No. 203828, date unknown; and No. 203352, shipped May 12, 1937.

Apart from this, both the SP and the SP Skeet and Upland remained unchanged for the next few years. The Skeet and Upland gun last appears in the catalogues in 1939, and from 1940 through 1946, only the standard SP and SPE grades are listed.

The Sterlingworth Skeet and Upland held out longer, making its last catalogue appearance in 1945. By then, some Sterlingworths had undergone a major design change, the first such change made to the Fox gun in more than twenty years. At some point in the mid-'30s, Savage engineers revised the Sterlingworth frame and stock so that the two could be fastened together with a through-bolt rather than the traditional tang screws. This arrangement saves the stockers considerable time, because it eliminates virtually all need for hand-fitting. It also makes a tight fit between the stock-head and the frame easier to achieve and maintain. Roe Clark tells me that "a few hundred" Sterlingworths

LIST PRICES OF REPAIR PARTS — FOX GUNS (Except Model B)

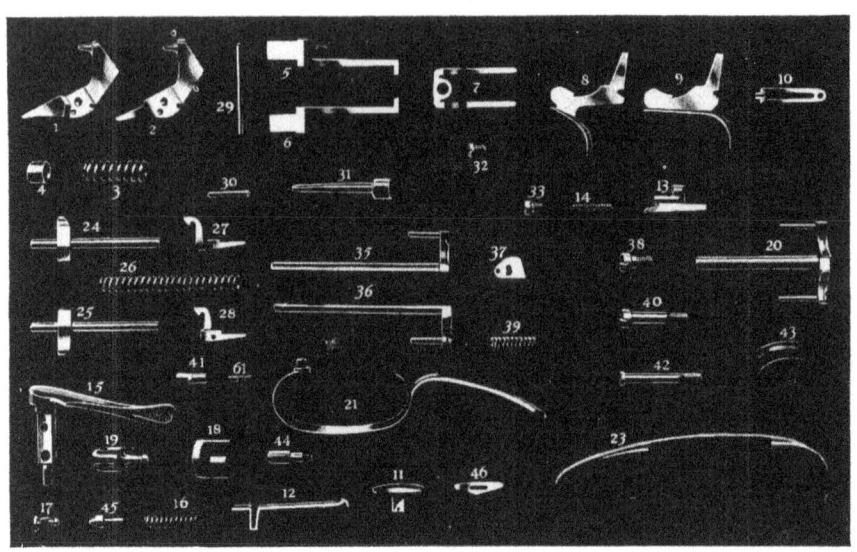

No.	Part	List Price	No.	Part	List Price
1	Hammer, R.	$3.00	25	Ejector Hammer, L.	$1.50
2	Hammer, L.	3.00	26	Ejector Spring	1.00
3	Mainspring	1.35	27	Ejector Sear, L.	1.50
4	Mainspring Follower	.50	28	Ejector Sear, R.	1.50
5	Sear, R.	1.50	29	Hammer & Sear Pin	.20
6	Sear, L.	1.50	30	Ejector Sear Pin	.20
7	Sear Spring	.85	31	Ejector Mainspring Follower	1.00
8	Trigger, R.	1.50	32	Sear Spring Screw	.20
9	Trigger, L.	1.50	33	Cocking Slide Screw	.20
10	Trigger Spring	.50	35	Ejector Extractor, R.	1.50
11	Safety Slide	1.35	36	Ejector Extractor, L.	1.50
12	Safety Spring	.50	37	Ejector Forend Latch	.50
13	Cocking Slide	1.50	38	Trigger Plate Screw	.20
14	Cocking Slide Spring	.45	39	Ejector Forend Latch Spring	.50
15	Top Lever	3.55	40	Front Tang Screw	.50
16	Top Lever Spring	1.00	41	Trip	.50
17	Top Lever Ball Screw	.50	42	Rear Tang Screw	.50
18	Bolt	2.55	43	Grip Cap	.50
19	Yoke	1.50	44	Yoke Screw	.50
20	Extractor	3.00	45	Top Lever Spring Follower	.25
21	Trigger Guard	3.00	46	Safety Tension Spring	.20
23	Butt Plate Straight	1.50	61	Trip Spring	.20
24	Ejector Hammer, R.	1.50		Other Springs, Pins, Screws	.20

All metal parts with exception of a few screws and springs are available in the rough only (unfinished) and therefore should be fitted by a gunsmith or gun returned to the factory for fitting.

Parts and repair price lists, October 1956

RETAIL PRICE LIST OF REPAIR -- FOX GUNS
Effective October 1, 1956

SAVAGE ARMS CORPORATION   CHICOPEE FALLS, MASSACHUSETTS

	Sterl. Worth	Sterl. Worth Ejector	Grade A Grade B Grade SP	Grades A & B & SP Ejector	Grade H Ejector	Grade C Ejector	REMARKS
* Beavertail forend assy. complete	$ 35.00	$ 50.00	$ 43.00	$ 65.00	$ 65.00	$ 65.00	
* Beavertail forend wood only	27.00	30.00	30.00	35.00	35.00	35.00	Note explanation of
* Standard forend assy. complete	25.00	40.00	33.00	55.00	55.00	55.00	the three asterisks.
* Standard forend wood only	17.00	20.00	20.00	25.00	25.00	25.00	
* Extra interchangeable barrels with							Repair to Fox Grade
extra matching forend (standard)	101.50	121.50	118.00	145.00	145.00	175.00	Guns not listed sub-
* Replace barrels using same forend	76.50	81.50	85.00	90.00	90.00	120.00	ject to quotation
* Remove dents and rebrown barrels	18.00	18.00	18.00	18.00	18.00	18.00	after factory in-
Rebrown barrels	10.00	10.00	10.00	10.00	10.00	10.00	spection.
*** OVERHAUL LOCKS (ACTION)	12.50	14.50	12.50	14.50	14.50	14.50	
* Recaseharden frame (refinish)	8.00	8.00	8.00	8.00	8.00	8.00	Time required to
* Butt Stock	39.50	39.50	49.50	49.50	49.50	59.50	complete repairs is
Refinish stock	14.00	14.00	19.00	19.00	19.00	26.00	indefinite and de-
Refinish forend	7.00	7.00	12.00	12.00	12.00	14.00	pends on repairs to
* Cut off or change pitch of stock	10.00	10.00	10.00	10.00	10.00	10.00	be made and if parts
* Change drop of stock 3/8" either way	15.00	15.00	15.00	15.00	15.00	15.00	are immediately
* Convert to Automatic Ejector							available.
including standard forend assy.	52.00		67.00				

* Requires return of the complete gun to the factory
** Can overhaul only if manufactured and fitted by Fox Gun Company or Savage Arms Corporation.
*** IN ADDITION TO REPAIRS REQUESTED OR REQUIRED, ALL GUNS SHIPPED TO THE FACTORY WILL BE SUBJECT TO LISTED CHARGE FOR OVERHAULING ACTION PLUS COST OF ANY MAJOR ACTION PART REPLACED.

* Furnish & fit Selective Single Trigger	$70.00	Extra for Monte Carlo stock	$20.00
* Convert single to double triggers	35.00	Recoil pad and fitting	8.00
* Reverse triggers	5.00	*Pattern gun	5.00
Remove dents without rebrowning per		Fit Ivory Sights per pair	2.75
barrel tube	4.40	*Fit safety to "no safe" gun	10.00
Cut off barrels, remuzzle and resight	8.40	Resolder ribs and rebrown barrels	14.50
Change choke per barrel tube	4.20	**Extra to overhaul gun with single trigger	5.00
Repolish both barrel tubes (inside)	8.40	Rechamber barrels for 2 3/4" shells and	
Extra for cast-off stock	20.00	proof test at owner's risk	7.00

Prices are f.o.b Chicopee Falls. All guns repaired at factory subject to $2.50, inspection/packing/handling charge. Authorization to proceed with repairs will constitute acceptance of delivery status. Suggest shipping to factory via insured parcel post or railway express prepaid.

ORIGINAL BARRELS AND FOREND must be included with shipment when gun is returned for fitting extra set. When fitting extra or replacement barrels, the customer should specify chokes desired.

were built on this new design, all in 12-gauge. A similar change was planned for the 20-bore but never put into regular production.

From its all-time low in 1932, the Depression economy slowly improved until 1937, when the Dow-Jones average slipped back to where it was at the beginning of 1935. By the middle of 1938, it was on the rise again, but the whole economy remained sluggish. German expansionism under Adolph Hitler was a growing cause for alarm. They were still not hopeful times in which to be a gunmaker. By 1939, production of Fox guns was at a virtual standstill. Savage had one last card to play, and it appeared in the catalogues and price lists of 1940, called the Model B, available in 12, 16 and 20 gauges and in .410-bore. The 1940 retail catalogue has this to say:

> *The new Fox Model B has the features of light weight, stream-line design, perfect balance and superior shooting qualities which distinguish our other Fox models. Large-volume production and the*

elimination of costly hand-operations enable us to supply this new Fox model at an astonishingly low price.

At $25.75 a copy, the price was low enough, but the Model B is a Fox in name only. Actually, it's a version of the old Stevens Model 311 double that was first manufactured in 1931. (Savage had owned Stevens since 1920.)

Little as it has to do with the real history of Fox, I confess that there's a soft spot in my heart for both the 311 and the Model B—since the first double gun I ever owned was a 20-bore Model 311, followed a year later by a 20-gauge Model B. With the Model B, which is one of the few guns I ever bought new, I felt I had arrived. My father, who thought doubles were pretty but couldn't imagine why anybody would want one when he could have a pump gun, felt I had taken leave of my senses. Considering how double guns have shaped my life since, he was right, in a way—but that's another story.

By 1940, the curtain was starting to come down anyway. The German invasion of Poland on September 1, 1939, was truly the beginning of the end for the Fox gun. The 1940 price list shows the Model B; the Sterlingworth in Standard, Ejector, Wildfowl, DeLuxe, DeLuxe Ejector, Skeet and Upland Game, and Ejector Skeet and Upland Game versions; the SP and SPE; and grades A, AE, HE, CE, XE, DE, and FE. No single trap guns are listed at all. The Sterlingworth Wildfowl and the FE Grade don't appear on the 1941 price list. By 1945, the HE was gone, and the last Fox price list of all, effective October 15, 1946, shows only the Model B, the Sterlingworth, Sterlingworth Ejector, SP, SPE, AE, and CE.

Earlier in 1946, Savage had moved all Fox production to the old Stevens plant in Chicopee Falls, Massachusetts. You'll find a few guns marked with the Chicopee Falls address, but most of them are guns that were sent in to have the barrels replaced or an extra set made. The barrels built at Chicopee Falls, Roe Clark tells me, were made of 4140 steel and were silver-soldered rather than soft-soldered, as Fox barrels always were before.

The last of all the Foxes sold to the sporting-goods trade left the factory on December 12, 1946. It was a 20-gauge SP Grade, No. 203974. In a world once again rebuilding itself and attempting to cope with the aftermath of the bloodiest, most destructive war in history, scarcely anyone mourned the passing of yet another double gun. The sporting world, populated by a generation of ex-GIs thoroughly steeped in the virtues of sheer firepower, already had turned to repeaters as the guns of the future.

Naturally, a few Foxes remained tucked away in the Savage plant, either as finished pieces or as component parts. Some went for such uses as the Herb Stewart and Wilfred Wright guns, and a few others were disposed of here and there, this way and that. Yet others—displayed in executive offices, in showcases at the plant, in the research and development section, and elsewhere—were sold off one by one over a period that extended to the late 1950s.

The last Fox to be sold new in the box from the warehouse was a 12-gauge Sterlingworth Skeet and Upland Game gun, No. 161127, with 28-inch barrels bored improved-cylinder and modified; Roe Clark bought it in the spring of 1956, at the Savage-employee price of $64.

By and large, Fox guns built during the Savage years are not as highly regarded as those made in Philadelphia. This is justified, to an extent, for those made in the mid- and late 1930s are noticeably less well-finished. Stocks especially are not so carefully shaped nor as nicely checkered. This does not, however, justify indicting Savage Arms for a lack of skill or a concern for quality. Savage simply attempted to turn out the best gun possible in extremely difficult circumstances, and in some cases—the SP Skeet and Upland, for instance—it succeeded better than any other gunmaker of the time.

The fact is, Savage inherited a standard of quality that already was reduced from earlier times, and if you want to establish a point where the standard starts to noticeably slip, you'll have to go back to Philadelphia and about 1927. The guns Savage built from 1930 through about 1933 are on the whole just as well done-up as the ones the A.H. Fox Gun Company turned out in the last three years before the sale.

Now, with this said, I offer a caution: Do not simply dismiss out of hand Foxes of the late '20s, the '30s, or even the early '40s. The overall trend is toward declining quality, but there are exceptions, so it's wise to evaluate these later pieces gun by gun.

Actually, almost the entire history of the Fox gun is a chronicle of steady decline in the amount of hand-work that went into it. Everyone who made the Fox faced the same problem—how to make the best gun possible under circumstances that always seemed to array themselves against it.

To my mind, the peak of quality came early on. The loveliest guns of all are those built before about 1912, in the years when Ansley Fox was in charge. But even he knew full well that it was a level of quality the company could not sustain if it hoped to survive. In some ways, it's a wonder the Fox gun survived at all, for as long as it did.

DE Special 20-gauge by Burt Becker WILLIAM W. HEADRICK

20

SPECIALS & ODDMENTS

Apart from attempting to identify a Skeeter using nothing but catalogue illustrations from the early 1930s, scarcely anything in Foxdom is a greater source of confusion than the guns identified as Specials. In some cases, the "Special" designation appears on the gun itself, stamped or engraved on the water table; in others, it's noted only in the paperwork—on the work- or shipping-order card. Either way, Specials can be almighty confusing.

The word *special* occurs from the earliest days of the Fox Gun Company to the last years of production under Savage Arms, and it is unquestionably the most loosely used word of any associated with the Fox gun, for over the course of Fox history it has five distinctly different meanings. The fact is, though, only two of these uses denote guns that should properly be thought of as true Specials; the rest are merely words, either on paper or stamped in steel.

True Specials first.

One kind of Special is a gun that's decorated in a way completely different from any standard pattern. It is therefore a gun of no particular grade. Fox No. 35, built for Fox Company director Louis H. Eisenlohr, is an early example. The water table is stamped "CS," which might stand for "Custom Special." On the other hand, there is evidence to suggest that Fox had not yet built any guns of higher grade than C, so it might mean "C Special." The engraving is indeed laid out something like the format of the very earliest C Grade guns, but in coverage and detail, it is far more elaborate than any

CS Grade ejector gun, built in 1905 for Fox Company director Louis H. Eisenlohr, is an early example of a true Fox Special.   WILLIAM W. HEADRICK

standard C Grade—more elaborate, in fact, than any standard D Grade and almost the equivalent of a first-generation F.

That it was built for a company director lends a certain historical significance, but it is an exceptional gun in its own right. It's the earliest Fox I know of that has ejectors, for one thing. Its wood is truly magnificent—better in color and figure, in fact, than some FE Grades I've seen. As I mentioned in an earlier chapter, the bird-dog scene on the bottom of the frame is identical to the scene engraved on the Philadelphia Arms E Grade built for William Haywood. I have no problem at all believing those two guns were engraved by the same hand, and a brilliantly skillful hand at that. Eisenlohr's signature is inlaid in gold on the trigger guard in a patch of scroll so tiny that at first glance it looks like stippling. Had I not seen the FE Grade built for exhibition at the 1909 Grand American, No. 35 would get my vote as the finest American gun of my experience; to my mind, it comes in second to FE No. 13291, but not by much.

If No. 35 is an early gun of no particular grade, then the single trap gun built for Herb Stewart in the 1950s and identified as a Trap Grade Special is a late one. (This name has nothing whatever to do with the Trap Grade that Savage built in the mid-1930s, which makes it also an example of how loosely some of the grade names were used.)

Specials of the no-particular-grade sort—the "raised-gold" or "Gough" Specials, for instance—oftentimes are thought of as guns of higher grade than FE. No doubt they cost more than the FE Grades of their time, and they certainly are different from FEs. In terms of the amount of hand-work that went into them, they're not quite the equivalent of a first-generation FE, but they do show more hours of hand-work than an FE of the second generation. To get the best grasp on understanding these guns, think of them as fancier than second-generation FEs, though different—but not necessarily a higher grade. And don't think of Specials as GE Grades; they are not

Now, the other type of true Special is a gun you might well think of as "graded special." These exist in every grade from A to F, and they are decorated in some way that is unlike the standard patterns of their grades. In these, the amount of hand-work is about the same that would go into a standard gun of its particular grade, but the results look different.

The most striking example I know is FE Grade No. 26097, a 12-bore shipped to Mr. Jacob H. Dilts on July 20, 1922. I ran across this gun years ago, in the workshops at Griffin & Howe in New York City. That it was a Fox was obvious from across the room, but even in hand I couldn't have said what grade it was, for it showed very little engraving; what it had was beautifully done English scroll—there just wasn't much of it. I found "FE Special" engraved on the water table.

That an FE Grade should have relatively large areas of its frame unengraved struck me as decidedly odd. But that, I've since learned, is in the nature of the graded Special.

Predictably, the work-order cards for FEs tend to show more detailed specifications than those for lower grades, and the card for No. 26097 is no exception. Among other items, it calls for a skeleton-steel butt plate, special checkering around the fore-end latch, and bone case-hardening, a process that Fox had abandoned six or seven years earlier—and which by the time I saw the gun, had faded almost entirely. Mr. Dilts clearly was particular about his guns.

On the back of the card is written "special inglish style ingraving," and therein lies the key: A graded Special is simply a gun with a different pattern of engraving—not necessarily more of it and, in fact, sometimes less. I've seen guns marked "A Special," "B Special," "C Special," and so on, that fit this definition perfectly.

As I said, these two types are the only guns that strike me as being true Specials, and if they were the only ones to which the word was applied, the matter of Specials wouldn't be nearly so screwy. But of course they weren't. Both the Fox Gun Company and Savage Arms tossed *special* around as if it were a Frisbee, and that's where things get mixed up.

In many cases, the word is associated with perfectly ordinary Foxes, either in the paperwork or on the guns themselves. By "ordinary" I don't mean to imply any judgement on quality, only that these guns are Foxes typical of their grade but for one reason or another are called Specials. These are the instances when *special* does not denote a unique gun but instead is simply a word.

"Special" pops up frequently in reference to XE Grades. Remember, in fact, the XE originally was called the Special Trap Gun, and the first one built would qualify as a true Special under the first definition—because it was unlike anything Fox had made before. But for some reason, the word stuck to the XE. A lot of early specimens are identified in the paperwork as "Special X" or "X Special," and this continues to appear long after it was officially known as XE Grade.

For instance, gun No. 22006, which was shipped to Mr. Claude Seagreaves on June 15, 1918, shows on the work-order card as "XES," but only the word *Special* appears on the gun itself. And yet, except for having a somewhat thicker fore-end than the usual Fox splinter, it is a typical XE in every respect. Five 20-bores shipped in the 1920s are even later examples of standard XE Grades that are identified in the paperwork as Specials: No. 201530, shipped January 11, 1921; No. 201540, shipped in 1924; No. 201541, shipped July 20, 1922; No. 201544, shipped July 14, 1924; and No. 201546, shipped in 1921.

One reason why some guns are marked "Special" is simply that the customer asked for it. You'll find this noted on the work-order cards of otherwise completely ordinary, decidedly un-special guns.

It gets murkier yet. Both the Fox Company and Savage Arms used work-order cards with "Fox Special" printed at the top. In some instances, you can see that the gun one of these cards describes would qualify as a true Special, but more often it wouldn't. In these cases, *special* seems to mean "special work," "special attention," "special alteration," "special order not fillable from inventory or warehouse stock," or something similar. Even stock dimensions that don't meet standard specifications may show up on one of these "Fox Special" cards. AE Grade 20-bore No. 203192, shipped to Abercrombie & Fitch October 17, 1930, is a good example. The only thing even remotely unusual about it is a note on the work order indicating that A&F asked for 2 3/4-inch chambers. Otherwise, it's as typical an AE Fox as you could imagine, and yet the card is marked "Special"—clearly a case in which the word simply means "in some way different from standard."

Similarly, gun No. 27800 is an HE Grade Super-Fox that was shipped October 20, 1922. The work order identifies it as "Special" and bears these notes: "Stock fairly thick for thin face man. Special boring, same as the Askins gun, pitch

2 1/4". Single trigger, intermediate position. Stock to be 14" from trigger to center of butt. Chamber for 2 3/4" shell. Regular engraving and checkering. Engrave name Dr. H.H. Leibold on trigger guard."

What's special here? Special stock work, special boring. The *regular* engraving and checkering is the key. To my thinking, non-typical engraving is central to the definition of a true Special. But almost any departure from standard specifications seems to have been enough to sometimes prompt the use of *special* in the paperwork, less often on the gun itself.

In later years particularly, even guns ordered with standard options appear as "Specials" in the paperwork. No. 203760 was the last FE 20-gauge built, and possibly the last FE Grade of all. It was shipped September 11, 1935. The work-order, which is written on one of Savage's "Fox Special" tags, calls for a number of optional features—vent rib, beavertail fore-end, single trigger, skeleton-steel butt plate, and the name E.A. Grim, M.D. inlaid in gold on the trigger guard with the serial number in gold on the tang, and ivory beads. (It also has Chromox barrels, which must have been one of the very last sets in inventory.)

Is this gun a true Special? Not to my mind, not by the definitions I suggested in the beginning. All the options are standard catalogue items—even the gold-work, in FE Grade—and standard options alone do not make a gun different from any other grade nor even substantially different from others of its own grade.

As one final use, remember that the SP Grade was also called the Fox Special.

Determining why any Special is so called isn't always easy and should properly be done on a gun-by-gun basis. Two important things to remember: Specials are not GE Grades, and the mere appearance of the word does not necessarily make any gun worth a premium price. Evaluating Specials requires enough familiarity with Foxes to be able to recognize what's typical and what isn't, but once you reach that point, the Specials won't seem quite so mystifying.

Nor will the fabled pieces in the 450000 serial-number range. Time has a way of evolving the extraordinary into legend, especially, it seems, in the gun world—and everybody loves a mystery.

Some Savage-era Fox guns are numbered in a series apart from the usual number blocks, a series that begins with No. 450000. Naturally, it has been tempting to assume that such "special" pieces must be exceptionally fine or remarkably ornate—shades of the Parker Invincible. Human nature being what it is, we seem to prefer that the unusual also be exotic.

Some have suggested that this number block was reserved for GE Grades, but this definitely is not the case. Another suggestion is that these guns were built especially for company executives; this may be true, but they weren't "presentation" pieces in the common sense of the word. Actually, the only thing intrinsically unusual about the 450000-series guns is the number-block itself.

Roe Clark suggests that Savage built these guns as experiments in cost-effectiveness, trying to determine, in the face of the Depression, just what it could accomplish with the newly acquired Fox gun at reasonable manufacturing cost. I believe Roe is absolutely right about this.

I've seen factory records for ten guns in the 450000 range. Not surprisingly, there are some anomalies in the paperwork. No. 450000, for example, appears twice. In one instance, it's described as an AE Grade choked cylinder and cylinder; in the other, it's called "Skeet" with cylinder and improved-cylinder chokes. This is not, however, a case of the same number being assigned to two different guns. Instead, it's a case of Savage executives brain-storming for new ideas, since there is good evidence to suggest that Nos. 450000, 450001, and 450002 were the prototypes for what Savage later would call Skeeter and Trap Grade. The confusion over the chokes simply is a minor error of bookkeeping.

No. 450005 also appears twice, and the descriptions show some minor contradictions in chokes and stock dimensions. These may represent changes the owner asked for, since the gun apparently was returned to Savage in the late 1930s, or it may be another instance of careless measuring and bookkeeping. In any event, these undoubtedly are two descriptions of the same gun. Remember, these were experimental guns and Savage was, after all, looking for ways to survive as a company, not create meticulously documented heirlooms. Minor omissions and errors in paperwork occur throughout the history of Fox, and it's one of the reasons why a lot of researchers and collectors have gray hair, or none at all.

Here's what the records say about the 450000-series guns:

No. 450000: AE Grade/"Skeet," 12-gauge, 30-inch barrels choked cylinder and cylinder or cylinder and improved-cylinder, vent rib, single trigger, straight-hand stock with 14 $1/4$-inch pull, 1 $5/8$-inch bend at comb and 2 $1/4$ inches at heel; beavertail fore-end; vent rib; shipped November 29, 1931, card marked "office sample."

No. 450001: "No. 2 Skeet," HE engraving, 12- gauge, 30-inch barrels, full-pistol-grip stock with 14 $1/4$-inch pull, vent rib, single trigger, beavertail fore-end; shipped April 24, 1931, card marked "office sample."

No. 450002: "No. 3 Skeet," HE engraving, 12-gauge, 28-inch barrels choked improved-cylinder and improved-modified, half-pistol-grip stock, dimensions: 14 $^1/_2$-inch pull, 1 $^1/_2$ inches bend at comb, 2 inches at heel, beavertail fore-end, vent rib, single trigger; no date, card marked "office sample."

No. 450003: A Grade, 20-gauge, 26-inch barrels, choked improved-cylinder and modified, straight-hand stock with 14 $^1/_2$-inch pull, 2 $^5/_8$ inches bend at heel, single trigger; shipped March 10 or 13, 1940.

No. 450004: AE Grade, 12-gauge, 32-inch barrels, full chokes, straight-hand stock with 14-inch pull, 2 $^5/_8$-inch bend at heel, vent rib, single trigger; shipped 1940.

No. 450005: AE Grade/Skeeter, 12-gauge, 28-inch barrels choked modified and improved-cylinder or improved modified and improved-cylinder, full-pistol-grip stock with 14- or 14 $^1/_8$-inch pull, 1 $^5/_8$-inch bend at comb and 2 $^1/_4$- or 2 $^5/_8$-inch bend at heel, vent rib, beavertail fore-end; shipped first on April 14, 1931, and again on June 15, 1939.

No. 450006: A Grade, 12-gauge, 30-inch barrels choked full and full, full-pistol-grip stock, dimensions: 14 $^1/_2$-inch pull, 1 $^5/_8$-inch bend at comb, vent rib, single trigger, beavertail fore- end; shipped April 23, 1931.

No. 450010: AE Grade, 12-gauge, 28-inch barrels choked modified and full; shipped 1939.

Savage clearly was tinkering with ideas for new grades. In fact, No. 450001 is the gun that appeared in Fox catalogues as illustration of the Skeeter—and thereby caused a measure of confusion, because its engraving is A Grade, not Skeeter.

We'll probably never know exactly how many guns actually were numbered in the 450000 series. It's reasonable to suppose that Nos. 450007, -008, and

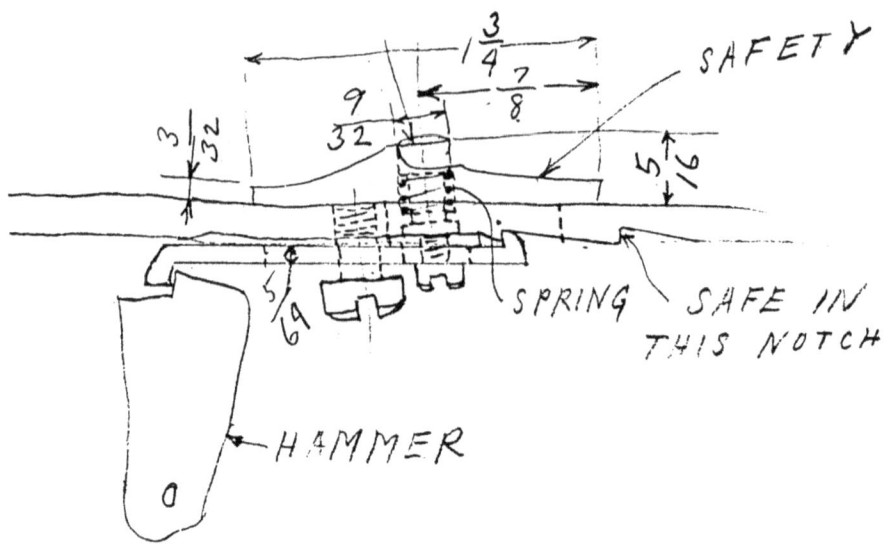

A sketch of the safety mechanism from the Fox Gun Company file on the proposed over/under gun. Presumably, the spring-loaded button in the slide was intended as a safety-lock, much like the system currently used by Krieghoff.

-009 were assigned, but no record of them has turned up so far.

We do know, however, that the old assumption of these guns being unusually fine has no basis in fact.

Another old assumption is that the Fox Gun Company tinkered with the notion of building an over/under, and this one is absolutely true. Many years after the Fox gun went out of production, a desk drawer in the Fox Products Company offices yielded an old and well-worn manila envelope. On it, in pencil, is written:

OVER-UNDER GUN

OR

VERTICAL BARREL SHOTGUN

Inside is a thin sheaf of magazine clippings, some mechanical sketches, computations, and a few notes—all indicating that someone at the Fox Gun Company was taking an interest in an over/under. Exactly when this occurred is impossible to say, although I suspect it was the early 1920s. The earliest clipping is from a British magazine, *The Country Gentleman and Sporting Gazette* of January 10, 1914, and it's an article on the Lang over/under—or as the English say, the under and over. From *The Shooting Times* of July 8, 1922, is a brief piece on the

SPECIALS & ODDMENTS

Westley Richards Ovundo, and from *The Field* of May 24, 1923, a story and ad for the Beesley Shotover.

From *Field & Stream* are a general review of English over/unders by Paul Curtis (April 1923) and ads for the Westley Richards Ovundo (October and November 1924). Among the items showing no dates are ads for over/under guns by Boss, Simson and August Schuler, and a page from a Woodward catalogue, showing the Woodward over/under.

Many of these clips carry notations on prices and certain dimensions of the various guns. Other notes, hand-written and much faded by time, are somewhat disjointed:

Woodward frame 2 ³⁄₈ deep.

It has been found that a gun of the under and over type is very troublesome to shoot with if the ordinary highly polished and rounded surface of the top barrel is allowed to prevail. It forms a reflecting medium that the light from the sky takes advantage of to the extent of practically obscuring the barrel, so proving that subconsciously the shooter must see the barrel in relation with the bird.

The shadows cast by the rib lying between the two barrels of the ordinary bun makes a break in the light-reflecting surfaces and so forms the required aiming guide. One of the new guns is the over and under single-trigger gun, constructed on a new system. A single

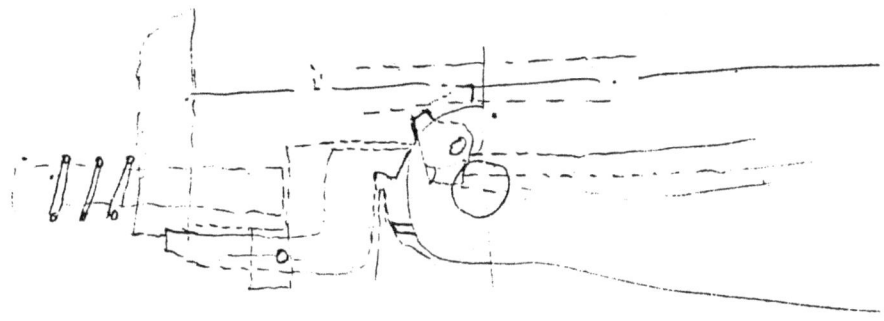

Also from the proposed over/under gun file, presumably a sketch of the ejector-sear mechanism.

barrel gun seems to possess advantages over the double barrel side-by-side gun in its freedom of handling and its wider view and the single barrels, when arranged one of the other, appear to acquire the qualities we have referred to of the single barrel.

Anyone who has used and over-and-under gun will freely admit that this is so.

Under barrel should corresponding with the right of the ordinary gun.

Most of this reads like advertising or catalogue copy, so I can only conclude that the company was taking the over/under idea seriously—although ad copy would have been more than a little premature if the drawings are any indication. As you see from the reproductions here, they are simply sketches, and since they show only the safety and what I take to be the ejectors, they offer no more than maddeningly brief glimpses of what a Fox over/under might have been. The safety apparently was to feature much the same sort of spring-loaded lock that Krieghoff has used for many years.

It's tempting to wonder if the over/under wasn't an offshoot of the single trap gun, at least insofar as the single trap offers a start on designing a frame tall enough to accommodate vertically-paired barrels. Unfortunately, we'll probably never know.

In working with the remaining factory records, Roe Clark has found one card referring to an over/under gun. The serial number is listed at 5072—a six-pound, five-ounce 12-gauge with 28-inch barrels bored modified and full. The card is stamped August 11, 1932, and in Roe's opinion it does not refer to a Fox gun but rather to some over/under belonging to a Savage company official who sent it to the shop for repair or alteration of some sort.

From the beginning, the Fox Gun Company offered its customers great latitude in specifying features and details of the guns they ordered. Some options were noted in the catalogues: recoil pads, skeleton-steel butt plates, ivory beads, ejectors, single trigger, vent rib, beavertail fore-end, and the like. Repair price lists from the early 1910s even include fitting sling-swivels and straps. These also note that safeties could be removed and the safety slot filled in; you could also order a new gun made with no safety. Safetyless guns were popular among pigeon and trap shooters.

Special-order chokes and stock dimensions show up frequently in the work orders, and some are amusingly picky. One man insisted that his gun pattern

An example of exhibition- or presentation-grade wood available from Fox on special order.

WILLIAM W. HEADRICK

fifty-two percent from the right barrel and sixty-five percent from the left. Mr. Sam Church, who ordered B Grade 12-bore No. 14692, was pickier still: The work-order reads "Right barrel must pattern 275. Left barrel must pattern 300." And presumably he was satisfied with what the factory did, because there's no record of the gun being returned after it was shipped in July 1909. Yet another fan of high-performance shooting apparently had to see some evidence; the card for gun No. 202655, a CE 20-gauge shipped May 1, 1928, specifies "barrels choked (strong) improved cylinder and (strong) modified. Pattern gun, return patterns."

Stocks were a veritable can of worms where special dimensions are concerned. One man ordered a half-hand stock with 15 ³/₄-inch pull, two inches of bend at the comb and four inches at the heel—which the work order understates as being "for a long armed, long necked man." Another specified everything in metric dimensions: 370mm pull, 70mm drop at heel, eight to ten millimeters cast, with a total gun weight of three kilograms.

Some customers were choosy about weight. The card for the very first 16-gauge Fox, DE Grade No. 300001, reads, "To be lightest weight possible." Mr. J.A. Johnson was more specific when he ordered BE 20-gauge No. 201002: "Strike 3-4 ounces off barrels, bore out stock 2-3 ounces." Mr. Johnson apparently had other concerns as well, for the card also bears the notations, "As dark curley grained wood in stock as possible at regular price" and "extra fine shooter in pattern and penetration." When the gun left Philadelphia on October 25, 1917, it weighed five pounds, six ounces—which apparently was light enough to suit, and we can only assume that Mr. Johnson was satisfied with how it shot.

Yet others were choosy about almost everything, like the man who ordered No. 22818. It's an A Grade with 32-inch barrels and three-inch chambers. The card reads: "For Duck Shooting; trigger pulls to be Left—5 lbs.: Right 4 ¹/₂ lbs.; chamber for 3" cartridge, to shoot 3 ¹/₂ drams Dupont, 1 ¹/₄ ounce charge of #4 or #5 shot; cast off ¹/₂" to shoot from left shoulder; balance 2 ¹/₂" forward of standing breech (See that this is well balanced)." It was shipped to a sporting-goods dealer in the Boston area on March 15, 1916.

Fox also was willing to supply all sorts of custom features besides the options listed in the catalogues, and there are some factory-original guns floating around that were made with checkered, gold-plated triggers; with stocks made with the diamond-shaped wrist popular in England; with gold and silver shields and ovals fitted to stocks and fore-ends; with frames filed in the scalloped, "fancy-back" style; with special checkering patterns and stock carvings. My friend Shelly Snyder has a Super-Fox, built in the 1920s, that was ordered with a swastika worked into the fore-end checkering. Since the symbol itself is far older than the

German National Socialist Party—used by the ancient Greeks, Celts, Buddhists, and Indians of both North and South America—this doesn't necessarily mean the man who ordered it was a Nazi sympathizer. He may simply have been a shooter who wanted a good-luck symbol on his gun. On the other hand, the traditional good-luck swastika's arms are bent anti-clockwise, and the one on Shelly's gun has the arms bent the other way, which was the Nazi style...so who knows? Stranger things have happened.

Predictably, a lot of customers took the company up on its special-features offer, and many work orders are a pastiche of special instructions, as in these examples:

No. 11532, C Grade 12-gauge, shipped December 1, 1910: "Very thick comb; $2\,^7/_8$" muzzle pitch; very thick grip $4\,^1/_8$" circumference; take off safety and plug slot; skeleton butt."

No. 18931, C Grade 12-gauge, shipped August 19, 1911: "Large grip thick stock back of grip; engrave gold oval 'Made expressly for Dr. Mascil 1911.'"

No. 32021, DE Grade 12-gauge with two sets of barrels, shipped October 20, 1927: "Skeleton butt plate; 3" pitch; circumference of grip $4\,^1/_2$", flat on sides making it oval in cross section; checker both triggers; independent safety; both pair of barrels to have flat ribs; 26" barrels to be chambered for 2 5/8" shells, 30" barrels for 3" shells; right trigger pull $3\,^1/_2$ to 4 pounds, left trigger pull 4 to $4\,^1/_4$

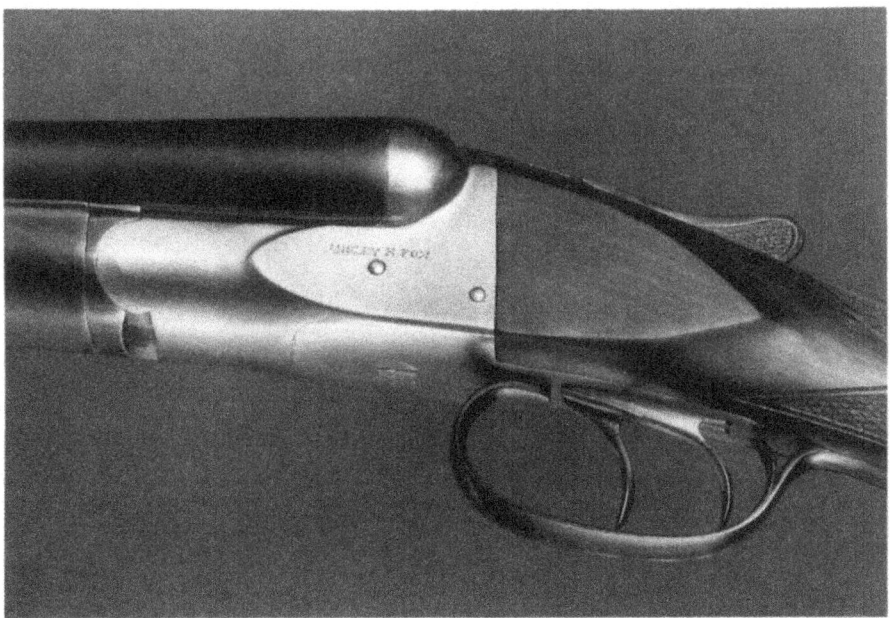

Fox No. 200644, an AE Grade special-ordered without engraving   WILLIAM W. HEADRICK

pounds; make patterns and send with gun marking which is 26" and which is 30"; make comb concave on left side; checkering to be sharp and coarse 16."

Gun No. 200644 is an excellent example of how far Fox was willing to go in accommodating customers' wishes, no matter how odd. The specs for this 20-bore, which was shipped July 7, 1914, begin with exacting though not unusual stock dimensions, followed with the note "Must be exactly like this." Then come notes specifying 30-inch barrels with full choke in both, an overall weight of six pounds, ten ounces, and "select nice stock." For this, the stockmaker chose a piece of European walnut of a quality about what you'd find on a C Grade of the period. None too odd so far, but then there's a note that says "No engraving on action or barrels."

The customer, one Mr. R. McDougal, apparently wanted a small-bore pigeon or target gun, for No. 200644 has no safety. It also has a Sterlingworth-type fore-end. In order to end up with a well-balanced 20-gauge of nearly seven pounds, the Fox craftsmen left the barrels—which are Krupp steel, by the way—quite thick at the breech-end, struck them with straight rather than curving taper, and used a top rib noticeably wider than the usual Fox 20. The rib is also hollow and swamped, which is unusual among Foxes. The heavy barrels, in turn, required a slightly oversized frame, and the whole effect is a gun that looks more like a 16 than a 20.

Both gun and work-order are marked AE Grade, but Mr. McDougal asked for no engraving, and that's what he got. "Ansley H. Fox" is engraved on each side of the frame, but there is otherwise not a line nor squiggle of engraving anywhere on the gun. In terms of decoration, or the lack of same, it certainly would qualify as a Special—but in this instance the word isn't used anywhere, neither on the gun nor in the paperwork. All in all, the whole thing is odd to the borderline of weird.

Several cards bear the notation "Have Mr. Fox select wood." FE Grade No. 17132, shipped July 24, 1912, is an example, and Ansley Fox may indeed have picked out the wood for this one before he departed the Fox Gun Company scene. It's doubtful, however, that he was able to comply with a similar request for B Grade No. 17254; it was shipped July 28, 1913, and Ansley Fox was long gone by then.

Standard Fox barrel lengths always ranged from twenty-six to thirty-two inches in even increments. Nonetheless, some customers wanted other lengths, and the company was happy to oblige. Thirty-four-inch tubes never were catalogue options, but a few guns have them. Roe Clark has turned up several cards specifying 29- and 31-inch barrels and one for a Sterlingworth Brush gun ordered with 24-inch tubes choked cylinder and modified.

Specials & Oddments

Odd-length barrels on American guns are always suspect, and by far the majority are indeed hacksaw jobs; some, however, truly are factory-righteous. Not many, but a few. To make things cloudier still, the factory was always willing to shorten barrels in the repair shop, and this sort of alteration typically would not be noted in the records.

In a very few instances, highly knowledgeable customers insisted that Burt Becker build their Foxes, especially after Nash Buckingham made Becker a minor deity. Perhaps the most notable of these are a pair of DE Grades that Becker made for a U.S. Senator who, along with Buckingham and Ding Darling and Henry Bartholomew, was active in the conservation movement of the 1930s. The first gun, No. 203603, is a 20-bore with 26-inch barrels chambered for 2 $^3/_4$-inch cartridges, and a single trigger. The card notes, "Work to be done by Mr. Becker. Must be very pretty piece of work, 8 weeks delivery." It was shipped May 11, 1931.

The Senator apparently liked what he got, for he ordered a companion gun two years later. This one is No. 203660, described in the records as a Special DE. It, too, is a 20-gauge with single trigger and full-pistol stock and is bored with 2 $^3/_4$-inch chambers. The barrels, however, are thirty inches, for it was, as the card says, "wanted for wildfowl shooting." The card also notes,

DE Special 20-gauge wildfowl gun by Burt Becker   WILLIAM W. HEADRICK

Pair of AE Grade guns ordered with the same serial number: 34233 and 34233/2.

"Stock dimensions to be exact duplicate of Gun number 203603." It was shipped September 18, 1933.

For the second order, there was no need to specify a pretty piece of work, but that's just what the Senator got. I haven't seen the short-barreled piece, but I have spent some time with the wildfowl gun, and only one word can truly describe it—exquisite.

In a few instances two guns were inadvertently assigned the same serial number. Since that sort of thing can happen rather easily in a busy factory, you'll find similar glitches among guns by other American makers as well. But it's rare to find two guns that clearly were given the same number on purpose.

Fox No. 34233 is a standard AE Grade with 28-inch barrels and full-pistol stock. It left factory inventory in October 1934. Gun No. 34233/2 is also an AE, but it has 30-inch barrels, and its checkering pattern is a hybrid incorporating elements of both DE and FE designs. Most likely, both guns were built for a Savage executive or one of the company salesmen. One thing's for sure: You won't see many guns like them.

Foxes with two sets of barrels are not especially rare, although instances in which the second set was built at the same time the gun was made are scarce,

A Grade two-barrel set: one set 16-gauge, the other 20.   WILLIAM W. HEADRICK

indeed. Most often, the second set was added some years later, so it's not particularly unusual to find a gun with one set each of Krupp and Chromox tubes—nor a gun with one pair of Philadelphia barrels and another bearing Savage Arms stamps. The second set typically will be the shorter of the two.

Multi-gauge barrel sets are extremely rare, in my experience. One of the niftier specimens I know of is No. 302797—a lightweight A Grade 16-bore shipped on November 12, 1929, which makes it one of the last guns sent out from Philadelphia. In the early 1960s it belonged to a man who was a friend of a foreman at Savage. The foreman told the owner about a pair of 20-gauge Fox barrels, Chicopee Falls vintage, that had turned up in the plant, so No. 302797 went in for a job of restoration and retrofit and is now a 16- and 20-bore on one frame.

Niftier still, in some ways, are a few 20-gauges made up at Savage with extra sets of barrels that have no chambers. They're made that way because a 20-gauge barrel with no chamber will shoot a 28-gauge cartridge fairly efficiently, and these guns probably represent another of Savage's experiments to see how versatile the Fox gun could be.

I've always thought the small-bore Fox frame, diminutive as it is, would make a splendid 28-gauge, and it's a pity that circumstances weren't such in the 1930s to allow Savage to go all the way and bring out a proper 28-bore Fox. Sales in the Depression would never have justified the cost, but my soul, what lovely things they would have been.

CE Grade 20-gauge   WILLIAM W. HEADRICK

21
Matters of the Heart: Velma

In the fall of 1942, with the world awash in the tumult of war, Ellen Fox's health began to fail. She was fifty-seven.

She entered Temple University Hospital in Philadelphia on November 20, and within a few days the diagnosis was clear—cancer of the colon and bladder. Dr. Joseph Farrell, who attended the case, did what he could, but available treatments were few and by that point, futile. She died at thirteen minutes past eight o'clock on Christmas morning.

Her body was turned over to William H. Battersby's Sons, morticians, of 3316 North Broad Street, Philadelphia, where on December 26 Ansley Fox made burial arrangements and signed an agreement to pay $432 in funeral costs.

The burial service was scheduled for two o'clock on Tuesday afternoon, December 29, at the Harleigh Cemetery in Camden, New Jersey, just across the river from Philadelphia. Ellen was buried next to her mother, in lot No. 2 of the five-grave plot.

Although Ansley Fox maintained both an apartment and an automobile in the city, he customarily traveled between Pleasantville and Philadelphia by train and frequently dined at the station restaurant. There I'm told he became acquainted with Velma Shank, a woman in her late 30s who was working as a waitress. Perhaps they met during the month when Ellen was hospitalized, when Ansley Fox made frequent trips into the city, or perhaps they'd met before. No one knows.

The outcome, however, is clear. Ansley Fox was not one who cared to be without the companionship of a woman, and Velma Shank became the third Mrs. Ansley Fox, the one who would bury him.

DE Grade 12-gauge, vintage 1909 WILLIAM W. HEADRICK

22

SUNSET AND EVENING BELL

Ansley Fox turned seventy-one just before the last Fox gun was shipped out of Utica. He was retired from the world of business that had occupied so many years of a long and busy life. As Europe struggled to rebuild amid the shambles of war, the world seemed poised on the brink of yet another new age. The first successful pilotless rocket missile and the first electronic brain were built in 1946, the same year Chester Carlson invented the process of xerography. The following year, Chuck Yeager became the first pilot to fly a plane faster than the speed of sound, P.M.S. Blackett suggested that all massive rotating bodies are magnetic, and Jackie Robinson became the first black man to sign a contract with a major-league baseball team.

To a man born a year before the debacle at the Little Big Horn, into a world that scarcely knew electricity, much less the automobile or the flying machine, it must all have been a wonder.

In the summer of 1948, the world looked forward to the first Olympic Games to be held since the ominous, highly politicized 1936 Games in Berlin. On Ansley Fox's seventy-third birthday, June 25, the Republican Party nominated New York Governor Thomas Dewey as its presidential candidate and California Governor Earl Warren as his running mate. That same evening, Joe Louis knocked out Jersey Joe Walcott in the eleventh round to maintain his title as Heavyweight Champion of the World, a repeat of his performance against Primo Carnera on the same date in 1935.

At the Olympic Games in London, the United States would claim thirty-eight medals altogether, twenty-one more than her nearest rival, Sweden. On August 6, seventeen-year-old Bob Mathias captured the world's attention by winning the decathlon with a stunning total of 7139 points.

Three days later, Ansley Fox suffered a stroke. Upon examination, Dr. Isabel G. Wilcox found him hemiplegic, one side of his body paralyzed, and, probably at his own request, allowed him to remain at home.

The paralysis led to hypostatic pneumonia within a few days, as fluids gathered in his lungs. At 5:42 in the afternoon on Sunday, the 15th of August, his heart finally stopped. Ansley Fox had lived seventy-three years, one month, and twenty-one days.

Mortician B.W. Cunningham of Pleasantville took charge of his body.

On the 17th, the same day local registrar Mary Havenstein recorded his death certificate, *The New York Times* published an obituary datelined Atlantic City, August 16:

> *Ansley H. Fox, inventor of the A.H. Fox shotgun, died last night at his home, 214 South Palermo Avenue, in West Atlantic City. His age was 73.*

The end of the search for Ansley Fox – and the beginning of a book. The author at Ansley Fox's grave in Camden, New Jersey, June 1986.

The following day, the *Atlantic City Press* had this to say:

> FOX—Of West Atlantic City, on August 15, 1948, ANSLEY H., husband of Belma [sic] L. Fox. Relatives and friends, also Franklin Lodge No. 134, F. and A. M., are invited to attend funeral services Wednesday, 7:30 p.m., at Cunningham Funeral Building, 400 S. Main St., Pleasantville. Interment Harleigh Cemetery, Camden, N.J., at the convenience of the family.

The family found it convenient to bury Ansley Fox on August 19, next to Ellen in Lot No. 755, Merion Section, at Harleigh Cemetery, just a few hundred yards from where the bones of Walt Whitman repose. The last two graves in the 180-square-foot plot would be occupied by Ansley Fox's old friend and former brother-in-law William Gerou on August 4, 1977, and by William Gerou's wife Millie on June 13, 1984.

Seen through the scrim of history, the picture of the man alternately sharpens and fades. Ansley Fox was quintessentially American, endlessly fascinating. He was a risk-taker, volatile, brilliant, demanding, probably even arrogant. Whatever internal tides moved him, he clearly sought to leave behind something of quality, something that would endure. The search must have been painful at times, both for himself and for those whose lives touched his. The world he knew changed and changed again, and its currents often seemed to run against him. He must have felt some bittersweet satisfaction in seeing the company he founded continue to produce the gun he had created and named, and he surely would have felt some pride, had he been able to read his own obituary, in knowing that the gun would be history's remembrance of Ansley Fox.

Now, the Harleigh Cemetery is a shady, peaceful island amid the urban sprawl of Philadelphia and Camden. Where Ansley Fox lies is an unimposing place, simply five flat stones laid out in a row in the close-cropped grass. If you step back a few yards, the stones look much like the traps in an old-time pigeon ring, and from his place, on the left end, you might well imagine Ansley Fox as a hard driver, headed for the boundary fence.

"Campfire" catalogues, 1907-1912　　　　　　　　　　　WILLIAM W. HEADRICK

The last Fox catalogues, 1937-1942　　　　　　　　　　WILLIAM W. HEADRICK

Appendix I
The Paper Trail

Factory-published paper goods—catalogues, price lists, brochures, and such—can be both wonderfully useful and maddeningly difficult tools. On the one hand, catalogues can be excellent windows on the past, showing the evolution of both a gun and a company year by year, reflecting in turn prosperity and recession, struggle and success. On the other, however, they can be utterly misleading, can be tempting snares that lull a researcher into the sort of complacency that goes before a massive fall.

What appears in catalogues is difficult not to believe, even in the face of evidence to the contrary; this, in turn, invites assumptions that often prove to be riddled with pitfalls. The researcher who would use factory literature as primary sources does well to bear in mind a few simple but extremely important facts. First among them is that factory literature is an end product, the last step in the process by which a new model or grade of gun is created and offered for sale. This was as true of the gun trade's approach two or three generations ago as it is today, perhaps even more so. Catalogues and other such documents are planned and printed months in advance, so while it is tempting to assume that a gun appearing for the first time in the 19-umpteen catalogue was conceived and developed that very year, logic and sense insists that it cannot be so. Logic and sense say the gun was established and in production the previous year, if not before. Companies out to turn a profit announce new models when they have sufficient inventory to meet demand, not when the idea first strikes.

This would be simple enough if makers were careful to publish a fully updated, precisely current catalogue every year. Nowadays, when gun companies employ publications staffs of their own or contract the work through advertising agencies, that may be the case. But it certainly wasn't fifty or seventy or a hundred years ago.

In those days, when marketing and advertising weren't the complex, sophisticated sciences they are now, gunmakers took a much more straightforward approach: They printed a supply of catalogues and used them until the supply was gone, regardless of how the product line changed in the mean time.

This is true of Fox catalogues almost from the beginning, and it becomes an especially important consideration in the 1930s, when Savage Arms was literally fighting for its life. In the early days, some catalogues appear to have been reprinted once or twice, sometimes fitted with newly designed covers, sometimes not; simple frugality dictated that an expensive set of printer's plates should be used as long as what was on them bore any reasonable semblance to reality. In the gut of the Depression, pennies saved or wasted might make the difference between survival and bankruptcy.

Interesting as factory paper goods can be in their own right, a researcher is therefore wise to remember that catalogues are not necessarily accurate resources.

Which leads to still another problem. I have yet to see a Fox catalogue, of any period, that was printed with a date of issue, so it's sometimes difficult to know exactly what year any given piece was meant to represent. From 1908 through 1912, the catalogues were numbered, beginning with No. 21 and ending with No. 25, which is some help—but only if you know how the years and numbers correspond. For the most part, Fox catalogues must be dated on the basis of internal evidence. If catalogues were expected to serve for years on end, price lists were not, because price lists had a more direct impact upon sales. Until World War I, Fox printed prices in the catalogues, but from about 1919 on, price lists were printed as separate sheets and inserted, loose-leaf, into whatever catalogues were being used, or used up, at the time.

As historical documents, these lists are much more reliable than the retail catalogues. They were almost always dated, and the company seems to have revised them each year—in some cases even more often.

Paper is impermanent stuff, and putting together a complete collection of Fox catalogues, price lists, and brochures probably would be impossible. I know serious collectors who've been at it for twenty years or more, but I don't know any whose supply of paper goods doesn't show some gaps. The following, therefore, has some gaps in it, too, but it's more complete than not.

From 1906 through 1942, Fox retail catalogues essentially comprise eight distinct series, identifiable by the cover design or by trim size. In this list, these series are identified by cover slogan or illustration, or in some instances, both.

SERIES 1: *"The Finest Gun in the World,"* 1906-1907

Catalogue, 1906
6 1/4 by 3 1/2 inches, 18 pages plus cover, cord-bound with tassel. Cover green, foil-stamped with "The Finest Gun in the World." A, B, and C grades pictured; D and F grades described but not pictured. "Not connected with Philadelphia Arms Co." printed on pages 1, 2, and 14. Address listed as Wayne and Bristol Streets.
Prices:

Grade A	$ 50.00
Grade B	$ 75.00
Grade C	$100.00
Grade D	$200.00
Grade F	$500.00

Catalogue, early 1907
6 1/4 by 3 1/2 inches, 24 pages plus cover, cord-bound with tassel. Same cover as 1906. A, B, C, and D grades pictured; F Grade described but not pictured. "Not connected with Philadelphia Arms Co." appears on pages 2 and 14. Address listed as 18th Street and Windrim Avenue.
Prices:

Grade A	$ 50.00
Grade B	$ 75.00
Grade C	$100.00
Grade D	$200.00
Grade F	$500.00

SERIES 2: *"Campfire"* Cover, 1907-1912

Catalogue, mid-1907
6 by 9 inches, 24 pages plus cover, cord-bound with tassel. Cover illustration a camping-scene applique. Ansley H. Fox "signature" flypage. A, B, C, D, and F grades pictured.

Prices:

A Grade	$ 50.00
B Grade	$ 75.00
C Grade	$100.00
D Grade	$200.00
F Grade	$500.00

Catalogue, 1908
6 by 9 inches, 24 pages plus cover, cord-bound. Campfire-scene applique on cover. Page 1 printed "Catalogue No. 21."
Prices:

A Grade	$ 50.00
B Grade	$ 75.00
C Grade	$100.00
D Grade	$200.00
F Grade	$500.00

Catalogue, 1909
Campfire-scene cover applique. Page 1 printed "Catalogue No. 22."

Catalogue, 1910
Campfire-scene cover applique. Page 1 printed "Catalogue No. 23."

Price List, January 12, 1910.
Prices same as Catalogue No. 21.

Catalogue, 1911
6 by 9 inches, 28 pages, cord-bound. Campfire-scene cover applique. Page 1 printed "Catalogue No. 24." This is the last catalogue issued during Ansley Fox's tenure. It is the first full-scale catalogue to show the Sterlingworth.
Prices:

Sterlingworth	$ 35.00
with ejectors	$ 50.00
A Grade	$ 50.00
AE Grade	$ 65.00
B Grade	$ 75.00
BE Grade	$ 90.00
C Grade	$100.00
CE Grade	$115.00

D Grade	$200.00
DE Grade	$215.00
F Grade	$500.00
FE Grade	$515.00

In 1911, the Fox Company bought a three-sheet, six-page insert in *National Sportsman* magazine. This little item—printed in two colors on slick paper and trimmed to 6 1/2 by 9 1/2 inches—illustrates the full line of guns from Sterlingworth to FE and, indeed, amounts almost to a catalogue in itself.

Catalogue, 1912

6 by 9 inches, 28 pages plus cover, cord-bound. Last of the "campfire" cover catalogues. Page 1 printed "Catalogue No. 25." First full-scale catalogue to list 16- and 20-gauge guns. In the 1960s, the Fox Products Company reprinted this catalogue—with a different cover—presumably as a nostalgia piece to hand out among its customers.

Prices:

Sterlingworth	$ 35.00
with ejectors	$ 50.00
A Grade	$ 50.00
AE Grade	$ 65.00
B Grade	$ 75.00
BE Grade	$ 90.00
C Grade	$100.00
CE Grade	$115.00
D Grade	$200.00
DE Grade	$215.00
F Grade	$500.00
FE Grade	$515.00

Dealers' Confidential Price List, January 1, 1912

3 1/2 by 6 inches, single-fold. "Notice and Guarantee" printed on back licenses dealer or agent purchasing gun for re-sale to sell at net prices only. Any lower price "will be an unauthorized sale and an infringement of the above patents, and the ownership of the gun shall revert to the A.H. Fox Gun Co." Prices same as 1912 catalogue.

A.H. FOX

Small-bore Booklet, 1911-1912

3 ½ by 6 ¼ inches, 8 pages, printed in two colors, saddle-stitched with two wire staples. A promotional piece for the newly introduced 16- and 20-bore guns, the pamphlet is titled "Complete Description of the A.H. Fox 16 and 20 Gauge Guns / 1912 Model / The Most Perfectly Proportioned Small-Gauge Guns Ever Built."

SERIES 3: *"A Fox Gets the Game,"* full-size, 1913-1917

Catalogue, 1913

9 ½ by 6 ½ inches, 24 pages plus flysheets plus cover, saddle-stitched with two wire staples. This is the first catalogue upon which the slogan "A Fox Gets the Game" appears. The cover, gray paper with blue trim, is embossed and foil-stamped in gold; the illustration is a color applique. Printed in two colors. This catalogue lists the Special Trap Gun that soon would become the XE Grade. Only net prices are included, encouraging potential buyers to order guns directly fron the factory.

Net prices:

Sterlingworth	$ 25.00
with ejectors	$ 37.50
A Grade	$ 37.50
AE Grade	$ 49.50
B Grade	$ 50.00
BE Grade	$ 62.00
C Grade	$ 70.00
CE Grade	$ 82.00
D Grade	$140.00
DE Grade	$152.00
F Grade	$350.00
FE Grade	$362.00

Catalogue, 1914

9 ½ by 6 ½ inches, 24 pages plus covers, saddle-stitched with two wire staples, printed in two colors; "Fox Gets the Game" applique; cover is gray with blue trim, gold-foil-stamped. This is the first catalogue to include the XE Grade, the first to mention "guns built to order," and the first in which grades C, X, D, and F are offered with ejectors as standard equipment. A separately printed brochure

advertising the new Fox-Kautzky single trigger appeared as a loose insert in some 1914 catalogues.

Only net prices are listed.

Prices:

Sterlingworth	$ 25.00
with ejectors	$ 32.50
A Grade	$ 37.50
AE Grade	$ 45.00
B Grade	$ 52.50
BE Grade	$ 60.00
CE Grade	$ 75.00
XE Grade	$100.00
DE Grade	$150.00
FE Grade	$350.00

Fox-Kautzky Single Trigger Brochure, 1914

4 3/4 by 6 1/4 inches, 4 pages. Titled "The Premier of Single Triggers," this brochure was issued to promote the Kautzky single trigger, for which the Fox Gun Company had recently purchased patent and manufacturing rights.

Catalogue, 1915

9 1/2 by 6 1/2 inches, 28 pages plus flysheets plus cover, saddle-stitched with three wire staples, printed in two colors. "Fox Gets the Game" applique on cover, which is brown with black trim, embossed and gold-foil-stamped. This is the most elaborate of all Fox catalogues, produced for distribution at the Panama-Pacific Exposition in San Francisco, where the Fox gun won a gold-medal award for double guns and single trigger. It features a center-spread quoting Teddy Roosevelt's letter to Ansley Fox and a two-page illustration of an FE Grade gun—but not, in fact, of Roosevelt's FE. The order blank is a separate, loose sheet; the verso is devoted entirely to listing the virtues of the Fox-Kautzky trigger.

Only net prices are included.

Prices:

Sterlingworth	$ 25.00
with ejectors	$ 32.50
A Grade	$ 37.50
AE Grade	$ 45.00
B Grade	$ 52.50
BE Grade	$ 60.00

A.H. FOX

CE Grade	$ 75.00
XE Grade	$100.00
DE Grade	$150.00
FE Grade	$350.00

Catalogue, 1916

9 1/2 by 6 1/2 inches, 24 pages plus cover, saddle-stitched with three wire staples, printed in two colors. Cover brown with black trim, embossed and gold-foil stamped. "Fox Gets the Game" applique; a printed reproduction of the Panama-Pacific Exposition blue ribbon and medal also pasted on cover. Roosevelt FE Grade center-spread. This catalogue is now quite scarce.

Export Price List, November 15, 1916

A single sheet glued to the first page of some retail catalogues; heading reads "IMPORTANT—Change of Prices, Export Effective November 15, 1916." Unlike later, Savage Arms export lists in which prices were hand-written for specific foreign currencies, prices on this list are printed and presumably represent the amount in U.S. dollars that Fox required after conversion to foreign currencies. For unknown reasons, FE Grade is not included.

Sterlingworth	$ 42.00
with ejectors	$ 54.00
A Grade	$ 60.00
AE Grade	$ 72.00
B Grade	$ 90.00
BE Grade	$102.00
CE Grade	$120.00
XE Grade	$150.00
DE Grade	$240.00

Catalogue, 1917

9 1/2 by 6 1/2 inches, 24 pages plus cover, saddle-stitched with three wire staples, printed in two colors. "Fox Gets the Game" cover applique. Some catalogues issued in 1917 have the ribbon-and-medal cover applique. All have the Roosevelt FE Grade center-spread and loose-leaf order blank with Fox-Kautzky trigger information on the verso.

This was the last large-format Fox catalogue issued until about 1927.

Net prices:

Sterlingworth	$25.00
with ejectors	$32.50
A Grade	$37.50
AE Grade	$45.00
B Grade	$52.50
BE Grade	$60.00
CE Grade	$75.00
XE Grade	$100.00
DE Grade	$150.00
FE Grade	$350.00

SERIES 4: *"A Fox Gets the Game,"* pocket-size, 1918-1924

Fox produced more of the so-called "pocket" catalogues than any other factory publication and used the small, 6- by 3 ½-inch, format for many years. Covers are printed in three colors—brown, black, and gray—and the texts in two colors. Some editions contain as many as forty pages. These little catalogues were designed for maximum mileage and were reprinted several times.

Despite the popular name, the small size wasn't really intended to fit into a pocket but rather into what was the standard, letter-sized envelope of the day. Net prices are printed in some; in others, prices are listed on separate, tipped-in sheets.

Establishing the precise year in which many of these catalogues were issued can be difficult if not virtually impossible, but using internal evidence, you can sort them at least as follows:

1918: B Grade included; single trap guns not included
1919-1922: B Grade not included; single trap guns included; HE Grade appears only in price list
1924: B Grade not included; single trap guns included; HE Grade included in text.

Catalogue, 1918

6 by 3 ½ inches, 32 pages, self-cover, saddle-stitched with two wire staples. This is the last Fox publication to include the B Grade.

Net prices:
    Sterlingworth $ 37.50

with ejectors	$ 45.00
A Grade	$ 45.00
AE Grade	$ 54.00
B Grade	$ 63.00
BE Grade	$ 72.00
CE Grade	$ 90.00
XE Grade	$120.00
DE Grade	$180.00
FE Grade	$350.00

Price List, 1919
Doubles:

Sterlingworth	$ 55.00
with ejectors	$ 67.50
A Grade	$ 66.00
AE Grade	$ 78.50
CE Grade	$100.00
XE Grade	$150.00
DE Grade	$225.00
FE Grade	$500.00

Singles:

J Grade	$130.00
K Grade	$150.00
L Grade	$200.00
M Grade	$500.00

Price List, February 1, 1920

Includes jobber, dealer, and consumer prices, the latter with tax. Fox clearly anticipated a possible price change later in the year, as the last line of this price list reads, "Orders for delivery after July 1st, 1920, will be accepted at prices ruling at time of shipment."

Consumer prices:
Doubles:

Sterlingworth	$55.00
with ejectors	$67.50
A Grade	$68.25
AE Grade	$80.75
CE Grade	$115.00
XE Grade	$175.00

	DE Grade	$275.00
	FE Grade	$500.00
Singles:		
	J Grade	$155.50
	K Grade	$180.00
	L Grade	$250.00
	M Grade	$500.00

Price List, January 1, 1921
Doubles:

	Sterlingworth	$ 55.00
	with ejectors	$ 67.50
	A Grade	$ 68.25
	AE Grade	$ 80.75
	CE Grade	$115.00
	XE Grade	$175.00
	DE Grade	$275.00
	FE Grade	$500.00
Singles:		
	J Grade	$155.00
	K Grade	$180.00
	L Grade	$250.00
	M Grade	$500.00

Price List, January 1, 1922

This is the first price list to include the GE Grade.

Doubles:

	Sterlingworth	$ 48.00
	with ejectors	$ 60.50
	A Grade	$ 62.00
	AE Grade	$ 74.50
	CE Grade	$115.00
	XE Grade	$185.00
	DE Grade	$275.00
	FE Grade	$500.00
	GE Grade	$1100.00

Singles:

	J Grade	$155.00

A.H. FOX

K Grade	$180.00
L Grade	$250.00
M Grade	$500.00

Price List, January 1, 1923
First list to include the HE Super-Fox, in 12-gauge only. Curiously, two versions were printed; both bear the same date, but one lists the HE at $100, the other at $125.

Doubles:

Sterlingworth	$48.00
with ejectors	$60.50
A Grade	$62.00
AE Grade	$74.50
CE Grade	$115.00
XE Grade	$185.00
DE Grade	$275.00
FE Grade	$500.00
GE Grade	$1100.00
HE Grade	$100 / $125

Singles:

J Grade	$139.00
K Grade	$180.00
L Grade	$250.00
M Grade	$500.00

Super-Fox Brochure, 1923, 1925, early 1930s
3 1/2 by 6 1/4 inches, 20 pages, saddle-stitched with two wire staples; printed in two colors, second as spot color. The A.H. Fox Gun Company published two versions. The first, put out in 1923, shows the Super-Fox available in 12-gauge only; the second, published in 1925, is identical except for listing the 20-gauge as well. The first—and possibly both—contains a loose-leaf sheet promoting Super-X three-inch cartridges. This is printed in black on blue paper.

Savage Arms reissued the 1925 version in the early 1930s, with a slightly redesigned cover and, naturally, Savage Arms cited as the manufacturer.

Price List, January 1, 1924

Doubles:

Sterlingworth	$ 48.00
with ejectors	$ 60.50
A Grade	$ 62.00
AE Grade	$ 74.50
CE Grade	$115.00
XE Grade	$185.00
DE Grade	$275.00
FE Grade	$500.00
GE Grade	$1100.00
HE Grade	$100.00

Singles:

J Grade	$125.00
K Grade	$153.00
L Grade	$210.00
M Grade	$500.00

SERIES 5: *"Wood-Grain"* Covers, 1925-1927

In 1925, Fox brought out a new cover design comprising simply the words "The FOX GUN / The Finest Gun in the World" against a background of walnut grain. The 1925 version is the most expensively printed, although it amounts to the 1924 catalogue text with the new cover. The 1926 and '27 versions were printed in the less-expensive self-cover approach—that is, the cover is printed on the same paper as the text rather than on heavier paper.

Typically, these catalogues are 6 1/4 by 3 1/2 inches, 40 pages, saddle-stitched with two wire staples, printed in black and brown. The HE Super-Fox is noted as available in 12 and 20 gauges. Prices are shown on separate sheets.

"How to Buy a Gun," 1920s

3 1/4 by 6 inches, 16 pages, self-cover, saddle-stitched with two wire staples, printed in black and green. A delightful little brochure that Fox produced as a promotional piece and often referred to in magazine advertising.

A.H. FOX

"Have a Healthful Hobby," mid-1920s

Single sheet four-folded into ten panels; folded size 3 5/8 by 6 1/4 inches. This is one of the first Fox publications to use photographs rather than engravings. An interesting piece, although it never gets around to explaining exactly what the health benefits of owning a Fox gun might be.

Price List, March 1, 1926

Doubles:

Sterlingworth	$ 36.50
with ejectors	$ 48.40
A Grade	$ 52.50
AE Grade	$ 64.50
HE Grade	$ 79.60
CE Grade	$107.30
XE Grade	$172.60
DE Grade	$256.60
FE Grade	$466.50
GE Grade	$1026.00

Singles:

J Grade	$112.00
K Grade	$140.53
L Grade	$185.00
M Grade	$466.50

Catalogue, 1927

6 1/4 by 3 1/2 inches, 40 pages, self-cover, saddle-stitched with two wire staples, printed in black and brown. Another version of the small-format, "wood-grain" cover catalogue. Uses a slightly smaller, lighter-weight typeface for headings than the 1926 version, but text, illustrations, and pagination are all identical.

Price List, January 1, 1927

Doubles:

Sterlingworth	$ 36.50
with ejectors	$ 48.40
A Grade	$ 52.50
AE Grade	$ 64.50
HE Grade	$ 79.60
CE Grade	$107.30
XE Grade	$172.60

        DE Grade $256.60
        FE Grade $466.50
        GE Grade $1026.00
Singles:
        J Grade $125
        K Grade $150
        L Grade $185
        M Grade $466.50

FOX PLAY GUN LITERATURE, c.1927-1933

Beginning about 1927, Fox issued a number of one-and two-fold pieces advertising the various toy guns, cannons, targets, cartridges, and extra bags of the wooden balls the guns were meant to fire. Establishing precise dates for them is well-nigh impossible, except that those published before 1930 often bear the A.H. Fox Gun Company imprint, while those issued afterwards are cited as products of the Fox Manufacturing Company or simply the Fox Company.

Here's a sampling of prices, taken from magazine ads and brochures:
       1927: double-barrel, $3.75
       c.1928: double-barrel, $3.50
           extra shells, 50¢
           wooden balls, 15¢ per bag
       1929: double-barrel with target and ammunition, $3
       1931: double-barrel, $3
           Ranger repeating cannon, $2.25
           wooden balls, 15¢ per bag
       c.1931: double barrel, $3
           "Model 31" 15-shot repeater, $3.90
           "Model 32 Western Scout" 7-shot repeater, $2.25
           "Model 33 Indian Chief" single-shot, $1.75
           wooden balls, 15¢ per bag
       1933: double-barrel, $2
           15-shot repeater, $3
           7-shot repeater, $2
           single-shot, $1.50
           Ranger repeating cannon, $1.50

A.H. FOX

SERIES 6: *"Wood-Grain/Fox Head"* Covers, 1928-1929

The last gun catalogues issued by the A.H. Fox Gun Company are 6- by 9-inch vertical-format pieces, 12 pages, self-cover, saddle-stitched with two wire staples, printed in two colors, black and brown. The covers show a wood-grain panel at the top with "The FOX GUN / The Finest Gun in the World" inside it. A vignette of a fox's head inside a circle is at the center, and at the bottom is printed "Manufactured by A.H. Fox Gun Company, Philadelphia, Pa." Prices were printed on separate sheets.

Price List, January 1, 1928

$6\,^3/_4$ by $6\,^1/_4$ inches, medium-green paper printed on both sides in black ink. Headed "For Dealers Only." Dealer and consumer prices and prices for parts are shown on the front, costs for repairs on the verso.

Consumer prices:

Doubles:

Sterlingworth	$ 36.50
with ejectors	$ 48.40
A Grade	$ 52.50
AE Grade	$ 64.50
HE Grade	$ 79.60
CE Grade	$107.30
XE Grade	$172.60
DE Grade	$256.60
FE Grade	$466.50
GE Grade	$1026.00

Singles:

J Grade	$125.00
K Grade	$150.00
L Grade	$185.00
M Grade	$466.50

Price List, January 1, 1929

$6\,^1/_4$ by 7 inches, single-fold, yellow paper, printed in black on both sides. Headed "For Jobbers Only." Front shows jobber, dealer and consumer prices, and prices for parts; repair costs on verso.

Consumer prices:

Doubles:

Sterlingworth	$ 36.50
with ejectors	$ 48.40
A Grade	$ 52.50
AE Grade	$ 64.50
HE Grade	$ 66.50
CE Grade	$100.00
XE Grade	$172.60
DE Grade	$256.60
FE Grade	$466.50
GE Grade	$1026.00

Singles:

J Grade	$125.00
K Grade	$150.00
L Grade	$185.00
M Grade	$466.50

Repair Price List, January 1, 1929

6 1/4 by 7 inches, single fold, slick white paper, printed in black on both sides. Front shows prices for parts, cost of repairs on verso. The specimen I've seen was issued by A.H. Fox Gun Company but bears Savage Arms overstamps.

Fox Reels, 1931-1932

8 1/2 by 11 inches, 8 pages, self-cover. Published by Fox Company; describes full line of Fox fishing reels. Printed in black and green; photo of Fox plant on cover.

SERIES 7: Lynn Bogue Hunt Covers, 1930-1934

The first Fox catalogues issued by Savage Arms are 7 3/8 by 9 inches, 24 pages, saddle-stitched with two wire staples, printed in two colors. The covers are black with silver-gray trim and feature a Lynn Bogue Hunt duck-shooting scene as a full-color applique. This format remained in use through 1934.

A.H. FOX

Price List, January 2, 1930

Doubles:

Sterlingworth	$ 36.50
Sterlingworth DeLuxe	$ 39.30
Sterlingworth Ejector	$ 48.40
A Grade	$ 52.50
AE Grade	$ 64.50
HE Grade	$ 66.50
CE Grade	$100.00
XE Grade	$172.60
DE Grade	$256.60
FE Grade	$466.60
GE Grade	$1026.00

Singles:

J Grade	$125.00
K Grade	$150.00
L Grade	$185.00
M Grade	$466.50

Price List, 1930

Single tip-in sheet, no date; retail prices same as January 2 price list.

Jobber's Price List, January 15, 1931

8 ½ by 11 inches, 8 pages, Savage Arms Form 38-31. According to the terms and conditions specified, the company deducted two percent if accounts were paid in ten days and offered a quantity allowance of $.50 per gun to any jobber purchasing twenty or more Fox guns during 1931. Jobbers could save an additional $.50 per unit on Fox guns shipped before August 1, provided the factory actually shipped ten guns or more and the jobber ordered twenty guns or more prior to the same date. All jobbing prices were "guaranteed against our own decline during 1931." Retail prices same as January 2, 1930, price list.

Wholesale Price List, January 15, 1931

8 ½ by 11 inches, 8 pages, Savage Arms Form 43-31. Intended for use by wholesalers only. Specifications and retail prices same as January 2, 1930, price list.

"Fox Trap Guns," 1932

10 1/8 inches by 6 1/4 inches, two-folded to form six panels, printed in two colors—black and red. Describes Trap Grade double and single trap gun.

Wholesale Price List, January 25, 1932

8 1/2 by 11 inches, 8 pages, Savage Arms Form 43-32. SP, SPE, and Trap grades listed, along with non-selective single trigger.

Retail prices:

Doubles:

Sterlingworth	$ 36.50
Sterlingworth Ejector	$ 48.40
Sterlingworth DeLuxe	$ 39.50
Sterlingworth DeLuxe Ejector	$ 51.50
SP Grade	$ 45.00
SPE Grade	$ 57.00
A Grade	$ 52.50
AE Grade	$ 64.50
HE Grade	$ 66.50
Trap Grade	$125.00
CE Grade	$100.00
XE Grade	$172.60
DE Grade	$256.60
FE Grade	$466.50

Singles:

J Grade	$125.00
K Grade	$150.00
L Grade	$185.00
M Grade	$466.50

Price List, June 21, 1932

Single sheet, listing new retail prices for all guns.

Doubles:

Sterlingworth	$ 39.50
Sterlingworth DeLuxe	$ 43.00
Sterlingworth Ejector	$ 52.50
Sterlingworth DeLuxe Ejector	$ 56.00
SP Grade	$ 48.50
SPE Grade	$ 61.00
A Grade	$ 57.00

AE Grade	$ 70.00
HE Grade	$ 72.00
CE Grade	$110.00
Trap Grade	$135.00
XE Grade	$185.00
DE Grade	$275.00
FE Grade	$500.00

Singles:

J Grade	$135.00
K Grade	$160.00
L Grade	$200.00
M Grade	$500.00

Fox Special/SP Grade brochure, 1932

12 ½ by 18 inches, single-fold, printed in black and red on white paper, one side only. Headed "Announcing the New Fox Double with Single Trigger." Left side describes SP Grade with non-selective trigger; right side devoted to Savage rifles.

"The Fox Sterlingworth" brochures, undated

6 by 10 ¼ inches, twice folded, printed in three colors (black, brown, and blue) on white paper. Savage issued at least two versions of this, possibly more. Of the two I've seen, the Sterlingworth is listed at $39.50 and other Fox guns priced from $57 to $500, which suggests that it was issued between 1932 and 1935. The other shows the Sterlingworth at $42.85 and other guns from $60 to $525; those prices were current in 1937.

Jobber's Price List, March 15, 1933

8 ½ by 11 inches, 8 pages; Savage Arms Form 31-33. Retail prices same as price list of June 21, 1932.

Wholesale Price List, March 15, 1933

8 ½ by 11 inches, 8 pages; Savage Arms Form 43-33. Retail prices same as price list of June 21, 1932.

Retail Price List, March 1, 1934

Doubles:

Sterlingworth	$ 39.50
Sterlingworth DeLuxe	$ 43.00
Sterlingworth Ejector	$ 52.50
Sterlingworth DeLuxe Ejector	$ 56.00
Sterlingworth Wildfowl	$ 62.50
SP Grade	$ 57.00
SPE Grade	$ 70.00
SP Skeet	$ 92.00
A Grade	$ 57.00
AE Grade	$ 70.00
HE Grade	$ 72.00
CE Grade	$110.00
Trap Grade	$135.00
XE Grade	$185.00
DE Grade	$275.00
FE Grade	$500.00

Singles:

J Grade	$135.00
K Grade	$160.00
L Grade	$200.00
M Grade	$500.00

"New Fox Special," 1934

14 by 6 1/4 inches, three-folded to form eight panels, printed in two colors—black and orange. Savage Form 23. Describes SP and SPE grades.

Jobber's Price List, March 1, 1934

8 1/2 by 11 inches, 8 pages, printed in black on blue paper. Savage Arms Form 31-34. Retail prices same as price list of March 1, 1934.

A.H. FOX

SERIES 8: *"Traditionally Fine Doubles,"* 1935-1942

The final series of Fox catalogues all use the same cover design—a handsome piece in the Art Deco style. All are 7 3/8 by 9 1/8 inches, self-cover, saddle-stitched with two wire staples. Interiors, all printed in black, the covers in several different colors. All use the title "FOX / TRADITIONALLY FINE / Double barrel Shotguns."

Catalogue, 1935
Cover green and black, leatherette-texture, gold-foil stamped.

Retail Price List, February 20, 1935
Doubles:

Sterlingworth	$ 39.50
Sterlingworth Ejector	$ 52.50
Sterlingworth DeLuxe	$ 43.00
Sterlingworth Deluxe Ejector	$ 56.00
Sterlingworth Skeet &Upland Game	$ 44.50
Sterlingworth Skeet &Upland Ejector	$ 57.50
SP Grade	$ 57.00
SPE Grade	$ 70.00
SP Skeet & Upland Game	$ 70.00
A Grade	$ 57.00
AE Grade	$ 70.00
HE Grade	$ 72.00
CE Grade	$110.00
Trap Grade	$135.00
XE Grade	$185.00
DE Grade	$275.00
FE Grade	$500.00

Singles:

J Grade	$135.00
M Grade	$500.00

Wholesaler-Jobber Price list, 1935
8 1/2 by 11 inches, 12 pages. Prices same as February 20 price list. This catalogue lists the Sterlingworth Wildfowl ($62.50), however, while the February 20 price list does not.

Catalogue, 1936
Cover blue and black, linen-finish, gold-foil stamped.

Retail Price List, February 10, 1936
Doubles:

Sterlingworth	$ 48.25
Sterlingworth DeLuxe	$ 46.25
Sterlingworth Ejector	$ 55.75
Sterlingworth DeLuxe Ejector	$ 59.25
Sterlingworth Skeet &Upland Game	$ 48.00
Sterlingworth Skeet &Upland Ejector	$ 90.00
SP Grade	$ 60.00
SPE Grade	$ 73.00
SP Skeet & Upland Game	$110.00
SPR Grade	$140.00
A Grade	$ 60.00
AE Grade	$ 73.00
HE Grade	$ 75.00
CE Grade	$117.00
Trap Grade	$140.00
XE Grade	$200.00
DE Grade	$300.00
FE Grade	$525.00

Singles:

J Grade	$140.00
M Grade	$525.00

Jobber's Price List, February 6, 1936
8 1/2 by 11 inches, 12 pages, Savage Form 31-36. Sterlingworth Wildfowl listed at $59.25.

Catalogue, 1937
Cover medium-brown, black, and white.

Retail Price List, January 2, 1937
Doubles:

Sterlingworth	$ 42.85
Sterlingworth Ejector	$ 55.75
Sterlingworth DeLuxe	$ 46.25

A.H. FOX

Sterlingworth DeLuxe Ejector	$ 59.25
Sterlingworth Skeet &Upland Game	$ 48.00
Sterlingworth Skeet&Upland Ejector	$ 61.00
SP Grade	$ 60.00
SPE Grade	$ 73.00
SP Skeet & Upland Game	$100.00
A Grade	$ 60.00
AE Grade	$ 73.00
HE Grade	$ 75.00
CE Grade	$117.00
XE Grade	$200.00
DE Grade	$300.00
FE Grade	$525.00

Singles:

J Grade	$140.00

Catalogue, 1938
Cover and text identical to 1937 catalogue.

Distributor's Price List, February 1, 1938
8 ½ by 11 inches, 8 pages, Savage Form 27-38.

Doubles:

Sterlingworth	$ 35.00
Sterlingworth Ejector	$ 45.00
Sterlingworth Wildfowl	$ 48.00
Sterlingworth DeLuxe	$ 37.75
Sterlingworth DeLuxe Ejector	$ 48.00
Sterlingworth Skeet &Upland Game	$ 39.00
Sterlingworth Skeet &Upland Ejector	$ 49.75
SP Grade	$ 49.00
SPE Grade	$ 59.50
SP Skeet & Upland Game	$ 81.75
A Grade	$ 49.00
AE Grade	$ 59.50
HE Grade	$ 61.00
CE Grade	$ 96.00
XE Grade	$165.00
DE Grade	$245.00
FE Grade	$425.00

Singles:
J Grade	$115.00

Wholesale Price List, February 1, 1938
8 1/2 by 11 inches, Savage Form 28-38. Prices same as Distributor's list.

Catalogue, 1939
Cover and text identical to 1937 and 1938 catalogues.

Price List, February 1, 1939
Doubles:

Sterlingworth	$ 44.75
Sterlingworth Ejector	$ 57.75
Sterlingworth DeLuxe	$ 48.25
Sterlingworth DeLuxe Ejector	$ 61.25
Sterlingworth Skeet &Upland Game	$ 50.00
SP Grade	$ 60.00
SPE Grade	$ 73.00
SP Skeet & Upland Game	$100.00
A Grade	$ 60.00
AE Grade	$ 73.00
HE Grade	$ 75.00
CE Grade	$117.00
XE Grade	$200.00
DE Grade	$300.00
FE Grade	$525.00

Singles:
J Grade	$140.00

Export Catalogue, March 1, 1939
8 1/2 by 11 inches, 28 pages, Savage Form 31-39. A curious little document, four pages of which are devoted to Fox guns. No prices are printed. The copy I've seen has "British Isles Export Prices" hand-written on the cover and prices hand-written with a fountain-pen, prices clearly adjusted to reflect the exchange rate between the dollar and the pound. Presumably for the sake of crisp communication via trans-Atlantic cable, each model and grade is given a five-letter code name, as follows:

Sterlingworth	"Pound"
Sterlingworth Ejector	"Matic"
Sterlingworth Wildfowl	"Tonic'
Sterlingworth DeLuxe	"Luxor"
Sterlingworth DeLuxe Ejector	"Tudor"
Sterlingworth Skeet & Upland Game	"Quail"
Sterlingworth Skeet & Upland Ejector	"Stark"
SP Grade	"Speck"
SPE Grade	"Spade"
SP Skeet & Upland Game	"Stamp"
SP Skeet & Upland Game with single trigger	"Robin"
A Grade	"Adele"
AE Grade	"Argus"
HE Grade	"Henry"
CE Grade	"Manor"
XE Grade	"Index"
DE Grade	"Drain"
FE Grade	"Fruit"
J Grade single	"Jenny"

Catalogue, 1940
Cover orange, black, and white.

Price List, January 2, 1940

Model B	$ 25.75
Sterlingworth	$ 48.50
Sterlingworth Ejector	$ 61.25
Sterlingworth Wildfowl	$ 64.50
Sterlingworth DeLuxe	$ 51.50
Sterlingworth DeLuxe Ejector	$ 64.50
Sterlingworth Skeet & Upland Game	$ 53.50
Sterlingworth Skeet & Upland Ejector	$ 66.50
SP Grade	$ 63.50
SPE Grade	$ 77.00
A Grade	$ 63.50
AE Grade	$ 77.00
HE Grade	$ 80.00
CE Grade	$125.00
XE Grade	$210.00
DE Grade	$320.00
FE Grade	$565.00

Wholesale Price List, January 2, 1940

8 1/2 by 11 inches, 28 pages of which five are devoted to Fox guns. Savage Arms Form 28-40. Price list itself four pages, Form 28A-40.

Catalogue, 1941

Cover red, black, and white.

Wholesale Price List, January 2, 1941

8 1/2 by 11 inches, 24 pages, Savage Form 28-41. Four pages are devoted to Fox guns, although not all grades available at the time are listed. Retail prices (tax included):

Model B	$ 27.95
Sterlingworth	$ 52.65
Sterlingworth Ejector	$ 66.45
Sterlingworth Skeet &Upland Game	$ 58.05
Sterlingworth Skeet &Upland Ejector	$ 72.05
Sterlingworth DeLuxe	$ 55.90
Sterlingworth DeLuxe Ejector	$ 69.90
SP Grade	$ 68.80
SPE Grade	$ 83.60
AE Grade	$ 83.60
CE Grade	$135.45

Retail Price List, June 16, 1941

Model B	$ 29.30
Sterlingworth	$ 56.50
Sterlingworth Ejector	$ 72.00
Sterlingworth DeLuxe	$ 60.50
Sterlingworth DeLuxe Ejector	$ 75.70
Sterlingworth Skeet & Upland Game	$ 62.75
Sterlingworth Skeet & Upland Ejector	$ 78.00
SP Grade	$ 75.00
SPE Grade	$ 90.00
A Grade	$ 75.00
AE Grade	$ 90.00
HE Grade	$ 93.00
CE Grade	$149.00
XE Grade	$260.00
DE Grade	$400.00

A.H. FOX

Catalogue, 1942
Cover red, black, and white. This is the last Fox retail catalogue published.

Retail Price List, January 2, 1942

Model B	$ 33.70
Sterlingworth	$ 64.95
Sterlingworth Ejector	$ 82.80
Sterlingworth DeLuxe	$ 69.60
Sterlingworth DeLuxe Ejector	$ 87.00
Sterlingworth Skeet & Upland Game	$ 72.15
Sterlingworth Skeet & Upland Ejector	$ 89.70
SP Grade	$ 86.00
SPE Grade	$103.50
A Grade	$ 86.25
AE Grade	$103.50
HE Grade	$106.95
CE Grade	$171.00
XE Grade	$299.00
DE Grade	$460.00

Wholesale Price List, January 2, 1942
8 1/2 by 11 inches, 24 pages, Savage Form 28-42. Four pages devoted to Fox guns; Grades A, HE, XE, and DE are not listed.

Distributor's Price List, January 22, 1945

Model B	$ 34.50
Sterlingworth	$ 66.50
Sterlingworth Ejector	$ 84.75
Sterlingworth Skeet &Upland Game	$ 73.85
Sterlingworth Skeet &Upland Ejector	$ 91.85
Sterlingworth DeLuxe	$ 71.25
Sterlingworth DeLuxe Ejector	$ 89.00
SP Grade	$ 88.00
SPE Grade	$105.95
AE Grade	$105.95
CE Grade	$175.00
XE Grade	$306.00
DE Grade	$470.00

Distributor's Price List, October 15, 1946

Model B	$ 48.60
Sterlingworth	$ 89.90
Sterlingworth Ejector	$114.10
SP Grade	$118.75
SPE Grade	$143.60
AE Grade	$143.60
CE Grade	$236.00

Information and Ordering Guide, September 1993

9 $^{1}/_{2}$ by 7 inches, 4 pages, heavily textured paper, self-cover, saddle-stitched with two wire staples, printed in black and green. Cover printed with green background and a four-color reproduction of the "A Fox Gets the Game" illustration. Grades CE, XE, DE, FE, and Exhibition listed, grades CE and FE illustrated. This is the first of the new Fox catalogues published by the Connecticut Shotgun Manufacturing Company.

Price List, September 1993

CE Grade	$ 5,650.00
XE Grade	$ 8,500.00
DE Grade	$12,500.00
FE Grade	$17,500.00
Exhibition Grade	$25,000.00

Appendix II
CHRONOLOGY

1875: Ansley Herman Fox born, June 25, Decatur, Georgia

c. 1878: Fox family moves to Baltimore

1894: Ansley Fox granted patent No. 522,464 for hammerless break-action gun, July 3

1896: Ansley Fox granted patent No. 554,507 for car-brake, February 11
Ansley Fox granted patent No. 563,153 for improvements to 1894 design, June 30

1897: National Arms Company incorporated, December 9

1898: Ansley Fox and Fentress Keleher married, June 29
National Arms Company becomes National Gun Company, July
Fox Gun Company, Baltimore, incorporated, July 26; purchases Fox patents from National Gun Company
Ansley Fox wins Maryland Handicap live-pigeon shoot, October 14

1899: James Addison Fox born, December; dies as infant

1900: Ansley Fox leaves Fox Gun Company; joins Winchester Repeating Arms Company as professional shooter and sales representative

Fox Gun Company reorganizes as Baltimore Arms Company; in receivership, 1904

Ansley Fox competes in the Grand American Handicap tournament in New York; finishes with 96-percent average, highest of anyone who completed every event, April

Ansley Fox sets new world record for clay-target trap doubles (98 x 100), May 15

Ansley Fox competes in first Grand American Handicap tournament to use clay targets, June

Ansley Fox sets new club record for clay targets (109 x 110) at Westminster Gun Club, Carrol County, Maryland, August

Ansley Fox wins High Overall Average at Dixie Gun Club Tournament, Pensacola, Florida, September

Ansley Fox is high gun at Peters Cartridge Company's three-day target and live-pigeon tournament, Atlanta, October

1901: Ansley Fox moves to Philadelphia

Ansley Fox is high gun in Grand American Handicap Tournament, New York; loses Grand American event in miss-and-out shoot-off, April

1902: Ansley Fox competes in last Grand American Handicap tournament to use live pigeons, Kansas City, May-June

Philadelphia Arms Company incorporated in New Jersey, November 5

Ansley Fox granted patent No. 714,688 for breechloading gun, December 2

Ansley Fox resigns affiliation with Winchester, December

1903: Philadelphia Arms Company incorporated in Pennsylvania, October 27

1904: First Philadelphia Arms guns delivered, July

Harry H. Fox granted patent No. 767,557 for breechloading gun, August 16; assigned to Philadelphia Arms

Max Wirsing granted patent No. 767,621 for ejector system, August 16; assigned to Philadelphia Arms

Ansley Fox resigns from Philadelphia Arms, announces plans to manufacture new gun, December

1905: A.H. Fox Gun Company incorporated, April
Ansley Fox granted patent No. 796,119 for fastening system, August 1
Ansley Fox granted patent No. 801,862 for breechloading gun, October 17
First A.H. Fox Gun Company guns built, including prototype 16-gauge (No. 17)

1906: A.H. Fox hammerless gun formally announced, January; A, B, & C Grades advertised, D Grade mentioned
Ansley Fox granted patent No. 810,046 for fastening system, January 16
George A. Mosher appointed general manager of Fox Gun Company
A.H. Fox Gun Company buys Philadelphia Arms, November
Joseph Kautzky granted first patent, No. 827,242, for single trigger

1907: D and F grade guns appear in advertising
Ejectors advertised as optional features
Philadelphia Arms Company dissolved, March 15
A.H. Fox Gun Company incorporated in New Jersey, March 15
A.H. Fox Gun Company corporation dissolved in New Jersey; reincorporated in Pennsylvania, September 27

1908: George Mosher resigns; Adolph R. Roll hired as Eastern sales representative

1909: A.W. Connor hired as vice president/sales manager
Ansley Fox and George A. Horne granted patent No. 921,220 for ejector system for breechloading gun, May 11
Fox Gun Company becomes first gunmaker to display at the Grand American Handicap tournament

1910: Sterlingworth announced; described as "Model 1911"; approximately first 3000 guns marked "Sterlingworth Company," about 400 with Wayne Junction address; feature sculpted hinge-pin into 62000-number range; "chrome-nickel and vanadium steel" barrels mentioned
Sterlingworths built with leaf-spring fore-end latch
William H. Gough hired as chief of engraving department
Some graded 12-gauge guns stamped "Model 1910"

A.H. FOX

1911: Fox Gun Company announces it is "preparing to furnish" 16- and 20-gauge guns, January

Chromox steel first mentioned by name in company literature

Kremer fore-end latch first appears on Sterlingworths

Joseph Kautzky granted patent No. 990,562 for single-trigger mechanism, April 25

Frederick T. Russell granted patent No. 991,375 for ejector system, May 2; assigned to A.H. Fox Gun Co.

Sterlingworth referred to as "A.H. Fox Model 1911"; listed in catalogue as available in "Standard," "Field," and "Brush" versions; ejectors announced as being available for Sterlingworths; Sterlingworth fore-end latch changed to loop-tensioner system

Fox Gun Company exhibits 16- and 20-gauge guns at Grand American Handicap tournament, June 20-23

1912: Fox Gun Company announces that delivery of small-bores would commence by September 1; small-bores described as "Model 1912"

Earliest-known X Grade 12-gauge shipped, February 22

A.H. Fox Gun Company in receivership, March

Edward and Clarence Godshalk purchase controlling interest in Fox Gun Company, March 21

A.W. Connor leaves Fox Gun Company; Ad Roll becomes sales manager

Ansley Fox and John C. Kremer granted patent No. 1,029,374 for fore-end latch, June 11

First 20-gauge gun known shipped, September 17; CE Grade, No. 200011

Lowest-number 16-gauge production gun shipped, October 21; DE Grade, No. 300001

Early graded smallbores built with snap-on fore-ends, Kremer latch

20-gauge guns available with 3-inch chambers

Guns marked "Chromox Fluid Steel" appear

1913: Second-generation engraving styles begin to appear

Fentress Fox petitions for divorce, March

Special Trap Gun appears in catalogue

Sterlingworth "Trap" version appears in catalogue

Change from snap-on to Deeley fore-end latch for small-bores complete

First 20-gauge guns (6) marked "XE" shipped, September, October, December

1914: Second-generation engraving styles in place
New-style frame-filing for XE, DE, and FE Grades begins to appear
Fox gun Company purchases patent to Kautzky single trigger
"Special" guns first advertised, $750; probably reference to "Gough" or "raised-gold" Specials
Special Trap Gun becomes XE Grade in catalogue
Ejectors become standard for C, X, D, and F grades
Fentress Fox granted divorce, March 23
Ansley Fox and Ellen Gerou married, March 25
Ansley Fox granted patent No. 1,105,971 for vehicle spring, August 4; assigned to "Automobile Development Company"
Joseph Kautzky granted patent No. 1,109,632 for single- trigger mechanism, September 1

1915: Clarence Godshalk granted patent No. 1,137,477 for ventilated rib, April 27
Burt Becker begins supplying custom work for A.H. Fox Gun Company
At Panama-Pacific Exposition in San Francisco, Fox wins Gold Medal for double guns and for single trigger
Fox Gun Company produces barrels for Serbian Mauser rifles, barrels and magazines for Moisin-Nagant rifles
Ansley Fox granted patent No. 1,151,350 for automobile shock absorber, August 24; assigned to Fox Pneumatic Shock-Absorber Company
(c.) Fox Company changes from bone/charcoal to cyanide case-coloring process

1916: Ansley Fox granted patent No. 1,172,588 for shock absorber, February 22; assigned to Fox Pneumatic Shock-Absorber Company

1917: Ansley Fox organizes Ansley H. Fox Company, Inc.
Ansley Fox in Phil. Dir. as President, Fox Pneumatic Shock-Absorber Company; converts shock absorber company to Fox Motor Company
Fox Gun Company begins manufacturing Colt .45 parts

1918: Last appearance of B Grade in catalogues/price lists
Fox Gun Company awarded government contract to produce Very flare pistols, August

1919: Single trap gun announced; J, K, and L grades advertised
First single trap gun known shipped, July 19; J Grade, No. 400006
First L Grade single trap gun known shipped, August 29; No. 400083
First K Grade single trap gun known shipped, September 15; No. 400023
Ansley Fox granted patent No. 1,293,396 for gas-operated machine gun, February 4
Ansley Fox and Walter J. Rice granted patent No. 1,294,892 for gas-operated machine gun, February 18
Ansley Fox organizes Fox Motor Car Company; November 21

1920: M Grade single trap gun advertised
Ansley Fox and Walter J. Rice granted patent No. 1,335,677 for machine-gun cartridge-feeding device, March 30
Godshalks organize Fox Automotive Products Corporation as subsidiary to AHFGCo.

1921: First M Grade single trap gun known shipped, April 5; No. 400346
Ansley Fox granted patent No. 1,367,810 for air- cooling system for internal-combustion engines, February 8
Ansley Fox granted patent No. 1,388,856 for machine-gun, August 30

1922: GE Grade appears in price list, January 1, $1100
Fox automobile unveiled in New York City, January
Super-Fox developed
First 20-gauge Super-Fox shipped, December 14

1923: Super-Fox first appears in price lists, @ $100 in some and @ $125 in others
Fox Motor Car Company in receivership
Ansley Fox granted patent No. 1,464,357 for air cooling system for motor-vehicle engines, August 7

1924: Super-Fox first appears in catalogue
Clarence Godshalk granted patent No. 1,520,643 for automobile steering lock, December 23
Clarence Godshalk granted patent No. 1,521,239 for auto lamp, December 30
Ansley Fox organizes Fox Holding Company, April 5

1925: Clarence Godshalk and D. Behrsing granted patent No. 1,543,047 for tilting steering wheel, June 23

Clarence Godshalk and D. Behrsing granted patent No. 1,548,011 for push-button circuit breaker, July 28

Clarence Godshalk granted patent No. 1,550,689 for lock-nut apparatus, August 25

Clarence Godshalk granted patent No. 1,554,815 for automobile lock, September 22

Ansley Fox granted patent No. 1,556,506 for internal- combustion engine, October 6

Ansley Fox granted patent No. 1,563,477 for internal- combustion engine, December 1

Ansley Fox granted patent No. 1,563,478 for air-cooling system, December 1

1926: Clarence Godshalk granted patent No. 1,570,476 for lock-nut, January 19

Clarence Godshalk granted patent No. 1,570,477 for spare-tire lock, January 19

Clarence Godshalk granted patent No. 1,578,424 for means of securing gear-casing parts, March 30

Ansley Fox granted patent No. 1,579,759 for internal- combustion engine, April 6

Clarence Godshalk granted patent No. 1,601,912 for removable gear-case cap, October 5

Clarence Godshalk granted patent No. 1603,045 for locking steering wheel, October 12

Ansley Fox moves to Pleasantville, New Jersey; organizes Seaboard Development Corporation

1927: Frederick Henke granted patent No. 1,625,657 for spare- wheel lock, April 27; assigned to Fox Gun Company

Frederick Henke granted patent No. 1,625,658 for tire lock, April 27; assigned to Fox Gun Company

Clarence Godshalk granted patent No. 1,637,995 for lock-nut, August 2

Clarence Godshalk granted patent No. 1,640,700 for vehicle signaling device, August 30

Frederick Henke granted patent No. 1,644,058 for toy gun, October 4; assigned to Fox Gun Company

A.H. FOX

Fox Play Gun introduced as "The Finest Play Gun in the World"; stamped "A.H. Fox Gun Company" until 1930, then "Fox Company"

(c.) Double guns with vent rib and beavertail fore- end begin to appear

Fox Company buys John Lauterbach Company, manufacturer of fishing reels; reels subsequently manufactured under Fox name; stamped "A.H. Fox Gun Company" until 1930, then "Fox Company"

1928: Frederick Henke granted patent No. 1,649,590 for electric switch; assigned to Fox Gun Company

Godshalks organize Fox Manufacturing Company (golf accessories)

Walter R. Paxson granted patent No. 1,671,451 for toy shotgun, May 29; assigned to Fox Gun Company

1929: Ansley Fox granted patent No. 1,711,493 for internal- combustion engine, May 7

Frederick Henke granted patent No. 1,735,079 for toy- gun cartridge, November 12; assigned to Fox Gun Company

Walter R. Paxson granted patent No. 1,735,086 for toy- gun cartridge, November 12; assigned to Fox Gun Company

Savage Arms buys A.H. Fox Gun Company, November

1930: Vent rib and beavertail fore-ends appear in catalogue as options for double guns A Grade and above

Sterlingworth DeLuxe introduced

1931: First guns in 450000 serial-number range shipped

Skeeter introduced

Sterlingworth DeLuxe Ejector introduced

Last L Grade single trap gun known shipped, December 11; No. 400566

Ansley Fox granted patent No. 1,836,312 for cigarette lighter, December 15

Last K Grade single trap gun known shipped, December 26; No. 400372

1932: Skeeter becomes Trap Grade, exhibited at Grand American

SP Grade, or "Fox Special," introduced

Non-selective single trigger available

Last M Grade single trap gun known shipped, June 16; No. 400476

Fox sells fishing reel business to Ocean City, November

1934: 20-gauge Super-Fox discontinued
SP Skeet Grade introduced
K and L grade single trap guns discontinued
Sterlingworth Wildfowl Grade introduced

1935: Sterlingworth Skeet and Upland Game Gun introduced
SP Skeet and Upland Game Gun introduced; presented as centerfold in catalogue—first centerfold since Roosevelt gun of 1915
Ansley Fox granted patent No. 2,006,591 for container for self-lighting cigarettes, July 2

1936: M Grade single trap gun discontinued
Catalogue notes that all Fox barrels are made from "special alloy steel;" Chromox supply exhausted
SPR Grade appears in jobber's and retail price lists
Last J Grade single trap gun known shipped, January 31; No. 400559
Ansley Fox granted patent No. 2,040,733 for ignition element for self-lighting cigarettes, May 12

1937: Trap Grade discontinued

1939: SP Skeet and Upland Game Gun discontinued
J Grade single trap gun discontinued

1940: FE Grade discontinued
Sterlingworth Wildfowl discontinued
Model B introduced
(c.) Ansley Fox organizes Fox Munitions Company
Ansley Fox granted patent No. 2,200,420 for machine for attaching ignition bands to cigarettes, May 14

1942: Last Fox retail catalogue issued
Ellen Fox dies, December 25

1943: (c.) Ansley Fox marries Velma Shank

1945: Super-Fox discontinued
DE Grade discontinued
Last 12-gauge gun known shipped

1946: Last distributor's price list issued, October
       Last 20-gauge gun known shipped, December 12; SP Grade, No. 203974

1948: Ansley Fox dies, August 15

1956: Last Fox gun sold from warehouse—Sterlingworth Skeet and Upland Game Gun, No. 161127

1993: Connecticut Shotgun Manufacturing Company resumes manufacture of Fox guns in 20-gauge only, grades CE, XE, DE, FE, and Exhibition First guns completed as not-for-sale display pieces, December '93-January '94: CE No. 205504, XE No. 205503, DE No. 205502, and Special No. 205507

1994: New Fox guns on first public display at the Shooting, Hunting and Outdoor Trade Show, Dallas, Texas, January 13-16.

Appendix III
Grades & Models by Year

Distinguishing between grades and models is one of the most confusing aspects of studying Fox guns. The problem begins in 1910, with the appearance of the Sterlingworth, and comes to full flower in the mid-1930s, when Savage offered a profusion of Sterlingworth and SP Grade guns.

Essentially, the amount of hand-work—fit, finish, filing, and engraving—and the quality of materials (especially wood, sometimes barrels) are what separate one grade from another. Models, on the other hand, are different from others of their grade in having certain features—ejectors, single trigger, a vent rib, and the like—that the others do not. So, strictly speaking, a CE is not a different grade from C but rather only a C Grade with ejectors.

Still, both the A.H. Fox Gun Company and Savage Arms implied such differences simply by calling one an A Grade and the other an AE Grade. Gun-fanciers do the same, and it really doesn't matter except in a sort of academic way. For the record, though, the Fox grades are as follows:

Sterlingworth	X/Special Trap
SP/Fox Special	D
SP Skeet & Upland	F
Skeeter/Trap Grade	G
A	J
B	K
H	L
C	M

The HE has the dubious distinction of being the only Fox gun that is both a grade and a model—a grade because of its decoration and a model because it's built on a frame different in size from any other Fox. Moreover, you could get it in grades other than H. Take this to its logical conclusion, and I suppose we'll have to say the same in part for the Super-Fox 20-gauge, which is a model because it's built on a unique frame but not a separate grade because it's decorated the same as the 12-gauge version...and to tell you the truth, I'd just as soon Fox had never built any Super 20s at all because they make my head hurt when I try to be academic...

So much for grades and models. What should be more useful is to know when they were all in production. For quick reference, this chart shows when each grade and model appeared in price lists or catalogues, which is about as close as we'll ever get to an accurate picture. In making it, I have used the most reliable sources, which are price lists and such publications as jobber's and wholesaler's catalogues; if you've read my comments in Appendix I, you already know why.

You should be aware, however, that guns often remained in inventory for some time after being officially discontinued, so these terminal dates don't necessarily indicate when the last gun of a given grade actually was taken out of warehouse stock. Sometimes, in fact, certain grades appeared in the catalogues for several years after the last specimen was sold. The few instances in which I happen to know the actual date of last shipment are noted in parentheses.

DOUBLE GUNS

Sterlingworth Standard.	1911-1946
Sterlingworth Field	1911-1946*
Sterlingworth Brush	1911-1946*
Sterlingworth Trap	1911-1946*
Sterlingworth Ejector	1911-1946
Sterlingworth DeLuxe	1930-1945
Sterlingworth DeLuxe Ejector	1931-1945
Sterlingworth Wildfowl	1934-1940

*The names *Field*, *Brush*, and *Trap* were used only until 1930, but Sterlingworth guns were built to the same specifications until the end.

Sterlingworth Skeet and
Upland Game 1935-1945 (1956)
Sterlingworth Ejector Skeet
and Upland Game 1935-1945
SP 1932-1946
SPE 1932-1946
SP Skeet 1934
SP Skeet and Upland Game 1935-1939
SPR 1936
A 1905-1942
AE 1905-1946
B 1905-1918
BE 1905-1918
C 1905-1913
CE .... 1905-1946, resumed 1993
Skeeter 1931
Trap 1932-1936
HE 12 1923-1942
HE 20 1925-1931
  (first shipped 1922, last 1940)
Special Trap 1913
XE .... 1914-1945, resumed 1993
D 1906-1913
DE .... 1906-1945, resumed 1993
F 1906-1913
FE .... 1906-1940, resumed 1993
GE 1922-1930
Exhibition 1993-

SINGLE TRAP GUNS

J 1919-1939 (1936)
K 1919-1934 (1931)
L 1919-1934 (1931)
M 1919-1936 (1932)

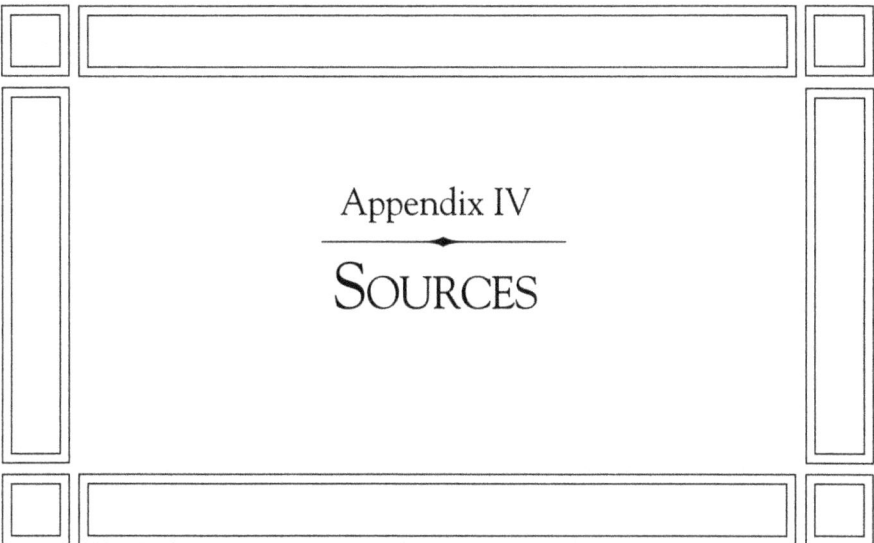

Appendix IV

Sources

Those of us who fancy the Fox gun are extremely fortunate in having an excellent resource for information from what factory records still exist. Roe Clark, Savage Arms historian, provides research services on specific guns for a fee of $15 per gun.

The work-order cards, which are virtually all that remain of Fox factory records, typically indicate grade, original specifications, and the shipping date. To obtain this information, write to:

        Roe S. Clark
        R.D. 1, Otis Stage Road
        Blandford
        Massachusetts 01008

Be sure to identify each gun by serial number.

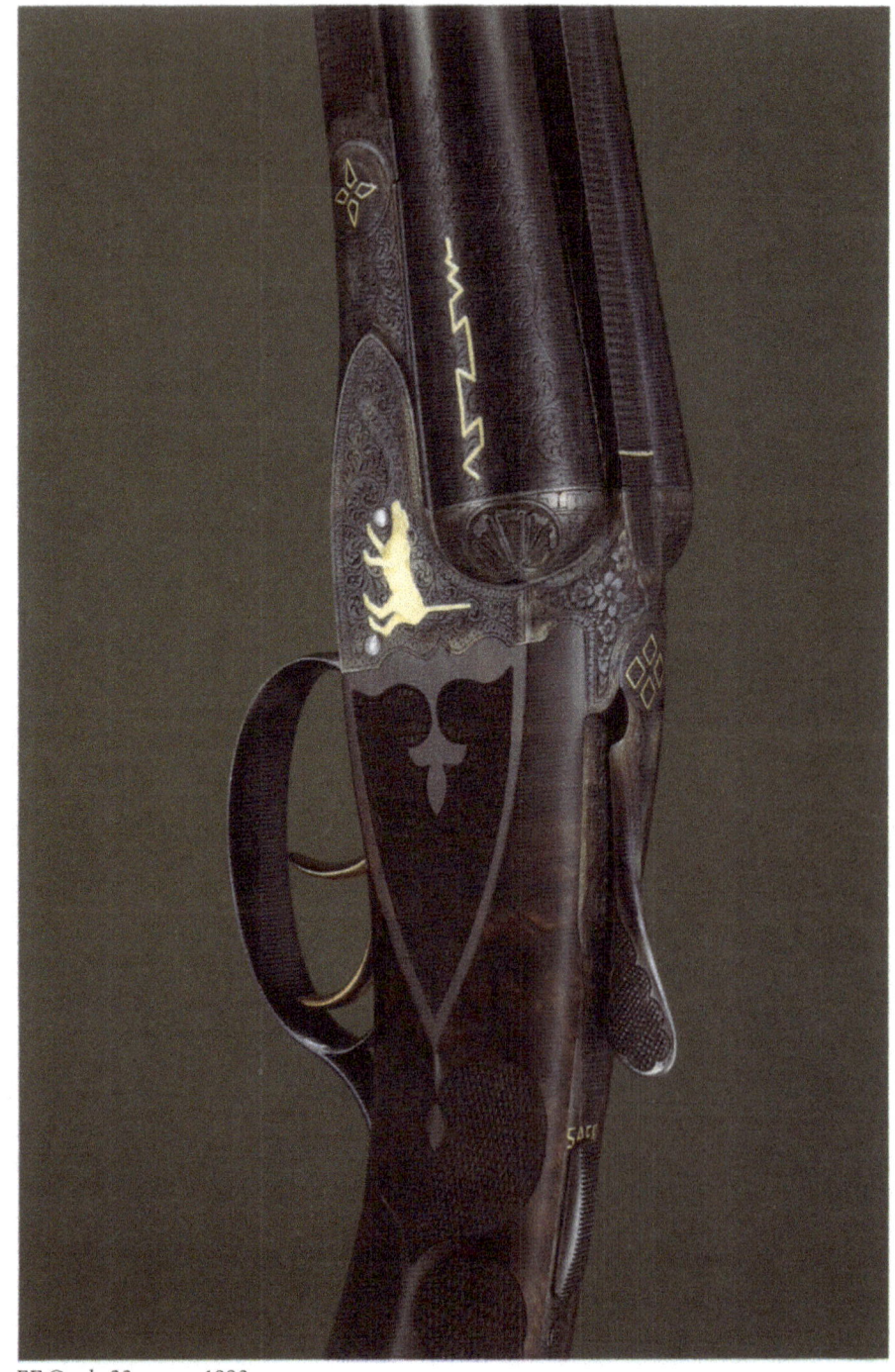

FE Grade 20-gauge, 1993   CONNECTICUT SHOTGUN MANUFACTURING CO.

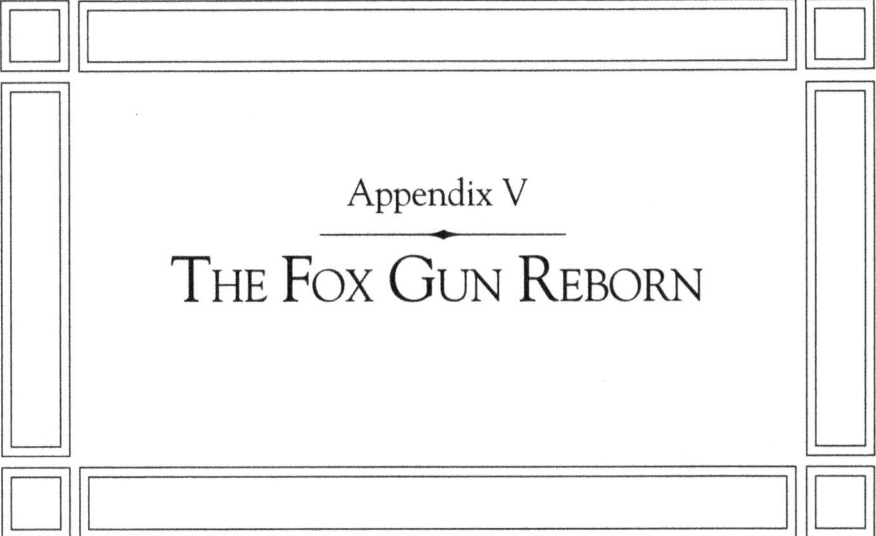

Appendix V

THE FOX GUN REBORN

The thing about history, someone once remarked to me, is that tomorrow there'll be more of it. To this truism I can only add that what becomes history tomorrow may not be what we'd predict judging from the history that accrued yesterday or the day before.

We have, for instance, more than a generation of yesterdays in the American gun trade from which to conclude that the manufacture of high-quality double guns in the United States is a phenomenon long past. The seeds of its demise sprouted even before Ansley Fox quit the gunmaking scene more than eighty years ago, and they came to full flower at the close of World War II. One by one, history claimed the American classics—Lefever in 1915, Parker and the Remington Model 32 in 1942, Fox in 1946, Ithaca in 1948, L.C. Smith in 1950. Only the Winchester Model 21 remained, surviving solely because John Olin refused to let it go—despite the fact that no factory-produced Model 21 ever sold for a profit. Finally, in December 1959, it too was taken out of regular production and consigned to the Winchester Custom Shop.

The same forces felled them all—escalating production costs, changing tastes, technological advances that allowed manufacturers to produce durable, reliable repeating guns at a fraction of what even the plainest doubles cost to build. American-made doubles simply were unable to claim any substantial share of the mass market.

Interest began to revive in the 1960s, among collectors and shooters alike. The one sent prices for old American doubles on a spectacular inflationary binge, and the other provided a steadily growing market for relatively inexpensive guns built in Europe and Japan. The remarkable success of the Japanese-built Parker Reproduction in the mid-1980s showed that the demand existed but at the same time offered no evidence that a similar gun made in America could be economically viable. Remington's ill-fated attempt at manufacturing Parkers in this country a few years later only served to underscore the point.

But the Parker Reproduction sowed a seed of its own, nurtured by a clearly developing trend in which more and more shooters proved willing to spend larger and larger amounts for good guns. In the late 1980s and early 1990s, a number of gunmakers began mulling over the notion of reviving some aspect of the American trade. Those who asked my opinion on which American classic would be the most likely candidate for resurrection all got the same answer: If the choice were mine, it would be for the simplest and best mechanically, and the handsomest of them all—the Fox. As I have made no secret of my regard for Fox guns, I'm sure it came as no surprise to any of them.

Antony Galazan was not one of those who asked, but he came to the same conclusion, for the same reasons. And, as it turned out, he was the one who carried the idea from speculation to reality.

Tony Galazan is a young man who combines an appreciation for genuine quality in gunmaking, a thorough understanding of how to accomplish it, an excellent aesthetic sense, and a streak of brilliance as a toolmaker and machinist.

The new Fox guns' debut at the 1994 SHOT Show in Dallas. From left: Michael McIntosh, Dick Perrett, Antony Galazan, gunsmith Walter Koluth, transportation director Rich Wengle.

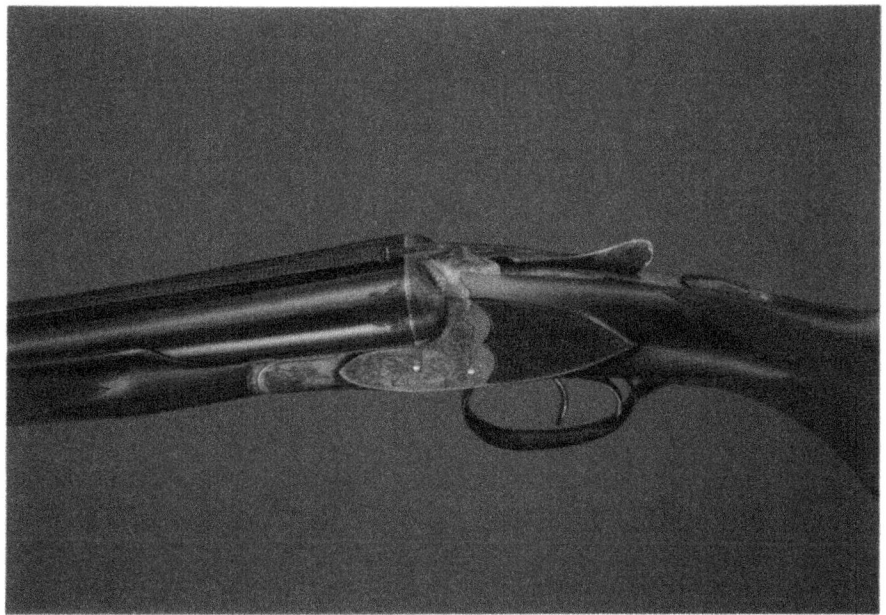

CE Grade 20-gauge, 1993 CONNECTICUT SHOTGUN MANUFACTURING CO.

In some of these, he is not greatly different from Ansley Fox himself. He, too, is a risk-taker—as anyone attempting to manufacture high-quality double guns in the United States during the closing years of the twentieth century would have to be—but unlike Ansley Fox, Tony Galazan has not set out to be all things to all segments of the gun market, and that at least makes the risk a calculated one.

In mid-1992, after negotiating an agreement with Savage Arms for use of the patents and trade names, Galazan organized the Connecticut Shotgun Manufacturing Company in New Britain, Connecticut. He serves as CEO and director, Dick Perrett as president.

The enormously complex task of setting up a gun factory began with a crucial round of decisions. All told, the older Foxes were built in more than two dozen grades and models—an approach that only a handful of gunmakers in the world can successfully carry off today. The smaller the operation, the narrower the focus needs to be, and Tony Galazan ultimately decided that he would initially manufacture 20-bores only, in grades CE, XE, DE, FE, and an Exhibition Grade reminiscent of the guns the A.H. Fox Company built for display at the Panama-Pacific Exposition in 1915.

Moreover, he intended from the start that every phase of the manufacturing process should be carried out in the United States—and to every practical extent, in the small factory building at 35 Woodland Street, New Britain.

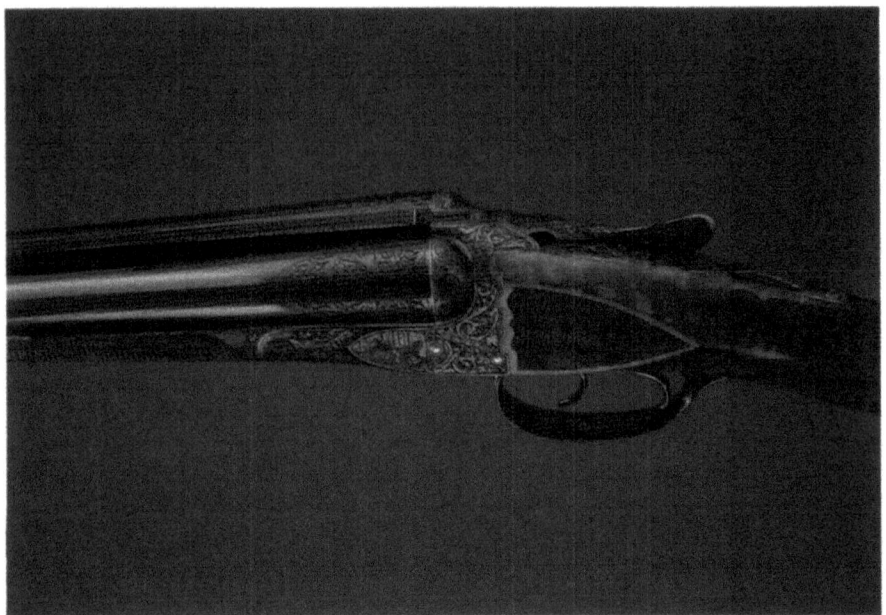

DE Grade 20-gauge, 1993   CONNECTICUT SHOTGUN MANUFACTURING CO.

    Current technology offers opportunities, undreamt of three generations ago, that would have sent Ansley Fox into raptures. In the old days, Fox guns were built from forgings, rough blocks of metal hugely oversized and showing only faint semblance of their final shapes. Though the milling machines on which the parts were worked down to size were state-of-the-art for their time, they were primitive compared with the computer-controlled machinery available today. And now, even the rough parts can be remarkably precise, thanks to the process of investment casting, in which molten steel is injected into complex, high-precision molds.

    As the first step, Galazan and his team of machinists disassembled a number of old 20-bore Foxes and measured every part. "In the end," he says, "we had to pull averages for every dimension. Virtually no two of the older ones are exactly the same."

    With dimensions established, they made and refined molds for every part except barrels, ribs, screws, springs, trigger guard, and the various components of the cocking system. Then came the even more complex process of programming and setting up the mills, grinders, and other machinery; of designing and making a vast array of jigs and fixtures; of establishing the protocol by which each step is performed—all to achieve maximum efficiency and precision in transforming the castings into close-tolerance gun parts, and in transforming these, in turn, into finished guns.

All told, the preparations took about a year and a half, but the returns should prove worth the effort.

Tony Galazan: "I intend to do as much work by machine as possible, in order to give the gunsmiths the nearest thing to a finished product that I can. I want them to be able to put all their efforts into the final fitting and finishing—the things that have to be done by hand to achieve a genuinely top-quality gun. If we can combine the best castings, the best machining, and the best gunsmithing, we'll have the best gun."

As I write this in February 1994, production is about to begin in earnest. Having visited the factory, met the craftsmen, studied the parts and the first of the guns, it seems to me we're on the threshold of a moment in history not unlike some of those on which Ansley Fox's life so often turned. It's an exciting prospect.

As often is the case when history changes direction, the new Fox guns will require a shift in how we think of them. The heyday of the classic American gun was a very long time ago; up to now the Parker Reproduction and the Winchester Model 12 and Model 42 reproductions made by Browning amount to our only recent experience with the reintroduction of older guns, and from them we have come, rightly, to draw a distinction between original guns and reproductions.

The Foxes, on the other hand, represent something quite different, something unique, something we haven't seen in many, many years—original guns brought back to production. The new Foxes are not "reproductions" in the

Most of the new Fox parts are investment cast.   MICHAEL McINTOSH

Many of the milling operations are carried out by computer-controlled machinery.   MICHAEL McINTOSH

way the Parker Reproduction or the Brownings are. They are instead simply Foxes, as "original," if you will, as those made in Philadelphia or Utica or Chicopee Falls.

The difference is subtle, perhaps—and I don't bring it up to take anything away from the reproduction guns that now exist—but I believe it's important to see the Foxes in a proper context.

All Parker guns built before the end of World War II are original Parkers, and so are all Foxes made in the same era—regardless of whether they were built by Parker Brothers or Remington Arms, by the A. H. Fox Gun Company under Ansley Fox, by the same company under the Godshalks, or by Savage Arms. The Connecticut Shotgun Manufacturing Company simply is one more entity in the series of companies that have built A.H. Fox guns. The only difference is that the hiatus lasted for forty-odd years instead of the few months that elapsed when production was shut down in Philadelphia and subsequently resumed in Utica. Neither time nor company ownership define originality, but the continuity of production within the American gun trade certainly does.

So, let's think of these guns as they are—A.H. Foxes, real Foxes, stamped with the same patents and built to exactly the same mechanical design. Even the serial numbers resume the sequence the Fox Gun Company started in 1912 with No. 200001. The highest number for a graded 20-gauge in the Savage records is No. 203974—an SP Grade shipped December 12, 1946. To avoid duplicating a higher number that may have been assigned but not recorded, Galazan began the new Fox numbers with No. 205501. (That particular number exists as a frame only and will remain so; the lowest-numbered finished gun is No. 205502, which I'll describe presently.)

What is different between the new Foxes and the old ones has to do with manufacturing technique and materials. All investment-cast parts are of 8620 steel, fine-grained stuff with a high nickel content. As the procedures for melting, stress-relieving, and other processes were perfected only in relatively recent times, this steel is purer and more consistent in composition than any that was available when Foxes were in production before.

Along with what's new comes much of the Fox tradition. The new guns, for instance, are available with both Krupp and Chromox barrels. Both arrive at the factory as solid billets—those of Chromox from an American supplier and the Krupps, obviously, from Germany—and are bored, machined, joined, ribbed, and chambered in-house.

Actually, virtually every operation is performed in-house, right down to making screws and winding springs. The machinists work their wizardry on one side of the building, refining the castings and milling the non-cast parts from solid stock. All the parts are then hand-fitted and assembled by five Austrian gunsmiths whose workbenches are on the other side. In between are the parts

Lukas Geiger, one of the five Austrian gunsmiths who fit and assemble new Foxes   MICHAEL McINTOSH

One of the milling rooms MICHAEL McINTOSH

room, polishing room, stocking room, and a glass-walled cubicle where barrels and other parts are rust-blued.

The only work farmed out is the investment casting, the color case-hardening, and some engraving—and even these are done in the United States. In fact, apart from the Krupp barrels, stock wood is the only component imported from outside the country.

And it's lovely wood, indeed—Turkish walnut that ranges in figure from handsome to spectacular. Even in semi-planed form, the blanks stacked in the tiny, low-ceilinged storage room upstairs are enough to set a walnut-lover salivating.

Although the frame is the same size and shape as the small-bore Fox frame always has been, there are some small differences in detail. As were those of XE Grade and higher from about 1914 on, the new Fox frame is rebated at the top and bottom tangs, CE Grade included. In XE, DE, FE, and Exhibition grades, the top of the standing breech is shaped to follow the arc of the barrels curving in toward the rib, just as it was in the old days. Now, however, all grades feature the Becker-style fancy-back scalloping on the rear edges of the frame, a treatment previously given only to a few DE and FE grade pieces.

Such details certainly enhance the guns' aesthetic appeal, but the rebates and scallops have some practical advantages as well. By allowing wood and metal literally to interlock, these bearing surfaces prevent any movement between frame and stock head, assuming the stock is properly fitted.

Proper fitting is a safe assumption, as each gun will be stocked by hand to customer specification. Custom dimensions always were available, but not many older Foxes actually were headed up by hand. Higher-grade guns were hand-fitted, certainly, but the basic inletting was done by machine, which under mass-production conditions tended to remove relatively large amounts of wood from the one part of a gunstock where every square millimeter of bearing surface makes a substantial contribution to durability. Doing the heading-up entirely by hand creates not only the closest possible fit but maximum stability as well.

Connecticut Shotgun Manufacturing Company published its first Fox catalogue and price list in September 1993 (details and prices are in Appendix I), but owing to the gremlins that inevitably plague the start-up of any operation so complex, the first guns were not completed until December 1993 and January 1994, just before their public debut at the Shooting, Hunting and Outdoor Trade Show in Dallas, January 13–16, 1994. There are four of them, three lettered grades and a Special; they were built as display pieces, and the company does not plan to offer them for sale. For the sake of historical interest, they are as follows:

> *No. 205502, DE Grade; 26-inch Krupp barrels; straight-hand stock with skeleton steel buttplate, splinter fore-end; two triggers; ivory front and middle beads; engraved and signed by Kurt Horvath.*

> *No. 205503, XE Grade "Special"; 30-inch Krupp barrels; straight-hand stock with checkered butt, splinter fore-end; two triggers; ivory front and middle beads; engraved and signed by J.R. Demunck.*

> *No. 205504, CE Grade "Special"; 28-inch Chromox barrels; pistol-grip stock with grip cap and hard-rubber buttplate, beavertail fore-end; two triggers; ivory front bead; engraved and signed by J.R. Demunck.*

> *No. 205507, "Special"; 28-inch Krupp barrels; half-hand stock with skeleton steel buttplate, splinter fore-end; ivory front and middle beads; two triggers, gold-plated; engraved and gold-inlaid by an engraver who prefers to remain anonymous and did not sign the gun. Although this gun is in many respects similar to an FE Grade, it is marked only as a Special and is so listed in the factory records.*

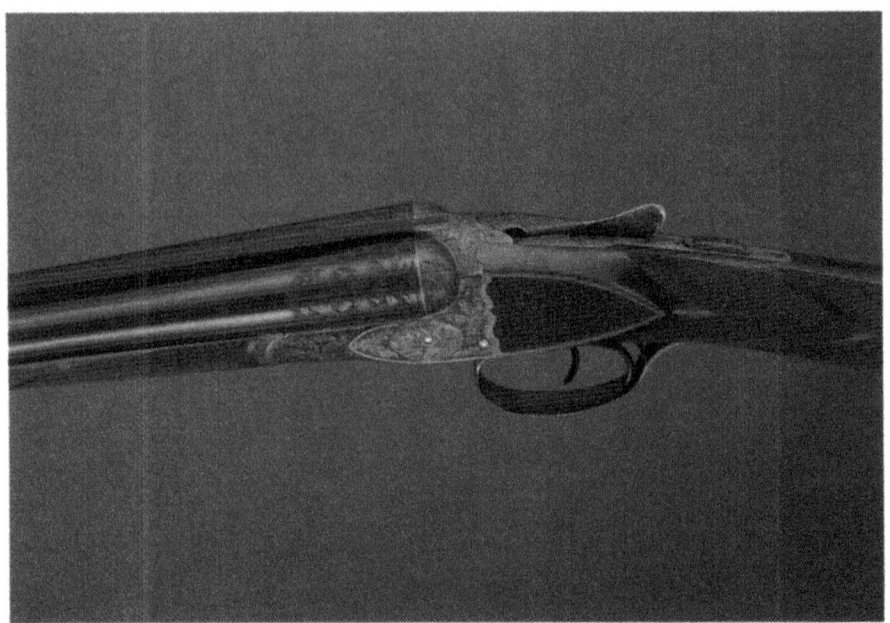

XE Grade 20-gauge, 1993   CONNECTICUT SHOTGUN MANUFACTURING CO.

As they were meant to do, these four guns show not only the various grades but also the range of barrel lengths, stock designs, and other features available. Some, like the Krupp barrels, beavertail fore-end, checkered butt, and skeleton steel buttplate, are additional-cost options. Standard features for each grade include automatic safety, ejectors, double triggers, 26-, 28-, or 30-inch Chromox barrels choked to customer specification, splinter fore-end, ivory beads, the choice of grip style, and the choice of a hard-rubber buttplate or old-style red rubber pad. In all grades but CE, the standard splinter fore-end is the longer, second-generation style, fitted with a buffalo-horn wedge and shaped to a slight schnabel.

Some sort of personalizing is also standard for FE and Exhibition grades—initials engraved on a gold stock oval, engraved or gold-inlaid on the trigger guard, your signature gold-inlaid on the guard, or "Made for" and your name gold-inlaid on the barrels. These are optional in the other grades.

Other options include Monte Carlo stock, cheek-piece, extra sets of barrels, and a leather-covered trunk case with oil bottle, cleaning rod, jag, mop, bore brush, and snap caps. The Fox-Kautzky single trigger is also available—the third (and best) version, patented in 1914 and subsequently purchased by the Fox Gun Company.

As I said earlier, the success of any new gun company these days depends in part upon the scope of its operation. Concentrating on only mid- and high-grade guns of a single gauge is obviously an attempt to avoid the pitfalls created by too much diversity, but even so, it's an ambitious undertaking. As plans now stand, production will amount to roughly a hundred guns per year; this is minuscule compared with what the A.H. Fox Gun Company turned out, yet it's a greater volume than that of any maker in the world who builds guns to a similar level of quality. In filling the orders already in hand, Connecticut Shotgun will make no guns for inventory for at least the first year, possibly longer.

Because both 20- and 16-gauge Foxes are built on the same frame and share most of the same internal parts, new 16-bores are a virtual certainty. But not in the immediate future. As company president Dick Perrett told me, "I imagine we will add 16s in a couple of years; it's mainly just a matter of making 16-gauge barrels. Right now, though, we already have a full plate building 20s. And we might eventually offer 28-gauges, although the 20-gauge frame is a bit larger than an ideal 28 would be.

"One thing I'm sure we won't do is build 12-bores. That would require a complete new set of molds and machining programs, and it would be prohibitively expensive. Besides, the majority of older Foxes are 12s, and lots of them still exist in good, shootable condition.

"We also aren't going to make any 20s with three-inch chambers, nor do we have any plans at this time to build guns for use with steel shot. We're

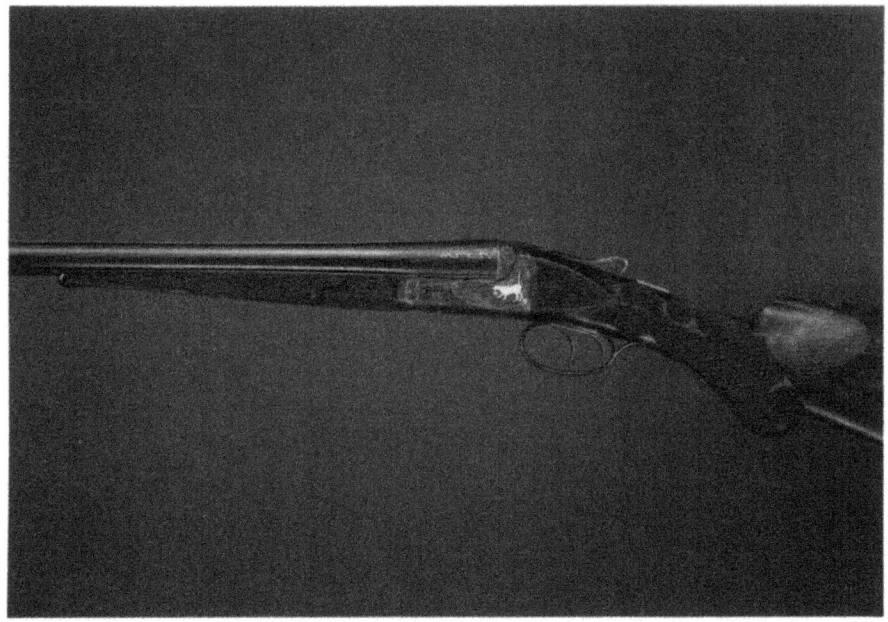

FE Grade 20-gauge, 1993   CONNECTICUT SHOTGUN MANUFACTURING CO.

concentrating solely on lightweight, nicely balanced upland guns that we can custom-build just for our customers."

Nor does Connecticut Shotgun offer repair or rebarreling services for older Foxes. Dick Perrett: "We get a lot of calls about this. We try to help people find good sources for the work they want done, but we don't have the capacity to do it here, not and turn out new guns as well."

New guns, of course, are the whole point—new guns and perhaps a new era of American gunmaking, an era in which we regain one of the best aspects of our heritage as a manufacturing nation. Despite Ansley Fox's claim, neither his nor any other American gun was the finest in the world, but there was a time when we built the finest factory-made guns of all, and if only in a small way, the Connecticut Shotgun Manufacturing Company has brought a part of that to life once again.

At the 1994 SHOT Show, I spent four days at the A.H. Fox booth, talking to people and watching the reactions as they got a first-hand look at a gun that's literally come back from the grave of history. For four days they came in a continuous stream to look at and handle the guns. Some returned again and again, as if not quite certain they could actually believe what they saw.

What they saw were guns in some ways decidedly better than the majority of Foxes ever were—made of better materials, more carefully fitted, better finished inside and out, more skillfully engraved, gun for gun, than ever before.

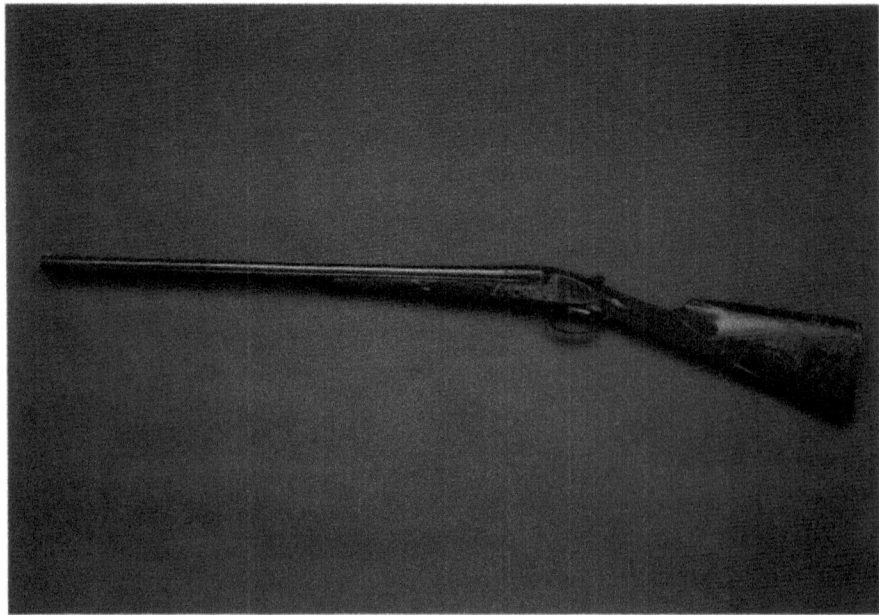

DE Grade 20-gauge, 1993   CONNECTICUT SHOTGUN MANUFACTURING CO.

And more than once I felt a pang of regret that Ansley Fox couldn't be there to see them, too. Of all the things he made in his busy life, he was proudest of the gun, and he would be proud of these, I'm sure—possibly even a bit envious, because in large measure they are his vision fulfilled. These are what he always wanted the Fox gun to be.

For catalogues, price lists, and order forms, contact Connecticut Shotgun Manufacturing Company, Postal Box 1692, New Britain, Connecticut 06051-1692; the phone number is 203-225-6682, telefax is 203-832-8707. Catalogues are $3.50 each.

INDEX

A

Abercrombie & Fitch	310
Altoona Rod and Gun Club	49
American Shooting Association	42
Andrews, William	223
Anson & Deeley	29
Askins, Charles Sr.	212-214, 216, 218
Aubrey, A.J.	118

B

Baer, Larry	184
Baker Gun Works	25, 181
Baltimore Arms Company	35-36
Baltimore Gun Club	43
Baltimore Shooting Association	41, 43, 45, 54, 57
Barthmaier, Frank J.	83, 85, 95
Bartholomew, Henry	222, 321
Batavia Gun Works	213
Bates, _____	49
Bates, Howard D.	44, 53
Becker, Burt	213-214, 217-218, 221, 222, 227, 239, 321-322
Beesley Shotover gun	315

Bielin, Mitzie	283
Blackett, P.M.S.	329
Blaisdell, George	273
Bogardus, Adam	42
Boss over/under gun	315
Bowen, Hal	227, 229
Bowers, F.A.	132
Brewer, J.L.	85
Bridges, H.C. ("Tarheel")	43
Briley, Jess	235
Brooks, Berry	222
Brown, Alexander	61
Brown, Eliza	39
Browning Arms Company	385-386
Browning, John	50
Buckingham, Nash	213, 214, 221, 222-223, 227, 229, 321
Budd, Charles	42
Burhans & Black	93
Burton, Arthur	85
Buxton, Edward	99

C

Calmette, Gaston	161
Campbell, L.H. Jr.	275
Carlson, Chester	329
Carnera, Primo	329
Carver, F.W.	42
Castle, Thomas	30
Churchill, Winston	93
Clark, Roe S.	144, 146, 186, 240, 301, 304, 305, 312, 316, 320
Cobb, Ty	173-174
Coleman, Fred	85
Colt Patent Firearms Company	32, 118
Connecticut Shotgun Manufacturing Company	383ff
Connor, Albert W.	97, 102-106, 109, 110, 111, 117, 118, 124, 128, 135, 137, 162
Coolbaugh-Macklin Motor Company	206
Coolidge, Calvin	211
Cornell, Henry G.	103

Craveroiler Company	209
Crenshaw, E.M.	35
Crosby, William R.	42, 52, 53, 55
Crossman, E.C.	33, 123, 184, 220, 221, 223-224, 227, 235, 299
Cunningham, B.W.	330
Curtis, Paul	315
Custer, George Armstrong	xvii, xviii

D

Darling, J.N. "Ding"	321
Daubt, Douglas S.	65
Davis, Charles L.	54-55
Dellmuth, Carl	273
DeMunck, J.R.	389
Dewey, Thomas	329
Diesel, Rudolf	191
Dilts, Jacob	309
Disney, Walt	61
Dixie Gun Club	49
Duesenburg automobile	200
DuPont, Philip F.	65, 68, 69
Durant Billy	93
Duchess of Hohenburg	161

E

Eastman, George	61
Eastman Kodak Corporation	61
Edwards, Manley	39
Edwards, Virginia	39
Eisenlohr, Louis H.	85, 95, 307, 308
Elliott, Bob	56
Elliott, Dave	56
Elliott, James A.R.	34, 42, 45, 50, 53, 56
Elliott's Shooting Park	56-57
Ellis, Havelock	244
Eyster, James H.	85, 95

F

Fanning, John	42, 51, 52, 55

Farrell, Joseph	327
Ferguson, Chapin A.	32
Florists' Gun Club	57
Flues, Emile	61
Forbes, _____	49
Ford, Henry	161, 192, 194
Ford Motor Company	161, 244
Fort, Samuel	30

A.H. Fox Guns

(References to the various Fox grades and models are made virtually throughout the text and appendices. The following citations refer to specific discussions of the subjects listed; other references may be found on following pages (ff) or throughout the remainder of the text (passim)).

Barrel weights	149-154
Beavertail fore-ends	247, 282-283ff
Chromox steel	137-139, passim
Cutaways	83-84
Ejectors	86-90, 117, 124
Engraving	117-123, passim
Fore-end latches	113-115, 139-140
Fox-Kautzky single trigger	167-170, 172, 295
GE Grade	237-241, 309, 311
HE Super-Fox	211-235
Model 1910	123-124
Model 1911	123-124
Model 1912	127
Model B	303-304
Over/under	314-316
"Pin" guns	113
Serial-number blocks	117
Single-barrel trap guns	181-189, passim
Skeeter Grade	280ff
Small-bore guns	124-126, 135-146, passim
SP/SPE	295ff
SP Skeet Grade	299ff
SP Skeet and Upland Game gun	300ff
Specials	307-311
Special Trap Gun	156ff
SPR Grade	301

Sterlingworth	111, passim
Sterlingworth DeLuxe	280ff
Sterlingworth DeLuxe Ejector	280ff
Sterlingworth Skeet and Upland Game gun	300ff
Sterlingworth Wildfowl Grade	229
Trap Grade	290ff
Trap Grade Special	241, 308
Ventilated rib	181-183, 247, 280, 282
X Grade	156-160ff
Fox, Addison C.	21, 22, 32
Fox, A.H., Gun Company	58, 65, 72, 73, 75, 77, passim
Fox, Amos	21, 22
Fox, Ansley H., Company	194, 196
Fox Automotive Products Company	261
Fox, Beaulah	22
Fox, Ellen Gerou	131-132, 263, 269, 327
Fox, Fentress DeVere Keleher	39, 131, 132
Fox Gun Company (Baltimore)	32-35, 44
Fox, Harry H.	22, 65
Fox Holding Company	209
Fox, James Addison	39, 48
Fox, Louisa Ansley	21
Fox Manufacturing Company	249, 261
Fox Motor Company	196-197, 209
Fox Motor Car Company	197-209
Fox Munitions Company	275
Fox Play Gun	247-253
Fox Pneumatic Shock-Absorber Company	194
Fox Products Company	261, 314
Fox, Raphael	22
Fox, Sharon	22
Fox, Velma Shank	327
Francis Ferdinand, Archduke	161
Franklin automobile	200, 204
Franklin, H.H., Company	203
Frazier, Mary Bella (Cunningham)	131, 132
Freud, Sigmund	244
Fugger, Josep	240
Fulford, Elijah	165, 168

Furst, William S.   194

G

Galazan, Antony   382ff
Gamble, Clara   39
Gandhi, Mohandas   211
Geiger, Lukas   387
Geiji, Joseph A.   30
General Motors Corporation   93, 246
George, J.M.   45
Germane, F.J.   197
Gerou, Millie   132, 263, 269, 331
Gerou, William H.   131
Gerou, William H., Jr.   131, 263, 273, 331
Gilbert, Fred   34, 42, 51, 52, 53, 54, 55
Gillette, King   61
Glascock, Bedford   35, 36
Godfrey, Charles J., Company   36
Godshalk, Clarence A.   135, passim
Godshalk, Edward H.   128, 135, passim
Golding, Frank H.   203
Gough, Leaphy C.   119
Gough, William H.   118-123, 157, 158, 184
Green, Cliff   222
Green, G.F.   xvii
Greener, W.W.   29
Griebel, Arnold   240
Griffin & Howe   309
Griffith, Eugene C.   54, 56
Griffith, J.D.   184
Grim, E.A.   311

H

Haywood, C. William   64, 65, 69, 73, 74, 308
"Hazel"   50
Headrick, William W.   184, 235
Heikes, Rolla   34, 42, 47, 48, 51, 52, 53, 55
Henke, Frederick   247, 249
Heringe, Augustus   85

Higgins, W.D.	277, 291
Hildebrand, E.	263
Hirschey, H.C.	57
Hitler, Adolph	269, 303
Hollenbeck, Frank	35, 118
Holmes Automobile Company	203
Hoover, Herbert	246, 256
Horne, George A.	86, 88
Horvath, Kurt	389
Hozier, Clementine	93
Hummer, Ernest E.	32
Hummer, J.C.	39
Hunt, Lynn Bogue	277
Hunt, Walter E.	95
Hunter Arms Company	34, 86, 165
Hunter One-Trigger	165, 167

I

Illinois State Sportsmen's Association	54
Infallible Single Trigger	165
International Silver Company	118
Interstate Association	42, 47, 49, 55, 84
Interstate Manufacturers & Dealers Association	42
Inventions Holding Company	273
Ithaca guns	61, 81
Ithaca Gun Company	93, 125, 165, 181, 189, 212, 221

J

Jenkins, Harry L.	85
Johnson, J.A.	318
Jung, Karl	244

K

Kautzky, Joseph	165-170
Kelly, James	269, 273, 275
Kibbee, Guy	269
King, Charles Brady	194
Kingsbury, Henry F.	64
Koluth, Walter	382

Kremer, John C.	115, 139, 140
Krieghoff over/under gun	316
Kumbak Putting Green	253

L

Lancaster Arms Company	165
Landsettel, C.H.	263
Lang over/under gun	314
Lard, Allen	165, 168
Lauterbach, John, Company	253
"Leader"	47
Leibold, H.H.	311
Lefever Arms Company	34, 84, 125, 181, 381
Lefever, Dan	25, 34, 61, 165, 181, 213
Letterman, William C.	184
Lewis, Spencer K.	127, 135
Ligowsky Clay Pigeon Company	42
Ligowsky, George	42
Lincoln, Abraham	95
Lindig, William	84
Louis, Joe	329
Lueker, Claude	174
Lupos, H.E.	47

M

Malone, James R.	44, 47
Marmon automobile	200
Marshall-Wells Hardware Company	112, 158
Mathias, Bob	330
McCormack, Denis	275
McDougal, R.	320
McKinley, William	61, 95
McMurchy, Harvey	42
Mercer automobile	200
Meriden Arms Company	86
Middleton, A.C.	237
Mills, Joseph W.	85
Minier, David	61
Money, Harold	53

Monumental Shooting Park	43, 46
Mooney, Julia	39
Moore, Charles	85
Morgan, J. Pierpont	85-86
Morrison, J.L.D.	54
Mosher, George A.	84, 90

N

Naracom, William	216
National Arms Company	30-32
National Gun Company	32
New England Westinghouse	86, 174
New Interstate Park	44, 50, 51, 55, 56
New Jersey State Sportsman's Association	54
Newport Gun Club	48
Nice, Budd G.	197
Nicholson, T.R.	200, 206

O

Ocean City Manufacturing Company	254, 256
Ohio Trap Shooters' League	54
Olds, Ransom	194
Olin, John M.	212, 214, 218, 220, 381
O'Shaughnessy, P.J.	196
Otto, N.A.	191
Overbaugh, Harry	172

P

Panama-Pacific International Exposition	171-172, 176, 383
Parker Brothers	25, 118, 125, 146, 149, 181, 189, 221, 237, 386
Parker gun	34, 35, 44, 47, 68, 69, 70, 71, 81, 112, 115, 168, 184, 311, 381, 382, 386
Parker Pen Company	135
Parker Reproductions gun	382, 385
Parmelee, Frank	42, 52
Patterson, J.M.	132
Paxson, Walter	247, 249, 256
Peden, J. Lyle	135
Perrett, Dick	382ff

Peters Cartridge Company	50, 54
Philadelphia Arms Company	36, 57, 64-75, 77, 84, 85, 86, 111, 112, 113, 137
Philadelphia Arms guns	64-75, 308
Philadelphia Shooting Academy	158
Philip Gross Hardware Company	105
Picasso, Pablo	34
Pleasants, Joseph Burton	32
Polk, Henrietta	22
Porsche, Ferdinand	206
Poth, H.A.	95
Potter, Sheldon	197
Powell & Clement Company	102
Princip, Gavrilo	161
Prudhomme, E.C.	240
Purdey gun	29

R

Reed, William C.R.	85
Reily, Frank	95
Remington Arms	25, 213, 218, 382, 386
Remington Model 32	381
Rice, Walter J.	196, 197
Richards, Burr Howard	32-35
Richards, Burr Howard Jr.	32-36
Richards, Westley	61, 295, 315
Roberts, G. Brinton	95
Robinson, Jackie	329
Robson, A. Roy	197
Roll, Adolph R.	92, 100, 110, 135, 162, 175, 221
Roosevelt, Edith Carow	99
Roosevelt, Kermit	101
Roosevelt, Theodore	61, 70, 95, 99-106, 124, 126, 162, 163, 191
Rosebrugh, W.R.	158
Russell, Frederick T.	117, 124

S

Sanders, Bunny	184

Savage Arms Corporation	102, 118, 137, 146, 184, 188, 189, 220, 229, 238, 239, 240, 256, 261, 277 passim, 383, 386
Sayles, J.H.	209
Schrenck, Frank H.	196, 197
Schuler over/under gun	315
Schultz, _____	49
Scott, Henry J.	132
Seaboard Development Corporation	263
Seagraves, Claude	310
Sears Roebuck	118
Self Lighting Cigarette Corporation of America	273
Selfridge, Thomas	92
Selous, Frederick	99
Shaner, Elmer	53
Shannon, Alfred P.	64
Sheldon, Harold	222
Sherritt, M.A.	197
Simmons Hardware Company	102
Simon, Ed. W., Company	246
Simson over/under gun	315
Smith, L.C., guns	25, 34, 61, 65, 88, 125, 149, 160, 165, 181, 183, 189, 221, 381
Smithsonian Institution	99
Sneider, Charles Edward	25
Snyder, Sheldon	318, 319
Sousa, John Philip	168
Southard, Melvin E.	209
Spoorns, Frank	118
Standard Gun Club	45
Sterlingworth Company	111-113
Sterlingworth Railway Supply Company	112
Stevens Arms Company	304
Stewart, Herbert A.	238, 239, 240, 241, 299, 304, 308
Storr, E.H.	47
Street & Finney, Inc.	135
Stutz automobile	200
Supplee Biddle Hardware Company	221
Swanson, H.O.	203

Sweeley, E.M.	212
Syracuse Arms Company	34, 35, 84, 86, 88

T

Tabb, John Prosser	32
Taft, William Howard	95, 103, 104
Thomas, William H.	85
Toulouse-Lautrec, Henri	61
Trimble, Ralph	54
Triune Corporation	273
Tryon, E.K., Company	184

V

Van Dyke, Henry	244
Very flare pistol	176

W

Walcott, Jersey Joe	329
Walsh, Roy	269
Warner, George	222
Warren, Earl	329
Washington, Booker T.	61
Waters, Hood	44, 47
Welch, R.A.	50
Wells, T.E.	49
West, Steve	235
Western Cartridge Company	212-213
Westminster Gun Club	49
White, Alvin	240
Whitman, Walt	331
Wilcox, Isabel G.	330
Wilkes, John	81
Williams, H.N.	196
Wills-St. Claire automobile	200
Wilson, Woodrow	105, 171, 174, 175-176, 191-192, 194
"Winchester"	47, 55
Winchester guns	50, 81, 240, 292, 299, 381, 385
Winchester Repeating Arms Company	32, 47, 49, 57, 64, 118, 176, 244
Winton, Alexander	194

Wirsing, Max	65, 75
Wolters, Richard A.	249, 253
Woodward over/under gun	315
Wright, M.H.	22, 77
Wright, Orville	92
Wright, Wilfred	238-239, 241, 299, 304
Wrigley, E.W.	194

Y

Yaeger, Chuck	329

www.ingramcontent.com/pod-product-compliance
Lightning Source LLC
Chambersburg PA
CBHW061123070526
44584CB00033B/4203